Review of the Convention on Contracts for the International Sale of Goods (CISG)

1998

Review
of the
Convention on Contracts
for the
International Sale of Goods (CISG)

1998

EDITED BY:
Pace International Law Review

KLUWER LAW INTERNATIONAL
The Hague • London • Boston

Published by Kluwer Law International,
P.O. Box 85889, 2508 CN The Hague, The Netherlands.

Sold and distributed in the U.S.A. and Canada
by Kluwer Law International,
675 Massachusetts Avenue, Cambridge, MA 02139, U.S.A.
tel: (617) 354-0140; fax: (617) 354-8595

In all other countries, sold and distributed
by Kluwer Law International,
P.O. Box 85889, 2508 CN The Hague, The Netherlands
tel: 31 70 308 1562; fax: 31 70 308 1555

ISBN 9041193529

Kluwer Law International incorporates the publishing programs of
Graham & Trotman Ltd, Kluwer Law and Taxation Publishers,
and Martinus Nijhoff Publishers.

Contents

PART II
TRANSLATIONS

Table of Abbreviations

A.C.	Appeal Cases
Act.Jur.Hung	Acta Juridica Academiae Scientiarium Hungaricae (Hungary)
All E.R.	All England Law Reports
Am.J.Comp.L.	American Journal of Comparative Law
Ariz.J.Int'l & Comp.L.	Arizona Journal of International and Comparative Law (USA)
Aust.Bus.L.Rev.	Australian Business Law Review
BB	Der Betriebsberater
BGB	Bürgerliches Gesetzbuch (Germany)
Bus.Law	The Business Lawyer (USA)
Cah.de Dr.	Les Cahier de Droit (Canada)
C.L.J.	Cambridge Law Journal (UK)
Can. Bus.L.J.	Canadian Business Law Journal
ch	Chapter
CIF	cost, insurance, freight (Incoterm)
Cir.	Circuit
CLOUT	Case Law
CISG	Convention on Contracts for the International Sale of Goods (U.N. Doc. A/CONF.97/18, Annex I)

CMR Convention relative au Contrat de transport international de marchandises par route/Convention on the Contract for the International Carriage of Goods by Road

C.V.I.M. Convention des Nations Unies Sur Les Contrats de Vente Internationale de Marchandises (U.N. Doc. A/CONF.97/18, Annexe I)

Doc. Document(s)

Colum.L.Rev	Columbia Law Review (USA)
Cornell Int'l.L.J.	Cornell International Law Journal (USA)
Cornell L.Rev.	Cornell Law Review (USA)
Dig.Com.L.	Digest of Commercial Laws of the World (USA)
ECJ	Court of Justice of the European Communities
E.C.R.	European Court Reports
ed(s)	editor(s)/edition
e.g.	*exempli gratia* (Lat.=for instance)
et seq.	*et sequen(te)s* (Lat.=and the following pages(s))
EuZW	Europäische Zeitschrift für Wirtschaftsrecht (Germany)
EwiR	Entscheidungen zum Wirtschaftsrecht (Germany)
F.	Federal Reporter (USA)
F.3d	Federal Reporter, Third Series (USA)
Fed. Ct. Rep.	Federal Court Reporter (Australia)
Fed. Supp.	Federal Supplement (USA)
Fordham L. Rev.	Fordham Law Review (USA)
Ga.J.Int'l & Comp.L.	Georgia Journal of International and Comparative Law (USA)
Harv.Int'l.L.J.	Harvard International Law Journal (USA)
Harv.L.Rev.	Harvard Law Review (USA)
Hastings Int'l & Comp.L.Rev.	Hastings International and Comparative Law Review (USA)
ICC	International Chamber of Commerce
Incoterms	Incoterms 1990. International Commercial Terms of the ICC, ICC publication no. 460.
i.a.	*inter alia* (Lat.=among others)
id.	*ibidem* (Lat.=in the same place)
Int'l.Bus.Law.	International Business Lawyer (UK)
Int'l&Comp.L.Q.	International and Comparative Law Quarterly (USA)
Int'l Law.	The International Lawyer (USA)

I.L.M. International Legal Materials (ed. American Association of International Law, Washington D.C.)

Int'l Tax & Bus.Law. The International Tax & Business Lawyer (USA)

Int'l Trade & Bus. L. A. International Trade & Business Law Annual (Australia)

IPRax Praxis des Internationalen Privat- und Verfahrensrechts (Germany)

J.L.& Com. Journal of Law and Commerce (USA)

J.Bus.L. The Journal of Business Law (UK)

J.D.I. Journal de Droit International (France)

JuS. Juristische Schulung (Germany)

JZ Juristenzeitung (Germany)

Limitation Convention 1974 Convention on the Limitation Period in the International Sale of Goods (U.N. Doc. A/CONF./63/15), YB V(1974), 210-215.

L.Q.R. The Law Quarterly Review (UK)

NJW Neue Juristische Wochenschrift (Germany)

N.J.L. New Law Journal (UK)

1978 Draft Convention UNCITRAL Draft, 11th Plenary Session (New York 30 May-16 June 1978), YB IX (1978), 14-21

N. Number(s)

No. Number(s)

Nw.J.Int'l L. & Bus. Northwestern Journal of International Law & Business (USA)

N.Y.St.B.J. New York State Bar Journal (USA)

N.Y.L.J.Int'l &Comp.L New York Law School Journal of International and Comparative Law (USA)

Ohio St.L.J. Ohio State Law Journal (USA)

O.J. Official Journal of the European Communities

Pace Int'l L. Rev. Pace International Law Review (USA)

Q.B. Law Reports, Queen's Bench Division (ULK)

RabelsZ Rabels Zeitschrift für ausländisches und internationales Privatrecht (Germany)

RCDIP	Revue critique de droit international privê (France)
Rev.jur.Univ.Puerto Rico	Revista jurídica de la Universidad de Puerto Rico (USA)
RIW	Recht de Internationalen Wirtschaft (Germany)
Rec. Dall. Sir	Receuil Dalloz Sirey (France)
RSDIE	Revue suisse de droit international et de droit européen (Switzerland)
SGA	Sales of Goods Act 1979
SZIER	Schweizerische Zeitschrift für Internationales und Europäisches Recht (Switzerland)
Stan.J.Int'l L.	Stanford Journal of International Law (USA)
Temple Int'l & Comp.L.J.	Temple International and Comparative Law Journal (USA)
Tex.Int'l.L.J.	Texas International Law Journal (USA)
Tul.J.Int'l&Comp.L.	Tulane Journal of International and Comparative Law (USA)
UCC	Uniform Commercial Code (USA)
UCC L.J.	Uniform Commercial Code Law Journal (USA)
U.Chic.L.Rev.	Uniform of Chicago Law Review (USA)
U.N.	United Nations
U.N.Doc.	U.N. Documents
UNIDROIT	Institut International pour l'Unification du Droit Privé/International Institute for the Unification of Private Law
Uniform L.Rev.	Uniform Law Review (UNIDROIT, Rom)
U.Pa.J.Int'l.Bus.L.	University of Pennsylvania Journal of International Business Law (USA)
U.Pitt.L.Rev.	University of Pittsburgh Law Review (USA)
Wash.L.Rev.	Washington Law Review (USA)
Wash. U.L.Q.	Washington University Law Quarterly (USA)
W.L.R.	Weekly Law Reports (UK)

Yale L.J.	The Yale Law Journal
YB UNCITRAL-Yearbook, New York : United Nations Publications (1971 et seq.)	
ZeuP	Zeitschrift für Europäisches Privatrecht (Germany)
ZIP	Zeitschrift für Wirtschaftsrecht (Germany)

PART I

Articles

CHAPTER ONE

A Comparison of Buyer's Remedies Under the CISG with the Latin American Legal Tradition

by Alberto L. Zuppi*

I. INTRODUCTION
II. SIMILARITIES AND DIFFERENCES
III. BUYER'S REMEDIES
   A. Remedies Which Seek to Save the Contract
      1. Fixing an additional time for performance
      2. Requiring performance
      3. Demanding substitute goods or repair
      4. Reducing the price
      5. Postponing buyer's performance
   B. Remedies Under Latin American Legislation
      1. Deferring performance in general
      2. Refusal to accept delivery before fixed time or in different quantities than contractually agreed
      3. Postponing payment
      4. Claiming damages
   C. Remedies Which Seek the Contract's Termination
      1. Declaring the contract avoided because of sellers' fundamental breach
      2. Avoidance in case of non-performance within the additional period

* University of Buenos Aires (Arg), Dr. fur., University of Saarland (Ger). A first German draft of this article, though different in many aspects, was part of the Swiss Feschrift Neumayer. I wish to thank my friend Al Kritzer for his suggestions on this paper.

I. Introduction[1]

The UN Convention on Contracts for the International Sale of Goods[2] has received considerable attention in Latin America. Representatives of eleven Central and South American states participated in its development at the Vienna Diplomatic Conference, and seven of those nations later ratified the Convention.[3] Today in those countries, the CISG has been addressed in domestic case law, scholarly articles, and other related literature.[4] The CISG reflects a successful compromise of different legal traditions, reached after two generations of international negotiations, where the Latin American perspective was introduced and incorporated representing both the civil law tradition and the laws of developing countries.[5]

Scholars and practitioners of all countries are often confronted with the CISG's advantages and disadvantages. In spite of some initial reluctance by the international community to accept CISG contractual application,

---

[1] Main abbreviations used in this article: Codigo Civil = CC, Codigo de Comercio = CCo. After the related code the abbreviation of the Nation of the cited text will be added: Arg =Argentine, Bra = Brazil, Bol = Bolivia, Col = Colombia, Chi = Chile, CR = Costa Rica, Cub = Cuba, RDom = Dominican Republic, E= Spain, Ecu = Ecuador, ESal = El Salvador, Ger= Germany, Gua = Guatemala, Hon = Honduras, Per = Peru, Par = Paraguay, Pan = Panama, Nic = Nicaragua, DFMex = Federal District Mexico, ROU= Uruguay, Ven= Venezuela.

[2] United Nations Convention on Contracts for the International Sale of Goods, Apr. 11, 1980, U.N. Doc. A/CONF. 97/18, Annex I, reprinted in 19 I.L.M. 668 [hereinafter CISG].

[3] Argentina ratified the CISG on 7/19/83 and it's been in force there since 1/1/88. Chile ratified 2/17/90, in force since 3/1/91, Cuba ratified 11/2/94, in force since 12/1/95, Ecuador ratified on 01/27/92, in force since 2/1/93 and Mexico ratified 12/29/87, in force since 1/1/89. Venezuela signed the Convention but ratification is still pending. In Peru and Uruguay, the CISG will be in force in April 2000 and January 2000, respectively.

[4] *See* Pace Internet database on the CISG, <*http:/www.cisg.law.pace.edu*>; RABEL Internet database on the CISG <*http:/ra.irv.uit.no/trade_law/documents/sales/cisg/txt/cisg.complete.html*>. For Spain and Latin America see <*http://www.uc3m.es*>. See generally Michael R. Will, CISG International Bibliography 1995, which has many Latin American references, UNILEX (*International Case Law and Bibliography on the UN Convention on Contracts for the International Sale of Goods*) 1996 and the CISG bibliographies published by UNCITRAL.

[5] *See* Alejandro Garro, *Reconciliation of Legal Traditions in the U.N. Convention on Contracts for the International Sale of Goods*, 23 The Int'l Lawyer 443-83 n. 2 (1989).

more than 10 years of international application has proved its merits as a fair and acceptable accommodation of different legal cultures and interests. This paper compares CISG remedies with Latin American law in the case of a seller's breach of duty. The objective of the comparison is to try to foresee where difficulties may arise and the direction regional case law is likely to follow.

Often in this paper I refer to a Latin American civil law tradition. This reflects the specific influence and reception in Latin America of the Roman law system, the former Spanish colonial legal culture, and the strong impact of the French Civil Code. This basic framework also incorporates legal influences from Germany, Italy, the Civil Code of Louisiana, and some Creole institutions.

One word needs to be said concerning legal text translations used in this paper: All translations from Spanish into English were done by the author. In the description of legal situations, the CISG's English vocabulary is frequently used, despite the accuracy of better translations found, for example, in the UNIDROIT Principles.[6] This has resulted in a monochordic legal text but, hopefully, one that is nevertheless accurate and preserves the CISG's international idiom.

The first part of this paper briefly examines the main points of similarity and difference between the CISG and the Latin American legal tradition. The second part focuses on a specific CISG subject: buyer's remedies in case of seller's breach of the contract. CISG remedies will be compared and classified according to three different types of objectives: A) remedies which attempt to save a failing contract; B) remedies which seek to declare the contract avoided or cancel the contract; and C) remedies which pursue compensation of damages. In the last part of this paper, some Latin American remedies that were not considered by the CISG will be discussed.

II. Similarities and Differences

A sellers' main duties are stated in CISG Art. 30: He must deliver the goods, hand over any related documents and transfer the title in the goods. National law regulates the process of transferring title, any warranties con-

---

[6] International Institue for the Unification of Private Law, Principles of International Commercial Contracts (Rome 1994) [hereinafter UNIDROIT Principles].

cerned with the claims or rights of third parties, and the standard for a defect-free condition of the purchased merchandise. Usually, Latin American codes declare that obligations of the seller are reduced mainly to two: Delivery (or *traditio*) and warranty.[7] Some Civil Codes, like the Bolivian and Paraguayan laws, further describe seller's duty: He must transfer title of the goods to the buyer, if this was not an immediate effect of the contract.[8] The Peruvian Civil Code states as a seller's fundamental duty to perfect (*"peffeccionar'*) the transfer of title in the goods.[9] This point is seen by other Latin American law texts as a consequence of the goods' delivey (*"traditio"*) as is the case of Guatemala's Civil Code.[10] Some Commercial Codes list a set of circumstances that are considered cases of symbolic delivery of merchandise (*"enfrega simbólica"*).[11]

Delivery of documents related to the merchandise is specifically regulated by Bolivian, Chilean, Ecuadorean, and Peruvian law. Other Latin America law refers indirectly to delivery of documents when regulating the delivery of accessories of the purchased goods.

The law of Argentina, Bolivia, Dominican Republic, Guatemala, Panama and Paraguay require, as a seller's duty, that the seller maintain merchandise in the same shape and condition as that of the time when it

---

[7] *But see* RAÚL DIEZ DUARTE, LA COMPRAVENTA EN SEL CÓDIGO CIVIL CHILENO 148 (1988), who makes a semantic distinction between *"entrega"* or delivery and *"tradición"* or Latin *"traditio:"* the former is general; the latter is specific. An example of this manner of introducing seller's obligation is found in Chapter IV of the Uruguayan Civil Code. It contains only one article — 1686 CCROU — which states: "Las obligaciones del vendedor se reducer en general a dos: la entrega o tradición, y el saneamiento de la cosa vendida. La tradición se verifica conforme a las reglas establecidos en el Título III del Libro Tercero." The same text may be seen in Art. 1824 CCChi, Art. 1880 CCCol and Art. 1791 CCEcu. Art. 1486 CCVen contains the same text although without the last paragraph related to *traditio.* However, the immediate section after this article addresses that subject. Art. 1070 CCCR refers only to delivery.

[8] See Art. 614 CCBol, which states "[El] vendedor tiene respecto al comprador, las obligaciones principales siguientes: 1) Entregarle la cosa vendida; 2) Hacerle adquirir la propiedad de la cosa o el derecho si la adquisición no ha sido efecto inmediato del contrato; 3) Responderle por la evicción y los vicios de la cosa." *See also* Art. 759 CCPar.

[9] *See* Art. 1549 CCPer for the Spanish *"perfeccionar."*

[10] *See* Art. 1809 CCGua.

[11] *See, e.g,* Art. 149 CCoChi, Art. 466 CCoCR, Art.355 CCoNic, Art. 763 CCoPan, Art. 529 CCoROU, Art. 923 CCoCol, Art. 149 CCoVen, Art. 194 CCoEcu, Art. 200 CCoBra and Art. 463 CCoArg.

was sold. Delivery expenses are charged to the seller by all considered Latin American legislation.

Latin American law does not speak of "fundamental breach" as does CISG Art. 25. Nor does it refer to the remedy of delivering substitute goods or making up deficiencies in the goods. These rules, however, are found by the general remedies against hidden vices or redhibitory defects.[12] A similarity to fundamental breach is, however, contained in the 1994 Peruvian Civil Code, which refers to a seller's "fundamental duty" to perfect the transfer of title in the goods.[13]

A claim for damages in Latin America always means a combination of "*daño emergente*" — damages that can be expected to result from a breach — on one hand, and on the other hand, "*lucro cesante*" — future earnings lost as a result of contract avoidance. However, the Latin American texts add such specific elements to the damage description as legal costs ("*costas y costos*"), taxes ("*impuestos*" or "*tributos*" or "*tasas*") and moral damages or compensation for pain and suffering ("*daño moral*").

Only the Commercial Code of Uruguay contains a clause similar to CISG Art. 2(a), listing a set of non-commercial sales.[14] But all Latin American countries distinguish between civil and commercial sales. As a general principle, when the subject is not commercial, it will be regulated by the Civil Code; when it is commercial, the Civil Code regulates all questions not covered by the applicable commercial law. This distinction between civil and commercial sales is not merely formal. It has a bearing not only on the applicable law in a specific transaction but also on the applicable statute of limitations and the jurisdiction and competency of the tribunal to address conflicts that might arise between parties. Although there have been some attempts to unify this system, until now the division between civil and commercial sales remains.

Despite being an international compromise — a text involving several legal traditions — from the Latin American point of view, the CISG

---

[12] According to the BLACK'S LAW DICTIONARY 1150 (5th ed. 1979) "redhibitory defect" or "vice" means in the civil law tradition "a defect in an article sold, for which the seller may be compelled to take it back; a defect against which the seller is bound to warrant."

[13] "Es obligación esencial del vendedor perfeccionar la transferencia de la propiedad del bien." Art 1549. The adjective used in Latin America will usually be "esencial." *See* Art. 751 CCoHon and Art. 143 CCoVen.

[14] *See* Art. 516 CCoROU

brought not only concessions to common law, like the general principle of revocability, but also some novelties such as Articles 35(1) and 35(2)(d), which govern the way goods must be contained or packaged. The only reference to this in Latin America can be seen in the extended comment to "general practices," which appears in legislation and has generated some specific case law.[15] The same can be said for time periods, which under the CISG are longer than under many Latin American codes. For example, the time established for the buyer to examine the goods under Art. 38(1) — "[w]*ithin as short a period as is practicable in the circumstances*" — provides greater latitude than many Latin American codes.[16] This concession to reasonableness was encouraged by scholars of developing countries.[17]

The extent of performance from a Latin American perspective deserves special comment. A buyer's claim for non-delivery could be referred to as partial or total non-performance (Art. 51(1) CISG). In case of total non-performance, the buyer's situation, despite his problems, generally is clear: The seller did not send what was purchased, meaning a fundamental breach of his duties that allowed the buyer to declare the contract avoided and to claim damages. However, questions may arise where there is partial performance. In most Latin American codes there is a rule stating that a buyer who agreed to buy an entirety may refuse to accept partial deliveries. Upon this refusal, the buyer may transform seller's partial performance into total non-performance.[18] However, if the buyer has accepted partial delivery, the contract is regarded as performed only with respect to that part, without prejudice to buyer's rights arising from seller's failure to perform

---

[15] *See* "Safra," CNPenal Ecnico, Sala II, [1984-C], f1. 64.

[16] Time periods to inspect covered merchandise varies throughout Latin America. It is 3 days in Argentina, (Art. 472 CCoArg,), Chile (Art. 159 CcoChi), Uruguay (Art. 520CCoROU), and Panama (Art. 772 CcoPan); 4 days in Honduras (Art. 772 CcoHon); 5 days in Costa Rica (Art. 450 CcoCR); 8 days in Venezuela (Art. 145 CcoVen), Ecuador (Art. 192 CcoEcu), and El Salvador (Art. 1019 CcoESal); and 10 days in Brazil (Art. 211 CcoBra).

[17] *See* K. Date-Bah, *The Convention on the International Sale of Goods from the Perspective of the Developing Countries, in* LA VENDITA INTERNAZIONALE 29 (Giuffrè ed. 1981).

[18] *See* Art. 375 CCoMex, Art. 1835 CCChil, Art. 157 CCoChi, Art. 1638 CCSal, Art.462 CCCR, Art. 775 CCoPan, Art. 537 CCoROU, Art. 927 CCoCol, Art. 200 CCoEcu, Art. 203 CCoBra and Art. 468 CcoArg. For example, the first paragraph of Art. 468 CCoArg states: "El comprador que haya contratado por junto una cantidad determinada de efectos, aunque sea por distintos precios, pero sin designación de partes o lotes que deban

future deliveries.[19] Consistent with this, when the contract is partly performed, the buyer retains all available options against all unfinished parts of seller's performance. CISG Art. 51 applies this same principle.

Some Latin American texts state that in the case of sale by installments, the contract cannot be declared avoided if the buyer has paid 25% of the price or has made improvements to the purchased item that equates to 25% of the price. This is the rule in Paraguay.[20] In Peru, the required percentage needs to reach 50%.[21] According to the Argentinian Civil Code,[22] if the sale was made on credit and the buyer does not pay the price, the seller cannot declare the contract avoided, but instead will have the right to demand payment of interest.

Some Latin American commercial texts govern the situation in which the seller issues a warranty against malfunction in the goods. In this case, the law gives the buyer 30 days to inform the seller of the malfunction.[23]

All considered Latin American legislation has a specific reference to *fructus civiles.* These are the natural value increases in the purchased merchandise that are caused by the passage of time and recognized under the law. The CISG omits every reference to these time revenues or natural value increases; instead, the passing of risk of Chapter IV is concerned solely with loss and damage. Only the Commercial Codes of Costa Rica, Honduras and El Salvador[24] state specific rules on INCOTERMS.[25]

III. Buyer's Remedies

Under the CISG, a buyer's remedies against non-performance by a seller may be classified into three groups according to the objective of each. The first group of remedies seeks to salvage the contract. The second group con-

---

entregarse en épocas distintas, no puede ser obligado a recibir una porción bajo promesa de entregarle posteriormente lo restante." *Id.*

[19] Art. 468 CCoArg further states: "Sin embargo, si espontáneanente conviniere en recibir una parte, queda irrevocable y consumada la venta, en cuanto a los efectos que recibió, aún cuando el vendedor false a la entrega de los demás. . . ." *Id.*

[20] *See* Art. 782 CCPar.

[21] *See* Art. 1562 CCPer.

[22] *See* Art. 1429 CCArg.

[23] *See* Arts. 932-33 CCoCol and Art. 1021 CCoESal.

[24] *See* Arts. 473 and 475 CCoCR, Arts. 786-90 CCoHon and Arts. 1029-35 CCoESal.

[25] International Chamber of Commerce, INCOTERMS 1990 (ICC Publication No. 460).

cerns avoidance of the contract. The last group seeks to repair or to control the damage done. Here, we will analyze the buyer's remedies under the CISG and under Latin American legislation according to these general categories.

A. *Remedies Which Seek to Save the Contract*

References to "salvaging the contract" relate to the general tenor of the CISG, which favors preservation of a failing contract rather than its termination. The philosophy of the CISG is that the high expenses usually associated with an international sale should deter a severe reaction, like recission, in response to an obligor's non-performance. The CISG provides a spectrum of different methods to achieve this goal.

1. Fixing additional time for performance

Art. 47(1) of the CISG states that a buyer may set an additional period of reasonable length for a seller's performance. Under civil law tradition, a provision such as this belongs implicitly to the nature of the so-called "consensual contract" or a contract that is made complete based on the party's consent, as is the case with the contract of sale.[26] However, in Latin America, provisions such as these are not undisputed. For example, in Argentina, if the additional period was not explicitly agreed to in the contract, it is not accepted under some case law doctrine. Applying the Latin rule *"ubi lex non distinguit, nec nos distinguere debemus"* ("where the law does not distinguish, neither may ought distinguish us"), in the case of a seller's temporary inability to deliver due to circumstances outside his control, case law provides that a buyer is not expected to have to wait until the situation is resolved.[27]

Mexican scholar Jorge Barrera Graf states that Mexican law does not contemplate a buyer's option to concede to seller any additional performance period. He is of the view that such circumstances could bring procedural difficulties related to statute of limitations and time warranties.[28]

[26] See Art. 1140 CCArg, which provides that consensual contracts are perfected as to the operation of their particular terms at the moment the parties mutually express their consent.

[27] See, among other cases, 75 Jurisprudencia Argentina 910 (1941), 5 L.L. 41.

[28] *See* Jorge Barrera Graf, *La Convención de Viena sobre los contratos de compraventa internacional de mercaderías y el derecho mejicano, in* ANUARIO JURÍDICA 925, n.13, T. II (Universidad Nacional Autonoma de Mexico ed. 1981).

However, this way of thinking does not persuade one that giving an additional period of time to perform the contract should depend only on the will of the contracting parties. In addition, it must be recognized that fixing additional periods of time for performance is not totally unknown in Latin American legal texts. For example, in Argentina, Art. 216 CCoArg states that obligees *may* concede to obligor an additional period to perform his duty. The óbligee may decide to concede nothing; he may prefer instead to declare the contract avoided. But under Argentine law, if he agrees to an additional period of time, the additional time period should not be less than fifteen days, and setting such a period does not mean the obligee relinquishes a possible damages claim. The Argentine's time limitation does not apply in cases where there exist different customs or usages between the parties, nor does it apply where there is a specific clause in the contract agreeing to a reduced period of time for performance.[29] Similar conclusions result from the application of Art. 1204 CCArg, which regulates the implied resolutory condition discussed below. Article 1204 CCArg provides that in case obligor's duty was not performed, obligee may demand fulfillment within no less than 15 days, unless usage or an express agreement mandates a shorter period.[30]

Art. 950 CCoESal recognizes periods of grace for commercial duties only when the period is expressly established by law. In contrast, Art. 694 of the Commercial Code of Honduras states that periods of grace to perform are unacceptable in commercial transactions. However, the Honduran Civil Code provides that the party who did not perform can be requested to perform within a convenient period, no less than 15 days.[31] Only the Commercial Code of Colombia treats the existence of a period of grace as an

[29] The Spanish text reads: "[N]o ejecutada la prestación, el acreedor podrá requerir al incumplidor el cumplimiento de su obligación en un plazo no inferior a 15 días, salvo que los usos o un pacto expreso estableciera uno menor, con los daños y perjuicios derivados de la demora. Transcurrido el plazo sin que la prestación haya sido cumplida, quedarán resueltas, sin más, las obligaciones emergentes del contrato con derecho para el acreedor al resarcimiento de los daños y perjuicios." Art. 216 CCoArg.

[30] Art. 1204 CCArg, second paragraph, states: "No ejecutada la prestación el acreedor podrá requerir al incumplidor el cumplimiento de su obligación en un plazo no inferior a quince dies, salvo que los usos o un pacto expreso establecieran uno menor. . . ." *Id.*

[31] "El que incumple podrá ser requerido por la contraparte para que cumpla su obligación dentro de un plazo conveniente, no inferior a quince días, a no ser que la naturaleza del contrato, los usos o el pacto perrnitieren un plazo menor." Art. 748 CCoHon.

extension of the original term established in the agreement. To be recognized, the setting of this period must be made prior to maturity of the original term.[32]

The rule stated in CISG Art. 45(3) — "No period of grace may be granted to the seller by a court or arbitral tribunal when the buyer resorts to a remedy for breach of contract" — is known in Latin America, but with considerable differences. For example, Bolivia,[33] Panama,[34] and Uruguay[35] permit a judge to set a period of grace in an avoidance claim depending on the specifics of the case. However, the commercial codes of Mexico[36] and Ecuador[37] do not accept periods of grace if they are not admitted by the contract or by law.

2. Requiring performance

CISG Art. 46 states that the buyer may require the seller to perform his obligations unless he has resorted to a remedy that is inconsistent with this requirement. This is the main rule. But the CISG provides an exception to this principle: CISG Art. 28 states that a court is not bound to enter a judgement for specific performance unless the court would do so under its own law with similar contracts of sale not governed by the CISG. This provision, inserted at the request of common law countries, is less relevant to the Latin American nations analyzed here. These countries follow the civil law tradition of giving high priority to the requirement of performance.

Which remedies are inconsistent with CISG Art. 46(1) requirements? Certainly they include the declaration of avoidance pursuant to CISG Art. 49 and the requirement of delivery of substitute goods pursuant to Art. 46(2). It has also been said that applying the remedy of price reduction is inconsistent with requiring the seller to perform.[38] Rules in Latin America consistently state that avoidance can be declared despite the requirement of performance, but a party cannot be required to perform once avoidance has

[32] *See* Art. 829, para. 2, CCoCol.
[33] *See* Art. 568.1 CCBol.
[34] *See* Art. 1009 CCPan.
[35] *See* Art.1431 CCROU.
[36] *See* Art. 84 CCoDFMex.
[37] *See* Art. 153 CCoEcu.
[38] *See* KARL. H. NEUMAYER AND CATHERINE MING, CONVENTION DE VIENNE SUR LES CONTRATS DE VENTE INTERNATIONALS DE MERCHANDISES 330 (1993).

been declared.[39] Bolivian law applies the same principle, adding that the party who has not performed can no longer be required to perform once an avoidance request against him was served by the court.[40] *Contrario sensu*, the period between the factual declaration of avoidance and the notice by the court of the related request, favors the party that has not performed, because performance can be validly carried out during this period. This can sometimes be a meaningful period.

In Chile, the majority rule is that, if he so elects, the buyer can resign the avoidance remedy chosen first and then demand performance.[41] In Venezuela, it is understood that a declaration of avoidance is not entirely the option of the buyer; a judge may rule that preservation of the contract is more consistent with the circumstances of the case and such a ruling will prevail against a buyers' desire to avoid the contract.[42]

Under the CISG, the buyer's right to select the remedy is founded in the Article 46 word "may" *("podrá")*. The practicality of the avoidance remedy will likely depend upon the possibility of obtaining due performance. The Civil Code of Uruguay stresses the performance remedy by stating that the buyer may require performance "whenever possible."[43]

3. Demanding substitute goods or repair

Both Art. 46(2) and 46(3) of the CISG state that if goods do not conform to the contract, the buyer may require the seller to deliver substitute goods or to remedy the lack of conformity by repair. In both cases, buyer's request must be in conjunction with notice given under CISG Art. 39 within a reasonable time.

Usually, Latin American codes state that a seller must deliver that which was agreed upon in the contract.[44] The codes have detailed provi-

---

[39] *See* Art. 1204 CCArg, Art. 216 CCoArg, Art. 1949 CCDFMex, and Art. 376 CCoMex.

[40] See Art. 568 II CCBol, which states: "Si se hubiere demandado solamente la resolución, no podrá ya pedirse el cumplimiento del contrato; y el demandado, a su vez, ya no podrá cumplir su obligación desde el día de su notificación con la demanda."

[41] *See* Luis Claro Soler, *Explicaciones de derecho civil chileno y comparado, in* 10 JURÍDICA DE CHILE 171 (1979).

[42] *See* JOSÉ MELICH ORSINI, LA RESOLUCIÓN DEL CONTRATO POR INCUMPLIMIENTO 297 (1979).

[43] See Art. 1431 CCROU, which states; "cuando sea posible. . . podra exigir el cumplimiento de la obligation."

[44] *See, e.g.*, Art. 1884 CCCol or Art. 1426 CCArg.

sions on conformity of the goods and on that which must be warranted. Such provisions are contained in the Mexican Civil Code of the Federal District (Art. 2283 III CCDFMex) and in other Latin American codes like those of Colombia,[45] Ecuador,[46] Chile,[47] El Salvador,[48] Argentina,[49] Dominican Republic,[50] Guatemala,[51] Paraguay,[52] and Venezuela.[53] Other codes set forth seller's duty to remedy hidden defects in separate chapters or sections, as is the case in Peru and Brazil.

Latin American rules place upon the buyer the burden of proving the existence of hidden defects. These rules are more detailed than the CISG. Defects that should be apparent are excluded from seller's warranty to remedy hidden defects. The Latin American rule is that receiving clearly defective goods without protest is equivalent to implicit acceptance of the defective merchandise. There are qualifications to this rule, for example in sales by sample or by model, or sales by destination ("*venta por envío*").

Art. 46(3) of the CISG states that if goods do not conform to the contract, the buyer may require the seller to remedy this by repair, unless this is unreasonable under the circumstances. Under Latin American law, requiring a seller to repair defective goods is not specifically listed among a buyer's remedies. However, in some cases this can be an element in a claim for price reduction.

4. Reducing the price

Art. 50 of the CISG provides that if the merchandise does not conform to the contract, the buyer may reduce the price in the same proportion as the difference between the price of the delivered goods at the time of the delivery and the value that conforming goods would have had at that time. The second paragraph of this article states that if the seller has remedied any failure to perform in accordance with Art. 37 or Art. 48, or if the buyer refused performance under these articles, he cannot reduce the price. These

[45] *See* Art. 1880 CCCol.
[46] *See* Art. 1791 CCEcu.
[47] *See* Art. 1824 CCChi.
[48] *See* Art.1627 CCESal.
[49] *See* Art.1414 CCArg.
[50] *See* Art. 1603 CCRDom.
[51] *See* Art. 1809 CCGua.
[52] *See* Art. 759(d) CCPar.
[53] *See* Art.1486 CCVen.

rules are known and accepted under Latin American law in cases of acceptance of partial delivery and in cases of hidden vices or defects.

The laws of Argentina and Brazil differentiate willfulness of a seller's fault, when goods are partially or entirely damaged. The Argentine Civil Code states in Art. 611 CCArg that when goods are partially damaged or lost without seller's fault and the price was previously fixed, the buyer has a right to demand the undamaged or unharmed remainder of the merchandise, with the related price reduction. In the alternative, he may declare the contract avoided. However, if goods were lost or deteriorated because of seller's fault, the buyer has the right to demand the remaining merchandise that is not damaged or lost. Additionally, he may claim damages for the lost or deteriorated part, or he may declare the contract avoided with damages.[54] Argentine law has no counterpart to the Art. 51(2) CISG rule that the buyer can declare the contract avoided in its entirety only if the failure to make delivery completely or in conformity with the contract amounts to a fundamental breach.[55] An analogous rule is encountered, however, in Arts. 866 and 867 CCBra.[56]

5. Postponing buyer's performance

Buyer's main duties are to receive the goods and to pay for them. Additionally, he will be in charge of examining the delivered merchandise and the payment of all expenses produced by transferring the title in the goods.

The CISG allows a party to postpone performance in three cases:

---

[54] Art. 611 CCArg states: "Si se perdiese o deteriorase sólo en parte, sin culpa del deudor, el acreedor tendrá derecho para exigir la entrega de la cantidad restante y no deteriorada, con disminución proporcional del precio si estuviese fijado, o para disolver la obligación." *Id.* Art. 612 CCArg states: "Si se perdiese o deteriorase sólo en parte por culpa del deudor, el acreedor tendrá derecho para exigir la entrega de la cantidad restante y no deteriorada, y de la correspondiente a la que faltare o estuviere deteriorada con los perjuicios e intereses, o para disolver la obligación con indemnización de perjuicios e intereses." *Id.*

[55] *See* Art. 469 CCoArg.

[56] Art. 866 CCBra states: "Deteriorada a coisa, nâo sendo o devedor culpado, podera o credor resolver a obrigacão, ou aceitar a coisa, abatido ao seu preço o valor, que perdeu." *Id.* Art. 867 states: "Sendo culpado o devedor podera o credor exigir o equivalente ou aceitar a coisa no estado em que se acha, com direito a reclamar, em um ou em outro caso, indenização das perdas e danos." *Id.*

i. Art. 71 CISG states that a party may suspend his own performance if, after the conclusion of the contract, it is clear that the other party will not perform his duties as a result of a serious deficiency in his ability to perform or in his creditworthiness, or if his behavior shows that he will not perform.
ii. Art. 52 CISG declares that buyer may refuse to accept a delivery that is early or in greater quantity than provided in the contract.
iii. Art. 66 CISG make it clear that buyer can suspend the payment of the price when loss or damage to the goods was due to an act or omission of the seller.

B. *Remedies under Latin American Legislation*

1. Deferring performance in general

Provisions similar to CISG's deferment of performance can be found in some Latin American codes. Usually, these texts only provide that the seller may postpone his due performance in clear cases of buyer's insolvency.[57]However, the buyer will also have the right to postpone his remaining duties where there is a clear risk that he may lose the acquired property.[58]

Under Bolivian law, such provisions are broader. Art. 576 CCBol states that each party may postpone performance when the other party's situation jeopardizes fulfillment of his obligations, unless sufficient assurance has been received.[59] A similar rule exists in the Peruvian Civil Code.[60] The Civil

[57] *See, e.g.*, Art. 1131 CCBra, Art. 2286 CCDFMex, Art. 1073 CCCR, Art. 1826 CCChi and Art. 1688 CCROU.

[58] *See, e.g.*, Art. 1530 CCVen. It states: "Si el comprador fuere perturbado o tuviere fundado temor de serlo por una acción, sea hipotecaria, sea reivindicatoria, puede suspender el pago del precio haste que el vendedor haya hecho cesar la perturbación o el peligro, a no ser que e l vendedor de garantía suficiente , o que se haya estipulado que, no obstante cualquiera contingencia de esta clase, el comprador verifique el pago." *Id.*

[59] Art. 576 CCBol states : "(suspensión del cumplimiento del contrato) Cada una de las partes puede suspender el cumplimiento de su prestación si las condiciones patrimoniales de la otra parse llegan a ser tales que ponen en peligro de no cumplir la contraprestación debida, a menos que preste una garantía suficiente." See also Art. 623.II CCBol, which describes the case of buyer's insolvency after the sale.

[60] *See* Art. 1427 CCPer.

Code of Guatemala[61] and the Civil Code of Brazil[62] also have such provisions, but add that the damaged party may declare the contract avoided and claim damages. Art. 1168 CCVen is less clear: Each party may refuse performance of his obligations, if the other party does not perform "[u]nless different dates have been set for the performance of their respective obligations."[63] Under the laws of Costa Rica[64] and El Salvador,[65] a buyer who fears he may lose possession of the goods may deposit the price with the Courts. Buyer's rights along these lines appear in many Latin American texts but with differences. For example, the Civil Code of Chile provides that when buyer has reason to believe that seller has hidden the existence of a prior claim against the goods or that his title in the goods will be otherwise disturbed, he may deposit the price with the court.[66] The deposit will remain with the court until seller has provided sufficient assurance of his performance or when, through seller's intervention, the claim against the property has been satisfied. Similar texts exist in Venezuela,[67] Mexico,[68] Dominican Republic[69] and Uruguay.[70]

2. Refusal to accept delivery before fixed time or in different quantities than contractually agreed

Latin American codes usually state that goods must be delivered at the time and in the quantity specified in the contract.[71] There is much attention

[61] *See* Art. 1540 CCGua.

[62] *See* Art. 1092 CCBra.

[63] Art. 1168 CCVen: "En los contratos bilaterales, cada contratante puede negarse a ejecutar su obligación si el otro no ejecuta la suya, a menos que se hayan fijado fechas diferentes pare la ejecución de las dos obligaciones." *Id.*

[64] *See* Art. 1088 CCCR.

[65] *See* Art. 1674 CCESal.

[66] *See* Art. 1872 CCChi.

[67] *See* Art. 1530 CCVen.

[68] *See* Art. 2299 CCDFMex.

[69] *See* Art.1653 CCRDom.

[70] *See* Art.1730 CCROU.

[71] *See, e.g.*, Art. 1884 CCCol which states that a seller is obliged to deliver what was agreed in the contract ("El vendedor es obligado a entregar lo que reza el contrato"). Similar provisions are found in Art. 1828 CCChi, Art. 1795 CCEcu and Art. 1689 CCROU.

to quantity, e.g., dimensions in code provisions dealing with the sale of real estate,[72] while less specific attention is given to the subject in the context of movable goods. Examples include the Civil Codes of Chile (Art. 1835 CCChi with reference to Art. 1832 and 1833 CCChi), Colombia (Art. 1891 CCCol with reference to Arts. 1888 and 1889 CCCol), and Ecuador (Art.1802 CCEcu with reference to Arts. 1799 and 1800 CCEcu). The Civil Code of El Salvador (Art.1638 CCESal in connection with Art.1635 and 1636 CCESal) is similarly drafted. In two consecutive articles it refers to the sale of a plot ("*predio*") the measurement of its dimensions. Another article applies this concept to sales of movable goods. In every case in which the dimensions of the "*predio*" are as much as 10% less, then the buyer is permitted to reduce the price to compensate for the discrepancy or to demand the contract avoided. Articles 1626 and 1627 of the Civil Code of Honduras refer to price reduction for dimensions 10% less, and a price increase for 5% more. However, these rules apply only to the sale of real estate.

The Peruvian Civil Code has a provision titled "sale by measurement" ("*compraventa sobre medida*"). It states that for sales of goods priced by unit of volume or length, the seller is required to deliver to the buyer the exact quantity established in the contract. If this is not possible and an excess quantity is delivered, the buyer is obliged to pay for the excess of the contract quantity provided. However, if there is an excess or shortcoming of more than 10%, the buyer may declare the contract avoided.[73] With certain differences between sales of real estate and movable goods, the Civil Code of the Dominican Republic refers to discrepancies in the amount of 20%.[74]

Buyer's interests are especially protected when the time for delivery is not specified in the contract. Accordingly, Art. 1409 CCArg states that seller *must* deliver purchased goods at the time specified in the contract. However, if a date was not agreed upon, delivery must take place when buyer asks for it. If seller does not deliver the purchased goods in the contractually fixed time, the buyer may declare the contract avoided or demand delivery, and if the seller is unable to deliver, the buyer may demand

---

[72] *See, e.g.*, Arts. 601-05 CCBol, Arts. 748-51 CCPar and Art. 1691 CCROU, all of which are applicable only to real estate. For more detailed attention to this subject see Art. 1344 CCArg.

[73] *See, e.g.*, Arts. 1574 and 1575 CCPer. *See also* Arts. 1076-80 CCCR and Art. 1822 CCGua

[74] *See* Arts. 1619 and 1624 CCRDom

immediate restitution of the purchase price.[75] The Civil Code of the Dominican Republic provides more details than any other Latin American text. For instance, there is a clause in Art. 1602 CCRDom under the chapter "seller's duties," which states that seller "must explain his obligations clearly. Anything obscure or ambiguous agreement, will be construed against him."[76] The Commercial Codes of Costa Rica,[77] Nicaragua,[78] Mexico,[79] Ecuador,[80] Panama,[81] Uruguay,[82] Colombia,[83] and Argentina[84] go so far as to state that unless otherwise agreed, the seller must hand over merchandise within 24 hours after the conclusion of the contract.[85]

3. Postponing payment

As previously stated, construing CISG Art. 66 *contrario sensu* as a remedy of the buyer entitles him to postpone payment of the price in the event of loss or damage to the merchandise that occurs after risk has passed when it is due to an act or omission of the seller. In Latin American legal tradition, there is a well-known Latin principle related to the passing of risk: *res perit domino* or "the thing is lost for its owner." In the event of loss or damage to the goods, the proprietor of the goods assumes the risk for loss or damages. Angelici[86] regards this principle as inadequate under a system

[75] *See* Arts. 1412-13 CCArg.

[76] "El vendedor debe explicar con claridad a lo que se oblige. Cualquier pacto oscuro o ambiguo, se interpreta contra el vendedor." Art. 1602 CCRDom.

[77] *See* Art. 465 CCoCR.

[78] *See* Art. 352 CCoNic.

[79] *See* Art. 379 CCoMex.

[80] *See* Art.189 CCoEcu.

[81] *See* Art. 758 CCoPan.

[82] *See* Art. 530 CCoROU.

[83] *See* Art. 924 CCoCol.

[84] *See* Art. 464 CCoArg.

[85] For example, Art. 924 CCoCol states: "El vendedor deberá hacer la entrega de la cosa dentro del plazo estipulado. A falta de estipulación debera entregarla dentro de las veinticuatro horas siguientes al perfeccionamiento del contrato, salvo que la naturaleza del mismo o de la forma como deba hacerse la entrega se desprenda que pare verificarla se requiere un plazo mayor."

[86] *See* Carlo Angelici, *La disciplina del pasaggio dei rischi, in* LA VENDITA INTERNAZIONALE 221-22 (Giuffre ed. 1981).

such as the CISG. Latin American laws uniformly hold that until the moment of delivery or "*traditio,*" all risks must be borne by the seller.[87]

In summary, if seller fails to perform the contract on time or without defect, and the buyer has not yet paid the price, Latin American laws usually permit the buyer to postpone payment until the seller has provided sufficient assurance of performance or has been ordered to eliminate the concern.[88]

4. Claiming damages

Notwithstanding damage reparation, which will be further explained as a third remedy group, the buyer's right to claim damages could also be seen as an adjunct to preserving a failing contract. As seen in Art. 45(1)(b) and 45(2) of the CISG, in the case of breach of contract by the seller, buyer has the right to claim damages as provided in CISG Arts. 74-77. The buyer will not be deprived of his right to claim damages by exercising his right to any other remedy. Art. 925 CcoCol has the same effect. This article states that buyer has the right to request damages in the event of seller's non-delivery. This right may be exercised without pursuing any other remedies.[89]

C. Remedies Which Seek the Contract's Termination

In cases addressed thus far, the buyer-obligee wishes to maintain the relationship with his obligor-seller counterpart. For this purpose, the buyer seeks to give the contract another chance. Remedies with an entirely different objective will now be reviewed: remedies used to destroy the contract when the obligee believes that his best approach is to get out of it.

---

[87] See Art. 577 CCArg, which states: "*Antes de la tradición de la cosa, el acreedor no adquiere sobre ella ningún derecho real.*" A Chilean scholar has made a distinction between the general concept -"delivery" or "entrega" in Spanish- and the specific "traditio." In all cases, *traditio* meant delivery, but not all delivery could be defined by the term *traditio. See* RAÚL DIEZ DUARTE, LA COMPRAVENTA EN EL CÓDIGO CIVIL CHILENO 201(1988).

[88] See among others already quoted, Art. 1872 CCChi and Art. 1730 CCROU.

[89] "El comprador tendrá derecho a exigir el pago de perjuicios por el incumplimiento del vendedor a su obligación de hacerle tradición válida, sin necesidad de instaurar previamente cualquiera de las acciones consagradas en el artículo 1546 del Código Civil y 870 de este Libro." Art. 925 CcoCol.

1. Declaring the contract avoided because of seller's fundamental breach

Article 49 of the CISG is the cornerstone of the buyer's annihilation remedies. It states that the buyer may declare the contract avoided if the failure by the seller to perform any of his obligations under the contract or the CISG "[a]mounts to a fundamental breach of contract."[90]

Avoidance does not follow automatically from the seller's breach of contract: Art. 46(2) of the CISG states that if the non-conformity of the delivered goods by the seller amounts to a fundamental breach of contract, the buyer may require delivery of substitute goods. One of the main principles of the CISG seeks to strengthen the possibility to rescue the contract as a first alternative whenever possible. When such rescue is not possible, this extreme remedy comes into play.

What are the seller's obligations under the CISG when his failure to perform amounts to a fundamental breach of the contract? When will a partial delivery be understood as non-performance and when will it be looked upon as a start of performance? These questions, as a general rule, cannot be answered without looking into each specific case.

This subject was always a critical point and continues to be so no matter under which legal tradition the question arises. From a scholarly point of view, it is not always easy to determine whether we are facing a seller's total non-performance or the beginning of a delayed performance. This subject has gained special attention regarding the CISG and international interpretation. For example, when having purchased a chemical product for human use called "Human Sulfat," we receive the product, but in a state which is only useful for beast or plants. It could be difficult to understand whether we are facing a fundamental breach of seller's duty to deliver a final product or a case of partial performance. The same question perhaps will receive different answers in Latin America and in Europe.

For example, purchasing a final product under Argentine law may create a pure and simple seller's obligation: to deliver an entirety called "car." The simplicity of such entirety is not affected by the complexity of the many assembled parts and functions implicitly included in the meaning of the noun "car." The turning point will be the certain and specific determi-

[90] Art. 49(1)(a) (CISG).

nation of the purchased thing and this determination will not be affected by the complexity of it.

In Germany the question under Geman law would be resolved by the German Civil Code Art. 462 BGB. Under this rule of the so-called "*Wandelung*" the buyer may demand an action for redhibition terminating the contract. But even though German case law applying the CISG in a sulfate case resolved to maintain the contract by construing it through an international lens, it was very conflictive and difficult to understand from the perspective of the Latin American legal tradition.[91]

Elqueta Anguita refers to the same problem in Chile.[92] One part of the Chilean doctrine and the main domestic case law understands that any kind of breach of the contract, including breach on secondary duties, will be sufficient to declare the avoidance (so Alessandri Rodríguez, Meza Barros and Vio Vázquez). The other part of the doctrine, adhered to by Elgueta himself and Claro Solar, maintains the opposite opinion.

The same problem was seen in Mexico. Barrera Graf[93] understands that Mexican law provides that no kind of non-performance, except produced damage, will allow the avoidance of the contract. Sánchez Medal Urquiza[94] maintains the contrary position: Alleged non-performance must have a special significance, especially bearing in mind obligee's interests. This was the idea represented by Ramella[95] in Argentina and Melich Orsini[96] in Venezuela. But both scholars recognized that this conclusion was not accepted by domestic case law, which admitted any non-performance as a reason for the avoidance.

The Bolivian Civil Code sets forth in Art. 572 CCBol a principle entirely compatible with the CISG: It will not be possible to declare the avoidance of the contract, if the seller's (not performed) duty has no significance

---

[91] *See* ALFREDO COLMO, DE LAS OBLIGACIONES EN GENERAL 216 (1920). *But see* Burghard Piltz, *Neue Entwicklungen im UN-Kaufrecht*, Neue Juristische Wochenschrift 2768 (NJW) 1996.

[92] *See* Augusto Elquita Angüita, *Resolución de contratos y excepción de pago, in* EDITORIAL JURÍDICA DE CHILE § 31 ff (1981).

[93] *See* Graf, *supra* note 28, at 945.

[94] *See* SÁNCHEZ MEDAL URQUIZA, LA RESOLUCIÓN DE LOS CONTRATOS POR INCUMPLIMIENTO 109 (1980).

[95] *See* ANTEO RAMELLA, LA RESOLUCIÓN POR INCUMPLIMIENTO § 57 (1975).

[96] *See* ORSINI, *supra* note 42, at 176.

in comparison to buyer's interest.[97] Similarly, the Civil Code of Paraguay[98] states that the declaration of avoidance will not be accepted if the lack of performance of the other party is of little importance or does not affect the other party's interest.

Articles 51(2) and 73 of the CISG concern the essence of the breach in cases of partial non-performance and sale by installments. In Argentina, Art. 468 CCoArg states that cases in which the buyer has purchased as a whole a certain quantity of goods without the seller's determination that certain parcels or parts must be delivered at different times, the buyer cannot be required to accept a portion of the goods under the promise to deliver the rest later. However, when a portion has been accepted, the sale is perfected concerning the delivered portion, regardless of the seller's failure to deliver the rest — the remedy for which can be a reduction of the price.[99]

Until 1968, the Argentine Civil Code provided in Art. 1204 CCArg what was known in Spanish as *"pacto comisorio expreso."* This legal expression refers to an expressly resolutory condition that produces the termination of the contract in case something happens, like the obligor's non performance.[100] After a Civil Code's reform that year by law Nr. 17.711, the implied resolutory condition or *"pacto comisorio tácito"* was accepted in place of the former expressly resolutory condition. This legal expression means that in contracts with reciprocal obligations, either party may de-

---

[97] See Art. 572 CCBol, under the title "Gravedad e importancia del incumplimiento," which states: "No habrá lugar a la resolución del contrato si el incumplimiento de una de las partes es de poca gravedad o de escasa importancia teniendo en cuenta el interés de la otra parte."

[98] *See* Art. 724 CCPar.

[99] "El comprador que haya contratado por junto una cantidad determinada de efectos, aunque sea por distintos precios, pero sin designacion de parses o loses que deban entregarse en epocas distintas, no puede ser obligado a recibir una porcion bajo promesa de entregarle posteriormente lo restante. Sin embargo, si espontaneamente conviniere en recibir una parse, queda irrevocable y consumada la yenta, en cuanto a los efectos que recibi6, aun cuando el vendedor false a la entrega de los demas, salvo, por lo que toca a estos, la opcion que le toca el articulo precedente." Art. 468 CCoArg.

[100] The former Art. 1204 CCArg stated: "Si no hubiere pacto expreso que autorice a una de las partes a disolver el contrato si la otra no cumpliere, el contrato no podrá disolverse, y sólo podrá pedirse su cumplimiento." (If there is no express agreement that authorizes one of the parties to declare the contract avoided if the other party has not performed its duty, the contract cannot be avoided).

clare the contract avoided if the other party has not performed his duty.[101] In spite of the fact that the Argentine Civil Code permits this solution, Art. 1374 CCArg prohibits it on sales of movable goods. The suitability of this restriction has been questioned[102] and, in any event, this prohibition is not applicable to commercial sales of movable goods.[103]

Many Latin American codes permit automatic avoidance and accept the declaration of avoidance without further requirements. Phrases such as "*ipso facto*" or "*sin mas*" are encountered in these codes. Argentina is an example. Art. 1204 CCArg states at the end of its second paragraph, that if due obligation is not performed in the additional period, all remaining duties emerging from the contract will be understood as finished without needing further steps.[104]

Uruguay, Brazil and Honduras take the opposite position. In these countries, the contract will not terminate *ipso facto* but, instead, an obligee must pursue this through a judicial process.[105] In Honduras, Art. 749 CCoHon provides that for an avoidance to be effective there must be prior notice to the counterparts. The Brazilian Commercial Code goes further: to put his obligor in default, the obligee must judicially demand the fulfillment of the obligation.[106] In Chile the law is unclear due to conflicting provisions of the Code.[107]

---

[101] The first paragraph of new Art. 1204 CCArg provides: "En los contratos con prestaciones recíprocas se entiende implícita la facultad de resolver las obligaciones emergentes de ellos en caso de que uno de los contratantes no cumpliera su compromiso. . . ." *Id.* This is the position provided by Art. 1124 CCCub, Art. 1532 CCEcu, Art. 199 CCoEcu, Art. 1092 CCBra, Art. 202 CCoBra, Art. 1009 CCPan, Art. 754 CCoPan, Art. 725 CCPar, Art. 1428 CCPer, Art. 1546 CCCol, Art. 870 CCoCol, Art. 534 CCoROU, Art. 156 CCoChi, Art. 1949 CCDFMex, and Art. 376 CCoMex.

[102] *See* JORGE J. LLAMBIAS, CÓDIGO CIVIL ANOTADO 441, Vol. III-A.

[103] *See* Art. 216 CCoArg and Art. 451 CCoArg.

[104] "[T]ranscurrido el plazo sin que la prestación haya sido cumplida, quedarán resueltas, sin más, las obligaciones emergentes del contrato. . . ." Art. 1204 CCArg.

[105] *See* Art. 1431 CCROU.

[106] *See* Art. 205 CCoBra, which states: "Para o vendedor ou comprador poder ser considerado em mora, é necessario que preceda interpelaçâo judicial da entrega da coisa vendida, ou do pagamento do preço."

[107] Art. 1489 CCChi declares the implied resolutory condition. The second paragraph, after referring to the non performance of duties, provides: "pero en tal caso podrá el otro contratante pedir a su arbitrio o la resoluciónо el cumplimiento del contrato, con indemnización de daños y perjuicios."

2. Avoidance in case of non-performance within the additional period

Art. 47(1) of the CISG provides that the buyer may fix an additional period of time of reasonable length for performance by the seller of his obligations. This is the so- called *"period of grace"* or *"Nachfrist,"* the latter being the German terminology. Art. 49(1)(b) of the CISG provides that buyer may declare the contract avoided if seller does not deliver within the additional period of time or declares that he will not deliver within that period.

Latin American legislation incorporates all prior considerations introduced above when the grace period or additional period in question is also used as a device to keep the contract alive.

The Bolivian Civil Code refers to the additional period in Art. 570.1 CCBol. This provision describes the giving of a period of grace similar to the one stated in the CISG. This Bolivian text provides that the party that has already done his duty may demand, through a notarial document sent to the party that has not performed, performance in a fixed reasonable period of time that cannot be less than 15 days. In case of non- performance, he will declare the contract avoided in the same way as under Art. 49 of the CISG.[108] This text is entitled "avoidance by request" (*"resolución por requerimiento"*). A similar provision is seen in the Peruvian Civil Code in Arts. 1428 and 1429 CCPer related to the sale contract by Art. 1559 CCPer.

Another implied recognition of the additional period appears in the second paragraph of Art. 1826CCChi. The related text states that if the seller, by his own fault, delayed delivery, the buyer may persist on the con-

---

Elgueta Anguita understands the expression *"pero en tal caso podrá... pedir,"* as the opposite of what was previously provided in the Code, because Arts. 1487 and 1488 CCChi provide for termination of the contract by application of the implied resolutory condition as an *ipso facto* result. *See* Elgueta Anguita, *supra* note 87, at 85. However, that phrase translated to English as "but in that case he may. . .request" shows that termination is not *ipso facto*. Main Chilean case law and doctrine is inclined to accept that only a judicial decision will declare the termination of the contract. Other opinions understand that termination was already obtained with the introduction of the claim.

[108] Art. 570(1) CCBol states: "La parte que ha cumplido su obligación puede requerir a la parte que incumple mediante note diligenciada notarialmente, que cumpla la suya dentro de un término razonable no menor a quince días con apercibimiento de que, en caso contrario, el contrato quedará resuelto."

tract or desist from it, in both cases claiming damages. But the quoted paragraph expressly states the contract's termination as a consequence of seller's delay and as a result of persisting in the contract without success or declaring its termination.

3. Anticipatory repudiation: declaring in advance the termination of the contract

CISG Art. 72 states that if it is clear prior to the date fixed for contract performance that one of the parties will commit a fundamental breach of the contract or declare that he will not perform his obligation, the other party, giving notice, if time allows him do so, may declare the contract avoided.

The concept of a declaration of avoidance prior to the date for performance in the manner recognized by the CISG is virtually unknown in Latin American law. The right to suspend payment is more customarily accompanied by the right to avoid the contract, for example, in cases of breach of warranty on the legal and peaceful possession of the goods or in the case of hidden defects.[109]

Usually, the Latin American texts permit only sellers to declare contract avoidance in advance. This is especially true where the seller has grounds enough to presume buyer's insolvency or radical changes in buyer's patrimony.[110] An equivalent buyer's right is practically unknown. Notwithstanding this, Paraguayan Art. 720 CCPar refers to both parties, allowing a party to postpone performance until sufficient assurances are given. But if such assurance is not provided, avoidance is permitted.

---

[109] For example, the Bolivian Civil Code admits that in case seller does not free the purchased goods from any pledges or other impediments in a judicially fixed additional period, buyer may declare the avoidance of the contract and claim damages. Art. 638(2) CCBol provides: "Cuando la cosa vendida se encuentra gravada con garantías reales o sujetas a vínculos de embargo o secuestro, caso en el cual además, si el vendedor no libera la cosa en el término que debe fijar el juez, el comprador puede demander la resolución del contrato y el resarcimiento del daño conforme al artículo 596." *Id. Compare* Art. 1088 CCCR and Art. 638(2) CCBol.

[110] *See* Art. 623.2 CCBol, Art. 2287 CCDFMEx, Art. 1131 CCBra, Art. 1793 CCEcu, Art. 1826 CCChi, Art. 1882 CCCol, Art. 1629 CCESal, Art. 1688 CCROU, Art. 1493 CCVen, Art. 1467 CCCub, Art. 1073 CCCR, Art. 1613 CCRDom, Art. 1624 CCHon, Art. 2594 CCNic, Art. 1419 CCArg, Art. 1237 CCPan. It is interesting to note that Art. 147 CCoChi. and Art. 448 CCoCR allow a buyer to demand delivery of cancelled invoices by showing seller's prior title.

The Spanish Civil Code and all those that follow it, like the Cuban Civil Code, provide something comparable to the CISG's provisions, but only in relation to sale of real estate.[111]

The obligations section of the Argentine Civil Code provides that an obligor in a state of insolvency cannot invoke a prior existent and agreed period, in order to perform his delayed obligations, after such declaration of insolvency was issued.[112] Under this rule, the fixed period or term ("*plaza*") is like a sort of benefit that insolvency negates.[113] This principle is recognized in other Latin American texts.[114]

Does it mean that one of the parties may declare the contract avoided when it is clear, prior to date of performance, that the other party will not perform? The anticipated fundamental breach may be clear either because of the actions of the obligor or because of situations of *force majeure*. Art. 72 CISG is much more directed to the anticipatory repudiation known by common law but also to cases of possible application of the clause "*rebus sic stantibus*," or changing by supervening causes, what is also known by the civil law tradition and will be analyzed below in this paper.[115]

Taken in the context of its related commentary, the expression "*when it is clear*," from the first sentence of Art. 72(1) CISG, must be understood in a broader sense than the Latin American normal meaning. The *Official Record* on the CISG describes that a clear future fundamental breach will constitute a contract repudiation or an objective fact "[s]uch as the destruction of the seller's plant by fire or the imposition of an embargo or of monetary controls which will render impossible future performance."[116] A

---

[111] See Art. 1503 CCEsp, which states: "Si el vendedor tuviere fundado motive para temer la pérdida de la cosa inmueble vendida y el precio, podrá promover inmediatamente la resolución de la venta." *Id.* Art. 1503 CCCub states that if seller has reasonable grounds to presume that sold real estate or paid price are at risk to be lost, he may promote immediate termination of the contract.

[112] *See* Art. 572 CCArg. "El deudor constituído en insolvencia y los que lo representen no pueden reclamar el plazo para el cumplimiento de la obligación." *Id.*

[113] *See* Camara Federal de Apelaciones 31 E. D. 30 (1970) (Revista Juridica El Derecho — Arg.).

[114] *See, e.g.*, Art. 315 CCBol, Art. 1188 CCRDom, Art. 1215 CCVen, and Art. 1015 CCPan.

[115] *See generally* JORGE MOSSET ITURRASPE, LA FRUSTRACIÓN DEL CONTRATO (1991).

[116] Commentary on the Draft Convention on Contracts for the International Sale of Goods prepared by the Secretariat, Document A/CONF.97/5, Art. 29, No. 5 — United

footnote recognizes that the non-performing party will be excused from damages by virtue of CISG Art. 65.[117] Latin American law resolves the objective fact with the notion of *"force majeure,"* which excuses non-performance in cases where causes are outside the control of the parties. But this subject, as is the case of unaccepted partial performance as fundamental breach for a Latin American law cultural inheritance, will be difficult to construe internationally with some uniformity.

D. Buyer's Remedies Which Seek Damages Reparation

The third group of the CISG's remedies analyzed in this paper will be those pursuing reparation for, control over, or a reduction in the harmful effects of all damages done by the seller.

1. Claiming damages

The CISG general rule appears in Art. 45.2: If the seller fails to perform any of his duties, the buyer may exercise his right to other remedies. By doing this the buyer is not deprived of any right he may have to claim damages. Art. 74 CISG calculates basic damages: a sum of money equal to the suffered loss including loss of profit. But the principle of the full recovery is subject to a limitation: damages may not exceed the loss that the party in breach foresaw or ought to have foreseen.

The *Official Records* state that "[t]he basic philosophy of the action for damages is to place the injured party in the same economic position he would have been in if the contract had been performed."[118] In the case of avoidance, the CISG differentiates between damages where there is and where there is not a substitute transaction.

In comparing the CISG with Latin American approaches to damages, it is appropriate to consider the reach or range of the concept of "damages." It is also appropriate to determine if the damage claim is ancillary to another claim or if it can be independently requested. Finally, in this section the Latin American concept of "moral damages" will also be discussed.

Nations Conference on Contracts for the International Sale of Goods, Official Records, New York, 1981 (A/CONF.97/19), 53 [hereinafter Official Records].

[117] *See id.*

[118] *Id.*

2. Measurement of the damage

The CISG has only one comprehensive category of damages. CISG Art. 74 states that:

> "Damages for breach of contract by one party consist of a sum equal to the loss, including loss of profit, suffered by the other party as a consequence of the breach. Such damages may not exceed the loss which the party in breach foresaw or ought to have foreseen at the time of the conclusion of the contract, in the light of the facts and matters of which he then knew or ought to have known, as a possible consequence of the breach of contract."[119]

To establish the range of damages caused by the non-performance, and determine which of the damages suffered will be taken into account to fix the compensation sum, it requires a prior classification to determine which were foreseeable results of the non-performance and which were not. To be compensable under the CISG, the damage must be foreseeable.

For the most part, foreseeability is also an element of Latin America law as is shown in Art. 345 and 346 CCBol, Art. 1059 — 60 CCBra,[120] Art. 1150 CCRDom, Art.1616 CCCol and Art.1601 CCEcu (the latter two drafted in a similar way), Art. 1321 CCPer,[121] Art. 2110 CCDFMex and Art. 992 CCPan. In Venezuela, Art. 1274 CCVen states that the party in breach is liable for damages that were foreseeable or that ought to have been foreseeable at the time of the conclusion of the contract, when the reason for non performance is not wrongful intent.[122] The CISG does not contain language limiting damages to losses which are the "immediate and direct" consequences of the breach. Various Latin American codes contain such language, for example, Art. 1275 CCVen provides — that even in case of

---

[119] CISG Art. 74

[120] "[a]lém do que ele efetivamente perdeu, o que razoabelmente deuixou de lucrar." Art. 1059 CCBra.

[121] However, it is not clear to the foreign reader which consequence the wrongful intent will bring.

[122] "El deudor no queda obligado sino por los daños y perjuicios previstos o que han podido proverse al tiempo de la celebración del contrato, cuando la falta de cumplimiento de la obligación no proviene de su dolo. . . ." Art. 1274 CCVen.

wrongful intent — damages cannot exceed the immediate and direct consequence of the breach.

Argentina, among other Latin American countries, has two rules, one of which addresses cases of wrongful intent *("dolo")*. Under Argentine law, the main rule limits damages to the immediate and direct consequence of the non-performance. But Art. 520 and Art. 521 CCArg go on to state that in case of willful and knowing breach, the seller can also be liable for the remote consequences *("consecuencias mediatas")* of the breach. Referring to casual acts, the Civil Code of Paraguay takes a similar position.[123]

3. Damages in conjunction with other remedies

As explained above, CISG Art. 45(2) provides that, by exercising his right to other remedies, the buyer is not deprived of any right he may have to claim damages. Similaraly, in Latin America, the obligee may request damages as an ancillary part of the main claim. In that case the subordinate claim's chances of success will depend upon the outcome of the main demand. However, apart from any other claim, damages may always be independently requested.

The Latin American legal tradition demands as a prerequisite for an independent claim, assertive seller's liability. This principle imports a liability compared with that model of behavior of the Latin *pater familiae,* which is equivalent to the CISG's *reasonable man.*[124]

4. Moral damages

In the Latin American legal tradition "moral damage" means intangible injury to feelings, honor, or moral principles, causing pain or suffering.

---

[123] See Art. 1856 CCPar., which states: "El obligado a indemnizar el daño que le sea imputable resarcirá todas las consecuencias inmediatas, y las mediates previsibles, o las normales según el curso natural y ordinario de las cosas, pero no las casuales, salvo que éstas deriven de un delito y debieran resultar según las miras que el agente tuvo al ejecutar el hecho." *Id.* It is not very clear which consequence could be "casual" but nevertheless foresaw by the perpetrator.

[124] Art. 947 CCoESal establishes another main principle: all commercial duties must be performed with the diligence of a good commercial man in his own business: "Las obligaciones mercantiles deben cumplirse con la diligencia de un buen comerciante en negocio propio." *Id.*

Such injuries originate in a tortious act. In spite of the difficulty of assessing moral damage because of its intangible nature, a judge may recognize the existence of such damages and award a compensatory sum of money.[125]

The Argentine Civil Code refers to *"agravio moral"* (Art. 522 CCArg), a specific and restrictive form of moral damage. The Civil Codes of Ecuador, Mexico,[126] Peru,[127] Bolivia,[128] and Venezuela[129] also contain specific rules on moral damages, establishing, however, different ways to measure it. In Ecuador, an un-numbered section of text added between Arts. 2258 and Art. 2259 CCEcu provides that, in case of extreme seriousness, an aggrieved party may seek payment of moral damages as an independent claim.

Other Latin American States, which traditionally follow the Spanish Civil Code, make no provisions on moral damages. This is the case in Panama, Chile, Colombia, Dominican Republic and Uruguay.

Clearly, such a specific emotional element would be very difficult to incorporate into an international multilateral agreement like the CISG. However, this absence does not mean that such results do not occur in international sales when a tortious act is committed. In a contract governed by the CISG in which the gap-filling law is that of a country that allows moral damages, the related party can obtain them.

5. Exercising the right to retain

CISG Art. 86(1) provides that the buyer who received the goods but intends to exercise any right to reject them must preserve them. However, he will be entitled to retain the merchandise until all reasonable expenses have been reimbursed by the seller.

The right to retain in Latin America is provided for in separate chapters or sections of the Civil Code or exists as a specific remedy in the deposit contract. In Argentina, for example, the retaining right appears immediately after the section describing privileges or credits' order of preferences. Under the title *"Del derecho de retención,"* Art. 3939 CCArg states that the

---

[125] *See* Art. 1916 CCDFMex. *See also* J.J. LLAMBIAS, COMPENDIO DE DERECHO CIVIL — OBLIGACIONES 107 (1971).

[126] *See* Art. 1916 CCDFMex.

[127] *See* Art. 1322 CCPer.

[128] *See* Art. 994 CCBol.

[129] *See* Art. 1196 CCVen.

right to retain belongs to the holder and entitles him to keep possession of it, until the payment of what is due is made for the same item.[130] The debt, as provided in this text, must be originated in the held item itself. On the other hand, the obligee cannot retain anything without prior agreement or without the help of a judicial ruling. This general position is also accepted by Art.1279 CCBra, Arts.1828 and 1832 CCGua, Art.1826 CCPar and old Art.1029 CCPer. The new Peruvian text allows a wider spectrum of uses of the right to retain the goods. Art 1123 CCPer has been applied in some specific cases in a way that requires that no direct connection must exist between the held item and the requested credit.[131] The same is provided by Art. 703 CCoHon and Art. 957 CCoESal.

Other civil law Latin American texts provide for the right to retain when they contemplate the contract of deposit. They recognize the power of the receiver to retain the deposited goods until his expenses are reimbursed. This form is seen in the law of Bolivia,[132] Colombia,[133] Costa Rica,[134] Dominican Republic,[135] Ecuador,[136] Panama[137] and Venezuela.[138] Chilean Civil Code specifically provides in Art.1872 CCChi the buyer's right to retain the price when seller has not delivered the purchased goods. The equivalent seller's right is provided in Art.151 CCoChi. But many Latin American Commercial Codes contain broader provisions on this topic than what was contemplated only as deposit by the Civil Codes.[139]

[130] Art. 3939 CCArg states: "El derecho de retención es la facultad que corresponde al tenedor de una cosa ajena, para conservar la posesión de ella hasta el pago de lo que le es debido por razón de esa misma cosa."

[131] Art. 1123 CCPer provides: "Por el derecho de retención un acreedor retiene en su poder el bien de su deudor si su crédito no está suficientemente garantizado. Este derecho procede en los casos que establece la ley o cuando haya conexión entre el crédito y el bien que se retiene." *Id.*

[132] *See* Art. 857 CCBol.

[133] *See* Art. 2258 CCCol.

[134] *See* Art.1357 CCCR.

[135] *See* Art. 1948 CCRDom.

[136] *See* Art. 2166, 2167 CCEcu.

[137] *See* Art. 1473 CCPan.

[138] *See* Art.1774 CCVen.

[139] This is the case with Art.196 CCoEcu, Arts.122 and 123 CCoVen, Art. 351 CCoNic, Art. 533 CCoROU and Art. 765 CCoPan.

Obviously, if a retainer's expenses were not reimbursed, he may request judicial sale of the held item. In that case, merchandise would be auctioned and the retainer could recollect his expenses from the proceeds of the auction. The rest would be returned to seller. Barrera Graf states that in case the buyer were a warehouse or storage house, he may proceed to sell the retained merchandise, and if it is the case, to destroy it when there is a risk to general health or security and it cannot be preserved without unreasonable expense.[140]

6. Requesting interest

In two specific cases the CISG recognizes the request of interest payment:

i. Art. 78 CISG states that if a party fails to pay any sum that is in arrears, the other party is entitled to interest on it, without prejudice to any claim for damages;
ii. Art. 84.1 CISG provides that if the seller is bound to refund the price, he must also pay interest on it, from the date on which the price was paid.

The CISG is silent on rate of interest. Historically, Latin American laws either specified a fixed interest rate between 6% to 12% yearly[141] or nominated a special organization to set the rate of interest. For example Art. 1244 CCPer[142] refers to the Peruvian Central Bank. But these positions were taken before the extraordinary wave of inflation that occurred in Latin America. In Argentina, for example, in 1989 the monthly inflation rate was a three-digit figure. The devastating effects of such economic disasters eroded the acquisitive power of money on a daily basis and called for new approaches to set rates of interest in the face of rampant inflation. Rates of interest were set based on new born terminology like the Spanish noun "*in-*

---

[140] *See* Graf, *supra* note 28, at 951.

[141] This is the case with Art. 1062 CCBra, Art. 1617 par. I CCCol, Art. 2395 CCDFMex and Art. 108 CCoVen. The Spanish Codigo de Comercio accepts that "today" the legal interest is fixed on 10%. *See also* Art. 341CCoE.

[142] Art. 1244 CCPer states: "La tasa del interés legal es fijada por el Banco Central de Reserva del Perú." *Id.* Other institutions are established by Art. 707 CCoHon and Art. 960 CCoESal.

dexación" or the Portugese expression "*corregao monetaria.*" These terms establish an increase in the money's worth equivalent to the increase of the cost of living.

In spite of the fact that inflation belongs mostly to the Latin American past, the danger of inflation remains latent like a vicious reciditive. Consolidation of democracy and the reality of community associations like Mercosur or NAFTA, with all their economic implications, should help control inflation.[143]

E. *Examples of Latin American Remedies for Breach of Contract Not Contained in the CISG*

Discussed below are four Latin American remedies that were not adopted by the CISG. The first two apply to the situation in which the buyer seeks to salvage a failing contract. The latter two are related to the avoidance remedy. These four Latin American remedies have in common the fact that a buyer can seek them without prior reference to them in the contract.

Other remedies can be set forth in the contract, for example, legal retraction or "*retracto legal*" or the property reservation clause.[144] However, such remedies are beyond the scope of this paper.

1. The right to obtain performance by a third party

Art. 77 CISG provides that a party who relies on a breach of contract must take such measures as are reasonable in the circumstances to mitigate the loss. Art. 28 CISG on the other hand states that a court is not bound to enter a judgment for specific performance unless the court would do so under its own law in respect of similar contracts of sale not governed by the CISG. May a court order specific performance by a third party when the obligor refuses to perform? Perhaps, under certain circumstances, performance by a third party may be seen under CISG Art. 77 as a form to mitigate the losses.

---

[143] In Argentina, for example, "indexación" was expressly prohibited in 1991 by law.

[144] Reserve of property is permitted by Art. 458 CCoCR and Art. 781 CCoHon. *See also* Section V, of the non-numerated article between Arts. 202 and 203 CCoEcu, and Art. 952 CCoCol. However see later Art. 954 CCoCol, which forbids reserve of property in commercial sales.

The Latin American position is very clear: Where seller does not perform, buyer's right to obtain performance from a third party in case of obligor's refusal of fulfillment of his duties, but charging the latter the cost of such performance, is recognized by all Latin American compared legislation, though with differences. Art. 505 (2)(a) CCArg provides for a obligee's right to procure performance from a third party and to charge the obligor the cost of it, but only with prior judicial waiver. This rule appears also in Art. 467 CCoArg. The same principle appears, among others, in Ecuador,[145] Peru,[146] Colombia,[147] and Paraguay.[148] Other texts, like Venezuela,[149] accept performance by a third party only when what it is due is the fulfillment of an obligation of doing something (*"obligation de dar"*).

Performance by a third party cannot be demanded when the obligation can be performed only by the obligor or it refers to a specific identified good.

2. The Argentine "astreintes."

The Argentine civil law reform in 1968 (Law n° 17.711) introduced a proceeding of French origin: the *"astreintes"* or proceeding to obtain a judicial fine, which could be on a daily, weekly, monthly, etc. basis, in case of non performance of a pending obligation.[150] The *"astreintes"* presumes the existence of an obligor's deliberately unfulfilled obligation. It is a compulsory judicial way to obtain performance. As such, it can be regarded as another remedy designed to preserve a failing contract.

3. Avoidance in instances of unforessable excessive hardship

Art. 79(1) CISG provides for cases of *force majeure*. Additionally, in some Latin American countries there is an opportunity to declare a contract avoided under the *"teoria de la imprevisión,"* when extraordinary and unforeseeable events arise which render performance excessively expensive.[151] Similar to the CISG's "reasonable man" standard, the Latin Ameri-

---

[145] *See* Art. 1596(1) CCEcu.

[146] *See* Art. 1219(2) CCPer.

[147] *See* Art. 1610(2) CCCol.

[148] *See* Art. 420(b) CCPar.

[149] *See* Art. 1266 CCArg.

[150] Art. 666 Bis CCArg. states: "[L]os jueces podrán imponer en beneficio del titular del derecho, condenaciones conminatorias de carácter pecuniario a quienes no cumplieron deberes jurídicos impuestos en una resolución judicial. . . ."

[151] *See* Paragraph 2, Art. 1198 CCArg.

can standard states that a reasonable head of family or a good *pater familae* should not, in normal circumstances, have been able to foresee the unexpected event.[152] This is a specific application of what in Europe is known as the result of a clause *rebus sic stantibus.* To understand this concept properly, it must be recognized that the objective is not to promote better business but to protect against a ruinous development. For example, in the past, a contract party in Latin America should expect cost increases because of inflation. That was normal and foreseeable. But, suddenly, a government devaluation of national currency could occur, starting a stampede in every exchange bureau, with customers trying to change national money against US Dollars. The stampede is uncontrollable, rocketing prices beyond all possible expectancies. The party in a contract with this country should expect some sort of contingency but what happened was unforeseeable and such lack of foresight is known as *"imprevisión."*

In Latin America this concept has various applications: some Civil Codes like those of Argentina,[153] Bolivia,[154] Honduras,[155] and Guatemala[156] refer to avoidance through excessive onerousness or *"resolución por excesiva onerosidad."* In these jurisdictions, in cases of bilateral commutative agreements or unilateral onerous contracts, where there has been neither fault nor delay by the concerned party, and extraordinary circumstances have arisen, he may seek to declare the contract avoided when the fulfillment of his pending duty would become so expensive that his performance is unbearable. The party expecting performance forestalls avoidance of the contract by offering to ameliorate the results.[157]

---

[152] *See generally* LILY R. FLAH AND MIRIAM SMAYEVSKY, TEORÍA DE LA IMPRECISIÓN (1989).

[153] Art. 1198 CCArg.

[154] Art. 581 CCBol.

[155] Art. 757 CCoHon.

[156] Art. 1330 CCGua.

[157] Art. 1198 CCArg states: "Los contratos deben celebrarse, interpretarse de buena fe y de acuerdo con lo que verosimilmente las partes entendieron o pudieron entender, obrando con cuidado y provisión. En los contratos bilaterales conmutativos y en los unilaterales onerosos y conmutativos de ejecucion diferida o continuada, si la prestacion a cargo de una de las partes se tornara excesivamente onerosa, por acontecimientos extraordinarios e imprevisibles, la parte perjudicada podra demander la resolucion del contrato. El mismo principio se aplicara a los contratos aleatorios cuando la excesiva onerosidad se produzca por causes extranas al riesgo propio del contrato. En los contratos de ejecucion continuada la resolucion no alcanzara a los efectos yo cumplidos. No procedera la resolucion, si el perjudicado hubiese obrado con culpa o estuviese en mora.

Followers of the Spanish Civil Code, on the other hand, like Colombia or Ecuador, have the concept of *laesio enormis,*[158] which is discussed in more detail below. Brazil, Mexico and Panama do not accept *laesio enormis,* although it can probably be introduced by case law.[159] The Civil Code of Uruguay does not expressly accept this concept.[160]

Countries that accept this doctrine require the fulfillment of three prior conditions:

i. The avoided contract should pertain to future performance; immediate performance is covered by the remedy of *laesio enormis.*
ii. The cost associated with changed performance due to extraordinary events should exceed all reasonable provisions made at the conclusion time of the contract.
iii. The performance of the obligation which now turned to be excessively expensive must be pending.

Bolivia accepts this concept only with respect to non-aleatory contracts in Art. 562 par. 1 and 2 CCBol. Even if Argentine law accepts the concept, the onerousness must be other than the normal risk of the contract. Where not expressly addressed in Latin American codes, principles of equity and good faith can make this concept a part of contract law.[161]

4. Laesio Enormis

In Latin America, usually this remedy is inapplicable to commercial contracts[162] or to the sale of movables,[163] but there are exceptions. Hon-

---

La otra parse podra impedir la resolucion ofreciendo mejorar equitativamente los efectos del contrato." *Id.*

[158] *Laesio enormis* means a disproportionate relationship between what one party is giving and the other is receiving.

[159] Brazil like Argentina, issued since 1971 a series of laws and executive decisions concerning this currency correction or *correção o reajuste monetario.*

[160] *See* Art. 1291 CCROU.

[161] *See* María Carreras Maldonado, *Revisión del contrato por cambio extraordinario e imprevisible de las circumstancias in,* LIBRO DEL CINCUENTENARIO DEL CODIOO CIVIL 37 (1978).

[162] *Compare* Art. 220 CCoBra which excepts fraud, error or simulation and Art. 385 CCoMex.

[163] *See* Art. 1858 CCEcu. However, compare with Art. 1949 CCCol.

duras Commercial Code accepts it in Art. 754 CCoHon but not for aleatory contracts.

Objective *laesio enormis* is explained in Velez Sarfield's footnote of Art. 943 CCArg with very interesting references. Subjective *laesio enormis* appears in Art. 954 CCArg. The second one, the subjective figure, describes a disproportionate result because one party took advantage of the lack of knowledge, inexperience or imprudence of the other party. The Peruvian Civil Code, for example, provides that a disproportion between obligations equal or superior to two thirds presumes exploitation.[164] The Bolivian Civil Code, as is the case with the lack of foresight theory, does not apply the doctrine of *laesio enormis* to aleatory contracts.

IV. Conclusion

In this paper we discussed buyer's remedies under two different perspectives: from an international agreement such as the CISG on one hand, and on the other hand, from the perspective of a specific Roman legal tradition, in our case, Latin American. We have seen similarities and differences and we can predict, with some degree of certainty, which decision likely could be issued in a Tribunal of this continent on some specific subjects. In spite of the possible different interpretations related to the extent of performance and in spite of some difficulties found in its wording, I believe that we have a fair and useful instrument to harmonize international commerce related to sale of goods.

[164] *See* Art. 1448 CCPer.

CHAPTER TWO

INCOTERMS and the UN Convention on Contracts for the International Sale of Goods*

by Prof. Dr. Burghard Piltz, Gütersloh

I. Introduction

In international trade, standardized abbreviations have long been used[1] to denote the obligations of buyer and seller that are typical of the export and import business. In European and related legal systems, the most commonly applied abbreviations are the INCOTERMS,[2] promulgated by the International Chamber of Commerce (ICC), which is situated in Paris. The INCOTERMS aim to provide internationally uniform rules for the interpretation of specific contact terms and clauses. In the past 60 years, the INCOTERMS have been amended and adjusted on several occasions to suit the development of technology. The present version, which has been in force since 1 July 1990, is that of the INCOTERMS 1990.[3]

Drafted as a set of rules independent of a particular area of trade, the INCOTERMS only deal with primary obligations imposed on a seller and buyer in the context of international contracts for the sale of goods. The INCOTERMS do not contain any detailed provisions on delivery times or on the buyer's obligation to pay the price. Also, the INCOTERMS do not

---

* Dedicated to Prof. Dr. Rolf Herber for his 70th birthday.

[1] For more detailed information see Andreas W. Renck, Der Einfluß der INCOTERMS 1990 auf das UN Kaufrecht, 5 (1995).

[2] International Chamber of Commerce, INCOTERMS 1990 (ICC Publication No. 460).

[3] For more detailed information see generally Bredow & Seiffert, INCOTERMS 1990, (2d ed. 1994); Vincent Heuzé, La Vente Internationale de Marchandises 197, 254 (1992); Jan Ramberg, Guide to INCOTERMS (ICC Publication No. 461, 1991); and Schneider, Recht der Internationalen Wirtschaft (RIW) 91 (1991).

regulate the conclusion of the contract of sale, the issue of title, the exemption from a party's obligation to perform, or the consequences of failure of performance. In the past, these aspects were always dealt with by applying the law referred to by the governing Private International Law.

Since the beginning of this decade, in the export and import business, the United Nations Convention on Contracts for the International Sale of Goods[4] has steadily replaced national sales laws. As of January 1999, the CISG is in force in 54 states.[5] As such, the INCOTERMS are now no longer embedded in a national sales law. Instead, their application must be considered in light of the CISG, which according to Art. 7, equally pursues uniform application.

II. Operation of the INCOTERMS

Although the INCOTERMS have been applied for decades, there is still no generally acknowledged legal opinion as to their legal status and basis of operation. Many scholars look for authority in customary law, usages, objective rules for interpretation, standard business conditions, soft law (laws that are non-binding, yet observed) or lex mercatoria.[6] However, among German legal scholars the view seems to prevail that the general principles of application of the INCOTERMS, as phrased by the ICC, are similar to those which determine the applicability of German standard business conditions.[7]

The INCOTERMS alter and supplement the provisions of the CISG. The authority to alter and supplement provisions of the CISG is principally

[4] United Nations Convention on Contracts for the International Sale of Goods, 19 I.L.M. 668 (1980) [hereinafter CISG].

[5] *See* United Nations Commission on International Trade Law (UNCITRAL), Current Status of Conventions and Model Laws (last modified Nov. 18, 1998) <http:/ www.un.or.at/uncitral/en-index.htm>.

[6] *See* Jürgen Basedow, *Die Incoterms und der Container oder wie man kodifizierte Usancen reformiert,* 43 RabelsZ 116, 125 (1979) and Renck, *supra* note 1, at 15.

[7] *See* Baumbach & Hopt, HGB (29th ed. 1995); Bredow & Seiffert, *supra* note 3; Berg-Erfurth, Menard & Fuchs, Das Kaufrecht No. 14 (4th ed. 1992); Joachim Quittnat, Das Recht der Außenhandelskaufverträge No. 234 (1988); Graf von Westphalen, Rechtsprobleme der Exportfinanzierung 168 (3d ed. 1987).

provided for by CISG Arts. 6 and 9.[8] Therefore, within the scope of application of the CISG, these articles form the starting point to determine the operation of the rules of interpretation of the INCOTERMS.

If the contracting parties agree on an INCOTERM by expressly referring to the INCOTERMS 1990, e.g. by incorporating a phrase into their contract such as "CIF New York — INCOTERMS 1990," the obligations of buyer and seller are determined by the rules of interpretation of the CIF clause provided for by the ICC.[9] However, it is known from experience that parties are usually not familiar in detail with the content of the rules of interpretation of the respective clauses. Furthermore, the rules of the INCOTERMS (hereinafter referred to as "the Rules") are not regularly exchanged between the parties. Instead, the parties are expected to independantly learn the implications of inclusion of an INCOTERM. This practice is disparate from other specific contractual agreements. Therefore, it is inappropriate to infer from the mere use of a three-letter-code together with the expression "INCOTERMS 1990" the incorporation of its entire catalogue of obligations into the contract as an individual agreement according to Art. 6 CISG. Instead, it seems more reasonable to interpret the reference to the Rules of a stipulated INCOTERM as a usage agreed to by the parties in accordance with Art. 9(1)CISG.[10] Though, in most cases it is not required to clearly distinguish between agreements concluded under Art. 6 CISG

[8] CISG Art. 6 states: "The parties may exclude the application of this Convention or, subject to article 12, derogate from or vary the effect of any of its provisions." CISG Art. 9 states: "(1) The parties are bound by any usage to which they have agreed and by any practices which they have established between themselves. (2) The parties are considered, unless otherwise agreed, to have impliedly made applicable to their contract or its formation a usage of which the parties know or ought to have known and which in international trade is widely known to, and regularly observed by, parties to contracts of the type involved in the particular trade concerned."

[9] *See* RENCK, *supra* note 1, at 16; DIETER MARTINY, INTERNATIONALES VERTRAGSRECHT No. 676 (5th ed. 1996).

[10] *See* JOHN O. HONNOLD, UNIFORM LAW FOR INTERNATIONAL SALES No. 114 (2d ed. 1991); Alfonso Calvo Caravaca, *La Compraventa Internacional de Mercaderias, in* DIEZ-PICAZO Y PONCE DE LEON 138 (1998); Werner Melis, *in* KOMMENTAR ZUM UN-KAUFRECHT Article 9, No. 7 (Heinrich Honsell ed., 1997); Joachim M. Bonell, *in* COMMENTARY ON THE INTERNATIONAL SALES LAW Art. 7, 3.5 (Massimo C. Bianca & Joachim M. Bonell eds. 1987); *But see* Holl & Keßler, Recht der Internationalen Wirtschaft (RIW) 458 (1995).

(and interpreted pursuant to Art. 8(3) CISG) and agreements concluded under Art. 9(1) CISG. As a consequence of the approach explained above, however, other contractual agreements, e.g. general business conditions, would prevail over the Rules of the INCOTERMS.

Since Art. 9(1) CISG requires an agreement between the parties, the aforementioned approach cannot be used if one of the thirteen codes laid down in the INCOTERMS, e.g. FOB, is incorporated into the contract when there is neither an explicit nor a tacit reference to the Rules, nor can such a reference be concluded from the practices that the parties have established between themselves. In such cases neither the Rules,[11] nor national interpretations simply can be applied.[12] From the perspective of the CISG, it first must be determined whether invoking the Rules does constitute a usage that the parties knew or ought to have known because, within international trade, it is widely known and regularly observed.[13] To assume that certain usages are relevant according to Art. 9(2) CISG, they need not be globally disseminated or in use for a long time.[14] The application of Art. 9(2) CISG is not excluded by the impossibility of finding common usages

---

[11] *See* Bundesgerichtshof (BGH) 917, 920 (1975) (This was, however, before the CISG came into force).

[12] *But see* WÖRLEN & METZLER-MÜLLER, HANDELSKLAUSELN IM NATIONALEN UND INTERNATIONALEN WARENVERKEHR 43 (1997).

[13] *See* CISG Art. 9(2) which states:

"The parties are considered, unless otherwise agreed, to have impliedly made applicble to their contract or its formation a usage of which the parties knew or ought to have known and which in international trade is widely known to, and regularly observed by, parties to contracts of the type involved in the particular trade concerned."

See also John A. Spanogle, *INCOTERMS and UCC Article 2 — Conflicts and Confusions,* INT'L LAW. 111, 113 (1997); Ulrich Huber, *Article 30, in* EINHEITLICHES UN-KAUFRECHT Art 30., No. 3 (Ernest von Caemmerer & Peter Schlechtriem eds., 2d ed. 1995); FRITZ ENDERLEIN, DIETRICH MASKOW & HEINZ STROHBACH, INTERNATIONALES KAUFRECHT: KAUFRECHTSKONVENTION, VERJAHRUNGSKONVENTION, VERTRETUNGSKONVENTION Article 9, No. 11 (1991); LE MASSON & STENAY, LA CONVENTION DE VIENNE SUR LA VENTE INTERNATIONALE ET LES INCOTERMS 39 (1990); ROLF HERBER & BEATE CZERWENKA, INTERNATIONALES KAUFRECHT art. 9, N. 16 (1991); J. VON STAUDINGER & ULRICH MAGNUS, UN-KAUFRECHT art. 9, N. 32 (1994); *But see* KARL H. NEUMAYER & CATHERINE MING, CONVENTION DE VIENNE SUR LES CONTRATS DE VENTE INTERNATIONALE DE MARCHANDISES Art. 9, No. 7 (1993).

[14] *See* STAUDINGER & MAGNUS, *supra* note 13, at No. 22 & 23.

that in detail comprise all the obligations of seller and buyer in relation to the relevant INCOTERM.[15] To invoke Art. 9(2) CISG, it is sufficient to determine a common usage that points towards the application of the Rules to interpret the stipulated three-letter-code.

In order to ascertain a usage pursuant to Art. 9(2) CISG, regard is to be had to an interpretation that is reasonably expected from all involved trade circles.[16] It can be assumed that Americans are often more familiar with the American Foreign Trade Definitions, which comprise three-letter-codes similar to those used by the INCOTERMS, but that differ significantly in content.[17] Therefore, in practice, reference in contracts to the rules of the INCOTERMS should be phrased explicitly.[18] Otherwise, the party invoking an INCOTERM must furnish evidence that reference to the Rules is to be regarded as a usage in accordance with Art. 9(2) CISG requirements.[19]

Interpreting the rules of the INCOTERMS according to German standard business conditions, as advocated by some scholars,[20] would possibly help in cases where German national law is applicable.[21] However, in order to incorporate standard business conditions into contracts governed by the CISG, parties must comply with strict requirements.[22] Regarding the Rules, these requirements rarely will be fulfilled. Internationally acknowledged rules of interpretation,[23] the relevance of the INCOTERMS as soft law[24] as well as their enforcement as lex mercatoria,[25] can hardly be integrated into the system of the CISG except for those cases where these approaches, e.g.

---

[15] See RENCK, *supra* note 1, at 22, 64, who therefore declines to accept Art. 9(2) CISG.
[16] *See* Werner Junge, *Article 9, in* KOMMERNTAR ZUM EINHEITLICHEN UN-KAUFRECHT Art. 9, No. 9 (Von Caemmerer & Schlechtriem eds., 2d ed. 1995).
[17] *See* Spanogle, *supra* note 12, at 111 and O'HARA, GUIDE TO THE INTERNATIONAL SALE OF GOODS CONVENTION ch. 107 (1993).
[18] *See* Ramberg, *supra* note 3, at 13.
[19] *See* STAUDINGER & MAGNUS, *supra* note 13, at Art. 9, No. 33.
[20] *See supra*, note 7.
[21] See, for reference to German standard business conditions, ULMER, ET AL., AGB-GESETZ § 2, No. 79 (8th ed. 1997).
[22] *See* STAUDINGER-MAGNUS, *supra* note 13, at Art. 14, No. 41.
[23] *See* RENCK, *supra* note 1, at 31 and NEUMAYER & MING, *supra* note 13, at Art. 9, No. 7.
[24] *See* RENCK, *supra* note 1, at 91.
[25] *See* KAPPUS, LEX MERCATORIA IN EUROPA UND WIENER KAUFRECHTSKONVENTION 1980 128 (1990).

pursuant to Art. 8(3) CISG, constitute relevant usages according to Art. 9(2) CISG. Furthermore, these approaches do not provide a convincing solution in cases where there are conflicts between the INCOTERMS and the American Foreign Trade Definitions.

III. Seller's obligation to deliver

As for the obligations of the seller, the CISG distinguishes between sales involving carriage of goods and other kinds of delivery.[26] Commentaries and materials on the CISG refer to contracts of sale into which "F" or "C" terms have been incorporated (shipment contracts), as well as to contracts for delivery containing a "D-clause" (destination contracts) as examples of sales involving carriage of goods as addressed in Art. 31 CISG.[27]

In certain provisions, the CISG intends specific regulations to be only applicable to sales involving carriage of goods, but not to other kinds of delivery. For example, Art. 31 CISG governs different types and places of delivery.[28] However, by using an INCOTERM, type and place of delivery are comprehensively determined in A.4 of the Rules (delivery) and, therefore, it is not necessary to resort to Art. 31 CISG.[29] The seller's obligation in the case of a sale involving carriage of goods, to provide for the transportation of the goods[30] according to Art. 32(2) CISG, can equally be found in A.3 of the Rules (transportation and insurance contracts). Finally, when using an INCOTERM, the provision governing the passing of the risk in sales involving carriage of goods, pursuant to Art. 67(1)1 CISG,[31] is replaced with the provision in A.5 of the Rules. It is therefore unnecessary to determine

[26] *See* Herber & Czerwenka, *supra* note 13, at Art. 31, No. 3.

[27] *See* Commentary on the Draft Convention on Contracts for the International Sale of Goods prepared by the Secretariat, Document A/CONF.97/5, Art. 29, No. 5 — United Nations Conference on Contracts for the International Sale of Goods, Official Records, New York, 1981 (A/CONF.97/19), 29.

[28] *See* Herber & Czerwenka, *supra* note 13, at Art. 30, No. 2 & Art. 31, No. 3.

[29] *See* Ole Lando, *Article 31, in* Commentary on the International Sales Law Art. 31, No. 2.4 (Massimo C. Bianca & Joachim M. Bonell eds. 1987).

[30] *See* Ulrich Huber, *Article 32, in* Kommerntar zum Einheitlichen UN-Kaufrecht Art. 32, No. 17 (von Caemmerer & Schlechtriem eds., 2d ed. 1995).

[31] *See* Herber & Czerwenka, *supra* note 13, at Art. 67, No. 3.

whether the relevant INCOTERM constitutes a sale involving carriage of goods according to the CISG. The rule laid down in Art. 67(2) CISG[32] is not only valid for sales involving carriage of goods, but is of general application[33] and furthermore is reflected in B.5 of the Rules.

By applying an INCOTERM, the obligations of the seller, as provided by the Rules, prevail over the provisions of the CISG.[34] Moreover, the Rules regulate all aspects of sales that involve carriage of goods that differ from other kinds of delivery. Therefore, it is unnecessary for a precise determination of the seller's obligation of delivery to consider the extent to which various INCOTERMS qualify as sales involving carriage of goods pursuant to Art. 31 CISG.[35]

It shall not be examined at this point, to what extent the other provisions of the CISG — which do not distinguish between different kinds of delivery — remain applicable or are eclipsed when using the INCOTERMS.[36] The analysis so far reveals no contradictions or inconsistencies of significance, except for the seller's obligation to give notice provided by Art. 32(1) CISG and in A.7 of the Rules. Whereas Art. 27 CISG is based on the dispatch-principle,[37] both this principle and the principle that a communication must be received, are advocated in provisions regarding notices in the INCOTERMS.[38] However, both of these legal opinions are too general, and therefore neither is convincing. According to the D-clauses of the

---

[32] CISG Art. 67(2) states: "Nevertheless, the risk does not pass to the buyer until the goods are clearly identified to the contract, whether by markings on the goods, by shipping documents, by notice given to the buyer or otherwise."

[33] *See* STAUDINGER-MAGNUS, *supra* note 13, at Art. 66, No. 3.

[34] Art. 30 and 31 CISG, irrespective of Art. 6 and 9 CISG, expressly point out that individual agreements prevail. *See* Huber, *supra* note 30, at Art. 31, No. 75 and STAUDINGER-MAGNUS, *supra* note 13, at Art. 31, No. 3 & 6.

[35] See less of a distinction in: Martin Karollus, *Article 31, in* KOMMENTAR ZUM UN-KAUFRECHT Art. 31, No. 12 (Heinrich Honsell ed., 1997); Huber, *supra* note 30, at Art. 32, No. 18; NEUMAYER & MING, *supra* note 13, at Art. 31, No. 7.

[36] For a more detailed analysis see generally RENCK, *supra* note 1 and Gunter Hager, *Article 67, in* KOMMERNTAR ZUM EINHEITLICHEN UN-KAUFRECHT Art. 67, No. 6 (Ernest von Caemmerer & Peter Schlechtriem eds., 2d ed. 1995).

[37] *See* STAUDINGER-MAGNUS, *supra* note 13, at Art. 27, No. 7; Peter Schlechtriem, *Article 27, in* KOMMERNTAR ZUM EINHEITLICHEN UN-KAUFRECHT Art. 27, No. 11 (von Caemmerer & Schlechtriem eds., 2d ed. 1995).

[38] *See* BREDOW & SEIFFERT, *supra* note 3, at 30. *But see* RENCK, *supra* note 1, at 158.

INCOTERMS, the place of destination for the carriage of goods is also the place where the responsibility regarding the performance of the contract passes from seller to buyer.[39] However, this evaluation is not in line with the dispatch-principle provided in Art. 27 CISG. The risk that the buyer will receive notice should instead be imposed on the seller, since otherwise compliance with the obligation to deliver can hardly be conceived.[40] On the other hand, according to the F and C clauses, the place where the risk passes from seller to buyer is where the principal carriage starts. The E clause refers to the seller's place of business.[41] In these instances it is not convincing that the exporter should be liable for the correct and punctual receipt of communications by the buyer, which the seller is obliged to furnish.

Today, the INCOTERMS must be interpreted in light of the CISG.[42] Since a different interpretation cannot be concluded from the Rules, the dispatch-principle of Art. 27 CISG also applies to the obligations to inform imposed by the INCOTERMS. Solely regarding a D-clause, the seller is — in contrast to Art. 27 CISG — responsible for the buyer's receipt of correct and punctual notice. This conclusion is based on the fact that the seller, by agreeing to a D-clause, has assumed additional obligations, which although not excluded, are not reflected within the structure of the CISG. Consequently, the interpretation of Art. 27 CISG must be adjusted to comply with this significant modification of the CISG.

IV. Buyer's obligation to pay

In B.1, the Rules regulate the buyers duty to pay the price as provided in the contract of sale. The Rules do not provide a specific obligation, but rather underline every buyer's self-evident principal obligation.[43] The INCOTERMS do not contain any further provisions concerning the obligation to pay the price. Therefore, unless agreed otherwise, practices or us-

[39] *See* Bredow & Seiffert *supra* note 3, at 21.

[40] Responsibility is imposed on the buyer to the same extent as to his obligation to give notice to the seller according to the F-clauses.

[41] *See* Bredow & Seiffert *supra* note 3, at 20.

[42] *See supra* section I., last paragraph.

[43] *See* Ramberg, *supra* note 3, at 26.

ages prevail and regard is to be had for CISG provisions that govern payment of the price.[44]

Pursuant to Art. 58(1) CISG, the price must be paid as soon as the seller has placed the goods or the documents controlling their disposition[45] "at the disposal of the buyer." Consequently, in sales involving carriage of goods, according to Art. 31 (a) CISG, payment of the price is due as soon as the last carrier offers the goods to the buyer at the place of destination of the carriage.[46] In contrast, § 271 BGB (German Civil Code) determines the time of payment independently from the disposal of the goods. Thus, regarding the BGB, the various types of delivery under the INCOTERMS do not raise any problems concerning the time of payment. However, it is still unclear which consequences follow from the rule in Art. 58(1) CISG, regarding time of payment, if an INCOTERM has been incorporated into a contract governed by the CISG.[47]

According to the E-clause, the seller is obliged to place the goods at the buyer's disposal at the place agreed on or usual place of delivery. According to the D-clause, the seller is obliged to place the goods at disposal of the buyer at the named place of destination, and the buyer is obliged to take delivery at that location (A.4 of the Rules). Therefore, according to Art. 58(1) CISG, the payment of the price is due as soon as the seller fulfills these obligations.

The F-INCOTERMS impose the obligation on the seller to hand over the goods not to the buyer, but to the carrier at the place where the principal carriage organized by the buyer starts (A.4 of the Rules). Irrespective of the intervening carrier, the buyer must take delivery of the goods at that place (B.4 of the Rules). Therefore, the place of delivery and the place of taking delivery coincide.[48] On the other hand, a sale involving carriage of goods according to Art. 31(a) CISG presupposes that the buyer's taking delivery of the goods is not to take place at the same place as where the seller

---

[44] *See* CISG Arts. 54 — 59.

[45] *See* Hager, *supra* note 36, at Art. 58, No. 10.

[46] *See id.* No. 7; STAUDINGER & MAGNUS, *supra* note 13, at Art. 58, No. 15. *See also* Schnyder/Straub, *Article 58, in* KOMMENTAR ZUM UN-KAUFRECHT Art. 58, No. 27 (Heinrich Honsell ed., 1997).

[47] *See* Rudolph, *Article 58, in* KAUFRECHT DER EXPORT UND IMPORTVERTRÄGE Art. 58, No. 9 (1996).

[48] *See* RENCK, *supra* note 1, at 176. For a different conclusion, see Sieg, Recht der Internationalen Wirtschaft (RIW) 101 (1995).

must fulfill his obligation to deliver.[49] Therefore, the F-INCOTERMS do not constitute a sale involving carriage of goods according to Art. 31 (a) CISG, although it has been stated otherwise in materials on the CISG.[50] Instead, as soon as the goods are handed over to the carrier they are placed at the buyer's disposal and thus the payment of the price is due according to Art. 58(1) CISG. The carrier who is — according to the F-clauses — contracted by the buyer (B.3 of the Rules) is simultaneously appointed to take delivery of the goods on his behalf.[51] If the parties, however, have agreed on the clause "FOB shipped"[52] or the seller himself has contracted with the carrier pursuant to A.3 (a) of the Rules to the FCA clause, the transaction equals a sale involving carriage of goods according to Art. 31 (a) CISG. Consequently, the payment of the price does not fall due before the carrier offers the goods to the buyer at the place of destination.

Contrary to the regulations in the F-INCOTERMS, according to the C-INCOTERMS, it is the seller who is obliged to contract with the carrier at his own expense (A.3 of the Rules). The risk passes when the goods are handed over to the carrier (A.5/B.5 of the Rules), just as it does according to the F-clauses. However, with respect to Art. 58 CISG, the passing of the risk is of no importance for determination of time of payment of the price. In general, the place of delivery does not change either, compared to the F-clauses (A.4 of the Rules). However, in contrast to the F-clauses, B.4 of the Rules on all C-clauses point out that the buyer must take delivery of the goods only at the place of destination of the carriage. Therefore, the goods are accepted by the buyer at a place different from that where the seller must fulfill his obligation to deliver. The carrier is thus not acting on behalf of the buyer in order to take delivery of the goods.[53] Since the seller is additionally obliged to contract with the carrier according to the C-INCOTERMS (A.3 of the Rules), all conditions of a typical contract of sale involving carriage of the goods are met.[54] Consequently, according to Art. 58(1) CISG, the price comes due as soon as the goods have arrived at the agreed place of destination, when a C-INCOTERM is incorporated into the contract.

---

[49] *See* BURGHARD PILTZ, INTERNATIONALES KAUFRECHT 108 § 4, No. 18 (1993).

[50] *See generally* SECRETARIAT COMMENTARY, *supra* note 27.

[51] *See* BREDOW & SEIFFERT *supra* note 3, at 81.

[52] *See id.* at 62.

[53] *See id.* at 71 & 81. *See also* RENCK, *supra* note 1, at 176.

[54] *See* PILTZ, *supra* note 46, § 4, No. 18.

V. Outlook

In practice, the INCOTERMS as well as the CISG are of fundamental significance for international transactions. However, the combination of both sets of rules raise numerous issues that still await well consolidated and acknowledged answers. Preliminary remarks or additional regulations in the Rules (in the planned year 2000 INCOTERMS revision) could point the way towards fostering orientation and would at the same time underline the strength of the CISG and the INCOTERMS as a combination of provisions suitable for international trade.

CHAPTER THREE

Comment on Roder Zelt- und Hallenkonstruktionen GmbH v. Rosedown Park Pty Ltd.

By Jacob S. Ziegel*

I. Introduction

Roder Zelt- und Hallenkonstruktionen GmbH v. Rosedown Park Pty Ltd.[1] ("Roder"), a decision of Judge Van Doussa of the Federal Court of Australia, South Australian District, is apparently the first reported Australian decision to address issues related to the United Nations Convention on Contracts for the International Sale of Goods.[2] This alone would justify a comment on the case, particularly given the paucity of CISG judgments in common law jurisdictions that have adopted the Convention.[3] There is however another and still stronger reason for this comment: the Australian court's decision squarely raises the issue (for the first time so far as I am aware) of whether the CISG applies to the seller's remedies under an installment sale[4] where the goods have been delivered and accepted by the buyer, and where the seller has retained title pending payment by the buyer of the price by agreed installments or otherwise.

* Professor of Law Emeritus, University of Toronto

[1] 28 April 1995, [1995] 57 Fed Court Rep 216-240; UNILEX database 1996; PACE CISG Caselaw <http:/cisgw3.law.pace.edu/cases/950428a2.html>.

[2] United Nations Convention on Contracts for the International Sale of Goods, 19 I.L.M. 668 (1980) [hereinafter CISG].

[3] By way of contrast, although Canada adopted the Convention in 1991, effective 1 May 1992, there is still no reported decision involving the Convention.

[4] Usually referred to in North America as a "conditional sale" or "conditional sale agreement."

My comment will focus primarily on this issue and deal summarily with several other CISG questions raised by the facts though not necessarily addressed by the judgment.

II. The Facts

Roder is a German manufacturer of tents and other prefabricated structures for public functions. Rosedown was in the business of renting out such equipment for large sports events in Australia. Roder agreed to supply Rosedown with its equipment needs and Rosedown agreed to pay the price by installments with interest after the equipment had been delivered in Australia. The agreement contained a title retention clause in Roder's favor and also provided that until the payments had been completed Rosedown was deemed to be a fiduciary agent and bailee of the equipment. The agreement also contained the usual provisions in a conditional sale agreement requiring Rosedown to keep the equipment insured and in a proper condition, not to sell it, and requiring Rosedown to account for the proceeds of sale or otherwise (sic) and to keep the proceeds separate from other property.

Rosedown fell seriously in arrears with its payments to Roder and was generally in acute financial difficulties. While in this condition, Rosedown's directors adopted a resolution appointing an administrator of Rosedown's business pursuant to the Commonwealth Corporations Law. Rosedown's creditors subsequently approved a Deed of Arrangement for the restructuring of Rosedown's business and the payment of its debts.

Following the appointment of the administrator, Roder initiated action claiming the return of its equipment on the ground that Rosedown had repudiated its contract because of the failure to maintain its interest payments and for other breaches of contract. This meant that Judge Van Doussa had to consider which law governed the interpretation of the parties' contract, including the title retention clause, and the rights and obligations of the parties under the contract. He also had to consider the effect of the administrator's appointment and the subsequent Deed of Arrangement on Roder's right to recover the equipment from the administrator, assuming there was a valid title retention clause to begin with.

The judge found that the contract of sale was governed by the CISG since both Germany and Australia had ratified the Convention. This meant that the parties' rights were governed by the Convention, including Roder's right to avoid the contract under arts. 61 and 64, because of a fundamental breach of contract by Rosedown. Judge Van Doussa held that the parties' pleadings were wrongly framed in the common law language of repudiation and should have alleged instead that the seller was entitled to avoid the contract and had done so, and was therefore entitled to return of the equipment.

In the judge's opinion, Rosedown's failure to maintain its interest payments did not constitute a fundamental breach because Roder had not complained about the missing payments before the administrator's appointment and had not invoked its right under article 63 giving Rosedown an additional period of time before avoiding the contract. He found however that the appointment of the administrator and the directors' resolution making the appointment, with its acknowledgment that the company was insolvent, resulted in such detriment to Roder as substantially to deprive it of what it was entitled to expect under the contract.

So far as the title retention clause was concerned, in the court's opinion its construction and meaning were governed by the CISG,[5] but the validity of the clause was governed either by German or Australian domestic law since the validity and property effects of a sale contract are expressly excluded from the Convention's scope.[6] He found that both German and Australian law recognized the validity of Romalpa clauses.[7] This also meant, once Roder exercised its right of avoidance, that it was entitled to recover its property because Rosedown no longer had any rights to the equipment under the contract. Conversely, Rosedown would be entitled to claim restitution for any payments made by it under the contract[8] although Roder would also have a claim against Rosedown for damages. The court also found that the administration and arrangement provisions in the Corporations Law did not change a creditor's property rights with respect to property in the administrator's hands, but that the creditor needed the court's permission to enforce its rights. Judge Van Doussa gave that permission.

---

[5] *See* CISG arts. 8, 11, 15, 18 and 29.

[6] *See* CISG art. 4(a) and (b).

[7] Romalpa clauses is the name given in England and Australia to title retention clauses in commercial installment contracts where the purchased goods consist of inventory to be resold or leased out by the buyer in the ordinary course of its business. The name Romalpa is derived from the English Court of Appeal decision affirming the validity of the clause in this context as well as in the more common context of goods used by the buyer as equipment. *See* Aluminium Industrie Vaassen B.V. v. Romalpa Aluminium Ltd. [1976] 1 Lloyd's Rep. 443 (Eng. C.A.).

[8] *See* CISG arts. 81 & 84.

III. Discussion

A. *Status of Installment Sales under the CISG*

The Roder case is an instructive example of the dynamic interplay between CISG law and domestic rules governing the validity of title retention clauses and the impact of a buyer's insolvency and restructuring. The Australian court's decision is however open to question on the following critical issue. Judge Van Doussa assumed, without discussion, that an installment sale (conditional sale agreement in North American parlance) in which the buyer obtains possession and use of the goods,[9] but the seller retains title until payment of the price or fulfillment of other conditions, is fully subject to the remedial provisions of the Convention just like any other contract of sale.

This is an unsafe assumption. From the turn of this century onwards, for at least some purposes, many US courts treated conditional sale agreements in which the buyer obtained possession of the goods and enjoyed most of the benefits of ownership, other than the bare title, as a short form of mortgage. The American Uniform Conditional Sales Act of 1918 recognized many of the special characteristics of conditional sales. Article 9 of the American Uniform Commercial Code (UCC) completed this assimilation with the adoption of the Code in the 1950s. Under Article 9 the seller in a title retaining contract merely retains a security interest in the goods and the buyer is treated as the beneficial owner of the goods.[10] If a buyer defaults in its payments the seller's remedies lie under Part V of Article 9 and not under Part VII of Article 2 on Sales.

In Canada, conditional sale agreements have followed a similar evolution[11] although the earlier history was more clouded than it was in the United States. All the common law jurisdictions in Canada have now

[9] Including, in the case of goods characterized as inventory, the right to sell or lease the goods in the ordinary course of the buyer's business.

[10] *See* UCC § 9-102 (1991) (scope of application), 1-201(37) (definition of security interest), and 9-107 (definition of purchase money security interest). In the spring and summer of 1998 the Code's sponsors approved a revised Article 9 but this is not expected to come into force in any state until January 1, 2001. The revised version of Article 9 retains all the basic features of existing Article 9.

[11] *See* R.M. Goode & J.S. Ziegel, Hire-Purchase and Conditional Sale: A Comparative Survey of Commonwealth and American Law 13-16 (1965).

adopted personal property security legislation (PPSAS) based on Article 9 of the Uniform Commercial Code.[12] In Canada, therefore, as in the United States, the seller in a conditional sale agreement merely retains a security interest in the goods. Consequently, the personal property security Acts and not the provincial sale of goods Acts regulate the seller's rights if the buyer defaults in its payments or other terms of the agreement.

The CISG does not define contract of sale and there is no provision expressly excluding conditional sale agreements from its scope. It must also be remembered that most other countries (including most other common law jurisdictions) do not subscribe to the North American characterization of conditional sale agreements.[13] In those countries such agreements are still treated as a special form of executory contract of sale. This is true even though the seller's remedies are often governed by statutory restrictions not essentially different from the consumer safeguards found in Article 9 and in the Canadian PPSAs.

These divergences in the national treatment of conditional sale agreements make it unclear how such agreements should be treated under the CISG. In my view, notwithstanding the uncertainties I have alluded to, the CISG's remedial regime is not appropriate once the buyer has obtained possession of the goods, and imposing the CISG rules "willy nilly" on conditional sale agreements will lead to fictions and distortions. Once the seller has performed its obligations under the agreement, I believe the security aspects should be treated as wholly outside the CISG and as governed by domestic law under the relevant conflict of laws rules.

The inappropriateness of the CISG provisions may be seen by asking what happens when the buyer is in default with its payments and by contrasting the consequences with the remedial regimes provided in Article 9

---

[12] *See* J.S. Ziegel, *The New Provincial Chattel Security Regimes,* 70 CAN. BAR REV. 681 (1991). Quebec also adopted some important features of Article 9 in the new Québec Civil Code of 1994, including the general recognition of non-possessory security interests in moveables and the requirement of perfection of such interests in a newly established and computerized registry system. However, the new chattel security regime does not apparently include conditional sales. *See also* M. Boodman & R. Macdonald, *How Far is Article 9 of the Uniform Commercial Code Exportable? A Return to Sources?* 27 CAN. BUS. L.J. 249 (1996).

[13] However, following an earlier strongly supportive report, the New Zealand government has announced its intention to adopt a Personal Property Securities (sic) Act along Canadian lines. A draft bill was circulated for discussion in October 1998.

and the Canadian PPSAs. Under the CISG, if the seller wants to repossess the goods it can apparently only do so by avoiding the contract if the buyer's failure to make a payment or to meet other conditions of the contract amounts to a fundamental breach.[14] If the contract is avoided, the seller loses the right to sue for the price but is remitted to a claim in damages.[15] The seller is, however, entitled to retain the goods as its own and, once the contract is avoided, the buyer has no right to redeem the goods regardless, it would seem, of how much of the price has been paid. The same preclusion will apply to the buyer's trustee in bankruptcy or liquidator if the buyer has become insolvent. Following avoidance of the contract, the CISG entitles the buyer to recover its payments[16] subject to the seller's right of set-off for the buyer's use of the goods while they were in the buyer's possession.[17]

All of this is terribly unreal. The seller's retention of title only serves a security function and by repossessing the goods and selling them the seller is only enforcing its security.[18] The contract is not meant to be avoided and the buyer should remain liable for the balance of the price. If there is a surplus after the resale, it should go to the buyer because this consequence too flows from the security function of the agreement. Given the true nature of the conditional sale agreement, Article 9 and the Canadian PPSAS also entitle the buyer to redeem the collateral prior to its sale by the seller unless after default the buyer has agreed to the seller retaining the goods in satisfaction of the seller's claims.

In all these respects, Article 9 and its Canadian counterparts are not only greatly superior to the CISG provisions but, in my view, they provide the only sound and workable conceptual structure. No doubt the same can be said of the many similar provisions in domestic systems specifically addressing the distinctive features of installment sales even though they do

[14] *See* CISG arts. 64 & 25. The contract could authorize the seller to repossess the goods and resell them, whether or not the buyer's breach amounts to a fundamental breach, and hold the buyer liable for any deficiency. Such provisions commonly appear in conditional sale agreements. However, at common law (and I assume in the civil law as well) such provisions raise troubling conceptual questions since it is difficult to explain in sales terms why the buyer should continue to be liable to pay the balance of the price if the seller has sold the goods and is no longer in a position to transfer title to the buyer.

[15] *See* CISG arts. 62, 74 & 81(1).

[16] *See* CISG art. 81(2).

[17] *See* CISG art. 84(2).

[18] *Cf.* Article 9, Part V, §§ 9-501 et seq., and Ontario Personal Property Security Act, Rev. Stat. Ont. 1990. c.P-10 as am., Part V, §§ 58-66.

not go as far as Article 9 in fully assimilating installment sales with other security devices. So far as I have been able to ascertain, only Prof. Peter Winship appears before me to have raised the status of installment sales under the CISG and then on a much more limited basis than what I have attempted to do.[19] In a footnote in an excellent chapter by him on the scope of the Convention, he notes that ULIS art. 5(2) subordinated the uniform law to mandatory national legislation protecting buyers who purchased by installment.[20] He goes on to report that at the 1980 conference, the Norwegian delegate questioned whether the Vienna text dealt adequately with the consequences of the buyer's failure to pay all installments and, upon being reassured that the settlement of accounts of parties to these contracts would be deemed excluded from the convention under article 6 (sic), the delegate withdrew an amendment to clarify the matter.[21]

Obviously the delegate should have been more persistent.

Let me make myself clear. I am not suggesting that the CISG has no application to installment sales. What I am saying is that the Convention should only apply to the sales component and not to the security aspects of the agreement. If this distinction is observed, the CISG will determine whether a sale agreement has been concluded, the terms of the agreement, and the seller's obligations with respect to the description and quality of the goods and their delivery. Once conforming goods have been delivered to the buyer, the security part of the agreement will be triggered and will determine the seller's and buyer's rights and obligations from this point onwards. This dichotomy is accepted in Article 9 and the Canadian Acts and works well in practice.

Thus UCC 9-206(2) provides that, "When a seller retains a purchase money security interest in goods the Article on Sales (Article 2) governs the sale and any disclaimer, limitation or modification of the seller's warranties." I see no difficulty in applying the reverse distinction to the CISG, that is that where the seller retains title to the goods after delivery pending payment of the price the validity of the title retention clause and related issues will be governed by non-CISG law.

---

[19] *See* Peter Winship, *The Scope of the Vienna Convention on International Sales Contracts, in* INTERNATIONAL SALES: THE UNITED NATIONS CONVENTION ON CONTRACTS FOR THE INTERNATIONAL SALE OF GOODS 1 — 24, n. 48 (Nina M. Galston & Hans Smit eds., 1984).

[20] *See id.*

[21] *See id.*

B. *Other Aspects of the Roder Decision*

1. Construction and meaning of the title retention clause.

As previously noted, Judge Van Doussa held that the CISG governed the construction and meaning of the title retention clause even though the validity of the clause was determined by German or Australian law. His approach is consistent with the structure of the Convention but it is also a little artificial. For example, the municipal law governing the validity of the title retention clause may require the contract to be evidenced in writing as a condition of the enforceability of the clause or the attachment of the seller's security interest.[22] If this is the case, I suggest the municipal rule must prevail regardless of any conclusion the court may reach with respect to the parties' intentions under art. 8 of the Convention. It may be argued that a distinction should be drawn between the validity of the clause inter parties and its validity with respect to third parties and that since art. 11 does not require CISG contracts to be in writing, the clause is effective between the parties. This solution too is strained. Since we are concerned here with the property effects of the contract, the better view, I believe, is that the forum should defer entirely to the requirements of the municipal law governing the seller's retention of a security interest.

2. Fundamental breach and avoidance of the contract.

There are two aspects here of the court's judgment that warrant consideration. The first arises from the judge's finding that Rosedown's failure to maintain its interest payments did not constitute a fundamental breach because Roder had not complained about the missing payments before the administrator's appointment and had not invoked its right under art. 63 giving Rosedown an additional period of time before avoiding the contract. The difficulty about this reasoning is that art. 63(1) is a discretionary provision and does not *oblige* the seller to give the buyer an additional period of time if the seller is satisfied that the delay that has already occurred amounts to a fundamental breach.

There may be circumstances — the facts in this case may be among them — where the breaching party can argue that it has been lulled into a

---

[22] *Cf.* UCC § 9-203(1)(a) (1991) (security interest does not attach and security agreement is not enforceable against debtor or third parties unless collateral is in secured party's possession or there is an agreement in writing).

false sense of security by the seller's failure to complain and that there was an implicit understanding between the parties, supported perhaps by prior usage and practice between them or by usages in the trade, that the seller would give notice before declaring the contract to be avoided. Unfortunately, given his initial holding, Judge Van Doussa did not explore these alternative avenues.

The second aspect of his judgment deserving further analysis is his finding that the appointment of the administrator and Rosedown's directors' acknowledgment that the company was insolvent amounted to a fundamental breach of Rosedown's contractual obligations. Article 25 of the Convention is strikingly silent in telling us anything about the type of conduct that may lead to a fundamental breach. Must it be volitional or may it be triggered by a condition, such as insolvency, totally unsought for by the allegedly breaching party? It seems safe to assume from art. 71(1) that the latter construction is the correct one. This is because art. 71(1) entitles a contracting party to seek assurance of performance if it appears that the other party will not be able to perform a substantial part of its obligations because of a "serious deficiency in his ability to perform or in his creditworthiness." If the buyer's insolvency is sufficient to trigger art. 71(1), it must surely also be sufficient to provide the basis for a fundamental breach claim.

Even conceding this, it is debatable whether the Australian judge invoked the right article. Since he had already held that there was no fundamental breach prior to Rosedown's declaration of insolvency, arguably art. 72 on anticipatory repudiation, and not art. 25, was the right article to invoke. It makes a difference because art. 72(2) requires the party intending to avoid the contract to give notice of its intention if time allows. In Roder there appears to have been no urgency, although notice to the administrator would probably have made no difference since the administrator was taking the position that the parties had not agreed on a title retaining clause.

A cognate issue also deserving of some consideration is the court's decision that the notice of avoidance required by art. 26 as the condition for an effective avoidance was satisfied by Roder's initiation of proceedings for the recovery of its property. Art. 26 does not stipulate any particular type of notice. Still, as CISG observers have noted, reasonableness is a pervasive behavioral norm throughout the Convention and one can visualize circumstances where issuing a writ is too blunt an instrument for giving notice of avoidance.[23]

---

[23] A possible example that comes to mind is where a buyer initiates proceedings to avoid a contract because of defective goods. Prof. John O. Honnold and other CISG scholars

3. Insolvency stay of proceedings and seller's rights under the CISG.

This is another feature of Roder that merits some attention. A standard provision in modern insolvency legislation is the imposition of a stay of proceedings and other action by creditors and other parties against the debtor. The stay may be exceedingly broad in its scope [24] and may include a stay on a seller's right to avoid a contract under an installment sale. So, for example, the Australian Corporations Law prohibited the initiation of proceedings against an administrator without the court's permission.

Judge Van Doussa did not consider whether these provisions created a conflict with the seller's right of avoidance under the CISG and the right of return of its property. Since the issue does not appear to have been raised, one can only speculate what his answer would have been. One possible answer is that the CISG is not concerned with the mechanics for the enforcement of the parties' rights but leaves this to be determined by the forum's law. The other, and in my view more persuasive, answer is that issues of insolvency law lie wholly outside the CISG's realm. This is because insolvency law involves the totality of a debtor's relationship with its creditors and not just one creditor (the seller), whereas the CISG only speaks to the rights and obligations of the parties to the particular contract.[25]

IV. Conclusion

My discussion of the legal issues arising from Roder is far from exhaustive but should provide much grist for other CISG commentators. Hopefully too other tribunals will have an opportunity to explore and refine the issues that were left untouched in the Australian judgment or were not adequately disposed of.

---

take the position that there is no fundamental breach where the seller makes a timely and credible offer to cure the nonconformity. Will the beginning of court proceedings deprive the seller of a right to cure? One hopes not, and that the seller should be able to argue that had the buyer adopted a more appropriate form of notice the court proceedings would have been unnecessary.

[24] *See, e.g.*, § 362 of the US Bankruptcy Code, 11 U.S.C. § 362 (1994). In Canada, the courts also have given a very elastic meaning to the scope of a stay order issued under § 11 of the Canadian Companies' Creditors Arrangement Act, Rev. Stat. Can. (1985).

[25] *See* CISG art. 4, opening sentence.

CHAPTER FOUR

Reasonable Time in Article 39(1) of the CISG — Is Article 39(1) Truly a Uniform Provision?

Camilla Baasch Andersen *

Table of Contents

* University of Copenhagen: Pace Essay Contest Winner — 1998.

reasonable

a. within the limits of reason; not greatly less or more than may be expected.

b. tolerable, fair.

I. Introduction

A. *The Definitions of a Term*

The science of law, like most other academic sciences, is one that depends very much on terminology. The precise definition of terms and the application of these terms are, essentially, at the core of judicial practice, and the words we work with can be elusive.[1] Defining and determining legal terms can often be made difficult by the fact that judicial science applies particular meanings to everyday words which are exclusive to the law, and which do not necessarily logically follow the linguistic definition of that word.[2] And the understanding of these terms can be further impeded by the fact that the semantics of different legal regimes differ from one another.[3]

The linguistic definition of the term reasonable is — as evidenced above — one based on expectations and toleration, and it is thus largely a subjective term. However, for the purpose of a legal context, a larger degree of objectivity is required of a term since it is a tool for many different practitioners. On the other hand, if the term becomes too objectively defined, its

[1] As Prof. Honnold so eloquently states: "We lawyers have to work with blunt, unreliable tools — words! . . . mushy ambiguous things even for ordinary communications." John O. Honnold, *The Sales Convention in Action — Uniform International Words: Uniform Application?* 8 J.L. & Com. 207 (1988).

[2] A good example would be the term "avoid," which linguistically is defined as not coming into contact with something, in the language of the 1980 United Nations Convention on Contracts for the International Sale of Goods means the ceasing of a contract which the parties have entered into. *See generally* CISG arts. 26, 49 and 51.

[3] The term "avoid" is exclusive to the regime of the 1980 United Nations Convention on Contracts for the International Sale of Goods. Other legal systems would use the term "terminate" or "cancel" to mean the same thing.

flexibility may be lost: It is the classic conflict of having to weigh individual (flexible) fairness against objective (rigid) predictibility — a compromise between the two ideals will often be required in order to accommodate both.

The present paper will focus on the meaning of the term "reasonable time" as understood by Article 39(1) of the 1980 United Nations Convention on Contracts for the International Sale of Goods[4] as well as provide an overview of caselaw in its application. This provision provides that a buyer notify the seller "within reasonable time" after he discovers or ought to have discovered that the goods do not conform to the contract. The objectivity of a term is especially important where the CISG is concerned, as this is a uniform law that must be interpreted and practiced uniformly. The aim of the determination of "reasonable time" in Article 39(1) will be to establish a pattern to the application of the provision, and assess whether the term is an autonomous term applied uniformly.[5] However, before delving deeper into the problems of Article 39(1), the uniform CISG should be properly introduced, as should the general use of the term "reasonable."

B. *The Uniform CISG*

1. A General Introduction to the CISG and Some of Its Problems

The CISG is a unique international uniform convention that has applied to contracts concerning the international sale of goods since 1988.[6] It has, at the present point in time, been ratified by 54 countries,[7] and this

[4] United Nations Convention on Contracts for the International Sale of Goods, Apr. 11, 180, U.N. Dox. A/CONF. 97/18, Annex I, reprinted in 19 I.L.M. 668 [hereinafter CISG].

[5] Please note that the determination of "reasonable time" in the present paper solely concerns Art. 39(1). The term as understood by other provisions of the CISG, such as Art. 46, must be interpreted and understood differently.

[6] Although drafted in 1980, the Convention could not enter into force until there were ten signatories to the Convention. With the accession to the Convention on Dec. 11, 1986 of China, Italy and the United States of America, a date for the application of the Convention could be set. This date was Jan. 1, 1988. *See Status of Conventions, infra* note 7.

[7] As of March 1, 1999, the Contracting States are: Argentina, Australia, Austria, Belarus, Belgium, Bosnia-Herzegovina, Bulgaria, Burundi, Canada, Chile, China (PRC), Croatia, Cuba, Czech Republic, Denmark, Ecuador, Egypt, Estonia, Finland, France, Georgia, Germany, Greece, Guinea, Hungary, Iraq, Italy, Latvia, Lesotho, Lithuania, Luxembourg,

makes it one of the most successful uniform international conventions to date. This success is not surprising. Preceded by the less successful 1964 Uniform Law of International Sale of Goods[8] and the Uniform Law for the Formation of Contracts on the International Sale of Goods,[9] the drafting of the CISG was conducted explicitly on the basis of forming more widely acceptable conventions,[10] which were later combined into one.[11] This, along with the ever-growing need to regulate international trade uniformly as the borders of the world become a little less discernible and international trade grows in volume, has made the Convention extremely popular.[12]

Mexico, Moldova, Mongolia, Netherlands, New Zealand, Norway, Poland, Romania, Russian Federation, Singapore, Slovakia, Slovenia, Spain, Sweden, Switzerland, Syria, Uganda, Ukraine, United States, Uruguay, Uzbekistan, Yugoslavia, and Zambia. *Status of Conventions and Model Laws,* United Nations Commission on International Trade Law, UN GAOR, 31st Sess., U.N. Doc. A/CN.9/449 (1998) [hereinafter Status of Conventions].

[8] Uniform Law on the International Sale of Goods (1964), reprinted in 3 I.L.M. 855 (1964) [hereinafter ULIS].

[9] Convention Relating to a Uniform Law on the Formation of Contract for the International Sale of Goods, July 1, 1964, 834 U.N.T.S. [hereinafter ULF], reprinted in JOHN HONNOLD, UNIFORM LAW FOR INTERNATIONAL SALES UNDER THE 1980 UNITED NATIONS CONVENTION 659-66 (2d ed. 1991).

[10] Please note that the ULIS and ULF have not been completely abandoned, but can still be applied between Contracting States if the CISG does not apply. *See, e.g.,* OLG München, 9 August 1995 [7 U 7143/92] (Germany) (UNILEX), <http://cisgw3.law.pace.edu/cases/950809g1.html> (Pace), which applied the ULIS to a contract between an Italian buyer and a German seller, since the CISG did not apply by virtue of Article 100, as the contract was drawn up before the entry into force of the Convention in Italy or Germany.

[11] *See Report of the United Nations Commission on International Trade Law on the Work of its Second Session,* U.N. GAOR, 24th Sess., Supp. No. 18, U.N. DOC. A/7618 (1969) (where the Working Group on the International Sale of Goods was established).

[12] Please note that in spite of this, the United Kingdom has not yet signed the Convention. *See Status of Conventions, supra* note 7. According to the Department of Trade and Industry, the issue was considered in 1989. *See* Dep't of Trade and Indus., Doc. No. U.R.N. 97-875. Although there was a majority in favor of accession, the Department felt this majority to be too slight for it to be brought to the legislature. *Id.* With the arrival of a new Government in May 1997, however, the new Ministry of Trade felt — in the light of the popularity of the Convention, especially amongst EU member States — that the U.K. was out of step with international trade law, and new consultations for a U.K. accession to the CISG are currently in progress. *See id.* This trend regarding the Consulta-

a. Travaux Préparatoires

The CISG was drawn up by the Working Group on the International Sale of Goods, established by the United Nations Commission for International Trade Law (UNCITRAL). Reports of the Working Group detail discussions, and show that suggestions by various representatives of participating nations were incorporated into the drafting. Moreover, a special report by the Secretariat[13] accompanied the final drafts of the Convention as an explanatory commentary. This latter document poses a unique problem. It is the equivalent to *travaux préparatoires*, since it comments on an earlier draft, but it is considered by some to be the next best thing to an official commentary.[14] However, the importance of *travaux préparatoires* in the CISG regime is somewhat uncertain. On the one hand, it might successfully be argued that as certain ratifying countries to the Convention have legal systems which do not prioritize *travaux préparatoires* as highly as legal sources (i.e., the common law countries),[15] it should not be given much weight. However, on the other hand, the Secretariat Commentary is extremely helpful in illustrating the intent of the drafters, and has been considered important by certain practitioners and scholars. For the purpose of the present paper, the Secretariat Commentary is considered significant, not only because it helps define the terms applied in the Convention irrespective of common law tradition, but also since it is the only source of law commenting on the CISG that has been recognized by all countries who participated in the drafting of the Convention. Thus, it represents internationally accepted theories behind the provisions, even though the Vienna Convention did not adopt any proposals to lend it official weight.

---

tion Document leans slightly towards the favoring of ratification, but the proposal to the legislature is not (yet) a reality.

[13] *See generally* Commentary on the Draft Convention on Contracts for the International Sale of Goods, prepared by the Secretariat, U.N. Doc. A/CONF.97/5 (1979), reprinted IN JOHN O. HONNOLD, DOCUMENTARY HISTORY OF THE UNIFORM SALES LAW (1989) [hereinafter Secretariat Commentary].

[14] *See* JOSEPH LOOKOFSKY, UNDERSTANDING THE CISG IN SCANDINAVIA 23 (1996).

[15] Although common law countries do not traditionally credit *travaux préparatoires* with much importance, some Courts have been known to look to that source for inspiration. *See* Chan v. Korean Airlines, 490 U.S. 122 109 S.Ct. 1676 (1989) (concerning the Warsaw Convention, where the Court stated that the "Convention's drafting history might be consulted to elucidate a text that is ambiguous"). *Id.* at 134.

b. Application without Supranational Control

The CISG also presents the practitioner with another problem, although this one is not so unique in the framework of the United Nations. The Convention forms part of the UN regime. As such, there is no supranational instance (such as the EEC Court) or Court of Uniformity before which cases can be brought. This means that problems of uniformity must be solved in the domestic realm. Discrepancies in domestic practice or misconstructions of the CISG cannot be brought before international CISG experts and rectified. However, the domestic practice of the Contracting States, as well as the practice from Arbitral Tribunals, is under a constant vigilance from international legal scholars, who are quick to subsequently point out any misunderstandings or problems which may have occurred — this can at least help prevent further mistakes from becoming precedents to others.[16] Although a tribunal monitoring its application would be preferable, the uniformity of the CISG and its terms would seem well protected to a certain degree.

c. Accessibility to Caselaw

The monitoring of caselaw is closely connected to yet another problem facing the practitioner as well as the scholar of international law — namely that of the accessibility of relevant foreign judgments. Paying heed to international precedents either directly or via scholars requires the caselaw in question to be accessible. Although great progress has been made in this field for the CISG with the arrival of databases on the Internet and collections of caselaw such as CLOUT and UNILEX,[17] this progress is primarily

---

[16] *See* John O. Honnold, *Uniform Sales Law — the Experience with Uniform Sales Laws in the Federal Republic of Germany*, 2 JURIKISK TIDSSKRIFT 3-14 (1990/91), where he explains how consideration and critique of case law in other jurisdictions, as well as help from scholars and comparative law centers, smooth any divergent interpretations of uniform law.

[17] See the Caselaw of UNCITRAL Texts, UN Doc. A/CN.9/SER.C/ABSTRACTS (date) or the UNILEX Database, edited by Prof. Bonell, from the Italian National Research Council (CNR), for a listing of Internet-sites. Another source for cases is the Pace University School of Law CISG Database [hereinafter Pace] (last modified, Feb. 1, 1999) <http://cisg.law.pace.edu> at <http://cisgw3.law.pace.edu/cases/980629u1.html>.

made within the legal systems of Central Europe and the United States. Caselaw from, for example, three of the official language texts of the Convention (Arabic, Chinese and Russian) is not yet available to the "western" scholar.[18] Such problems, and many others, would be greatly mitigated by establishing a center for research and documentation in all branches of the CISG, as proposed by prominent scholars such as Prof. Honnold.[19] Such a center is not a reality. Frequently international scholars will have better access to judgments available to them from their own country or related/similar legal systems,[20] and thus have greater opportunity to analyze and quote these. In turn, the domestic practitioners will be more prone to refer to international scholars of their own nationality in their own language,[21] and thus even the judge complying with his duty to apply international precedents will inadvertently apply precedents and theories that are more focused on domestic or similar practice in his interpretation of the terms of the CISG.

---

[18] Please note, however, that the database at Pace Univeristy School of Law recently has begun to report some cases from China and Russia. *See generally* (Pace).

[19] During a seminar on uniform sales law held on Feb. 16 and 17, 1987, Prof. Honnold endorsed the importance of establishing "a center for research and documentation in all branches of internationally uniform law, or, if this is considered too ambitious, the research center could be confined to UNCITRAL activities," as proposed by the Polish scholar Prof. Rajski. *See* John Honnold, *Uniform Words and Uniform Application. The 1980 Sales Convention and International Juridical Practice, in* EINHEITLICHES KAUFRECHT UND NATIONALEN OBLIGATIONENRECHT 140, 145 (Peter Schlechtriem ed. 1987). The activities of such a center would include documentation, research, legal training and expert advice. *See id.* Prof. Honnold added: "Surely the general entry into force of the Sales Convention should and will stipulate these developments" — sadly, that was not the case. *See id.*

[20] Although the international CISG scholars have cross-references to the practice from the countries of other scholars, this is still primarily restricted to the practice from the "western" hemisphere.

[21] For example, in the CISG regime the Courts of the United States refer to the theories of Prof. Honnold. *See, e.g.*, Delchi Carrier SpA v. Rotorex Corp., 71 F.3d 1024, 1028 (2nd Cir. 1995), *available in* <http://cisgw3.law.pace.edu/cases/951206u1.html> (Pace). Whereas, in German caselaw the scholarly commentary most frequently referred to is Prof. Schlechtriem. *See* LG Kassel, 15 February 1996 [11 O 4185/95] (Germany) (UNILEX), *available in* Pace (last modified, Feb. 1, 1999) <http://cisgw3.law.pace.edu/cases/960215g2.html>.

2. Interpretation of Terms in the CISG

The CISG is a uniform sales law which must be applied and interpreted uniformly, in accordance with Article 7(1).[22] This uniformity is at the very core of the Convention's existence, since the need for an international convention on sales of goods was prompted by the need for certainty in contracts on an international basis.[23] This uniformity means that it should ideally be applied in an identical manner in all courts and tribunals where it is adhered to.

The practitioner of the CISG has a duty, extrapolated from Article 7(1), to consider caselaw from other Contracting States and other states applying the CISG via Article 1(1)(b), as well as from Arbitral Tribunals.[24] The enactment of uniform laws will not suffice where these laws are not taken to mean the same.[25] Some leading scholars see the CISG as an opportunity to establish a legal *lingua franca* as well as common legal concepts to bridge the gap between international parties in trade.[26] This requires all terms to be

---

[22] Art. 7(1) of the CISG provides: "In the interpretation of this Convention, regard is to be had to its international character and to the need to promote uniformity in its application and the observance of good faith in international trade."

[23] The preamble to the CISG states "[t]he adoption of uniform rules which govern contracts for the international sale of goods and take into account the different social, economic and legal systems would contribute to the removal of legal barriers in international trade . . . ."

[24] *See, e.g.*, Joseph Lookofsky, *At fremme en ensartet anvendelse af CISG*, *in* BUGESKRIFT FOR RETSVAESEN (UFR) 139, 140, 144 (1996). "Man skal tage hensyn til den internationale præcedens, til hvad de forskellige domstole har sagt." [Consideration must be had to international precedents, to what the different Courts have said.] *Id.* at 140.

[25] *See e.g.*, Franco Ferrari, *Uniform Application and Interest Rates under the 1980 Vienna Sales Convention*, 24 GA. J. INT'L & COMP. L. 467, 470 (1995) ("In order to achieve uniformity in international trade law, however, it is not sufficient to enact uniform law conventions. It is equally important that its provisions . . . be interpreted the same way in various countries").

[26] Peter Schlechtriem, *Uniform Sales Law — The Experience with Uniform Sales Laws in the Federal Republic of Germany*, 1 JURIKISK TIDSKRIFT VID STOCKHOLMS UNIVERSITET 1, 28 (1991-92) "With the Uniform Sales Law there is a chance that for the first time since the medieval ages, when Roman law equipped most continental lawyers with their conceptual tools, that we not only have a common language but also common legal concepts to circumscribe the decisive issues." *Id. See also* Jan Hellner, *The UN-Convention on International Sales of Goods — an Outsider's View, reprinted in* Festschrift für Stefan Riesenfeld 71, 73 (1983).

understood uniformly and equally. Thus, for a term to be suitable to a uniform law, a determination of this term which transcends borders and assumes an objective meaning is required.

Some assistance in the interpretation of terms is found in Article 7(2), which prescribes that gaps are to be filled with the general principles underlying the Convention where such principles are present,[27] but this still is a tricky tightrope to walk. On the one hand, the problem of *faux amis* or labelling means that the drafter, practitioner, and scholar of uniform law should also beware of terms that seem precise but may have different domestic legal connotations for the court or tribunal interpreting them.[28] This may render them even more imprecise than the seemingly more ambiguous terms. On the other hand, a subjective definition of terms in a uniform law would render the uniformity of the law itself illusory, and imprecise terms can allow a margin of such subjective determination if they are not guided by criteria for their application. The term "reasonable" falls in the latter category of terms.

3. Reasonableness in the CISG

The subjectivity of the term "reasonable" is what makes it both suitable and unsuitable for application in a uniform law. It is flexible enough to avoid the problem of *faux amis*, but may also be too imprecise to ensure

[27] Art. 7(2) of the CISG provides:

> Questions concerning matters governed by this Convention which are not expressly settled in it are to be settled in conformity with the general principles on which it is based or, in the absence of such principles, in conformity with the law applicable by virtue of the rules of private international law.

According to Prof. Albert Kritzer, these general principles, reasoned by analogy of the Convention include: i) providing needed co-operation, ii) a duty to disclose material information, iii) reasonableness, and iv) equal treatment and respect for the different cultural, social and legal backgrounds of individual traders. *See* ALBERT KRITZER, GUIDE TO PRACTICAL APPLICATIONS OF THE UNITED NATIONS CONVENTION ON CONTRACTS FOR THE INTERNATIONAL SALE OF GOODS 79 — 84 (1989) (the latter with reference to the scholar Kastely).

[28] An example of such faux amis in the CISG-regime is found in art. 47(1), which the Secretariat labeled a "Nachfrist" rule in its commentary. However, this has misled some German practitioners to consider art. 47(1) a duty for the buyer as opposed to a right, by equating it to the domestic "Nachfrist" rule in HGB § 326 p.44, 45. *See* text with note 196 *infra* for examples of this unfortunate practice.

uniformity if left with no guideline or criteria for interpretation. Nevertheless, there are no fewer than thirty-seven provisions of the CISG that contain the word "reasonable."[29] One of these provisions, Article 8(2), prescribes that for the purpose of the CISG, a party is entitled to interpret actions of another party in accordance with the understanding that a reasonable person of the same kind would have, provided the intent of the action is not known to him.[30] In other words, the right to "reasonably" interpret actions applies to the entire Convention. Moreover, reasonableness is considered a general principle upon which the Convention is based, and so this standard applies to all issues governed by, but not settled in the CISG by virtue of Article 7(2) of the Convention.[31]

The following will examine what this abundance of reasonableness in the CISG entails and implies.

a. The Flexibility of Reasonableness in General

When considering the many references to the term "reasonable" in the CISG, it is important to keep in mind that the Convention represents a compromise of "equal ground" in transnational trade law, to make it capable of wide acceptance by countries of different legal, social, and economic backgrounds. Since the concepts of reasonableness, fairness, and justice are the cornerstones of all legal systems, the term "reasonable" is easily acceptable to all representatives due to its indication of justice and, not least, its flexibility.

The term, undoubtedly, holds a high degree of flexibility within the framework of legal science — the subjectivity of its linguistic definition spills over into its legal definition to the extent that it is generally taken to

---

[29] *See* CISG arts. 8(2), 8(3), 16(2)(b), 18(2), 25, 33(c), 34, 35(2)(b), 37, 38(3), 39(1), 43(1), 44, 46(3), 47(1), 48(1), 48(2), 49(2)(a), 49(2)(b), 60(a), 63(1), 64(2)(b), 65(2), 72(2), 73(2), 75, 76(2), 77, 79(1), 79(4), 85, 86(1), 86(2), 87, 88(1), 88(2), 88(3). *See also* extrapolations of the concept of the "reasonable person" in other parts of the CISG, for example arts. 9 and 24.

[30] Art. 8(2) of the CISG provides: "If the preceding paragraph is not applicable, statements made by and other conduct of a party are to be interpreted according to the understanding that a reasonable person of the same kind as the other party would have had in the same circumstances." This is largely an improvement of art. 13 of the ULIS, which stated: "For the purposes of the present Law, the expression "a party knew or ought to have known", or any similar expression, refers to what should have been known to a reasonable person in the situation." *See* <http://www.cisg.law.pace.edu/cisg/text/ulis.htm> (Pace).

[31] *See* KRITZER, *supra* note 27, at 79-84.

mean that all circumstances may be of influence when determining behavior in the eyes of the law. For instance, as opposed to other "yardsticks" against which good behavior has been measured (such as the *Bonus Pater Familias* and the *Vir Optimus* from tort law), the concept of the reasonable man does not prescribe rigid standards for perfect behavior, but takes everything into account. Similarly, no references to the term "reasonable" omit any criteria in the determination of fairness. This is the flip side to the flexibility of reasonableness; it is a very broad term that takes everything into account with no particular vantage point. It is extremely subjective, and easily subjected to circumstances which might be deemed legally irrelevant before some Courts and Tribunals. This subjectivity especially poses a problem where uniform law is concerned.

b. The Problem of Flexible Reasonableness in the CISG

The use of such a flexible term as "reasonable" in a CISG provision would seem to imply that the drafters of the CISG intended its application to vary, depending on the individual facts of each case.[32] It cannot, however, have been the intention of the drafters that the uniformity of the Convention should suffer under this flexibility,[33] as there is no margin of appreciation within the framework of the CISG for practitioners to adapt it to their own domestic legal systems.[34]

---

[32] Regarding "reasonable time," see *Report of the Secretary-General: obligations of the seller in an international sale of goods; consolidation of work done by the Working Group on the International Sale of Goods and suggested solution for unresolved problems*, [1972] IV UNCITRAL Y.B. 36, ¶ 85, at 48, U.N. Doc. A/CN.9/WG.2/WP.16. "[T]he Working Group concluded that the expression "within a reasonable time" was sufficiently flexible to adapt to the varying circumstances . . . ." *Id.*

[33] During the drafting of the CISG, a representative expressed concern that since the Uniform Law applies irrespective of the commercial or civil character of the parties, a lack of definitions of terms as viewed by international trade might lead to different approaches by Courts through the application of domestic or subjective criteria. *See Working Group on the International Sale of Goods; report on the work of the Second Session, 7-18 December 1970*, [1971] II UNCITRAL Y.B. 50, ¶ 94, at 59, U.N. Doc. A/CN.9/52. He further considered it necessary to have a definition of the term "reasonable time." *Id.*

[34] This margin of appreciation is a doctrine stemming from the regime of the European Convention on Human Rights (the ECHR), which the European Court of Human Rights has adopted to grant Contracting States "space" for their own assessment of cases since the ECHR does not set out to establish a uniform Europe. *See* European Convention for the Protection of Human Rights and Fundamental Freedoms, Nov. 4, 1950, 213 U.N.T.S. 222.

Although flexibility is a necessary prerequisite to fairness in legislation and practice, there must be a guideline and criteria for all flexible terms requiring reasonableness so they do not become too imprecise or the basis for seemingly arbitrary outcomes. Some provisions have such guidelines incorporated in the Convention.[35] In the absence of such a Convention guideline, or if it is still too imprecise, the practitioners, scholars, and jurists must step in. Since Article 7(1) of the CISG prescribes not only uniformity, but also that regard must be had to the international character of the Convention, each individual reference to the term "reasonable" should ideally be given its own autonomous meaning.[36] Any emerging judicial and arbitral definitions of these "reasonable" provisions, in practice as well as in theory, should reflect this and establish a pattern for the interpretation of the terms.

This brings me back to the focal point of the present paper, namely the determination of the term "reasonable time" in Article 39(1), and the assessment of its congruency in practice. Through an understanding of the provision itself and the scholarly interpretation of "reasonable time," as well as the all important international practice of the provision, such a pattern to the interpretation of Article 39(1) can, hopefully, be established, and the question of its uniformity can be settled.

---

[35] For example, with regard to the right to reasonably interpret actions in CISG art. 8(2), certain criteria for the determination of this particular reasonableness are listed in CISG art. 8(3). CISG art. 8(3) provides: "In determining the intent of a party or the understanding a reasonable person would have had, due consideration is to be given to all relevant circumstances of the case including the negotiations, any practices which the parties have established between themselves, usages and any subsequent conduct of the parties." Although somewhat vague and general, these criteria insure — to a certain extent — that the provisions which CISG art. 8(2) may in effect remain uniform while retaining the intended flexibility of reasonableness. This is one of the few provisions for which the Convention has set a guideline for the determination of its reasonableness.

[36] *See* M.J. Bonell, *Art. 7, in* COMMENTARY ON THE INTERNATIONAL SALES LAW — THE 1980 VIENNA SALES CONVENTION 74 (M.J. Bonnell & C.M. Bianca eds., 1987). "Yet, to have regard to the "international character of the Convention also implies the necessity of interpreting its terms and concept autonomously, *i.e.*, in the context of the Convention itself and not by referring to the meaning which might traditionally be attached to them within a particular domestic law." *Id.*

II. The Problems of Article 39

Of all the references to reasonableness in the CISG, the reference to "reasonable time" in Article 39(1) has captured the most judicial and arbitral attention. Indeed, Article 39 is one of the articles of the CISG that has been applied most by arbitrators and Courts.[37] There are numerous reasons for this richness in practice, the most significant of which is likely the vagueness of the term coupled with the fact that — unlike where Article 8(2) is concerned — criteria for determining this "reasonable" time period were never laid down in the Convention nor in the *travaux préparatoires.* It has thus been up to practitioners, scholars, and jurists to determine the meaning of the term "within reasonable time."

This has resulted in the fact that Article 39(1) poses an interesting problem. Not only in the definition of "within reasonable time," but also in the analysis of possible differences in practice: What are differences based upon? Are they significant? Has domestic law influenced the domestic Courts? Consequently, Article 39(1) is a well suited provision for analyzing and determining whether the reasonability factor is a suitable one for making a provision flexible, or whether it will endanger the uniformity of the Convention. The present paper will therefore focus on Article 39(1), and the meaning of "reasonable time," in an attempt to determine whether this is, indeed, an autonomous term which is understood uniformly. This will be illustrated by a comparative analysis of the practice from the Tribunals and domestic Courts on Article 39(1) of the CISG. In the process, the question of whether there is an emerging pattern for the determination of this term will be investigated and, hopefully, answered. First, an understanding of the provision is necessary.

---

[37] This tendency was also true for the CISG precedents, ULF and ULIS. *See* Peter Schlechtriem, *Some Observations on the United Nations Convention on Contracts for the International Sale of Goods, in* FRONTIERS OF LIABILITY 43 Vol. 2, (Peter Birks ed. 1994) "It was clear from our collection of judgments involving the Hague Sales Laws (ULIS and ULFIS) that about 1/5 of all the cases concerned questions of correct and timely notice and the consequences of failure to give notice." *Id.* However, where the CISG is concerned, art. 39 judgments represent more than 20 % of reported practice. *See* Pace, (visited Aug. 5, 1998) <http://www.cisg.law.pace.edu> (of 453 reported judgments, a total of 118 cases or 26% of the cases concern Art. 39).

A. *Introducing Article 39(1)*

Article 39 is part of Part III, Chapter II, Section II of the CISG, which is the section dealing with conformity of the goods and third party claims. It outlines an obligation for the buyer to communicate dissatisfaction in connection with other provisions of the CISG, and should therefore be viewed in that context. It has been considered one of the most important issues of the CISG by leading scholars.[38]

Article 39 states that:

> (1) The buyer loses the right to rely on a lack of conformity of the goods if he does not give notice to the seller specifying the nature of the lack of conformity within a reasonable time after he has discovered it or ought to have discovered it.
> (2) In any event, the buyer loses the right to rely on a lack of conformity of the goods if he does not give the seller notice thereof at the latest within a period of two years from the date on which the goods were actually handed over to the buyer, unless this time-limit is inconsistent with a contractual period of guarantee.

Article 39 is closely linked to other Articles of the CISG, most notably Articles 35, 38, 40, and 44. These provisions place Article 39 in its context, and help define and outline the duty to give notice.

1. Notice of Non-Conformity — Why?

A duty to reasonably notify of termination of a contract is well known in most legal systems.[39] However, the notification duty in Article 39(1) is

---

[38] *See* Franco Ferrari, *Specific Topics of the CISG*, 15 J.L. & COM. 1, 99 (1995). "One of the most important issues of the CISG . . . appears to be . . . the notice to be given to the seller in case of non-conformity of the goods" *Id.* "[T]he obligation to notify the seller in case of lack of conformity of the goods bought is one of the most important practical issues of the CISG." *Id.* at n.686 (quoting Ulrich Magnus, *Wiener UN-Kaufrecht (CISG) in*, VON STAUDINGERS KOMMENTAR ZUM BURGERLICHEN GESETZBUCH MIT EINFUHRUNGSGESETZ UND NEBENGESETZEN 39 (Heinrich Honsell ed., 12th ed., 1994)).

[39] *See* G.H. TRIETEL, REMEDIES FOR BREACH OF CONTRACT 400 (1988). "The prejudice which termination can cause to the defaulting party obviously increases the longer the aggrieved party delays in claiming this remedy; and most systems of law contain provisions designed to ensure that the right to terminate is exercised without undue delay." *Id.* ¶ 291.

not restricted to such cases of termination/avoidance, but concerns *any* remedy under the CISG. The failure to comply with this duty to notify of non-conformity will usually result in a complete loss of remedy, including the right to claim damages. This has been considered a drastic, and even disastrous, sanction by leading scholars.[40] The duty to notify applies to all buyers, regardless of their civil or commercial status.

As illustrated by the Secretariat Commentary, the purpose of the notification requirement in Article 39(1) is the protection of the seller. It prevents a buyer from any unreasonable reliance on alleged non-conformities from which the seller is not able to protect himself,[41] (e.g. in cases where the passage of time has met a burden of proof that is impossible to overcome) and protects the seller's interest in regarding the transaction as fully completed shortly after he has completed his end of the bargain. Moreover, according to some scholars, the notice requirement is also in the buyer's interest as it promotes a swift cure.[42] In addition to this, in the case of avoidance, Article 39(1) notice may be combined with notice of avoidance in accordance with

---

[40] The consequences of non-compliance with Article 39(1) have been considered drastic as well as disastrous. *See, e.g.*, Kazuaki Sono, *Failure to Notify — Art. 44, in* COMMENTARY ON THE INTERNATIONAL SALES LAW — THE 1980 VIENNA SALES CONVENTION 326 (C.M. Bianca & M.J. Bonell eds., 1987). "Under Article 39(1), the buyer's failure to give a timely notice of non-conformity of the goods will deprive the buyer of his right to rely on the lack of conformity against the seller. Thus, the sanction against the failure to give the adequate notice is drastic, i.e., the loss of remedy." *Id. See also* HERBERT BERNSTEIN & JOSEPH LOOKOFSKY, UNDERSTANDING THE CISG IN EUROPE 63 (1997) (who consider the sanction disastrous for the buyer).

[41] *See generally* Secretariat Commentary, *supra* note 13. "The purpose of the notice is to inform the seller what he must do to remedy the lack of conformity, to give him the basis on which to conduct his own examination of the goods, and in general to gather evidence for use in any dispute with the buyer over the alleged lack of conformity." *Id.* In LG Kassel of 15 February 1996 [11 O 4185/95] (Germany) (UNILEX), <http://cisgw3.law.pace.edu/cases/960215g1.html>, the Court stated that the purpose of the provision was not only the general interests of the industry to have a quick settlement of legal issues, but also first and foremost the seller's opportunity to undertake measures (which will become more difficult in time) to defend himself from claims such as damages. This latter consideration, however, is the driving force behind art. 39(2) according to the Secretariat Commentary, *supra* note 13, at art. 3, ¶ 5 (former draft to art. 39).

[42] *See* FRITZ ENDERLEIN & DIETRICH MASKOW, INTERNATIONAL SALES LAW CONVENTION 159-60 (1992). "It is in the interest of the buyer himself to inform the seller because the latter can do nothing to cure the lack before he becomes aware of it." *Id.*

Articles 26 and 49(2), and the notice then additionally serves the purpose of preventing the buyer from speculating at the seller's expense.[43]

Article 35 of the CISG requires the seller to deliver goods conforming to the specifications of the contract between the buyer and the seller.[44] Any lack of such conformity[45] may constitute a breach that will enable the buyer to exercise remedies under the Convention depending on the severity of the

---

[43] For instance, in the case of commodities which fluctuate greatly in value, the buyer should not be permitted "free options" of lengthy time-frames based on speculations of the increase in price versus his assessment of the significance of the non-conformity in question.

[44] Art. 35 of the CISG provides:

(1) The seller must deliver goods which are of the quantity, quality and description required by the contract and which are contained or packaged in the manner required by the contract.

(2) Except where the parties have agreed otherwise, the goods do not conform with the contract unless they:

(a) are fit for the purposes for which goods of the same description would ordinarily be used;

(b) are fit for any particular purpose expressly or impliedly made known to the seller at the time of the conclusion of the contract, except where the circumstances show that the buyer did not rely, or that it was unreasonable for him to rely, on the seller's skill and judgment;

(c) possess the qualities of goods which the seller has held out to the buyer as a sample or model;

(d) are contained or packaged in the manner usual for such goods or, where there is no such manner, in a manner adequate to preserve and protect the goods.

(3) The seller is not liable under sub-paragraphs (a) to (d) of the preceding paragraph for any lack of conformity of the goods if at the time of the conclusion of the contract the buyer knew or could not have been unaware of such lack of conformity.

[45] For a discussion of what constitutes lack of conformity under art. 35, see among others, Ferrari, *supra* note 38, at 101-104 and C.M. Bianca, *Conformity of the Goods and Third Party Claims — Art. 35, in* COMMENTARY ON THE INTERNATIONAL SALES LAW — THE 1980 VIENNA SALES CONVENTION 268, 273. (C.M. Bianca & M.J. Bonell eds., 1987). Generally, goods that do not conform to the specifications of the buyer or are unfit for ordinary purposes are non-conforming, the question of whether this includes the delivery of completely different goods (aliuds) is not finally settled. *Id.* Art. 33(1)(b) of the ULIS explicitly includes aliuds as non-conforming goods, but this provision was not restated in the CISG. Scholars are not in complete agreement as to the question under the CISG. *See, e.g.,* PETER SCHLECHTRIEM, UNIFORM SALES LAW 67 (1986) as opposed to C.M. Bianca, *Conformity of the Goods and Third Party Claims, in* COMMENTARY ON THE INTERNATIONAL SALES LAW — THE 1980 VIENNA SALES CONVENTION 268, 273 (C.M. Bianca & M.J. Bonell eds., 1987).

breach ensuing from the non-conformity.[46] These remedies vary from a right to fix a time for cure,[47] a reduction of price[48] and damages,[49] to the more drastic remedy of avoidance[50] of the contract where the breach is fundamental.[51]

---

[46] Any non-performance by the seller entitles the buyer to exercise his rights under the Convention or claim damages, see art. 45 of the Convention, which is a no-fault basis of contractual liability. For a comparative analysis of the fault and no-fault theories of contractual liability pursuant to the Danish Sale of Goods Act, the American Uniform Commercial Code and the CISG, see Joseph Lookofsky, *CISG: The Basis Of Liability*, 5 JUSTITIA 1-72 (1981).

[47] Art. 47 (1) of the CISG provides: "The buyer may fix an additional period of time of reasonable length for performance by the seller." Note that with respect to non-conformity, this is a right for the buyer and not the seller. Only where avoidance of a contract based on non-delivery is concerned may a buyer be obligated to have fixed such an additional period before avoidance. *See* CISG art. 49(1)(b).

[48] Art. 50 of the CISG provides:

> If the goods do not conform with the contract and whether or not the price has already been paid, the buyer may reduce the price in the same proportion as the value that the goods actually delivered had at the time of the delivery bears to the value that conforming goods would have had at that time.

However, if the seller remedies any failure to perform his obligations in accordance with CISG art. 37 or CISG art. 48 or if the buyer refuses to accept performance by the seller in accordance with those articles, the buyer may not reduce the price. For commentaries on CISG art. 50, see HONNOLD, *supra* note 9, at 309 and ENDERLEIN & MASKOW, *supra* note 42, at 195.

[49] Art. 74 of the CISG provides:

> Damages for breach of contract by one party consist of a sum equal to the loss, including loss of profit, suffered by the other party as a consequence of the breach. Such damages may not exceed the loss which the party in breach foresaw or ought to have foreseen at the time of the conclusion of the contract, in the light of the facts and matters of which he then knew or ought to have known, as a possible consequence of the breach of contract.

For commentaries on CISG art. 74, *see* HONNOLD, *supra* note 9, at 403 and ENDERLEIN & MASKOW, *supra* note 42, at 297.

[50] In the CISG regime, the term "avoidance" is applied for the termination of a contract. *See supra* text accompanying note 3. Avoidance by the buyer is regulated in CISG art. 49, which provides when such avoidance may take place (¶ 1), the time-frames for declaration of avoidance (art. 26), and when the buyer intends to avoid (¶ 2). CISG art. 49(1)(a) provides: "The buyer may declare the contract avoided: (a) if the failure by the seller to perform any of his obligations under the contract or this Convention amounts to a fundamental breach of contract." For commentaries, *see* HONNOLD, *supra* note 9, at 301; ENDERLEIN & MASKOW, *supra* note 42, at 189; and Michael Will, *Right to Avoid Contract — Art. 49, in* COMMENTARY ON THE INTERNATIONAL SALES LAW- THE 1980 VIENNA SALES CON-

However, in order to retain his right to rely on any given non-conformity, the buyer must — according to Article 39(1) — specify the lack of conformity to the seller "within reasonable time" after he discovers it or ought to have discovered it, or at least — according to Article 39(2) — within two years from delivery (unless a longer period of guarantee has been extended by the seller). So if a buyer does not wish to pay for faulty goods or pay in full for an incomplete shipment, he must give the proper notice.

2. Notice of Non-Conformity — How?

Article 39(1) requires the buyer to specify the nature of the lack of conformity to the seller.[52] Simply communicating that the goods do not conform will not suffice for the purposes of Article 39(1). If the goods suffer from more than one sort of non-conformity or defect, each must be duly notified to the seller in order for the buyer to rely thereupon.[53] If a notice is not specific enough, it will not be considered a satisfactory Article 39(1) notice, no matter how quickly it was communicated.[54] This is the only requirement regarding form.

VENTION 359 (C.M. Bianca & M.J. Bonell eds., 1987). Note that damages for loss under CISG art. 74 can still be awarded after avoidance (CISG art. 76(1)) as well as damages under CISG art. 75 for difference in price.

[51] The fundamentality of a breach is determined according to CISG art. 25, which provides:

> A breach of contract committed by one of the parties is fundamental if it results in such detriment to the other party as substantially to deprive him of what he is entitled to expect under the contract, unless the party in breach did not foresee and a reasonable person of the same kind in the same circumstances would not have foreseen such a result.

Scholars seem to agree that the substantiality of the breach is determined according to the individual facts of each case, Prof. Honnold includes the seller's right to cure, *see* HONNOLD, *supra* note 9, at 185. *See also* Michael Will, *Fundamental Breach, in* COMMENTARY ON THE INTERNATIONAL SALES LAW- THE VIENNA SALES CONVENTION 205 (C.M. Bianca & M.J. Bonell eds., 1987); and ENDERLEIN & MASKOW, *supra* note 42, at 111.

[52] *See* UN Doc. A/CN.9/SER.C/GUIDE/1 English 12 September 1995 (UNCITRAL Thesaurus) (which classifies this issue as 39A1, and the degree of specificity as 39A11).

[53] *See* LG Landshut, 5 April 1995 (54 O 644/94) (Germany) (UNILEX), explained in text accompanying note 209 *infra*.

[54] *See, e.g.*, LG Bielefeld, 18 January 1991 (15 O 201/90) (Germany) (UNILEX), where, although, notice was considered communicated to the seller within a reasonable time (3 days), it was not considered specific enough, with regard to one aspect of the non-conformity and therefore, could not be relied upon by the buyer.

Consequently, any kind of notice will suffice if timely and specific. A telephone call that details the non-conformity within reasonable time satisfies the requirement of Article 39(1) — at least in theory. It will, however, more often than not be impossible for the buyer to substantiate that such a timely call took place and that notice was communicated specifically to the correct person.[55] Consequently, a more easily proven means of communicating the notice would be preferable.

Moreover, notice must be communicated to the seller. If notice is given to a third party or someone associated with the seller but not directly identifiable with him (i.e., not directly in the seller's employ), the buyer must ensure that the seller receives it, and that could prove to be more difficult than delivering it to the seller in the first place. But, naturally, to notify of a non-conformity, the buyer needs to discover it first.

3. Notice of Non-Conformity — When?

Article 39(1) notification must be given within reasonable time after the buyer has "discovered" or "ought to have discovered" the non-conformity of the goods. This period within which notification must be given is measured in accordance with the following.

a. Start of "Reasonable Time" Period

Article 38 prescribes a duty for the buyer to inspect the goods delivered to him within a short period.[56] Since Article 39(1) relies not only on the time of discovery of a non-conformity but also on the time a buyer

---

[55] *See e.g.*, the Dutch judgment Arrondissementsrechtsbank Gravenhage, 7 June 1995, (94/0670)(Netherlands) (UNILEX), wherein the buyer failed to indicate when and how he gave timely notice.

[56] Art. 38 provides that:

> (1) The buyer must examine the goods, or cause them to be examined, within as short a period as is practicable in the circumstances. (2) If the contract involves carriage of the goods, examination may be deferred until after the goods have arrived at their destination. (3) If the goods are redirected in transit or redispatched by the buyer without a reasonable opportunity for examination by him and at the time of the conclusion of the contract the seller knew or ought to have known of the possibility of such redirection or redispatch, examination may be deferred until after the goods have arrived at the new destination.

Id.

"ought to have discovered it," these two provisions are closely intertwined. Indeed, Article 38 is prefatory to Article 39.

This relationship with Article 38 usually determines the point in time from when the reasonable time period is to be measured: as the reasonable time-frame pertains to the period *after* the non-conformity is discovered (or ought to have been discovered), amd is only related to the time of delivery via Article 38. The Article 38 examination need not be carried out immediately after the delivery of the goods (although this is recommended to avoid all doubts) nor within a set time-frame,[57] but without delay according to the objective circumstances of the case.[58] It is at this point that the buyer normally ought to discover the non-conformity.[59]

For the purpose of Article 39(1), it is irrelevant *when* the buyer in fact discovers a non-conformity if he neglects his duty to inspect the goods within as short a period of time as is practicable. Article 39(1) will be violated if notice is not given within reasonable time after the buyer ought to have discovered the non-conformity in accordance with an examination carried out under Article 38, even if notice is given immediately after he discovers it.

Only where a buyer can prove that a satisfactory examination would not reasonably[60] have revealed the lack of conformity is Article 38 not rele-

---

[57] *See* Ferrari, *supra* note 38, at 1105, who not only disagrees with Reishofer regarding the need for an immediate examination, but also rejects the rule of Piltz, according to which three to four days is generally considered a short period.

[58] *See* C. M. Bianca, *Examination of Goods — Art. 38, in* COMMENTARY ON THE INTERNATIONAL SALES LAW — THE 1980 VIENNA SALES CONVENTION 295 (M.J. Bonell & C. M. Bianca eds., 1987). The impediments influencing the permitted period for examination are limited to those that are "general and objective." *Id.* at 299.

[59] *See* Secretariat Commentary, *supra* note 13, at 34, § 2 (art. 36 — former draft to art. 38). "The time when the buyer is obligated to examine the goods under article 36 (current art. 38) constitutes the time when the buyer "ought to have discovered" the lack of conformity under art. 37 (current art. 39), unless the non-conformity is one which could not have been discovered by such examination." *Id.*

[60] The reasonableness of the extent of the duty to examine the goods can be reached through an application of the general principle of reasonableness via art. 7(2) gap-filling. *See* Peter Winship *Private International Law and the U.N. Sales Convention,* 21 CORNELL INT'L L.J. 487, 530 (1988); See also Kazuaki Sono, *Notice of Lack of Conformity, in* COMMENTARY ON THE INTERNATIONAL SALES LAW — THE 1980 VIENNA SALES CONVENTION 303, 309-10 (M.J. Bonell & C. M. Bianca eds., 1987) who also finds the expectations of the seller as a "reasonable person" in art. 8(2) relevant to what the examination may reveal.

vant to Article 39.[61] The question of whether it would be customary to discover the non-conformity in question in a particular trade may influence whether the non-conformity ought to have been discovered,[62] in accordance with Article 9(2),[63] as will the type of goods concerned and the facilities of the parties.[64] The Secretariat Commentary states that in such cases, the buyer must give notice within a reasonable time after he discovered the non-conformity in fact or ought to have discovered it in the light of the ensuing events, for instance, because the goods are taken into use, as mentioned in Secretariat Commentary example 37A.[65] However, such cases will be rare, as the duty to examine the goods in Article 38 is an extensive one.[66]

---

[61] See LG Paderborn, 25 June 1996 (7 O 147/94) (Germany) (UNILEX) wherein the non-conformities could only have been discovered by way of a detailed chemical analysis which the buyer could not have been required to carry out.

[62] *See* JOSEPH LOOKOFSKY, INTERNATIONALE KØB 62 (1981).

[63] Art. 9(2) provides: "The parties are considered, unless otherwise agreed, to have impliedly made applicable to their contract or its formation a usage of which the parties knew or ought to have known and which in international trade is widely known to, and regularly observed by, parties to contracts of the type involved in the particular trade concerned."

[64] *See* Secretariat Commentary, *supra* note 13, at 34, § 3 (art. 36, former draft of art. 38): "The examination which this article requires the buyer to make is one which is reasonable in the circumstances . . . That which is reasonable in the circumstances . . . will depend on such factors as the type of goods and the nature of the parties. For example, a party would not be expected to discover a lack of conformity of the goods if he neither had nor had available the necessary technical facilities and expertise, even though other buyers in a different situation might be expected to discover such a lack of conformity." *Id.*

[65] *Id.* at 35, (art. 37, former draft of art. 39), Example 37A: "The non-conformity in the goods was not such that Buyer ought to have discovered it in the examination required by article 36 (former draft of art. 38). However, the non-conformity was such that it ought to have been discovered once Buyer began to use the goods. In this case Buyer must give notice of the non-conformity within a reasonable time after he 'ought to have discovered' it by use." *Id.*.

[66] For example, in a Swiss judgment from 1992, the Court stated that the buyer ought to have discovered that the sofa cushions slid when the purchasers sat upon them and specifically pointed out that a buyer re-selling the goods must carry out his own thorough art. 38 testing of the goods and not rely on eventual customer complaints for the purpose of Art. 39(1). *See* Pretura delle Giurisdizione di Locarna-Campagna, 27 April 1992 (6252) (Switzerland) (UNILEX) (detailed in text accompanying note 231 *infra*). A similar conclusion is reached in the German judgment OLG Karlsruhe, 25 June 1997 (1 U 280/96) (Germany) (UNILEX), where the Court stated that the buyer should have

Logically, if a more detailed examination is required before the non-conformity can be determined, the Article 39(1) time-frame commences later. For instance, where an expert examination is necessary for the determination of non-conformity, the period of "reasonable time" does not start to run until the expert report is published, as this is then the time at which the non-conformity ought to have been discovered.[67]

Similarly, if a buyer can present an excuse for not having examined the goods in accordance with Article 38, and is otherwise justifiably unaware of the non-conformity,[68] he cannot be punished by Article 39 for not giving notice of this non-conformity within reasonable time since he ought not to have discovered it. If, on the other hand, the buyer discovers a lack of conformity before he "ought to," the reasonable time of the notice is counted from this time, even if this is before the delivery of the goods.[69]

It should be noted, that regarding the time from which reasonable time is to be calculated, it may be inferred that Prof. Sono seems to consider the time when the seller ought to have discovered the goods as an entirely separate issue from the examination duty in Article 38.[70] Prof. Schlechtriem has stated that it is to be calculated from the actual handing over of the goods.[71] These conclusions seem to contradict the Secretariat Commentary

---

discovered the short-comings of sticky film before selling it. *See infra* text accompanying note 183, where this judgment is analyzed.

[67] *See* Anna Veneziano, *Non-conformity of goods in international sales — A survey of current caselaw on CISG, in* Revue de droit des Affaires Internationales 1997 52 (1997) with reference to ICC Court of Arbitration (5713) 1989 (UNILEX).

[68] It should, however, be noted that such an excuse for not examining the goods will be hard to substantiate. For instance, the exception in art. 38(3) has been interpreted so restrictively that it solely applies where the buyer does not actually handle the goods himself at all; see OLG Saarbrücken, 13 January 1993 (1 U 69/92) (Germany) (UNILEX) where the deferment of the obligation to inspect the goods did not apply since the buyer took possession of the goods in order to redirect them. Consequently, since he should have examined them, he ought to have discovered the non-conformities and, therefore, he lost his right to rely on the non-conformity since he did not give notice thereof within reasonable time. *See id.*

[69] *See* Enderlein & Maskow, *supra* note 42, at 160. "If the buyer already discovers defects before taking over the goods, the reasonable time still commences at this time of discovery — i.e., before delivery." *Id.*

[70] *See* Sono, *supra* note 60, at 309, (where no mention of Art. 38 is made).

[71] *See* Schlechtriem, *supra* note 45, at 71-72. "The time limit for the notification of the defects is determined by the actual handing-over of the goods to the buyer." *Id.*

and the above-mentioned scholars. Moreover, by denying the interrelation of Articles 38 and 39, these conclusions fuel the confusion between the two articles.

i. The Mix-up of Articles 38(1) and 39(1)

To date, there has been some confusion in practice between the Article 38 and Article 39 time-frames, and these are often mixed together as a whole, counting from the time of delivery. These factors, which should ideally only determine when the non-conformities should be discovered, are taken to influence the period of reasonable time, and vice versa.

An isolation of the two time-frames will, admittedly, often be purely academic as the time when the goods are to be examined (and most non-conformities ought to be discovered) is dependant upon the time of delivery of the goods according to Article 38. Nonetheless, it would be preferable for Courts to determine separately: 1) upon which date the non-conformity ought to have been discovered (usually in connection with Article 38), and then 2) within which time-frame notice should have been given.

Such a determination would eliminate any doubt as to which factors influence the time of notification, an analysis that is difficult when Articles 38 and 39 are taken together. The confusion of the two articles will often cloud the elucidation of these factors. A typical example of this is the nature of the non-conformity. If the non-conformity is easily discernible, the reasonable time period will begin soon after the time of delivery, but ought not affect its actual span. However, scholars and practitioners alike deem the discernability of the non-conformity as a factor influencing the reasonable time period.[72] However, strictly speaking, that should not be so. This factor ought to influence the time that the non-conformity ought to have been discovered, not the length of time that it subsequently takes to give the notice.

Ideally, factors that influence the time between realization and communication of non-conformity should be limited to relevant considerations of communication and considerations regarding the perishable nature of the goods, special deadlines or similar aspects. These factors

---

[72] *See* Veneziano, *supra* note 67, at 51. "The interpretation of what is meant by 'reasonable time' has been — not surprisingly — one of the most frequent issues in case law . . . One important element taken into account by courts is whether the defects are easily discovered." *Id.* (with reference to an Italian judgment).

should apply in like manner regardless of how the lack of conformity is discovered or ought to have been discovered, as the time-frame of reasonable time pertains only to the time-span between (would-be) discovery and communication of the non-conformity.

b. End of "Reasonable Time" Period

A notice of non-conformity under Article 39(1) of the CISG is "given" in the sense of Article 39(1) and considered communicated at the time when it is appropriately sent, in accordance with Article 27 of the Convention.[73] The risk of delay or fault in the transmission does not compromise the buyer. In the words of Prof. Schlechtriem: *"Rüge reist auf Risiko des Empfängers"* — the notice travels at the recipient's risk.[74]

4. Notice of Non-Conformity — Exceptions to the Rule

All in all, the buyer must tread with caution. A thorough and expeditious examination of the goods, and a specific, documented notice of non-conformity following this examination, given directly to the seller, would seem the safest approach for a buyer wishing to retain the right to rely on any non-conformity of goods. The consequence of a failure to give such notice will normally be a complete loss of remedy under the CISG. The exceptions to this rule lie in Articles 40 and 44.

Article 40 provides that the seller cannot rely on the buyer's duty to give notice of non-conformity where the seller was aware, or could not have been unaware of the non-conformity in question.[75] This awareness on the seller's part is not always easily established, as the burden of proof is carried by the buyer.[76] Moreover, legal scholars do not agree as to the extent of the

---

[73] Art. 27 provides: "Unless otherwise expressly provided in this Part of the Convention, if any notice, request or other communication is given or made by a party in accordance with this Part and by means appropriate in the circumstances, a delay or error in the transmission of the communication or its failure to arrive does not deprive that party of the right to rely on the communication."

[74] *See* PETER SCHLECHTRIEM, INTERNATIONALES UN-KAUFRECHT 89 (1996).

[75] Art. 40 provides: "The seller is not entitled to rely on the provisions of Arts. 38 and 39 if the lack of conformity relates to facts of which he knew or could not have been unaware and which he did not disclose to the buyer."

[76] *See* Ingeborg Schwenzer, *Art. 40, in* KOMMENTAR ZUM EINHEITLICHEN UN-KAUFRECHT 370 (Ernst V. Caemmerer & Peter Schlechtriem eds., 1995). "Kenntnis oder nicht in Unkenntnis sein können des Verkäufers hat der Käufer zu beweisen." [The seller's aware-

phrase "could not have been unaware." Some believe it goes beyond gross negligence and must be something very obvious,[77] whereas others believe the phrase to encompass simple negligence and the failure to comply with the precautions and care that may be expected.[78] Reported practice on Article 40 is very scarce, and the outcome is rarely an assumption of the seller's knowledge where this cannot be certain.[79]

According to Article 44, specific remedies may be retained by the seller if a "reasonable excuse" for the failure to give notice within reasonable time can be proven.[80] Again, the term "reasonable" is used to imply flexibility. However, a reasonable excuse will more often than not be rather difficult to establish (especially where the buyer knew of the non-conformity [81] — unless he reasonably misjudged the significance of the non-conformity in

---

ness or inability to be unaware is for the buyer to prove]. The text has now been translated into English. *See* Ingeborg Schwenzer, *Art. 40, in* COMMENTARY ON THE UN CONVENTION ON THE INTERNATIONAL SALE OF GOODS 394 (Peter Schlechtriem ed. 1998).

[77] *See* Schwenzer, *supra* note 76, at 368-69. "Nicht in Unkentniss sein können ist mehr als grobe Fahrlässigkeit. Es muß sich vielmehr um ins Auge springende Vertragswidrigkeiten handeln." [Not being unaware requires more than gross negligence. It is rather a question of obvious undertakings which leap out at the eye]. According to Ulrich Huber, it is defined as "a little bit less than cunning and a little bit more than gross negligence." ENDERLEIN & MASKOW, *supra* note 42, at 164.

[78] *See* ENDERLEIN & MASKOW, *supra* note 42, at 164. "The wording of the CISG itself would, in our view, include simple negligence, which could also be described as a violation of customary care in trade." *Id.*

[79] *See* ICC (5713), 1989 (UNILEX) wherein the arbitrators stated that it clearly transpired from the files and materials of the case that the seller could not have been unaware of the non-conformity. In the famous judgment regarding maggots in mozzarella, Arrondissementrechtbank Roermond, 19 December 1991 (900366) (Netherlands) (UNILEX) the Court allowed the buyer time to prove that the maggots were in the cheese at the time of shipment, and added in an obiter dictum that if they succeeded the seller's knowledge would be presumed. Other judgments have been more restrictive in their findings for the buyer; Art. 40 was applied in LG Landshut, 5 April 1995 (54 O 644/94) (Germany) (UNILEX) since the seller had admitted knowledge of the non-conformity, and in LG Trier, 12 October 1995 (7 HO 78/95) (Germany) (UNILEX), since the addition of water in wine was clearly fraudulent and could not happen without the seller's knowledge.

[80] Art. 44 provides: "Notwithstanding the provisions of ¶ 1 of art. 39 and ¶ 1 of art. 43, the buyer may reduce the price in accordance with art. 50 or claim damages, except for loss of profit, if he has a reasonable excusefor his failure to give the required notice."

[81] *See* HONNOLD, *supra* note 9, at 261. "It seems difficult to justify a buyer's failure to give notice within a "reasonable time" after he knew of the non-conformity." *Id.*

question[82]). Practice on Article 44 has not yet found for a buyer claiming to have an excuse.[83] It would seem that German legal scholars and Courts agree that it is unlikely that fast-paced businesses can successfully present a reasonable excuse[84] — this would seem to exclude a substantial section of the modern business community.[85]

5. The Two Time-Frames of Article 39

With such a severe and drastic consequence as loss of remedy looming on the horizon, and a reasonable excuse so hard to come by, a buyer must understand which time-frame for notification lies before him if he wishes to rely on a non-conformity. The only time-frames to be considered are the absolute two-year time-frame for hidden defects in Article 39(2) and the more ambiguous one of "within reasonable time" in Article 39(1).

The absolute time-frame of two years poses no significant problems of interpretation.[86] Beyond two years after delivery of the goods, a buyer can-

---

[82] *Id.* "However, a buyer who notices a defect in the goods might reasonably consider the defect to be unimportant and only later discover the significance of the defect . . . ." *Id.*

[83] The burden of evidence for proving a reasonable excuse lies on the buyer, and a reasonable excuse is often rejected for lack of evidence. *See, e.g.*, ICC Court of Arbitration (7331), 1994 (UNILEX) and OLG Saarbrücken, 13 January 1993 (Germany) (UNILEX).

[84] *See* OLG München, 8 February 1995 (7 U 3758/94) (Germany) (UNILEX) where the Court agrees with Rolf Herber's conclusion in *Sphere of Application, in* COMMENTARY ON THE UN CONVENTION ON THE INTERNATIONAL SALE OF GOODS 13 (Peter Schlechtriem ed., 1998) (that when taking all things into account, a fast-paced business requires quick decisions and prompt actions and is thus unlikely to have an excuse, as opposed to single traders, artisans or free professionals).

[85] Such a differentiation between businesses would seem characteristic of the "inflexible flexibility" arising from the application of the term "reasonable" to uniform law. Although the considerations leading to the original conclusion of differentiation are fair in certain cases, formulating such a criterion for the presentation of a reasonable excuse (in the absence of criteria laid down in the Convention) may not, in fact, be reasonable when applied to all cases. If courts of another country were to feel bound by this aspiring criterion the same consideration might not rightly apply — but on the other hand, if this criterion solely applies to German law the "reasonable excuse" in art. 44 will be rendered non-uniform in practice. In the latter scenario, the unfortunate phenomenon of forum shopping would most certainly become attractive to buyers wishing to present a reasonable excuse, who would then be well advised to avoid a German forum. It is a delicate balance to maintain. The present paper will not, however, delve more deeply into the problems of art. 44.

[86] Interestingly, it has been applied in German domestic law as a "yardstick" for measur-

not rely on a hidden defect unless it is encompassed by a specific guarantee made by the seller. This applies even if the buyer can produce a satisfactory "reasonable excuse" in accordance with Article 44 of the Convention. Although greatly disputed during the drafting, the two-year period was adopted in order to prevent claims based on doubtful validity and evidence that would be hard to establish.[87] The period begins the moment the goods are handed over to the buyer, and is a straightforward term of exclusion that, absent agreement by the parties, cannot be tolled.[88] Although perhaps more controversial than Article 39(1),[89] Article 39(2) leaves little room for confusion or doubt regarding the time-frame.[90]

However, difficulties still abound with respect to the Article 39(1) time-frame of "reasonable time," which applies in the more common cases of more easily discovered non-conformities. The buyer cannot predict which time-frame he faces before his right to rely on the non-conformity expires. What is reasonable time? Must it be reasonable from the buyer's point of view or from the seller's? And how should the time-frame be determined?

Although a fixed time-frame for such a notice presents a clearer standard for both buyer and seller, this option was not chosen. The drafters' use of the term "reasonable time" would seem to represent a compromise between the certainty of contracts and the fairness of a case-by-case analysis. Even though the Convention is based on uniformity and predictability in

---

ing periods of guarantee; in a judgment from the German supreme Court from 1990, quoted in Schlechtriem, *supra* note 26, at 3, the court stated that a buyer's standard conditions could not extend the seller's warranties to exceed 2 years, with reference to art. 39(2).

87 *See* Sono, *supra* note 60, at 307.

88 *See* Enderlein & Maskow, *supra* note 42, at 161. "This is not a limitation period, but rather a period of exclusion. It may neither be checked nor interrupted, e.g., through repair." *Id.*

89 *See* Joseph Lookofsky, Consequential Damages in Comparative Context 261 n.36 (1989) "The more controversial of these provisions is Art. 39(2), with its absolute 2-year cutoff." *Id.*

90 Although the forseeability of the time-limit in Art. 39(2) is not a problem, this relatively short period of exclusion clashes with two other limitation periods: on one hand it may clash with shorter domestic limitation periods in, for example, German, Swiss and Austrian Law as well as longer periods which may apply under the U.S. UCC in the case of latent defects, and on the other hand it also causes problems in relation to the 4-year prescription period in the Convention on the Limitation Period in the International Sale of Goods (Art. 8 and Art. 10(2)). For more information see Sono, *supra* note 60, at 306 and Enderlein & Maskow, *supra* note 42, at 61.

international trade, its success also hinged on its acceptance by the representatives of the Working Group. The development of a fixed time-frame would have been a utopian undertaking, despite its obvious advantages of certainty, as illustrated by the history of the provision.[91]

B. A Brief History of Article 39(1)

Although Article 39(1) of the CISG is largely a restatement of the first line of Article 39(1) of the ULIS,[92] there has been a slight change in wording in that Article 39(1) of the ULIS required notification of non-conformity to be given "promptly" while Article 39(1) "within reasonable time." Several scholars [93] and practitioners [94] have taken this change in wording to indicate that the term "promptly" was thought too strict and that the drafters sought to make the time-frame in the new provision of the CISG more favorable to the buyer. In fact, Article 11 of the ULIS defined "promptly" as being within a short period "from the moment when the act could reasonably be performed,"[95] and therefore the change in wording of Article 39(1) would not seem overly significant.[96] It was amended because "promptly" was thought

[91] For an overview of the UN Documents on the drafting of this provision, *see infra,* Appendix B.

[92] Art. 39(1) of the ULIS provides: "The buyer shall lose the right to rely on a lack of conformity of the goods if he has not given the seller notice thereof promptly after he discovered the lack of conformity or ought to have discovered it."

[93] *See* Ferrari, *supra* note 38, at 108. "The time requirement of the ULIS was shorter." *Id.* See also Claude Witz, *Les Premières Applications Jurisprudentielles du Droit Uniforme de la Vente Internationale, in* UNDERSTANDING THE CISG IN SCANDINAVIA 24, n.82 (Joseph Lookofsky ed., 1996), who criticizes the German judges for their failure to recognize the difference between the two provisions.

[94] *See* LG Heidelberg, 2 October 1996 (O 37/96 KfH II) (Germany) (UNILEX), (wherein the Court stated — perhaps as a consequence of Witz's criticisms the year before — that art. 39 of the CISG is more buyer friendly than art. 39 of the ULIS as it does not require prompt notification). This judgment was subsequently reversed in OLG Karlsruhe, 25 June 1997 (1 U 280/96) (Germany) (UNILEX), but the statement regarding the ULIS was not commented on by the higher court.

[95] Art. 11 of the ULIS provides: "Where under the present Law an act is required to be performed "promptly," it shall be performed within as short a period as possible, in the circumstances, from the moment when the act could reasonably be performed."

[96] Profs. Enderlein and Maskow also conclude that the two timeframes are alike. *See* EN-

to be too rigid. Apparently the Working Group concluded that the expression "within a reasonable time" was sufficiently flexible to adapt to the varying circumstances in which inspection might be required."[97] The wording of the CISG therefore implies a greater degree of flexibility, but the initial time-frames set out in the two provisions would seem more similar than indicated by some commentators. Moreover, this accentuated flexibility might also conceivably be in the seller's favor in certain cases where the reasonability of a notice requires it to be provided more quickly than within a short time after it could reasonably have been given. The primary difference between the two Article 39 time-frames does not lie in the change of wording, but in the change of context. The nature of the CISG has enabled interpretations of Article 39(1) that represent generous international compromises.[98]

Despite the fact that Article 39 as a whole was a restatement of an existing provision, it was one of the most difficult provisions to agree upon. The controversy focused on the two-year cut-off period in what was to become Article 39(2), while very little attention was paid to the phrase "reasonable time." It was proposed both by the second session of the Working Group[99] and by the suggestion of Pakistan[100] when commenting on the Draft Convention, [101] that

---

DERLEIN & MASKOW, *supra* note 42, at 159 ("The reasonable time is in any case . . . like art. 39, ¶ 1 ULIS . . . ."), as does Ole Lando. *See* OLE LANDO, UDENRIGSHANDELENS KONTRAKTER 351 (1991) ("Hvor det drejer sig om eklamationsfristen ved mangler, er forskellen mellem CISG og ukbl næppe store") (where the notification time-frame for non-conforming goods is concerned, the difference between CISG and ULIS is not great).

[97] *See* Working Group on the International Sale of Goods; Report on the Work of the Second Session, 7-18 December 1970, II Y.B. UNCITRAL 1971, 50, U.N. Doc. A/CN.9/52, ¶ 91 (United Nations, New York 1972).

[98] *See generally* section III *infra.*

[99] *See id.* at ¶ 94. *See also Analysis of Comments and Proposals Relating to Articles 1-17 of the Uniform Law on International Sale of Goods* (ULIS) 1964: note by the Secretary-General, II Y.B UNCITRAL 1971 37, 47, U. N. Doc. A/CN.9/WG.2/WP.6, ¶ 72 (United Nations, New York 1972) in connection with the re-drafting of Art. 11 (which was later stricken from the Convention).

[100] *See Comments by Governments and International Organizations on the Draft Convention on the International Sale of Goods,* VII Y.B. UNCITRAL 1971, 109, 126, U.N. Doc. A/CN.9/125 (United Nations, New York 1978).

[101] *See Draft Convention on the International Sale of Goods,* VII UNCITRAL 1976, 89, 91, U.N. Doc. A/CN.9/116, Annex I (United Nations, New York 1977), (before the formation of contracts on international sale was incorporated into the Convention).

this term should be defined in the Convention. But, unfortunately, it was not, although a guideline for its determination is sorely needed.[102]

As mentioned above, the existing Article 39(1) is closely related to Article 38, which provides that a buyer must examine the goods delivered to him. During the drafting of the Convention, some representatives feared that the consequences of Articles 38 and 39 taken together would be too strict for the buyers within their country. They felt that, since examination and notification would not always be possible, the need for flexibility was critical. A firm or fixed notification time-frame could not be introduced in the compromise that the drafting of the CISG presented.

However, when considering the Convention as it is today, this reasoning would seem insufficient to bar the application of a fixed notification time-frame that would afford the buyer a larger degree of predictability and certainty as to his obligations. The specific situation of not being able to examine the goods properly would seem encompassed by the wording of Article 38 ("within as short a period as is practicable in the circumstances"), which the "ought to have had discovered" wording in Article 39(1) is dependant upon. At the very least, such a situation would be encompassed by the "reasonable excuse" wording of Article 44 that would allow such an unfortunate buyer to retain specific remedies. The application of a firmer or fixed time-frame would have been preferable and would not have caused developing countries the difficulties that they seemed to fear. It is interesting to note, however, that the flexible "reasonable time" time-frame was introduced before the exception of the present Article 44 and before the wording of Article 38 of the ULIS was changed from "promptly" to form the current Article 38.

Nevertheless, the fact remains that Article 39(1) of the CISG requires a buyer to specify non-conformity to the seller — not within an explicit fixed time-frame but "within reasonable time" after discovering a non-conformity or after he ought to have discovered it. This determination of "reasonable time" in Article 39(1)[103] is not at all straightforward, as the following theories from prominent scholars will evidence.

---

[102] If "reasonable time" had been defined in the Convention, an individual determination for each of the provisions applying the term would have been necessary, as they each pertain to different scenarios and cannot be determined equally. A general determination of "reasonable time" would have been too general and vague to be of much actual use in the practitioner's assessment of the individual timeframe — the guideline that is needed is a specific one.

[103] *See UNCITRAL Outline of the CISG [The UNCITRAL Thesaurus]*, U.N. Doc. A/CN.9/SER.C/GUIDE/1 English, September 12, 1995, (which classifies this issue as 39A2).

C. Scholarly Determinations of "Reasonable Time" in Article 39(1)

The Secretariat Commentary sheds no light on the definition of "reasonable time" in its commentary to Article 37 (the former draft of Article 39, the wording of which was kept). It elaborates on the consequences of failure to give notice, the relationship between Articles 36 and 37 (former drafts of the existing Articles 38 and 39), and the purpose of the two-year cut-off period and its relationship to periods of guarantee. There are no factors or guidelines for the determination of reasonable time to be found here or in the Convention,[104] and there were no such guidelines stated elsewhere during the drafting of the CISG, despite the urging of representatives that this term be determined.[105]

While there is nothing to be found to shed light on the concept of "reasonable time" in Article 39(1) of the Convention itself or in its *travaux préparatoires*, the term has been examined by numerous legal commentators and theoreticians analyzing the CISG as a whole or in part. Different scholars have suggested various definitions as to what the phrase may mean.

One leading scholar, Prof. Honnold, states that the assessment of "reasonable time" is one that must take into account a wide range of factors.[106] At a glance, this would seem a straightforward interpretation in keeping with the general legal definition of the term "reasonable" and in compliance with the drafters' use of this flexible term. It would also seem an objective solution to the question of whether the time-frame should be reasonable from the seller's or the buyer's point of view. While the purpose of the provision would seem to imply that the time-frame should be reasonable for the seller whose interests it protects, the fact that it represents a flexible compromise in the interests of the buyer would outweigh this consideration. By taking "a wide range of factors" into account, and thus the reasonableness of the time-frame from both the seller's and the buyer's point of view, a more

[104] Although it may well be argued that a right to reasonably interpret "reasonable time" pursuant to art. 8(2) would enable the application of criteria in art. 8(3), these do not help in the definition of a time-frame.
[105] *See supra* text accompanying notes 99 and 100.
[106] *See* HONNOLD, *supra* note 9, at 281. "The determination of the "reasonable period" for notice following the time when the buyer discovers (or ought to have discovered) the non-conformity would be influenced by a wide range of factors." *Id.*

subjective and fair solution can be reached in each individual case. But when applying this interpretation to a particular case, the practitioner should be aware that a wide range of factors does not mean all factors.

Not all factors are suitable for influencing the time-frame in question. The influence of factual elements must be considered legal misapprehensions in international trade rather than factors concerning reasonableness. For instance, what if these factors include purely domestic aspects? Keeping in mind the importance of trade usage in the CISG regime, it would be interesting to consider whether, for example, a domestic trade usage for longer notices[107] would grant the buyer more time to react to the non-conformity of the seller's goods than a buyer facing exactly the same circumstances without the domestic aspect.

Applying such a unique and subjective factor would seem to violate the uniformity of the CISG, and contradict the intention of the drafters. However, it might be unreasonable not to take into account those domestic factors that may have influenced the buyer, and of which the seller may well be aware. Moreover the importance of trade usage in commercial law is not to be underestimated. In such a situation, it would seem that the practitioner is faced with a choice between non-uniform, subjective fairness and objective uniformity where the term "reasonable time" has become too flexible and encompasses too much.

The application and interpretation of the provision itself — and not the reasonableness of the cases — is required to be uniform under the CISG. Consequently, it must be concluded that the uniformity must take precedence over the flexibility of the term "reasonableness" where undue domestic factors endanger the uniformity of the application of the Convention. Absent bad faith or reasonable assumptions by a party that domestic trade usage would influence the agreement, such considerations on the part of the buyer/seller should be considered legal misapprehensions in

[107] Art. 9(2) of the CISG provides only that international trade usages are impliedly made applicable to agreements between parties, and art. 9(1) solely binds the parties to trade usages they have agreed or previously established between themselves. In an Austrian judgment from OLG, November 9, 1995 (6 R 194/95) (Austria) (UNILEX), the Court found that a seller doing long-standing business in a particular trade in a particular country is bound by national trade usage. This conclusion should, however, be regarded as subject to a variety of conditions and not a sanctioning of the inclusion of national trade usage to art. 9.

the context of international trade. Not all purely domestic subjective factors can be considered.

As the example above illustrates, the term "reasonable time" can become too imprecise and subjective, and a firmer guideline for the determination of the time-frame is required. If the term were applied from the vantage point of a fixed period, which would then be influenced by predetermined or other reasonable factors, more uniform results would ensue and there would be greater predictability for both the buyer and seller in the determination of when a notice of non-conformity is due.

Other scholars have suggested such fixed guidelines for the determination of reasonable time. The Swiss scholar Schwenzer points out in Prof. Schlechtriem's Commentary that many German scholars consider reasonable time to be a period of about eight days where no special circumstances apply.[108] However, she goes on to state that other domestic legal systems have notice-requirements similar to Article 39(1) with time-frames that can be permitted to be much longer (as in France and the United States) and that should be considered. An appropriate compromise would seem to be a term of approximately one month to avoid discrepancies in international practice.[109] This compromise, which Schwenzer deems a "*Großzügiger Monat,*" [hereinafter referred to as the "noble month,"] is one that duly considers the need for uniformity while still retaining the flexibility of the time-frame as intended by the drafters by allowing individual factors to influence the point of reference. In accordance with Article 7(2), a compromise of legal systems is in keeping with the general principle of the Convention of equal treatment within the context of different legal backgrounds, [110] and would be thoroughly recommendable as an international guideline applied by all practitioners.

The problem with such a fixed guideline is, of course, establishing a "typical situation" that represents the norm. It would be impossible to

---

[108] *See* Schwenzer, *supra* note 76, at 362. "Deutsche Autoren wollen tendenziell einen Zeitraum von ca. acht Tagen zugrunde legen," *id.*, with references to Herber/Czerwenka, Piltz, Asam, and Reinhart in note 58.

[109] *See id.* "Will man allzu großen Auslegungsdivergenzen vorbeugen, erscheint eine Annäherung der Standpunkte unabdingbar. Als grobem Mittelwert sollte man deshalb wenigstens von ca. einem Monat ausgehen." *Id.*

[110] *See* KRITZER, *supra* note 27, at 79-84 and his reference to Kastely for the original source of this general principle.

imagine a situation where there were no factors that influenced the time frame, which could represent the situation against which all others could be measured. Nonetheless, such a perfectly typical situation does not necessarily have to be outlined for a guideline to apply equally to all notices subject to the standards of reasonableness.

Regarding factors that influence the timeliness, Schwenzer also points out that an individual analysis must be carried out for each specific case, and she names certain factors that may influence the notice period—namely the nature of the goods (whether the goods are perishable or seasonal) and the remedy the buyer chooses.[111] For instance, if the buyer is rejecting the goods, a more prompt communication may be required than if the buyer decides to keep them subject to damages.

Although not explicitly mentioned by Schwenzer, the application of the factors of perishability and seasonality would logically differ according to the remedy chosen. The perishable nature of the goods would seem relevant regardless of remedy, as the seller will need a swift notice to verify a defect before the goods "rot away," even if the buyer keeps them. However, if the buyer claims damages and keeps the goods, their possible seasonality would appear to be his problem. Provided that the tardiness of notice is not reflected in his claim against the seller, this need not influence the timeliness of the notice.

The latter factor of considering the remedy chosen was introduced by Prof. Sono, who explains that this might influence the notice because the seller should then be given an opportunity to protect his goods and his own interests.[112] Interestingly, proposals were made during the drafting of the Convention for this factor to be included by exempting price reductions from the loss of remedy ensuing from a failure to give notice,[113] but this

---

[111] *See* Schwenzer, *supra* note 76, at 274 (in English translation by Schlechtriem).

[112] *See* Sono, *Art. 39*, *in* COMMENTARY ON THE INTERNATIONAL SALES LAW- THE 1980 VIENNA SALES CONVENTION 309 (C. M. Bianca and M. J. Bonell, eds., 1987). "In such cases (rejection of the goods), a prompt communication may also be important to give the seller an opportunity to care for or redispose of the rejected goods and thus reduce the chance for loss or damage to the goods or the incurring of unnecessary expense." *Id.*

[113] This proposal was first made by the United States. *See Analysis of Comments and Proposal relating to Article 18-55 of the Uniform Law on the International Sale of Goods (ULIS): note by the Secretary-General,* UN Doc. A/CN.9/WG.2/WP.10, ¶ 49. The Austrian representative objected to this suggestion, however, and it was not drafted. A similar proposal was re-stated by the Czechoslovakian representative in UN Doc. A/CN.9/125. Interestingly, in the current re-drafting of the U.S. Uniform Commercial Code,

proposal was not drafted. Prof. Ferrari agrees with this factor of choice of remedy, and adds that the "perishability of the goods" and the terms of the contracts are also valid considerations.[114]

By mentioning "the need for impartial sampling or testing, and the possibility of cure by the seller" along with the perishable nature of the goods as considerations indicating the need for speed, Prof. Honnold would seem to focus on the mitigation principle (expressed in Article 77 for parties relying on breach) and the seller's interests of "damage control," but does not pronounce on the factor of choice of remedy.[115] However, Profs. Enderlein and Maskow, while stating that "[t]he reasonable time is . . . a short period," disagree with the factor of choice of remedy as an influence on timeliness, and state that the notice time-frame remains the same even if the buyer is relying on the non-conformity for damages.[116] The true importance of this factor can only be found in caselaw.

Many of these determinations of reasonable time glean their identity from the international practice of courts and tribunals when determining "reasonable time," and it is certainly here that the key is to be found. It is the actual application of the provision that ultimately defines it. Consequently, in the following section, judicial practice of Article 39(1) in several contracting states will be presented. This should enable a definition of criteria for the determination of the term, and a comparative analysis of the practices of different countries in the assessment of the uniformity of the provision.

---

such an amendment to restrict the consequences of failure to give notice has been introduced. See *infra* text accompanying notes 327 and 328.

[114] *See* Ferrari, *supra* note 38, at 109-10, with reference to Magnus, Schwenzer, Rohwer & Coe and Schlechtriem in notes 766 and 770. The terms of the contract will always supersede the CISG, by way of Art. 6, except in cases of invalid contract terms. The CISG does not concern the question of contract validity unless otherwise expressly provided, and this issue is to be settled by art. 7(2) gap-filling, i.e., otherwise applicable law and general principles of the Convention. Some examples of international principles for contract validity are found in the International Institute for the Unification of Private Law, Principles of International Commercial Contracts (Rome, 1994) [hereinafter UNIDROIT Principles]. See, for example, art. 2.20 on surprising contract terms.

[115] *See* Honnold, *supra* note 9, at 281.

[116] *See* ENDERLEIN & MASKOW, *supra* note 42, at 160. "The wording of this paragraph, however, requires the giving of notice within reasonable time also in this case. Furthermore, this view (Prof. Sono's choice of remedy criteria) underestimates the difficulties to prove a non-conformity which grows with time." *Id.*

III. Transnational Article 39(1) Practice

In the following, reported international Article 39(1) practice will be detailed[117] and analyzed. Due to the vastness of German caselaw, the judgments from this country will be analyzed separately, followed by caselaw from other countries and, finally, from international arbitral tribunals.

A. *Germany*

1. A Brief Introduction

a. The German Legal System and the CISG

Germany is divided into different legal districts, each of which has its own District Court (Landgericht) and Higher District Court (Oberlandesgericht). These districts are divided into smaller sub-sections that each have their own Petty Court (Amtsgericht). A case may be tried in either the Petty or District Court at the first instance, depending on the matter of the case, and appealed to the instance directly above. A case commencing in a District Court may be appealed twice to the level of the Supreme Court (Bundesgerichtshof), in disputes concerning matters of fundamental importance or case-matter over DM 60,000. The Supreme Court is situated in Karlsruhe and determines the last word in German legal issues. The decisions of all instances form precedents for the others to a certain extent, but naturally the hierarchy of the Court determines the value of the precedent of its judgments.

In German domestic law, commercial parties are subject to the Handelsgesetzbuch (HGB — Commercial Code) and the commercial buyer is required to notify the commercial seller of any non-conformity according to HGB Section 377 (regarding non-conformity) or HGB Section 378 (regarding goods that are *aliud* or delivered in wrong quantity). These provisions call for an "unhesitant" notice from the time of delivery (in case of obvious non-conformities) or from the time of discovery (in the case of

---

[117] For a brief overview of the case law mentioned in this section, *see infra,* Appendix A.

hidden defects). The term "unhesitant" should, according to Section 121 of the Bürgerliches Gesetzbuch (BGB — Civil Code) be defined as "with no blameworthy hesitation."[118] The wording of this time-frame is very similar to that of "reasonable time" set out in Article 39(1) of the CISG, the consequence of non-reliance if no timely notice is given is the same,[119] and there is no form-requirement of the notice.[120] In practice, this domestic time-frame is a flexible one that must be reasonable; however, this is usually stressed as reasonably brief, and notice periods of over two weeks will rarely be tolerated. The CISG was adopted by Germany in 1990, with an indirect reservation taken against its application.[121] German courts as a whole have had ample opportunity to decide cases involving the CISG, and there is certainly no lack of practice regarding Article 39.

b. Article 39(1) of the CISG in German Practice

The international practice of Article 39(1) is quite abundant when compared to the practice of other articles of the CISG. A majority of the published cases concerning this provision stem from the Courts of one country — namely Germany.[122] A direct reason for this may be difficult to find. However, some of the factors influencing this wealth of practice might include the nature of the codified German civil-law legal system, the fact that Germany has been accustomed to uniform international trade law

---

[118] *See* EUGEN KLUNZINGER, GRUNDZÜGE DES HANDELSRECHTS 249 (1994). "Untersuchung und Rüge müssen 'unverzüglich' erfolgen. Hierzu bestimmt die bekannte Definition in § 121 BGB: unverzüuglich bedeutet 'ohne schuldhaftiges Zögern.' Zeigen sich (verdeckte) Mängel erst später, so muß die Anzeige unverzüglich nach der Entdeckung gemacht werden." *Id.*

[119] The goods will be considered accepted by the buyer if correct notice is not given. *See* § 377 Abs. 3 HGB (regarding non-conforming goods).

[120] *See* GÜNTER POTTSCHMIDT & ULRICH ROHR, PRIVATRECHT FÜR DEN KAUFMANN 247 (1994). "Die Mängelanzeige ist nicht formbedürftig. Sie muß deshalb nicht schriftlich, sondern kann auch mündlich, telefonisch oder per Fernschreiben erklärt werden." *Id.*

[121] The Convention was signed by the former German Democratic Republic on August 13, 1981, ratified on February 23, 1989, and entered into force on March 1, 1990. Upon ratifying the Convention, Germany declared that it would not apply Art. 1(1)(b) in respect of any State that had made a declaration that that State would not apply art. 1(1)(b). *See* <http://www.cisg.law.pace.edu/cisg/countries/cntries-Germany.html> (Pace).

[122] For instance, of the 92 cases regarding art. 39 examined for the present paper, 71 are from German Courts, *see infra,* Appendix A.

through its application of the ULIS and the ULF,[123] and the extensive trading with Italy which takes place in Germany.

As mentioned above, the trade section of German law contains a provision which is similar to that of Article 39 of the CISG, namely HGB Section 377, which provides that notice of non-conformity be given within a flexible period of time. In contrast to this, Article 1495(1) of the Italian Civil Code provides a duty to notify of non-conformity within 8 days. This difference in domestic laws could make an Italian seller more accustomed to having the right to be properly notified of any non-conformity within a fixed narrow time-frame, whereas the German buyer according to his domestic law has a more flexible time-frame. Even where the parties are aware that their agreement is subjected to the CISG, this will often result in a discrepancy between the parties' expectations as to what "reasonable time" means in relation to the notice requirement, and they will take their differences to Court. Since the rules of International Private Law appoint the country of the defendant (according to the *actor sequitur forum rei* principle),[124] the German Courts are given ample opportunity to judge cases where the seller sues the buyer for the purchase price.[125] Indeed, a majority

---

[123] *See generally*, PETER SCHLECHTRIEM, VIENNA SALES CONVENTION 1980 — DEVELOPED COUNTRIES PERSPECTIVES (1994). In this book he introduces this theory as to the wealth of German practice. *Id.* He states that it took some years for the German Courts to become accustomed to ULF and ULIS, and that their experience may have made them more amenable to the CISG. *Id.* at 103. Previous ULF and ULIS practice was also largely focused on timely notice (one-fifth of it concerned such issues, *see supra* note 32, although not quite as predominantly as the CISG practice is focused on art. 39. *See id.*

[124] Codified in art. 2 of the Convention of September 27, 1968 on Jurisdiction and the Enforcement of Judgments in Civil and Commercial Matters (to which both Italy and Germany adhere). *See* Convention on Jurisdiction and the Enforcement of Judgments in Civil and Commercial Matters, Sept. 27, 1968, 1972 O.J. (L 299) 32, 8 I.L.M. 229 [hereinafter Brussels Convention]. However, this jurisdiction is not necessarily exclusive. Jurisdiction is also deemed to be present, according to art. 5(1), in the state where the domestic law applies to conflict of laws to be "the place of performance of the obligation in question . . . ." *Industrie Tessili Italiana Como v. Dunlop AG*, European Court of Justice Case 12/76 (1979) ECR 1473, (1977) 1 CMLR 26(B). In CISG cases of the seller suing the buyer for the purchase price, the obligation in question would be the payment of price, and the place determined by the contract, trade usage or art. 57(1)(a) of the CISG which primarily appoints the seller's place of business. So the seller might have the option to elect to bring a buyer to his own venue.

[125] German Courts will also have jurisdiction according to art. 5(1) of the Brussels Convention. *See* Brussels Convention, *supra* note 124, at art. 5(1).

of the German cases on Article 39 of the CISG stem from contracts between a German buyer and an Italian seller.[126]

In any event, the many German judgments concerning Article 39(1) make it possible to examine virtually all aspects of the application of the provision, and consequently a great part of the present paper will necessarily focus on the practice of the German courts. Although not all judgments or aspects of this practice will presently aid a transnational comparative study of Article 39(1) practice, since caselaw from other countries is less abundant, the following will attempt to outline a complete picture of the application of the provision in German law by analyzing all aspects of its interpretation. Thus, even though the present paper mainly focuses on the determination of when a notice is considered delivered "within reasonable time," an analysis of German practice of Article 39(1) will be incomplete without first determining what constitutes a notice with regard to specificity and form. The aspects of these requirements also influences the determination of reasonable time in some cases. Consequently, this section will first examine the content and form of the notices, and then examine the time-frames within which they are given, in an attempt to conclude what the German Courts determine to be "notice" and "within reasonable time."

2. Specificity and Form of the Notice of Non-Conformity

a. Specifying the Nature of the Non-Conformity

As mentioned above, notice must not only be delivered within reasonable time to the seller, but must also specify the nature of the lack of conformity in order to be in accordance with Article 39(1).[127] The requirement for the notice to be specific is highly significant as it influences whether notice is given.

This is illustrated by a 1995 judgment from the District Court of München concerning frozen bacon, where the Court found that a telex claiming "the goods are rancid" sent on the day of discovery of non-conformity did not meet the requirement of Article 39, and that the subse-

---

[126] Approximately half of the judgments from German Courts examined for this paper, concerned contracts with a German buyer and an Italian seller (32 of 68, *see infra,* Appendix A).

[127] *See supra,* Section I.

quent notice that specified it was not given within reasonable time.[128] The Court found that the buyer should not have hesitated to specify the non-conformity more carefully in the first notice. Another judgment from the same Court[129] pronounced that asking for assistance in identifying a problem with a computer program did not constitute proper notice of non-conformity.[130] An earlier judgment on fashion goods held that a reference to poor workmanship and improper fitting was an inadequate specification of the nature of the lack of conformity. [131]

Similarly, the Higher District Court of Koblenz recently found that the buyer's notice was not specific enough. [132] The buyer had communicated that five rolls of acrylic blankets were missing, but did not specify how he wished the seller to cure this defect, in the spirit of Article 39.[133] The Court found that although timely notice was given in regard to time-frame, in principle no notice could be said to have been given within reasonable time. This judgment seems to be a very harsh interpretation of the provision, and is currently pending before the Supreme Court.[134]

In a District Court judgment from Bochum from 1996,[135] the buyer notified the seller that the truffles delivered to him were "soft." This was not found to be a specific notice that the truffles contained worms, despite the

---

[128] LG München, March 20, 1995 (10 HKO 23750/94) (Germany) (UNILEX) <http://cisgw3.law.pace.edu/cases/950320g1.html> (Pace) (regarding the delivery of frozen bacon which proved to be rancid upon veterinary examination). In his comments to this judgment, Dr. Kindler criticizes the Court for not examining the (hypothetical) question of whether the veterinary examination revealing the rancidness could or should have been carried out sooner. *See* Peter Kindler, Praxis des Internationalen Privat- und Verfahrensrechts (IPRAX), VOL.1, 16-17 (1996).

[129] *See* LG München, February 8, 1995 (8 HKO 24667/93) (Germany) (UNILEX) <http://cisgw3.law.pace.edu/cases/950208g4.html> (Pace).

[130] *See id.*

[131] *See* LG München, July 3, 1989 (17 HKO 3726/89) (Germany) (UNILEX) <http://cisgw3.law.pace.edu/cases/890703g1.html> (Pace).

[132] OLG Koblenz, January 31, 1997 (2 U 31/96) (Germany) (UNILEX) <http://cisgw3.law.pace.edu/cases/970131g1.html> (Pace).

[133] The Court stated: "[s]pricht die Beklagte in ihrem u. a. die Fehlmenge rügenden Schreiben vom 8 (December) 1993 lediglich davon, daß fünf Rollen fehlten. Eine solche Angabe versetzt die Klägerin nicht in die Lage, eine Ersatz- oder Nachlieferung in die Wege zu leiten, was die Regelung von Art. 39 CISG u. a. bezweckt." *Id.*

[134] Pending before the Bundesgerichtshof, docket number ZR 64/97.

[135] LG Bochum, January 24, 1996 (Docket number not available) (Germany) (UNILEX) <http://cisgw3.law.pace.edu/cases/960124g1.html> (Pace).

fact that the buyer claimed that most professional truffle-vendors would know that softness implied a probable worm-infestation.[136] The Court stated that, regardless, the buyer should have added that the truffles "had worms due to their softness upon delivery" for the notice to be considered sufficiently specific.[137] The court also added that where notice of lack of conformity is not given personally to the seller, the buyer must ensure that the seller actually receives notice.[138] The fact that the notice must be specifically directed to the seller was also stated in a District Court judgment from Kassel from 1996 regarding the sale of marble.[139] A communication of the notice to a third party associated with the seller but not directly in the seller's employ will not suffice, as pointed out by the court.[140]

Another District Court judgment, this one from Bielefeld from 1991, is an example of how the court permitted the buyer to rely on part of the non-conformity of the delivered bacon, as this was properly specified in the timely (3 days after delivery) notice, whereas another aspect had not been sufficiently clarified and thus could not be relied upon.[141] Finally, the buyer in a 1995 District Court judgment of Marburg[142] had little luck with his notification of lack of conformity to the seller. The goods (an agricultural machine) were delivered to the buyer on June 26, 1992 and redirected to a client on July 22, 1992.[143] The machine immediately proved faulty and the

---

136 *See id.*

137 *See id.*

138 *See id.*

139 LG Kassel, February 15, 1996 (11 O 4185/95) (Germany) (UNILEX) <http://cisgw3.law.pace.edu/cases/960215g1.html> (Pace).

140 *See id.* Regarding the sale of marble the court stated: "Es genügt keineswegs die Mängelanzeige an irgendeine mit der Vertragsabwicklung befaßte Person zu richten." *Id.*

141 LG Bielefeld, January 18, 1991 (15 O 201/90) (Germany) (UNILEX) <http://cisgw3.law.pace.edu/cases/910118g1.html> (Pace), regarding the delivery of bacon which was unclean (properly specified) and not satisfactorily smoked (not properly specified).

142 LG Marburg, December 12, 1995 (2 O 246/95) (Germany) (UNILEX) <http://cisgw3.law.pace.edu/cases/951212g1.html> (Pace).

143 It is surprising that the Court does not seem to consider the fact that the buyer had a duty to examine the goods (according to Art. 38) and thus discover the non-conformity before redirecting the goods. Art. 38(3) should not apply where the buyer takes possession of the goods before they are redirected, and the duty to examine the goods should not have been deferred. *See* OLG Saarbrücken, January 18, 1993 (1 U 69/92) (Germany) (UNILEX) <http://cisgw3.law.pace.edu/cases/951212g1.html> (Pace). *See also supra* note 68.

buyer had to take it back.[144] Notice that the machine did not function properly was delivered on August 14, 1992 and August 31, 1992 with no response from the seller. The Court stated that these notices were not specific enough as neither of them specified the serial number of the machine nor its date of delivery — regardless of the fact that the buyer had only ever bought one such machine from the seller, the seller could not be required to search through sales ledgers to locate the documents for the machine in question.[145] The buyer further claimed to have telephoned specific notice to the seller, but since this could not be proven the Court found that this was not a valid notice.[146] The Court added that since no satisfactory notice had been given until the start of the proceedings (which were initiated by the seller when the buyer tried to set-off his claim for the machine from other obligations) the absolute time-limit in Article 39(2) had lapsed, and the buyer could not rely on the non-conformity of the machine.[147] With the application of Article 39(2), the buyer was excluded from presenting a reasonable excuse for the failure to give notice in accordance with Article 44.

It seems that German Courts are rather strict when interpreting whether the notices given by the buyer comply with the obligation to be specific. The flexibility of the term "reasonable time" has certainly not spilled over into the requirement to specify the nature of the lack of conformity. The prudent buyer must give very specific notice, detailing the lack of conformity on which he wishes to rely, directly to the seller.[148] And, as illustrated by the above judgment from Marburg, the form of the notice also holds a certain significance for the buyer's chance of success in relying on the notice.

b. Form of Notice

The manner in which a notice is communicated is not unimportant in practice, despite the fact that Article 39(1) does not prescribe a specific

[144] *See* LG Marburg, December 12, 1995 (2 O 246/95) (Germany) (UNILEX) <http://cisgw3.law.pace.edu/cases/951212g1.html> (Pace).

[145] *See id.*

[146] *See id.*

[147] *See id.*

[148] For those interested in comparing the judicial interpretations of the specificity requirement with the language of the U.S. Uniform Commercial Code (UCC), which distinguishes between rejection (§§ 2-602 and 2-605) and revocation (§§ 2-606, 2-607 and 2-608) of acceptance and the specificity required. *See* KRITZER, *supra* note 27, at 309-10.

form. Although perhaps an obvious one, the problem of notice-giving over the telephone has been brought before the German Courts several times. This form of notice is, in theory, acceptable, but poses a question of evidence. If the buyer cannot substantiate the call, the Court cannot take it into consideration unless the seller does not dispute it. Most buyers have been unsuccessful, but in a judgment from District Court of Frankfurt am Main from 1992, the Court found that notice was given satisfactorily since a shoe seller did not dispute that the call took place and that the non-conformity was specified.[149] Other judgments have generally been in accordance with the first judgment concerning the issue (which also concerned shoes), where the Court stated that notice by telephone *per se* was in accordance with Article 39, but that the buyer must indicate the date of the call and who took the call.[150] A more firm rule for notice by telephone was formed in a judgment from District Court of Frankfurt am Main from 1994 — concerning the sale of shoes, yet again — wherein the Court found that in order to recognize the notice, it must know *when* the buyer spoke to *whom* about *what*.[151] This rule of the buyer's burden of evidence has been enforced by all German courts so far.[152]

Another problem for the practitioner as to the Article 39(1) notice is the question of the implied notice: Article 39(1) must be logically said to prescribe a duty to actively notify the seller of the non-conformity. This was the conclusion in a 1993 District Court judgment of Aachen, where a German buyer of rare wood refused to pay the Nigerian seller and thought this an implied notice of non-conformity.[153] The court stated that the wording

---

[149] LG Frankfurt am Main, December 9, 1992 (3/3 O 37/92) (Germany) (UNILEX) <http://cisgw3.law.pace.edu/cases/921209g1.html> (Pace).

[150] *See* LG Stuttgart, August 31, 1989 (3 KfH O 97/89) (Germany) (UNILEX) <http://cisgw3.law.pace.edu/cases/890831g1.html> (Pace). This judgment is rather unique as it leaves open the question of whether art. 39(1) of the CISG or HGB § 377 applies, and concludes that neither requirement is fulfilled in the case at hand. *See also infra* note 171.

[151] LG Frankfurt am Main, July 13, 1994 (3/13 O 3/94) (Germany) (UNILEX) <http://cisgw3.law.pace.edu/cases/940713g1.html> (Pace).

[152] *See, e.g.,* OLG Frankfurt am Main, May 23, 1995 (5 U 209/94) (Germany) (UNILEX) <http://cisgw3.law.pace.edu/cases/950523g1.html> (Pace), LG Kassel, June 22, 1995 (8 O 2391/93) <http://cisgw3.law.pace.edu/cases/950622g1.html> (Pace), and Amtsgericht Kehl, October 6, 1995 (3 C 925/93) (Germany) (UNILEX) <http://cisgw3.law.pace.edu/cases/951006g1.html> (Pace).

[153] *See* LG Aachen, July 28, 1993 (42 O 68/93) (Germany) (UNILEX) <http://cisgw3.law.pace.edu/cases/930728g1.html> (Pace).

of the Article requires specific notice to be communicated, and that no notice was given within reasonable time.[154]

However, a more or less implied notice was accepted by the Court in a 1994 Petty Court judgment from Nordhorn, regarding the sale of shoes.[155] The Court found that a returning of the defective goods to the seller constituted a notice complying with Article 39.[156] The judgment was never appealed, but it would be interesting to note how a higher instance would consider such a notice. It can certainly be argued that a return of the goods implies dissatisfaction, but not unequivocally as it could also be a mistake or clerical error. Moreover, such a notice cannot be said to specify the nature of the lack of conformity of the goods as required by Article 39, unless the non-conformity of the goods is overwhelmingly self-evident. Even so, the conclusion of the Court appears surprising, especially when compared to the more formalistic reasoning of the court in the judgment from Marburg, above.[157] Perhaps the Court found the flexibility of the time-frame and the lack of form requirement inductive to considering the implied notice valid. All in all, it would be advisable for a buyer faced with a non-conformity to advise the seller of the specific details hereof by means of a form of communication which is easily documented and substantiated. And the buyer must do this within reasonable time.

3. Within Reasonable Time

The term "within reasonable time" has been translated to "*innerhalb angemesser Frist*" in German. Literally, this can be translated to "within an appropriate deadline." The German language text of the Convention is not an official text,[158] but the translation would seem well chosen because it is similar to the original term linguistically and is not a "label" from the do-

---

[154] *See id.* The judgment was subsequently reversed in OLG Köln, February 22, 1994 (29 U 202/93) (Germany) (UNILEX) <http://cisgw3.law.pace.edu/cases/940222g1.html> (Pace), but this was primarily due to the surfacing of a fax which proved that timely notice had been given. This fax is not mentioned before the first instance.

[155] Amtsgericht Nordhorn, April 20, 1994 (3 C 75/94) (Germany) (UNILEX) <http://cisgw3.law.pace.edu/cases/940614g1.html> (Pace).

[156] *See id.*

[157] LG Marburg, December 12, 1995 (2 O 246/95) (Germany) (UNILEX) <http://cisgw3.law.pace.edu/cases/951212g1.html> (Pace).

[158] The six equally authentic official language texts are: Arabic, Chinese, English, French, Russian and Spanish.

mestic notification regulations. There is a vast amount of German practice pertaining to the determination of "*angemessene Frist*," or "reasonable time." Very few of these judgments concerning Article 39(1) of the CISG find in favor of the buyer when assessing whether timely notice was given within reasonable time.[159] But here the similarities end.

In order to ease the overview of the many diverse judgments and their determinations of what constitutes reasonable time, the succeeding section will first examine the phenomena of agreed notices and the confusion of Articles 38 and 39, followed by an analysis of the applied time-frames. This analysis will be split into two sections: recent judgments from 1995 and after, and older judgments prior to 1995. This should help in determining any patterns, trends, or guidelines.

a. Agreed Time-Frames for Notification — Derogations of "Reasonable Time?"

The time-frames accepted by the German courts in relation to Article 39(1) vary greatly, and it is not always clearly discernible which factors the courts take into consideration when deciding whether the period of time in question was reasonable. There is, however, one criterion that is very clear. If the parties have agreed on a maximum period of notice, the courts have unequivocally stated that if notice is outside this agreed time-frame, it cannot be considered within reasonable time. This is an indisputably correct conclusion, for even where the time-frame specified is not considered by the courts to be an inter partes binding interpretation of "within reasonable time" as prescribed by Article 39(1), they will be free to choose another time-frame entirely in accordance with Article 6 of the CISG,[160] which allows agreed derogation from the CISG.

However, it may be possible to determine which of these agreed time-frames were considered within the "reasonable time" time-frame of Article 39(1) by the Courts, where the reasoning of the Courts is very detailed. The

[159] Of the 71 German judgments concerning art. 39(1) analyzed for the present paper, only eleven found that notice was given satisfactorily within reasonable time. *See infra*, Appendix A. One of these was subsequently reversed by a higher Court.

[160] Art. 6 states: "The parties may exclude the application of this Convention or, subject to article 12, derogate from or vary the effect of any of its provisions." Art. 12 prescribes that parties must agree in writing if declarations under art. 96 have been made — if no such declaration is made any agreement will suffice (where evidenced or not disputed).

distinctions between what the Courts consider derogations from the CISG via Article 6 and what they consider inside the framework of Article 39 in any event and not an actual derogation, may help to illustrate whether the time-frames involved would normally be considered reasonable. This requires highly detailed *ratio decidendi* in judgments, but the very detailed German caselaw sometimes makes it possible to conclude whether the courts would have considered the time-frame involved in accordance with Article 39(1) regardless of the fact that the time-frame agreed is binding between the parties. Consequently, it is interesting to note the agreed time-frames considered by the Courts to comprise a derogation from "reasonable time" and those that do not.

In a recent judgment from Higher District Court of München regarding the sale of clothing,[161] for example, the Court stated that in general the time-frame for notice-giving under Article 39 is a maximum of one month; however, they stated that the parties validly derogated from this by agreeing on a time-frame of two weeks.[162] In a 1991 District Court judgment from Baden-Baden[163] the seller of tiles agreed to the buyer's order in writing, adding that notice of non-conformity must be given within 30 days of delivery in accordance with general business terms. The Court found that this was not a material alteration of the offer, and that since this acceptance was undisputed by the buyer, it was part of the agreement.[164] The Court made no mention of any derogation from Article 39(1), but stated that since this agreed time-frame had elapsed, Article 39(1) prevented the buyer from relying on the non-conformity.[165] This would seem to strongly suggest that the Court did not find a time-frame of 30 days, less the time for examination and discovery, to derogate from the concept of "reasonable time" as understood by Article 39 of the CISG. Similarly, a 1993 judgment from the

[161] OLG München, March 11, 1998 (7 U 4427/97) (Germany) (UNILEX) <http://cisgw3.law.pace.edu/cases/980311g1.html> (Pace).

[162] *See id.*

[163] LG Baden-Baden, August 14, 1991 (4 O 113/90) (Germany) (UNILEX) <http://cisgw3.law.pace.edu/cases/910814g1.html> (Pace).

[164] This is in accordance with art. 19(2) of the CISG, which states: "(2) However, a reply to an offer which purports to be an acceptance but contains additional or different terms which do not materially alter the terms of the offer constitutes an acceptance, unless the offeror, without undue delay, objects orally to the discrepancy or dispatches a notice to that effect. If he does not so object, the terms of the contract are the terms of the offer with the modifications contained in the acceptance." *Id.*

[165] *See id.*

District Court of Hannover, regarding the sale of shoes accepts that the parties have agreed on a time-frame of 10 days, seemingly without considering this an Article 6 derogation.[166] It would seem, that even though the parties set their own (binding) time-frames, the courts considered that these conform with Articles 38 and 39 and were not a derogation from the Convention. However, the fact that the Court does not unequivocally state that there is an Article 6 derogation does not mean that there is none, and the conclusion is a frail one. In another judgment regarding agreed time-frames, this one from the District Court of Gießen from 1994, the court accepted that the parties had made a binding agreement that notice must be given within eight days of delivery.[167] This time, however, the Court specifically stated that it considered the agreement a derogation from the time-frame of "reasonable time" in Article 39, which was in accordance with Article 6, indicating that a period of eight days for examination and notice did not leave a "reasonable time" for giving notice in the sense of Article 39(1).[168]

These judgments may, at a glance, suggest that reasonable time as understood by Article 39 is considered approximately 10-30 days, since these periods do not represent a derogation from that provision. But barring the frailty of the conclusions, this is still not the case as the time-frames described above are from the time of delivery of the goods, and not from the time when the non-conformity is discovered or ought to have been discovered. They thus represent a combination of the two time-frames in Articles 38 and 39, and an isolation of the "reasonable time" period is difficult. This problem is not exclusive to the agreed time-frames, but permeates the entire application of Article 39.

b. The Mix-Up of Articles 38 and 39 in German Law

Articles 38 and 39 are closely intertwined.[169] Article 38 is a trigger which fixes the time for discovery of detectable non-conformities, and Article 39 is the yardstick with which the subsequent notices "within reasonable time" are measured. Ideally, the "trigger" and the "yardstick" should be

[166] LG Hannover, December 1, 1993 (22 O 107/93) (Germany) (UNILEX) <http://cisgw3.law.pace.edu/cases/931201g1.html> (Pace).
[167] LG Gießen, July 5, 1994 (6 0 85/93) (Germany) (UNILEX).
[168] *See id.*
[169] *See supra,* Section II, subsection 1.3.1.

separated in caselaw for the benefit of determining the respective time-frames. However, some German judgments appear to have confused the duty to examine the goods and the duty to notify of the non-conformity, and some have assessed them taken as a whole.[170] A possible explanation for this may be that the German domestic duty to notify of non-conformity in Section 377 of the HGB runs from the time of delivery, a fact which would accustom courts to just one time-frame from delivery until delivered notice. Moreover, it is understandable that a judge facing a notice which is obviously not timely when considering Articles 38 and 39 together will let the sleeping dog lie and mix the criteria for the two time-frames.[171]

The problem is not solely an academic one. For the purposes of the present paper, for example, the conjoined time-frames calculated from the date of delivery make a comparison of Article 39(1) notices rather difficult, since some Courts do not specify this time-frame separately.

---

[170] *See* LG Berlin, September 30, 1992 (99 O 123/92) (Germany) (UNILEX) <http://cisgw3.law.pace.edu/cases/920930g1.html> (Pace), (which takes into consideration that the non-conformity was easily discernible without mentioning art. 38) and LG Berlin, September 16, 1992 (99 O 29/93) (Germany) (UNILEX) <http://cisgw3.law.pace.edu/cases/920916g1.html> (Pace), (which makes no mention of art. 38 at all); *see also,* OLG Saarbrücken, January 13, 1993 (1 U 69/92) (Germany) (UNILEX) <http://cisgw3.law.pace.edu/cases/930113g1.html> (Pace), (which holds together art. 38 and art. 39), all of which assess the reasonable time of the notice from the date of delivery. The worst confusion was in LG Saarbrücken, March 23, 1992 (9 O 4048/89) (Germany) (UNILEX) <http://cisgw3.law.pace.edu/cases/920323g1.html> (Pace) regarding the sale of doors, where the Court suffered under the misapprehension that the duty to notify of the lack of conformity was implied by art. 38 (this confusion was, however, subsequently cleared up upon appeal of the case in OLG Saarbrücken, January 13, 1993 (1 U 69/92) (Germany) (UNILEX) <http://cisgw3.law.pace.edu/cases/930113g1.html> (Pace)).

[171] A good example of a mix-up can be found in a District Court judgment from Stuttgart, which left open the question of whether arts. 38 and 39 of the CISG or § 377 of HGB applied. In reasoning why notice 16 days after delivery was not timely, the Court stated that the fact that the defects of the shoes in question were easily discernible, combined with the fact that the seller had been forewarned as to possible defects by a previous defective shipment of shoes, prompted more swift notice. While these are certainly valid considerations in the case at hand, they solely concern the question of when the defects ought to have been discovered (i.e., art. 38), and not the reasonable period of time for giving notice. *See* LG Stuttgart, August 31, 1989 (3 KfHO 97/89) (Germany) (UNILEX) <http://cisgw3.law.pace.edu/cases/890831g1.html> (Pace). *See also supra* note 42.

In the following section, the time periods in question are noted as being after delivery (a confusion of Articles 38 and 39) if they are not after discovery (which means the actual discovery or the time when the buyer ought to have discovered the non-conformity), and observations by the Court that would help illustrate which period was the determining period have been included. This should at least hinder further confusion, and, where possible, help illustrate what these Courts consider to be reasonable time after discovery.

c. Reasonable Time After Discovery — the Time-Frame of Article 39(1)

The following concerns the determination of "reasonable time" in Article 39(1) as determined by German practice. The judgments from before 1995 will be analyzed first, followed by an analysis of more recent practice.

i. Practice Before 1995

The German practice on Article 39(1) has sent out some rather mixed messages. None more so than the practice that was pronounced before 1995. Very few of these "older" judgments found in favor of the buyer when determining whether the notice given was within reasonable time. Those that did mostly regarded notices that were quite obviously within reasonable time, and did not help establish a pattern concerning the determination of other cases. Examples of this are the notices in the judgments from District Court of Aachen, wherein the buyer notified the seller one day after discovery (which was the same day as delivery) that the shoes in question were non-conforming,[172] and District Court of Bielefeld, where the buyer of bacon notified 3 days after discovery.[173]

---

[172] LG Aachen, April 3, 1990 (41 O 198/89) (Germany) (UNILEX) <http://cisgw3.law.pace.edu/cases/900403g1.html> (Pace).

[173] LG Bielefeld, January 18, 1991 (15 O 201/90) (Germany) (UNILEX) <http://cisgw3.law.pace.edu/cases/910118g1.html> (Pace). However, although considered timely by the Court, notice was not considered specific enough and the buyer could not rely on the non-conformity. *Id.*

In a 1992 judgment from District Court of Frankfurt, regarding the sale of shoes, however, a notice given to the seller over the telephone nineteen days after delivery was considered by the Court to be undoubtedly within reasonable time (the Court did not comment on when the non-conformity was discovered or ought to have been discovered).[174] This seems surprising when considering the fact that another District Court judgment, this one from Mönchengladbach, had generally pronounced about six months earlier that notice regarding non-conforming textiles should have been given approximately two weeks after delivery, allowing one week for examination and one week for giving notice.[175] In other words, this latter judgment pronounced that reasonable time after discovery would be considered one week. The Court emphasized that the non-conformity was easily discernible, but that should only affect the time within which it ought to have been discovered.

The factors that convinced the District Court in Frankfurt that nineteen days was timely are not mentioned in the judgment, and no general guideline is pronounced. It is also unfortunate that the court does not specify within which time the non-conformity ought to have been discovered. The Court seems to find the timeliness obvious by finding the form of the notice acceptable, without mentioning the nature or discernability of the non-conformity, or why the notice is timely. The facts of the case, however, illustrate that the goods were not perishable, and that the buyer chose the remedy of reduction of price in repair of the non-conformity.

According to Sono, these factors should induce a longer timeframe,[176] and perhaps these factors motivated the Court. Another explana-

[174] LG Frankfurt am Main, December 9, 1992 (3/3 O 37/92) (Germany) (UNILEX) <http://cisgw3.law.pace.edu/cases/921209g1.html> (Pace). "Im Hinblick darauf, daß hier die Lieferung erst am 19 (October) 1991 erfolgt war und die telefonische Verständigung des Vertreters Mayer nach dem insoweit unbestrittenen gebliebenen Beklagtenvorbringen zwischen diesem Zeitpunkt und dessen nächster Vorsprache bei der Beklagten am 07 (November) 91 erfolgte, bestehen keine Zweifel an der Wahrung der Rügefrist." *Id.*

[175] LG Mönchengladbach, May 22, 1992 (7 O 80/91) (Germany) (UNILEX) <http://cisgw3.law.pace.edu/cases/920522g1.html> (Pace), (where a notice of a month was found to be untimely). "Selbst wenn man der Beklagten eine Frist von 1 Woche für die Untersuchung und eine Frist von einer weiteren Woche für die Absendung der Mängelrüge zubilligen wollte, wäre die mit Schreiben vom 7. (November) 1989 erhobene Mängelrüge auch für die Lieferung vom 6. Oktober 1989 nicht mehr rechtzeitig." *Id.*

[176] *See* Sono, *supra* note 112, at 309.

tion, however, may lie in the Courts application of Schwenzer's time-frame guideline of one "noble month."[177] Unfortunately, the Court did not divulge its reasoning.

Despite being the only one to find for the buyer where notice was given after more than a week, this judgment is not the only one to seemingly suggest a certain leniency in the determination of reasonable time. Although a 1994 District Court judgment from Köln rejected a time-frame of twenty-one days after delivery, the Court stressed that this was because the buyer knew that the seller had a deadline to comply with which would necessitate a speedier examination and notification.[178] The case involved the sale of business-catalogue space, and the Court stated that since the mistake in the twenty-two pages was discoverable within a few hours of delivery on 4 August 1992 and the buyer knew the seller had a deadline on 4 September 1992, an examination and notification should have been carried out sooner according to Article 38.[179] Since no notice was given within reasonable time after the mistake should have been found, the buyer could not rely on the non-conformity. The Court clearly stated that the Article 38 examination period could be set at a few days, but does not mention within which period the subsequent notice should have been delivered.[180] Nevertheless, the emphasis placed by the Court on the deadline in question would seem to suggest that a combined Article 38/Article 39 period of twenty-one days after delivery definitely was not considered untimely per se, but that the findings were based on the actual foreseeable detriment to the seller by the notice in question.

Most other German judgments before 1995 seem to lay down stricter guidelines. Some reach conclusions in favor of the seller which may be deemed obvious due to the extensive time-frames involved. For example, there are two 1992 judgments from the District Court of Berlin where notices were given two months and three and a half months, respectively, after delivery of goods with easily discernible non-conformities (both regarding shoes).[181] Other examples are a 1993 Higher District Court judgment, from

---

[177] *See generally* Schwenzer, *supra* note 76.

[178] LG Köln, 11 November 1993 (86 O 119/93) (Germany) (UNILEX) <http://cisgw3.law.pace.edu/cases/931111g1.html> (Pace).

[179] *See id.*

[180] *See id.*

[181] LG Berlin, 16 September 1992 (99 O 29/93) (Germany) (UNILEX) <http://cisgw3.law.pace.edu/cases/920916g1.html> (Pace) and LG Berlin, 30 September 1992

Saarbrücken, concerning the sale of doors, where notice was given two months after delivery as the buyer wrongfully believed the duty to inspect the goods was deferred, [182] a judgment from District Court of Düsseldorf where notice given four and twenty months after delivery was too late since the lack of conformity of the press-engines in question should have been discovered earlier,[183] and finally a Higher District Court judgment of Düsseldorf.

The latter judgment, from 1994, concerned a notice given two months after delivery of textiles that suffered from an easily discernible non-conformity.[184] Although reaching an obvious conclusion in the light of previous Article 39(1) practice, this judgment would seem to subtly hint at leniency. The Court found that through a *strict* construction of Articles 38 and 39, the buyer's notice two months after delivery was not reasonable.[185] It added that the determination of reasonable time hinges on whether a given notice is appropriate in each individual case. In order to determine this, the circumstances of each case ["*Umstände des Einzelfälles*"] and the opportunities of the contracting parties ["*Möglichkeiten der Vertragsparteien*"] must be analyzed. Since the non-conformity in question was easily discernible, it should have been discovered and notice given sooner. The Court did not add how much sooner, and did not separate the Article 38(1) time-frame from the Article 39(1) time-frame. Nevertheless, the fact that the Court considered the barring of a two-month notice to be a strict construction of the provisions in question implied that very generous notice time-frames could be considered reasonable.

(99 O 123/92) (Germany) (UNILEX) <http://cisgw3.law.pace.edu/cases/920930g1.html> (Pace).

182 OLG Saarbrücken, 13 January 1993 (1 U 69/92) (Germany) (UNILEX) <http://cisgw3.law.pace.edu/cases/930113g1.html> (Pace). *See also supra* note 148. This case was tried in the first instance in LG Saarbrücken, 23 March 1992 (9 O 4084/89) (Germany) (UNILEX) <http://cisgw3.law.pace.edu/cases/920323g1.html> (Pace), where the District Court mistakenly found the duty to notify the seller comprised by art. 38. The Higher District Court corrected the misconstruction of the CISG but affirmed the judgment. *Id.*

183 LG Düsseldorf, 23 June 1994 (31 O 231/94) (Germany) (UNILEX) <http://cisgw3.law.pace.edu/cases/940623g1.html> regarding 2 hydraulic press engines delivered 16 months apart. The court stated that even allowing longer time for the discovery of engine trouble (which was not easily discernible) the examination period was too long, and notice was untimely regarding both engines. *Id.* This judgment contains a very good explanation of the relationship between arts. 38 and 39.

184 *See id.*

185 *See id.*

Other German judgments have been entered which found in favor of the seller, without this conclusion seeming apparent. One of these judgments is a 1994 Petty Court judgment from Riedlingen, where the Court rejected a notice given twenty days after delivery of ham despite the obstructions facing the buyer due to the Christmas holiday closures in the period in question.[186] The Court stated that a period of three days for examination and discovery and a period of three days for notification would have been appropriate.[187] This judgment seems unnecessarily strict. Considering that nineteen days was acceptable in Frankfurt in 1992 and that twenty-one days was unacceptable in Köln in 1993 largely due to a deadline, the Courts conclusion that three days is the maximum time-frame for reasonable time seems harsh. Although the non-conformity was easily discernible (by the buyer's own admission, the ham was moldy a few hours after delivery), the buyer had paid the price in part and thus chose the remedy of price-reduction.[188] This ought to have made the time-frame for giving notice a little more flexible, and the fact that the goods were perishables in the present case ought not to have restricted the time-frame since the buyer chose to keep the goods. Since the seller did not deny or question the non-conformity itself, it would not seem relevant whether he had an opportunity to speedily ascertain the moldiness of the ham. The notice in the present case would not seem to have caused any detriment to the seller, and ought to have been considered reasonable in the light of previous practice.

An even stricter time-frame was pronounced by the Higher District Court of Düsseldorf in 1993.[189]The buyer would not pay the full price for a delivery in part of tinned gherkins. The Court found that a notice given within seven days of discovery was not considered within reasonable time.[190] The circumstances of this case are, however, unique. The parties had agreed that an examination of the goods take place upon delivery to the shipper and before redirection (thus rendering Article 38(2) inapplicable through derogation from the Convention in accordance with Article 6).[191]

---

[186] Amtsgericht Riedlingen, 21 October 1994 (2 C 395/93) (Germany) (UNILEX) <http://cisgw3.law.pace.edu/cases/941021g1.html> (Pace).

[187] *See id.*

[188] *See id.*

[189] OLG Düsseldorf, 8 January 1993 (17 U 82/92) (Germany) (UNILEX) <http://cisgw3.law.pace.edu/cases/930108g1.html> (Pace).

[190] *See id.*

[191] Art. 38(2) prescribes that the examination of goods in carriage may be deferred until they arrive at their destination.

This examination required the buyer's representative to approve the goods before shipment. The Court stated that since this factor was an important term of business to the seller, it implied that the seller required the non-conformity discovered and communicated to him at this time.[192] Although not actually constituting an agreed time-frame within which notice should have been given,[193] this agreed approval seems to have weighed heavily in the determination of the reasonable time of notice. A notice delivered seven days after the examination was thus not considered timely. The Court further stated that a delivery in part represents a non-conformity like any other under Article 39, and that the buyer could not rely upon it (thus the full purchase price should be paid for an incomplete shipment).[194] The Court reached this conclusion by equating Article 39 with Section 377 and Section 378 of the German Sales law. The similarities between Article 39(1) and Section 377 and Section 378 of the German HGB entail that any undue domestic influence will not necessarily jeopardize the uniformity of the CISG in the present case. However, the drawing of parallels between domestic and uniform international law is unsuitable in the application of international uniform law.[195]

A more severe equation to domestic law was made by the same Court in 1994, when the "*Nachfrist*"-type rule in Article 47(1), which is a right of the buyer, was equated to Section 326 HGB, which is a duty of the buyer.[196]

---

[192] *See* OLG Düsseldorf, 8 January 1993 (17 U 82/92) (Germany) (UNILEX) <http://cisgw3.law.pace.edu/cases/930108g1.html> (Pace).

[193] Such time-frames can be agreed between the parties and recognized by the Courts. *See supra* section I.

[194] *See* OLG Düsseldorf, 8 January 1993 (17 U 82/92) (Germany) (UNILEX) <http://cisgw3.law.pace.edu/cases/930108g1.html> (Pace).

[195] Moreover, any influence from § 378 HGB on the application of art. 39 may pose a severe problem, since the requirement of notice in the case of *aliuds* (i.e., whether the delivery of completely different goods is a delivery of non-conforming goods as understood by art. 35) is not completely settled under the Convention, whereas such notice is prescribed by § 378 HGB. This may already have influenced the Court in a judgment from BGHZ, 3 April 1996 (VII ZR 51/95) (Germany) (UNILEX) regarding the sale of cobalt sulphate <http://cisgw3.law.pace.edu/cases/960403g1.html> (Pace), which concluded that the CISG does not differentiate between *aliuds* and non-conforming goods.

[196] *See* OLG Düsseldorf, 10 February 1994 (6 U 119/93) (Germany) (UNILEX) <http://cisgw3.law.pace.edu/cases/940210g2.html>, regarding the sale of textiles from Italy to Germany. Unfortunately, in LG Duisburg, 17 April 1996 (45(19) O 80/94) (Germany) (UNILEX) <http://cisgw3.law.pace.edu/cases/960417g1.html> (Pace), a similar conclu-

The buyer was thus unjustly barred from relying on the non-conformity of the textiles delivered, and the question of the timeliness of the Article 39(1) notice was not discussed.

Yet another equation to German domestic law was made by the Higher District Court of Düsseldorf the previous year.[197] The Court made a direct analogy to Section 377 of the German sales law (the HGB) when deciding that notice given twenty-five days after delivery of textiles was not given within reasonable time.[198] It compared the considerations behind Article 39 of the CISG and Section 377 of the HGB, and stated that the interests of good business form the basis of the determination of a notice within reasonable time, as the notice should not give either party an unfair advantage and strive for a rapid settlement of differences.[199] The Higher District Court went on to state that twenty-five days could not be considered a short period of time, and that the buyer had not substantiated any difficulties in discerning the non-conformity.[200] The Higher District Court judgment made no mention of which general guideline it applied, nor did it explain why the notice should have been within a shorter period of time in lieu of a more generous one. This judgment also concerned the question of whether the seller had lost his right to rely on Article 39 if responding to an alleged late notice by taking back the goods to inspect them.[201] The Court found that a reasonable person, in accordance with Article 8(2), would not find an examination of the goods to verify a claim of lack of conformity sufficient im-

---

sion was reached: Although no notice of non-conformity had been given, the Court pronounced the lack of "*Nachfrist*" as an additional reason why the buyer could not rely on the non-conformity, by stating: "Hinzu kommt, daß die Beklagte die weiteren Voraussetzungen eines Schadensersatzanspruchs nach Artikel 45 ff. CISG, nämlich Fristsetzung zur Nachlieferung, nicht dargetan hat." This judgment was not appealed to the Higher District Court.

[197] OLG Düsseldorf, 12 March 1993 (17 U 136/92) (Germany) (UNILEX) <http://cisgw3.law.pace.edu/cases/930312g1.html> (Pace).

[198] *See id.*

[199] *See id.*

[200] The Court stated: "Eine Frist von 25 Tagen ist aber nicht mehr kurz bzw. angemessen im Sinne der Art. 38 und 39 CISG. Besondere Schwierigkeiten, die angeblichen Webfehler festzustellen, sind nicht ersichtlich." *Id.*

[201] *See* BGHZ, 25 June 1997 (VIII ZR 300/96) (Germany) (UNILEX) <http://cisgw3.law.pace.edu/cases/970625g2.html> (Pace). *See also* Internationalen Schiedsgericht der Bundeskammer der geweblichen Wirtshaft SCH-4318 <http://cisgw3.law.pace.edu/cases/940615a4.html> (Pace) and 4366 <http://cisgw3.law.pace.edu/cases/940615a3.html> (Pace).

plication that the seller considered the notice timely.[202] In that respect, a seller is entitled to "cover his bases" without "shooting himself in the foot," without taking out reservations against the timeliness of the notice.

ii. Recent Practice — 1995 and After

In 1995, the Higher District Court of München attempted to formulate a general guideline for the application of Article 39(1).[203] The case concerned a notice of non-conformity of plastic granules which was given three months after delivery, and was ruled not timely. The Court proclaimed, in an *obiter dictum*, that when determining reasonable time the individual circumstances of each case were to be taken into consideration, and that normally (in the case of non-perishable, non-seasonally dependant goods) a period of eight days would be a vantage point.[204]

Exactly one month later, the German Supreme Court (Bundesgerichthof) concluded its deliberations and pronounced its first judgment assessing Article 39(1).[205] The case concerned New Zealand mussels which, upon examination by the German buyer, contained higher levels of cad-

---

[202] *See id.*

[203] OLG München, 8 February 1995 (7 U 3758/94) (Germany) (UNILEX) <http://cisgw3.law.pace.edu/cases/950208g2.html> (Pace), regarding the sale of plastic granules, where the buyer waited 3 months after delivery to give notice: "Bei der bestimmung der "Angemessen frist" sind die Unstände des einzelfalles zu berücksichtigen; im Normalfall wird bei dauerhaften, nicht saisonabhängigen Waren ein Zeitraum von ca. 8 Tagen zugrundezulegen sein." By the *verbatum* reference to the time-frame in art. 39(1) it would seem likely that the Court means 8 days after discovery. The Court refers to the first observation by Schwenzer, *see supra* text accompanying note 109, but neglects to take the second (highly relevant) point of congruent international application and the "noble month" into consideration.

[204] *See id.*

[205] *See* BGHZ, 8 March 1995 (VIII ZR 159/94) (Germany) (UNILEX) <http://cisgw3.law.pace.edu/cases/950308g3.html> (Pace). The case was previously tried in LG Darmstadt, 22 December 1992 (14 O 165/92) (Germany) (UNILEX), (Pace) <http://cisgw3.law.pace.edu/cases/921222g1.html> (Pace) and OLG Frankfurt, 20 April 1994 (13 U 51/93) (Germany) (UNILEX) <http://cisgw3.law.pace.edu/cases/940420g1.html> (Pace). Both previous instances neglected to take art. 39 into independent consideration.

mium than prescribed in the recommended German guideline.[206] The Court stated that notice given a month after discovery (although a very generous time-frame)[207] may be considered reasonable time in the interests of differing international legal traditions.[208] Although the case concerned perishable goods, the hypothetically acceptable time-frame of Schwenzer's "noble month" guideline was not restricted to a shorter period in the present case — but since the case concerned a notice which was given more than six weeks after discovery, this endorsement of the "noble month" almost appears as an *obiter dictum* to serve as an outside starting point for determining the time-frame and any aspects which may prompt Courts to narrow it down. It would seem fair to assume that the Court considered the introduction of Schwenzer's "noble month" guideline necessary for Article 39(1) practice in Germany.

Nevertheless, in a judgment regarding the sale of sports clothes from the District Court of Landshut delivered one month later, the Court made the general statement that the time-frame for notification of defects which are not hidden could not be considered any longer than a few days after discovery.[209] This factor (the defect being easily discernible) seems especially confusing in an Article 39(1) context in the present case, since the Court

---

[206] The classification of the cadmium-mussels as fit for ordinary purposes since only great quantities would be hazardous for human consumption, in accordance with Art. 35(2)(a) of the Convention, is another interesting aspect of this case, and one which has been commented on widely. *See, e.g.*, Peter Schlechtriem, *Vertragsmäßigkeit der Ware als Beschaffenheitsvereinbarung, in* 1 PRAXIS DER INTERNATIONALEN PRIVAT-UND VERFAHRENSRECHTS 12-14 (1996), and LOOKOFSKY, *supra* note 14, at 58.

[207] The concept of the "noble month" [*Großzügiger Monat*] originates with the Swiss scholar Schwenzer for the sake of congruent international application. *See* Schwenzer, *supra* note 76, at 370 and accompanying text to note 109.

[208] The Court stated: "Selbst wenn man insoweit nach Auffassung des erkennenden Senats sehr großzügig wegen der unterschiedlichen nationalen Rechtstraditionen von einem "groben Mittelwert" von etwa einem Monat ausgehen wollte, war die Rügefrist vor dem 3. März 1992 abgelaufen." with reference to Schwenzer, *ibidem*. *See* BGHZ, 8 March 1995 (VIII ZR 159/94) (Germany) (UNILEX) <http://cisgw3.law.pace.edu/cases/950308g3.html> (Pace).

[209] LG Landshut, 5 April 1995 (54 O 644/94) (Germany) (UNILEX) <http://cisgw3.law.pace.edu/cases/950405g1.html> (Pace). "Eine Minderlieferung stellt keinen versteckten Mangel dar, so daß die Anzeigefrist nur wenige Tage läuft." *Id.* The case concerned sports clothes that suffered from three different non-conformities (color, shrinkage and wrong quantity).

stated that the lack of quantity should be discovered within a week, according to Article 38.[210] The obviousness of the non-conformity of the clothes in question had already been considered when determining when the non-conformity ought to have been discovered. It would seem that although the Court separated the Article 38 and Article 39 time-frames, the criteria are still confused, and, in any event, no attention was paid to the "noble month" applied in the earlier Supreme Court judgment. In a judgment of the Higher District Court of Stuttgart regarding the sale of machines from the same year, however, the Court referred to the Supreme Court judgment, and added that the Article 39(1) time-frame was — within the framework of the CISG in the light of the differing domestic legal traditions — approximately one month.[211] In other words, the "noble month" was considered to be more of a standard than an outside limit in this case concerning the sale of machinery.

The Petty Court of Augsburg clarified the nature of the "noble month" guideline in 1996, when it stated that the maximum period of time considered reasonable for the purpose of Article 39(1) was one month after discovery, and that certain factors — such as the seasonal nature of the goods, which in the present case concerned fashion wear for a particular season — would necessitate that the buyer give notice even sooner.[212] The buyer would not pay for the goods, and wished to avoid the contract.[213] Unfortu-

[210] *See id.*

[211] *See* OLG Stuttgart, 21 August 1995 (5 U 195/94) (Germany) (UNILEX) <http://cisgw3.law.pace.edu/cases/950821g1.html> (Pace). "Diese Frist beträgt im Rahmen des CISG im Hinblick auf die unterschiedlichen nationalen Rechtstraditionen etwa einen Monat." *Id.* However, in the present case, the buyer could not prove that he had given notice. For a commentary on this judgment, see Blume & Asam, *annotation to OLG Stuttgart,* Urteil vom 21.8.1995, 2 Praxis der Internationalen Privat- und Verfahrensrechts (IPRAX) 139 (1996) who does not criticize this application of the "noble month."

[212] Amtsgericht Augsburg, 29 January 1996 (11 C 4004/95) (Germany) (UNILEX) <http://cisgw3.law.pace.edu/cases/960129g1.html> (Pace). "Das Recht sich auf Vertragswidrigkeit — wie hier Verspätung der Lieferung — zu berufen, erlischt, wenn die Vertragswidrigkeit nicht innerhalb einer angemessenen Frist angezeigt wird. Insbesondere ist eine rasche Rüge bei Saisonwaren wie den vorliegenden geboten. Die maximale Frist beträgt einen Monat ab Kenntniserlangung von dem Mangel." *Id.* The latter part of the statement almost resembles an *obiter dictum* since the buyer waited 18 months to notify the seller.

[213] *See id.*

nately, this judgment is from a Petty Court and has not formed a precedent for other similar cases. This judgment sets a good example by explaining the importance of the maximum month used in the latest judgments, and the factors that influenced the Court's decision regarding whether a more restrictive time-frame should apply in the case at hand, while simultaneously separating the two time-frames of Articles 38(1) and 39(1).

The idea of the seasonal nature of the goods limiting the time-frame was also applied by the Petty Court of Kehl a few months earlier, when the Court examined the Article 39(1) time-frame although the notice could not be proven.[214] In this case, the buyer wished to avoid a contract that concerned fashion wear, and a notice given six weeks after the discovery of an easily discernible non-conformity (discoverable same day as delivery) was not found to be satisfactory.[215]

A judgment regarding notice given twenty-five days after discovery from the District Court of Heidelberg was recently reversed by the Higher District Court of Karlsruhe,[216] in a case regarding non-perishable, non-seasonally dependant sticky-film that did not stick properly. The buyer sued for damages. The District Court found that notice was given within reasonable time, and stated that since an exact time-frame for notice giving could not be pinpointed, the one month guideline suggested by Schwenzer should be applied in the present case.[217] No mention was made in the judgment, however, of the fact that the Supreme Court had already chosen to apply this "noble month" guideline in another Article 39(1) case. The Higher District Court reversed the District Court judgment.[218] It found that the goods should have been more thoroughly tested by the original buyer, and that

[214] Amtsgericht Kehl, 6 October 1995 (3 C 925/93) (Germany) (UNILEX) <http://cisgw3.law.pace.edu/cases/951006g1.html> (Pace), (regarding the sale of Italian fashion wear, where notice was given by telephone).

[215] *See id.*

[216] LG Heidelberg, 2 October 1996 (O 37/96 KfH II) (Germany) (UNILEX) <http://cisgw3.law.pace.edu/cases/961002g1.html> (Pace) and OLG Karlsruhe, 25 June 1997 (1 U 280/96) (Germany) (UNILEX) <http://cisgw3.law.pace.edu/cases/970625g1.html> (Pace).

[217] *See id.* The District Court also stated that Article 39 of the CISG represented a more buyer-friendly provision than Art. 39 of the ULIS. *See supra* text accompanying note 95.

[218] OLG Karlsruhe, 25 June 1997 (1 U 280/96) (Germany) (UNILEX) <http://cisgw3.law.pace.edu/cases/970625g1.html> (Pace).

these tests could have been carried out and the non-conformity discovered within a week.[219] Notice should then have been given three to four days later, with the maximum permissible period of time from delivery to notification amounting to a total of ten to eleven days.[220] The Higher District Court made no mention of the "noble month" applied by the District Court, nor did it explain why it considered the reasonable time period restricted to three to four days, despite the fact that the buyer wanted damages and not avoidance. It would seem that although the Courts agreed that the notification time-frame of 8 days after delivery agreed on by the parties should not apply in the case of hidden non-conformities, the Higher District Court has considered this agreement a legitimate factor in narrowing down the time-frame permissible for notification. Such an agreed time-frame should, admittedly, have alerted the buyer to make a thorough investigation of the goods within the prescribed time, and is an indication of an agreement for swiftness in the dealings between the parties. Nevertheless, it seems inappropriate for the Court not to consider or discuss the "noble month" guideline found applicable to the case at hand by the District Court before applying criteria to the time-frame, especially when considering that this guideline was introduced in German practice by the Supreme Court.

The Higher District Court of Köln, in a 1997 judgment concerning the sale of aluminium hydroxide machines,[221] affirmed the general rule of the "noble month," but stressed that this "noble month" is a vantage point by adding that the time-frame must be restricted in certain cases where the facts of the specific case reasonably prescribe it.[222] In this case, notice was given after the aluminum hydroxide provided by the seller had been placed in a large silo along with other shipments (and the buyer could not substantiate that all materials herein were provided by the seller).[223] The time

---

[219] *See id.*

[220] The Court stated: "Damit steht fest, daß bei einer der Klägerin oblegenen Probeverarbeitung nach maximal sieben Tagen Flecken festzustellen gewesen wären. Hätte die Klägerin mit der Probeverarbeitung nach drei bis vier Tagen begonnen, hätte sie den Mangel gegenüber der Beklagten spätestens nach zehn bis elf Tagen rügen können." *Id.*

[221] *See* OLG Köln, 21 August 1997 (18 U 121/96) (Germany) (UNILEX) <http://cisgw3.law.pace.edu/cases/970821g1.html> (Pace).

[222] The Court stated: "Eine solche Frist [Monatsfrist] kann freilich nur für Waren gelten, bei denen keine Veränderungen zu besorgen ist . . . ." *Id.* In this case a very swift notice was required to ensure that the seller could ascertain the non-conformity. *See id.*

[223] *See id.*

of the notice thus jeopardized the seller's possibility to ascertain the non-conformity. The Court restricted the flexible month to a shorter time-span with reference to the specific facts of the case, and the purpose of Article 39.

In 1996, the Supreme Court pronounced its second judgment pertaining to Article 39(1) of the CISG.[224] This case concerned a buyer of software who gave notice one day after discovering the non-conformity (which he did on the same day as the goods were delivered).[225] So, unfortunately, the Supreme Court found no cause to examine the time-frame more generally or pronounce a sorely needed *obiter dictum* on the determination of reasonable time. The only comment the buyer's notice warranted, was that it was undoubtedly timely.[226] The Supreme Court has only been given one other opportunity to pronounce judgment on and comment on Article 39(1) to date.[227] This judgment, from 1997, concerned a notice which was given almost seven months after the first delivery of Korean Steel suffering from lack of conformity.[228] The seller had indicated to the buyer that the written notice was timely, and the Court left the question of timeliness open and stated that the notice was reasonable as the seller had accepted it.[229]

It would seem that recent German practice regarding reasonable time in Article 39(1) does not paint a clear picture of the determination of the

---

[224] *See* BGHZ, 4 December 1996 (VIII ZR 306/95) (Germany) (UNILEX) <http://cisgw3.law.pace.edu/cases/961204g1.html> (Pace).

[225] *See id.*

[226] The Court stated: "Rechzeitigkeit der Rüge steht außer Frage." *Id.*

[227] *See* BGHZ, 25 June 1997 (VIII ZR 300/96) (Germany) (UNILEX) <http://cisgw3.law.pace.edu/cases/970625g2.html> (Pace).

[228] *See id.*

[229] The Court stated: "[d]ie Klägerin hat mit Schreiben vom 27. November 1992 die Materialbeanstandungen der Beklagten entgegengenommen und deren Weiterleitung an ihr Werk in Korea angezeigt; mit Schreiben vom 2. Dezember 1992 und 27. Januar 1993 hat sie weiter erklärt, sie werde, falls sich in den Vorräten der Beklagten wieder Ausschüsse zeigten und die Reklamationen berechtigt seien, "auch dafür geradestehen und ordentlich abwickeln." *Damit hat die Klägerin nicht nur hinsichtlich der Mängelrügen vom 5. November 1992 deren Rechtzeitigkeit anerkannt, sondern auch für spätere Beanstandungen auf den Einwand der nicht rechtzeitigen Rügeerhebung verzichtet* . . . ." (emphasis added). *Id.* According to an older judgment, OLG Düsseldorf, 12 March 1993 (17 U 136/92) (Germany) (UNILEX) <http://cisgw3.law.pace.edu/cases/930312g1.html> (Pace), such acceptance of the notice *must* be explicit; the seller did not signify that he found the notice timely if responding to an alleged late notice by taking back the goods to inspect them.

time-frame involved. A firm guideline for what constitutes reasonable time is lacking. The noble month maximum vantage point introduced into practice by the Supreme Court in 1995 seems to be taking hold in the Courts, but it will take more congruent practice to make it a legal guideline. It is uncertain whether such practice will emerge. Previous practice seems to indicate that inconsistent time-frames and discrepancies in proposed guidelines are not a new phenomenon.

4. Observations on the Practice of Article 39(1) in German Practice

Regarding the form, specificity and recipient of the Article 39 notice, there have been no discernible changes in German practice. The more recent judgments as well as the early ones are in complete agreement as to these requirements. A notice of lack of conformity must:

a) specify the nature of the lack of conformity and the goods in question very precisely,
b) be directed to the seller or someone directly employed by the seller, and not a third party or other associate, and
c) be delivered in such a way that it can be proven what was said to whom and when, in case the seller disputes it.

Furthermore, it would seem that a seller is cut-off from relying on Article 39 if he indicates that the notice was timely, but not if he takes back the goods to inspect them.

This state of affairs has remained unchanged throughout the relatively short period of the application of Article 39(1) by the German Courts, as has the fact that German Courts have not been predisposed to find in favor of the German party.[230] With regard to the concept of reasonable time, however, such a conclusion of stability is not so easily reached.

a. The Evolution of "Reasonable Time" in German Practice

Since there has never been a definite guideline that applies to all determinations of reasonable time in German practice, it is difficult to deter-

[230] *See* BERNSTEIN & LOOKOFSKY, *supra* note 40, at 63.

mine an evolution in the time-frame as determined by the German Courts when comparing recent and older practice. In addition to this, the confusion between the Article 38 and 39 time-frames fogs the issue of reasonable time to a certain degree. Even though some instances of differing practice seem to stand out and take on the guise of tendencies, there seems to be precious little progress in specific directions or discernible consequences of new turns in practice.

The Swiss scholar Schwenzer has stated that the early German judgments regarding Article 39(1) tend to lean towards the stricter time-frame of eight days.[231] However, the judgment from Frankfurt which accepted notice delivered nineteen days after delivery[232] and the judgment from Köln which stressed that twenty-one days was not acceptable due to the deadline ahead[233] would seem to suggest that a period of eight days was not necessarily the norm.

Any claim that the Courts have become more lenient in their recent application of Article 39(1) would seem to overlook that in 1995, the District Court of Landshut considered notice given nineteen days after delivery too late to be considered given within reasonable time,[234] whereas a few years before that exact same time-frame of nineteen days was considered reasonable by the District Court of Frankfurt regarding a notice given over the telephone.[235] The circumstances involved in the notification time-frames would not seem to isolate any factors which should require a stricter time-frame in the latter judgment.

On the other hand, it cannot be successfully argued that there is a general tendency towards more restrictive time-frames in the determination of reasonable time. There is no practice that evidences this. Judgments reject-

---

[231] *See* Schwenzer, *supra* note 76, at 362 (in German version). "Deutsche Autoren wollen tendenziell einen Zeitraum von ca. acht Tagen zugrunde legen. Auch die ersten deutschen Entscheidungen zum CISG weisen in diese Richtung." *Id.*

[232] *See* LG Frankfurt, 9 December 1992 (3/3 O 37/92) (Germany) (UNILEX) <http://cisgw3.law.pace.edu/cases/921209g1.html> (Pace).

[233] *See* LG Köln, 11 November 1993 (86 O 119/93) (Germany) (UNILEX) <http://cisgw3.law.pace.edu/cases/931111g1.html> (Pace).

[234] LG Landshut, 5 April 1995 (54 O 644/94) (Germany) (UNILEX) <http://cisgw3.law.pace.edu/cases/950405g1.html> (Pace).

[235] *See* LG Frankfurt, 9 December 1992 (3/3 O 37/92) (Germany) (UNILEX) <http://cisgw3.law.pace.edu/cases/921209g1.html> (Pace).

ing notices given over 20 days after delivery have been pronounced throughout the period of German practice of the CISG.[236]

The recent introduction of the "noble month" as a guideline for the sake of congruent international practice in 1995 by the Supreme Court [237] was an attempt at evolution, in keeping with the spirit of the CISG. It did not seem surprising or a radical change in previous practice, since practice was so changeable upon its introduction. It was pronounced in an *obiter dictum*-like fashion and was presumably meant as a general stable guideline — a vantage-point from which the individual circumstances of each case can create an individual reasonable time-frame.

The true surprise in the evolution of German practice is the lack of evolution, namely the fact that the subsequent judgments do not take this Supreme Court guideline into consideration and apply it. The fact that subsequent practice is as variable as the practice that preceded the introduction of this guideline is puzzling. It is especially surprising that a higher instance reversed a District Court judgment applying this guideline.[238] It must be concluded that the changes in practice are not set trends or tendencies, and that the variations in the findings of the Courts must be due to some other phenomenon.

Some leading scholars deem the requirements most German Courts impose on the buyer "overly harsh," and seem to be of the opinion that this may be due to their not having noted the difference between Article 39 of the ULIS and Article 39 of the CISG.[239] However, as mentioned earlier, [240]

---

[236] *See, e.g.*, LG Mönchengladbach, 22 May 1992 (7 O 80/91) (Germany) (UNILEX) <http://cisgw3.law.pace.edu/cases/920522g1.html> (Pace), regarding notice given 1 month after delivery and OLG Stuttgart, 21 August 1995 (5 U 195/94) (Germany) (UNILEX) <http://cisgw3.law.pace.edu/cases/950821g1.html> (Pace), also regarding notice given 1 month after delivery. In both cases, the lack of conformity was discoverable upon delivery, so the time-frames are equal.

[237] *See* BGHZ, 8 March 1995 (VIII ZR 159/94) (Germany) (UNILEX) <http://cisgw3.law.pace.edu/cases/950308g3.html> (Pace).

[238] *See* LG Heidelberg, 2 October 1996 (O 37/96 KfH II) (Germany) (UNILEX) <http://cisgw3.law.pace.edu/cases/961002g1.html> (Pace) and OLG Karlsruhe, 25 June 1997 (I U 280/96) (Germany) (UNILEX) <http://cisgw3.law.pace.edu/cases/970625g1.html> (Pace).

[239] See Witz, *supra* note 93, at 24, who criticizes the German judges for their failure to recognize the alleged difference between the two provisions. *See also* LOOKOFSKY, *supra* note 14, at 61.

[240] *See supra* Section II.

the difference in wording between the two provisions would only seem to regard the flexibility of the time-frame, and moreover, it would be surprising if the majority of domestic Courts fell prey to the same "mistake." In any event, the variations in practice regarding the determination of reasonable time do not indicate that the German Courts do not recognize the flexibility of the new Article 39. The problem is more likely to lie in the reluctance of practitioners to adopt interpretations from precedents and theories.

It would seem that the judges, when focusing on each individual case and its reasonableness, seem to forget the "bigger picture" of the need to keep uniform application of the CISG in mind. This results in somewhat arbitrary outcomes, especially where the international compromise of the "noble month" contrasts with more restrictive approaches. The reasonableness of each individual case is important. But since the uniformity is a tool for certainty in contracts, and since this certainty is also a necessary part of the overall reasonableness, the uniformity and the individual reasonableness must be combined. The variations have to be diminished — especially where they are due to a domestic vantage point.

b. The Influence of German Domestic Law upon "Reasonable Time"

Although there is no firm guideline for the German interpretation of Article 39, it would be fair to conclude that the approach is rarely a "buyer-friendly" one.[241] In many cases, the buyer must give a swift and specific notice for the Court to consider notification adequate in accordance with Article 39(1), even after the introduction of the "noble month."[242] This may, in part, be due to the influence of domestic law. The two provisions of Article 39 of the CISG and Section 377 of the HGB are so linguistically similar that it might seem to the German Courts that even if they allowed themselves to be unduly influenced, it would not jeopardize the uniformity of the Convention. And it might also seem harmless to equate the considerations behind the two provisions. However, once the connection between the two provisions is made, the essence of the domestic provision will undoubtedly influence the domestic judge. The considerations of uniform in-

[241] Prof. Lookofsky deems the interpretation of art. 39 by German Courts unusually demanding and seller-friendly. *See* LOOKOFSKY, *supra* note 14, at 61.

[242] *See supra,* Appendix A for an overlook of art. 39(1) caselaw results.

ternational provisions do not equal those of domestic law. Moreover, since the domestic time-frame is rarely deemed timely if over 2 weeks, and the international guideline of the "noble month" introduced by the Supreme Court doubles this acceptable time-frame, domestic influence may well be the reason for the findings of the judges opting for more restrictive time-frames. In light of the domestic time-frame they find a vantage point of a month unconscionable. Furthermore, it is likely that domestic German law is responsible for the confusion of the Article 38(1) and Article 39(1) time-frames, as Section 377 HGB time-frames begin at the time of delivery. Finally, the misconstructions of Article 47(1) that have led to an imposition of a duty for "*Nachfrist*" as opposed to a right, are most certainly the result of *faux amis* influence from the domestic "*Nachfrist*" rule in Section 326 HGB.

c. "Reasonable Time" in German Practice Today

Based on the caselaw outlined in the present paper, there are certain conclusions that may be drawn regarding what constitutes reasonable time as understood by Article 39 of the CISG in current German law. A notice in an Article 39(1) case brought before a German Court today would be divided into one of three categories: "almost always timely" (1-8 days after discovery), "almost never timely" (over 30 days after discovery), and a "grey area" of the periods in between the two which could be determined as "maybe timely." Unfortunately, in the latter category of cases, the determination would primarily seem to hinge on which Court the case is brought before. Some Courts have embraced the "noble month" and some have not. However, regardless of this battle between the "noble month" and the more restrictive time-frames, there are certain criteria extrapolated from the fact-patterns of the German cases that indicate common ground as to the determination of the time-frame of Article 39(1). The determination of "reasonable time" has been influenced in German practice by factors such as:

- the nature of the goods, i.e., whether the goods are perishable or diminishing in value, or connected to a certain season;
- the ease of discernability of the non-conformity — this factor should, however, ideally only influence the time of discovery and not the time of notice; [243]

[243] *See* discussion *supra* subsection 1.3.2.

- any deadlines facing the seller which are known to the buyer; and
- any aspect of the contract which implies the need for swiftness in the dealings between the parties.

With regard to the criteria of chosen remedy, the German Courts have not yet explicitly ruled on whether the consideration that avoidance requires swifter notice and damages is a valid one. There is a greater tendency to look at the seller's ability to ascertain the defect and cure it as well as the possibility of taking back the goods. Consideration of the seller's options are, predictably, primarily in focus before the Courts that favor shorter "seller-friendly" notices, and which have not embraced the "noble month."

The inconsistency of the German determinations of reasonable time poses a problem. Although it may not invite forum shopping, as the outcome of the judges' determination of reasonable time will not be predicable, the certainty in contracts which the CISG protects with its uniformity is at stake. The Convention must not only be interpreted uniformly internationally, but also domestically. Moreover, the incongruency of the German practice is all the more serious since the German Article 39(1) practice represents the bulk of caselaw, and thus the majority of international precedents. It would seem that a consistent application of a standard guideline (such as the noble month), with standard or individual factors influencing the timeliness (such as those mentioned above, and others which may influence timeliness) is sorely needed to prevent the German application of Article 39(1) from seeming slightly arbitrary. It is not enough for the Supreme Court to introduce such a guideline — it must be embraced by all German Courts. This must be done soon to ensure a uniform application of the CISG throughout Germany. Perhaps the Supreme Court will seize the opportunity to reinforce the "noble month" doctrine in an *obiter dictum* when pronouncing judgment in the appeal of the judgment from Higher District Court of Koblenz.[244] And perhaps this time the precedent will be followed.

The fact that this Supreme Court guideline of international compromise has not yet been embraced in all German Article 39(1) practice is disconcerting. If all German Courts do not pay heed to the precedents of their

[244] OLG Koblenz, 31 January 1997 (2 U 31/96) (Germany) (UNILEX) <http://cisgw3.law.pace.edu/cases/970131g1.html> (Pace), appealed as BGHZ ZR, 64/97 pending.

own Supreme Court, it seems unlikely that they will ever consider international precedents as they are required to do by Article 7(1).

B. Caselaw from Other Countries

Although the majority of international caselaw on Article 39(1) are from Germany, there is some practice regarding the determination of "reasonable time" that comes from Courts of other countries. An analysis of this caselaw in light of theoretic definitions and German caselaw will help establish the actual degree of international uniformity in the determination of "reasonable time" in Article 39(1) and possibly a pattern for this determination.

1. Austria

The Austrian legal system is a decentralized procedural regional system, very similar to that of Germany. Moreover, the Commercial Codes of Germany and Austria are almost identical, and the Austrian legal tradition looks to German caselaw for guides to interpretation.[245] Thus, Sections 377 and 378 of the Austrian Commercial Code contain the same notification requirements as Sections 377 and 378 of the German HGB.[246]

The CISG was adopted in Austria on January 1st, 1989.[247] Since then, there has been only one reported case regarding Article 39(1) before Austrian Courts. In a 1994 Higher District Court judgment regarding the sale of flowers, the Court found that the buyer could not establish that there was a non-conformity.[248] The decision went on to state that even if the buyer could establish a non-conformity, he would have lost his right to rely on it,

---

[245] *See* O.C.GILES, UNIFORM COMMERCIAL LAW — AN ESSAY ON INTERNATIONAL CONVENTIONS IN NATIONAL COURTS 35, note 29 (1970). "Germany and Austria provide an example of this [uniformity] in respect of their practically identical commercial codes. This uniformity has been maintained without compulsion, for since there is very little Austrian caselaw on the matters regulated by the Austrian code, Austrian lawyers largely rely on relevant German case law." with reference to Ferdinand Melchior in "Die Auslegung des HGB in Deutschland und in Österreich."

[246] For an explanation of these provisions, *see* Section III.

[247] Austria signed the Convention on 1 April 1980, ratified it on 29 December 1987 and it entered into force in Austrian law on 1 January 1989. Austria took out reservations against agreements not in writing. *See Status of Conventions, supra* note 7.

[248] *See* OLG Innsbruck., 1 July 1994 [4 R 161/94] (Austria)(UNILEX) <http://cisgw3.law.pace.edu/cases/940701a3.html> (Pace), decided in the first instance by LG

since he had failed to give the seller notice within a reasonable time after discovery of the defect.[249] The Court found that Article 39(1) was similar to Section 377 of the Austrian Commercial Code, but mixed the time-frames of Article 38 and 39 of the CISG by stating that Article 38 prescribed a duty to examine and give notice. Even allowing a period of two months after delivery of the goods for discovery of the lack of conformity, the reasonable time period for notification was considered shorter than the start of July until the end of July.[250]

This confusion of the two provisions of the CISG, well known from German practice, makes it difficult to discern within which period of time the Court considered notification timely after discovery of the non-conformity. The guidelines for the consideration of reasonable time are not divulged by the Court, but the conclusion is certainly similar to the domestic time-frame and the time-frames from the more restrictive German practice.

2. The Netherlands and Belgium

Although uniform in relation to some legislation, the Benelux Countries (Belgium, Netherlands and Luxembourg) do not share all laws. But the trade relations have always been very close, and the Civil and Commercial Codes of Belgium and The Netherlands are both based on the Napoleonic codes and share many traits, as do the decentralized regional procedural systems. It therefore seems surprising that The Netherlands was the only Benelux-country to accede to the CISG soon after its drafting.[251] The CISG has only recently entered into force in Belgium, following an accession in October 1996.[252]

Feldkirch, 29 March 1994 [5 Cg 176/92y = 64] <http://cisgw3.law.pace.edu/cases/940329a3.html> (Pace).

[249] *See id.*

[250] The Court stated: "Werde dem Beklagten eine Frist von zwei Monaten für die Erkennung des Mangels zugebilligt, hätte spätestens Anfang Juli der Mangel erkannt werden müssen. Da er aber erst gegen Ende Juli nach dem Urlaub gerügt habe, könne er sich weder auf Gewährleistungs- noch auf Schadenersatzansprüche berufen." *Id.*

[251] Netherlands signed the Convention on May 29, 1981, ratified it on December 13, 1990, and it entered into force in Dutch law on January 1, 1992. *See Status of Conventions, supra* note 7.

[252] Belgium acceded the Convention on October 31, 1996, and it entered into force on November 1, 1997. Note that the third Benelux-country, Luxembourg, acceded to the Convention on January 30 1997, with entry into force on February 1, 1998. *See id.*

There have been two reported instances of application of the CISG before Belgian Courts. Both were before the entry into force of the Convention and were decided by way of Article 1(1)(b), when the rules of Belgian private international law pointed to the laws of a Contracting State, Italy.[253] One of these cases concerned Article 39(1).[254] The notice in question was given to the seller nine months after delivery of shoes, and not surprisingly the Court found this unsatisfactory as the non-conformity should have been discovered and communicated sooner.[255] The Court did not distinguish between the time-frames in Articles 38 and 39, and it is hard to glean what is considered reasonable time, as the Court did not say when the non-conformity ought to have been discovered, nor when notice should have been given.

In Dutch practice, Article 39(1) has been applied several times. The first time was in 1990 in an interim decision from District Court of Dordrecht, which adjourned to give the buyer time to prove that timely and specific notice was in fact given in connection with the sale of textiles.[256] A year later, in the (in)famous "maggots-in-mozzarella" judgment,[257] the District Court of Roermond assessed a notice given two months after delivery of frozen mozzarella for resale. The Court declared that the buyer could not rely solely on the complaints of his customers, but should have noticed the maggots in the frozen mozzarella sooner by inspecting a defrosted sample of the cheese.[258] Moreover, a speedier notice of non-conformity was required since the goods were perishable foodstuff. Regrettably, the Court did not elaborate on what it considered a speedy notification. The case was adjourned to give the buyer a chance to prove that the maggots existed in the cheese at the time of shipment — if successful the Court would infer that

[253] By appointing the law of the seller's country pursuant to art. 4 of the 1955 Hague Convention on the Law Applicable to International Sales of Goods, to which Belgium is a party. *See* Hague Convention of June 15, 1955 on the Law Applicable to International Sales of Goods of June 15, 1955, 510 U.N.T.S. 147.

[254] *See* Trib. De Comm. Bruxelles, 5 October 1994. [RR 1.205/93] (Belgium) (UNILEX) <http://cisgw3.law.pace.edu/cases/941005b1.html> (Pace).

[255] *See id.*

[256] Rb Dordrecht, 21 November 1990 [2762/1989](Netherland) (UNILEX), <http://cisgw3.law.pace.edu/cases/901121n1.html> (Pace), (regarding the sale of textiles from a French seller to a Dutch buyer).

[257] Rb Roermond, 19 December 1991 [900366] (Netherland) (UNILEX), <http://cisgw3.law.pace.edu/cases/911219n1.html> (Pace).

[258] *See id.*

the seller "knew or ought to have known" of the non-conformity and bar reliance on Article 38 and 39 by way of Article 40.

Other Dutch judgments concerned a notice given three months after discovery of the non-conformity which was not considered timely,[259] and a case where the buyer did not specify a notice at all.[260] Neither case expanded on the determination of reasonable time.

These judgments from Belgian and Dutch practice contribute to the determination of reasonable time with the paradigms that perishable goods require swifter notice. A buyer re-selling the goods cannot rely on his customers to discover the non-conformity when he should have discovered it himself, and three months or more cannot be considered reasonable time. There is nothing surprising or controversial in these findings, and certainly no reason to suspect any undue influence of domestic law.

3. France and the Alleged Buyer-Friendly Approach

The French legal system is one of civil law, with roots in the Napoleonic Code Civile. The procedural system is uncomplicated. Depending on the subject matter, a case is heard in the first instance in local Inferior or Superior Court (tribunal d'instance/tribunal de grande instance), or in the case of commercial merchants in Commercial Court (tribunal de commerce). Appeal is to the local Court of Appeals (cour d'appel), and further appeals are to the Supreme Court (cour de cassation).

French domestic law is traditionally more buyer-friendly than that of most other European countries.[261] This is reflected by Article 1648 of the French Code Civil, which concerns the buyer's duty to notify the seller of a lack of conformity with a brief delay ("*dans un bref delai*"). In its interpretation of this Article, the Courts have allowed the buyer up to 2-3 years to give timely notices of non-conformity.[262] Given such generous notice timeframes and traditional buyer-friendliness in domestic law, it would perhaps

---

[259] *See* Rb Roermond, 6 May 1993 [920159] (Netherlands)(UNILEX), <http://cisgw3.law.pace.edu/cases/930506n1.html> (Pace) (regarding the sale of 20 kettles from an Italian seller to a Dutch buyer, 4 of which were defective).

[260] *See* Rb Gravenhage, 7 June 1995 [94/0670] (Netherlands)(UNILEX), <http://cisgw3.law.pace.edu/cases/950607n1.html> (Pace).

[261] See VENEZIANO, *supra* note 67, at 52, where she refers to France as "a country whose domestic law is traditionally more sympathetic to the buyer. . . ." *Id.*

[262] *See* Schwenzer, *supra* note 76, at 362 (in German version). "Dasselbe gilt für Frankreich, wo die Gerichte im Rahmen des Art. 1648 C.C. oft fristen von zwei bis drei Jahren

be a fair assumption that some of this might "rub off" on the interpretation of reasonable time as understood by Article 39(1). Such an influence from domestic law would jeopardize the uniform application of the CISG, and should be dissuaded if unearthed.

France was one of the first countries to adopt the CISG, and expressed no reservations against the provisions of the Convention.[263] There have been many judgments before French Courts dealing with the CISG,[264] but, the extent of French CISG caselaw regarding Article 39(1) is rather meager. In fact, to date there have been only two reported judgments which determine the extent of "reasonable time."

The first judgment concerned the sale of unwrapped cheese for resale. The cheese was not wrapped as required by French standards, and the buyer notified the seller of this non-conformity within one month after delivery of the goods and claimed damages.[265] The Court did not determine when the non-conformity was discovered or should have been discovered, but as the non-conformity was an obvious one the discovery was presumed to be almost immediately after delivery. The Court found that notice was given within reasonable time, but did not elaborate on its reason. When compared to other judgments from other Courts and Tribunals, this may appear slightly more buyer-friendly. For instance, it would be hard to imagine such a notice being considered acceptable by some of the more "seller-friendly" German Courts.[266]

---

für die Klageerhebung annerkennen," *Id.* (with reference to Gestin, Gestin/Desché and Audit in n. 62).

[263] France signed the Convention on August 2, 1981, ratified it on August 6, 1982, and it entered into force in French law on January 1, 1988. *See Status of Conventions, supra* note 7.

[264] According to Pace <http:cisgw3.law.pace.edu/cases>, there have been 39 French judgments concerning the CISG to date, several of these first instance judgments, however, have overlooked the Convention.

[265] *See* CA de Grenoble, 13 September 1995 [93/4126] (France)(UNILEX). <http://cisgw3.law.pace.edu/cases/950913f1.html> (Pace).

[266] Briefer notice-periods have been judged untimely by German Courts in: LG Mönchengladbach of 22 May 1992 <http://cisgw3.law.pace.edu/cases/920522g1.html> (Pace), OLGZ Düsseldorf ,12 March 1993 <http://cisgw3.law.pace.edu/cases/930312g1.html> (Pace), Amtsgericht Riedlingen, 21 October 1994 <http://cisgw3.law.pace.edu/cases/941021g1.html> (Pace), LG Landshut, 5 April 1995 <http://cisgw3.law.pace.edu/cases/950405g1.html> (Pace), OLGZ Stuttgart, 21 August 1995 <http://cisgw3.law.pace.edu/cases/950821g1.html> (Pace), and OLGZ Karlsruhe, 25 June 1997 <http://cisgw3.law.pace.edu/cases/970625g1.html> (Pace).

This judgment can be said to be in accordance with the "noble month" guideline applied in some German caselaw. Although the goods in the present case were perishable, which would normally induce a stricter time-frame, the buyer wanted damages and not avoidance. This would, according to some scholars, induce a longer time-frame. This judgment cannot *per se* be said to express any undue influence of French domestic buyer-friendly law.

The latest reported Article 39(1) judgment from French caselaw concerns a rather unique case in the sale of production machines.[267] Notice was found to be undoubtedly timely although the first substantiated notice of non-conformity after delivery was made three months after delivery was complete.[268] The non-conformities in question had been discovered *before* delivery during the buyer's inspection of the production of the machinery, and notice of non-conformity had been given immediately after the inspection in connection with the buyers Article 46 claim for performance. Notice was thus timely as it was given within reasonable time after discovery, regardless of the fact that discovery was before delivery. Moreover, based on the problems discovered during inspection, the buyer had taken possession of the goods under conditions of repair and upkeep by the seller's technicians. This judgment certainly does not evidence any buyer-friendliness, as the seller is not jeopardized in any way by the buyer's notice-giving.

4. Switzerland

The Swiss legal procedural system is a somewhat complicated one, due to the fact that the different ethnic sections of Switzerland have slightly different Courts. The Country is divided into Cantons and Districts, each of which has its own Courts. The Appellate Court decides cases based on the case-matter and the location of the Canton. The Supreme Court in Lausanne is the highest instance. In addition to this, there is a special Court for commercial matters in the Canton of Zürich.[269]

---

267 *See* CA Versailles, 29 January 1998 [95/1222] (France)(UNILEX),<http://cisgw3.law.pace.edu/cases/980129f1.html> (Pace).

268 *See id.*

269 The Swiss Courts are: Schweizerisches Bundesgericht (Supreme Court), Bezirksgericht, Pretore, Zivilgericht, Tribunal civil, Richteramt (District Courts), Apellationsgericht and Obergericht (Appellate Courts), Tribunal cantonal/Kantonsgericht (Canton Court) and finally the Handelsgericht (Commercial Court).

Although Canton law may vary throughout Switzerland, federal law applies identically. According to the federal Code of Obligations Article 370(3), notice of non-conformity must be given to the seller immediately after discovery (*"aussitôt qu'il en a connaissance"*) in Commercial trade. This period is interpreted by the Swiss Supreme Court to be a flexible one, but nonetheless usually quite brief (at least under 3 weeks).[270] The cut-off period for all claims is one year after delivery according to Article 210 of the Code of Obligations, unless the seller has sold the goods in bad faith or extended a longer period of guarantee.

The CISG did not enter into force in Switzerland until 1991, but no reservations against the provisions of the Convention were taken.[271] There has not been many cases regarding the CISG: The Swiss Supreme Court had one opportunity to interpret the Convention, and this case did not concern Article 39(1).[272] A total of 5 cases concerning the notification requirement have appeared before other Swiss Courts.

The first, concerning the sale of furniture, was decided by a Swiss-Italian District Court.[273] Similar to the above mentioned Dutch "maggots-in-mozzarella" judgment, the Court found that the buyer had violated his examination duty in Article 38 by relying on customer complaints, and that since the duty to examine the goods in accordance with Article 38 regulated the time from which a reasonable-time notice is to be given according to Article 39(1), notice given 4 months after delivery was not timely.[274] Apart from laying down strict guidelines for the examination duty in Article 38, this judgment also ensured that there would be no confusion in Swiss practice as to the time-frames of Articles 38 and 39. In its deliberations for the

[270] *See* Swiss Supreme Court of 12 May 1981 [107 II 172] *Gischig vs. Frölich Flachdach AG*, wherein the court states that the time-frame is considered "large" to let the buyer be sure of the consequences of the non-conformity, but that 3 weeks is the maximum in the present case. A more recent Supreme Court judgment of 17 February 1992 [118 II 142] refers to this paradigm and upholds it.

[271] Switzerland acceded the Convention on February 21, 1990, and it entered into force in Swiss law on March 1, 1991. *See Status of Conventions, supra* note 7.

[272] *See* Schweizerisches Bundesgericht of 18 January 1996 <http://cisgw3.law.pace.edu/cases/960118s1.html> (Pace) (In the case of *Firma T. S.r.l vs. Firma S. AG*, regarding Arts. 57(1) and 58).

[273] *See* Pretura delle guirisdizione di Locarno-Campagna, 27 April 1992 [6252] (Switzerland)(UNILEX),<http://cisgw3.law.pace.edu/cases/920427s1.html> (Pace), (regarding the sale of furniture from an Italian seller to a Swiss buyer).

[274] *See id.*

determination of notice, the Court stated that the provisions of Article 38 and 39 should apply more strictly to contracts between merchants, referencing a domestic scholar's writing on Swiss law.[275] This consideration does not seem in keeping with the spirit of the Convention,[276] especially since the Convention's main area of application is contracts between merchants. The Court concerned itself with how the late notice *actually* compromised the seller, and concluded that the buyer should have notified and permitted him to cure the defect, which he easily could have.

A more recent Swiss judgment on Article 39(1) regarding the sale of an isolation-tank[277] found it unnecessary to determine whether the buyer should have investigated the goods more thoroughly under Article 38, as the buyer admitted that he knew of the non-conformity for about four weeks before notifying the seller. The Court stated that it did not find this notice period reasonable, but did not mention which guideline it applied or which factors influenced its decision. However, the Court linked the Article 39(1) time-frame to the avoidance notification time-frame in Article 49(2)(b)(i),[278] which would seem a paradox since the buyer could only avoid the contract if he were permitted to rely on the non-conformity — which he was not.

Another Swiss judgment regarding Article 39(1), concerned the sale of furniture, and the burden of proof of notice-giving.[279] The Court stated that this burden was the buyer's since this is implicit in Articles 38 and 39, and reflects a general principle underlying the CISG in accordance with Article 7(2). It is unclear whether these first four Swiss judgments have been influenced by domestic law in the findings regarding Article 39(1), as they

---

[275] The Court stated: "Nella specie inoltre le parti sono entrambe commercianti e pertanto il dovere di verifica si impone con più rigore," with reference to Bucher in, OBLIGANTIONENRECHT, BESONDERER TEIL 93 (3rd ed.)

[276] According to the drafters, the Uniform Law applies irrespective of the commercial or civil character of the parties. *See* UN Doc. A/CN.9/52, ¶ 94.

[277] *See* HG Zürich, 26 April 1995 (HG 920670) (Switzerland) (UNILEX), <http://cisgw3.law.pace.edu/cases/950426s1.html> (Pace), (regarding the sale of an isolation-tank (fitness device) from a Swiss seller to a German buyer).

[278] Art. 49(2)(b)(i) provides: "(2) [t]he buyer loses the right to declare the contract avoided unless he does so: (b): in respect of any breach other than late delivery, within a reasonable time: (i): after he knew or ought to have known of the breach."

[279] *See* HG Zürich, 9 September 1993 (HG 930138 U/H93) (Switzerland) (UNILEX),<http://cisgw3.law.pace.edu/cases/930909s1.html> (Pace), (regarding the sale of furniture from an Italian seller to a Swiss buyer).

do not refer to the basis of their determination. The interpretations are certainly in accordance with Swiss domestic law, but they are not contrary to other applications of Article 39(1), so domestic influence should not be inferred. It is unfortunate that a distinction between commercial and civil parties has been introduced, with reference to a domestic scholar.

The most recent reported Swiss judgment on Article 39(1) from Obergericht Kanton Luzern in 1997 contained multiple references to CISG scholars.[280] The case concerned the sale of pharmaceutical goods (blood tubes), and the Court stated that there was an Article 38 duty to inspect the goods, despite their sterile packaging, and that Article 39(1) notice was to be given within a "noble month" after the non-conformities should have been discovered, with reference to Schwenzer.[281] This judgment mirrored the development in German law of favoring the "noble month" as a starting point for reasonable time, but as it stands alone (so far), it cannot yet be called a trend in Swiss law. Although reference in the above judgment to CISG scholars is a good path to removing doubts of undue influence, the best way to establish an international approach more in keeping with other determinations of reasonable time is to analyze current international practice in the determination of a CISG issue.

5. Italy and the International Approach

The roots of the Italian legal system date back to Roman law and Emperor Justinian's "*Corpus iuris civilis,*" which relied on early laws of contract similar to those applied today. It is a system of civil law which is fully codified in statutory law and unrelated to caselaw.[282] The procedural system of Italy is very similar to that of Germany, with regional jurisdiction at first instance and on appeal, and with one Supreme Court (situated in Rome). There are no specific Commercial Courts in Italy, all civil cases are heard by civil Courts.[283] A judge is not bound to follow the precedent of a superior

[280] Obergericht Kanton Luzern, 8 January 1997 [11 95 123/357] (Switzerland) (UNILEX), <http://cisgw3.law.pace.edu/cases/970108s1.html> (Pace), (which contains numerous references to KOMMENTAR ZUM EINHEITLICHEN UN-KAUFRECHT (Ernst von Caemmerer & Peter Schlechtriem eds., 1990)).

[281] *See* Obergericht Kanton Luzern, 8 January 1997 [11 95 123/357] (Switzerland) (UNILEX), <http://cisgw3.law.pace.edu/cases/970108s1.html> (Pace).

[282] *See* ROBERTO BARBALICH, ITALY — PRACTICAL COMMERCIAL LAW 1 (1991).

[283] The Italian Civil Courts are: Corte Suprema di Cassazione (Supreme Court), Corte di Appello (Court of Appeals), and Tribunale Civile (District Court).

Court (except where the findings of the Supreme Court must be followed under the "principle of law" where a specific case is remitted for final judgment in a lower Court). However, in practice the guidelines of the Supreme Court to the interpretation of the law are often considered by lower Courts.

The Civil Code of Italy of 1942 is a modernized version of the Napoleonic Civil Code. It provides, in Article 1495, that notice of non-conformity be given within a period of eight days after the lack of conformity with the goods is discovered, there is a one year cut-off period from the date of delivery.[284] Italy was one of the first countries to adopt the CISG, and did so without reservations.[285] Nevertheless, there is not a vast amount of Italian rulings on the CISG. To date there has been a total of eight reported judgments dealing directly with the CISG, and two containing *obiter* references to the CISG. Only one of these judgments concerns Article 39(1) and the determination of reasonable time.

In a 1966 judgment of the Tribunale Civile of Cuneo, the seller delivered sports clothes to the buyer which were in French sizes rather than Italian sizes as agreed upon.[286] Notice of this lack of conformity was given twenty-three days after delivery of the goods, and the Court clearly stated that the non-conformity was easily discernible, and that this would reduce the period of time acceptable from the date of delivery, i.e., technically reduce the time period acceptable under Article 38 and set the "ought to have discovered" time closer to the time of delivery.[287] The Court did not actually state when the non-conformity should have been discovered under Ar-

---

[284] *See* 6 MARIO BELTRAMO ET AL., THE ITALIAN CIVIL CODE, 75 (M. Beltramo ed., 2d ed. 1993) "Time limits and conditions of action. The buyer forfeits the right of warranty if he fails to notify the seller of the defects in the thing within eight days from their discovery, unless a different time limit is established by the parties or by law. Notification is not necessary if the seller has acknowledged the existence of the defect or if he has concealed it. In all cases, the action is prescribed in one year from delivery; but the buyer who is sued for performance of the contract can always plead the warranty, provided that the defect in the thing was notified within eight days from discovery and within one year from delivery." *Id.*

[285] Italy signed the Convention on September 30, 1981, ratified it on December 11, 1986, and it entered into force in Italian law on January 1, 1988. *See Status of Conventions, supra* note 7.

[286] Trib. di Cuneo, 31 January 1996 (45/96) (Italy) (UNILEX), (*Sport D'Hiver di Genevieve Culet v. Ets. Louyes et Fils*) <http://cisgw3.law.pace.edu/cases/960131i3.html> (Pace).

[287] *See id.*

ticle 38, so when it concluded that twenty-three days after delivery was not an acceptable notice time-frame, it is not easy to discern what the actual time-frame for notice-giving after discovery is. It would, however, seem safe to conclude that notice was not timely when delayed about twenty days after discovery of the lack of conformity. This was not considered a reasonable time by the Tribunale Civile. In determining reasonable time, the judge turned to caselaw from other countries on the same issue as precedents.[288]

By referring to international case law, the judge not only obtained guidelines for the determination of reasonable time, but also helped secure the uniformity of the Convention. If all domestic judgments on the CISG looked to international as well as domestic CISG rulings in the determination of CISG issues, a greater congruency of the Convention's international practice would be ensured.[289] Sadly, this is not so, although the practitioner is obliged to consider the decisions rendered in other Contracting States (and non-Contracting States applying the CISG) by way of Article 7(1). Nevertheless, a reference to foreign CISG practice is rare in domestic CISG caselaw.[290] There is however one forum where a transnational approach to CISG issues is almost certain. That forum is the International Arbitral Tribunal.

C. The International Arbitral Tribunal

The Arbitral Tribunal is an instance of justice that is becoming increasingly popular in international commercial law. As the primary form of alternative dispute resolution it presents an easily enforceable solution,[291]

[288] *See id.*

[289] *See* GILES, *supra* note 245, at 35. "How should Courts, in the day-to-day administration of justice, proceed. . . ? The best hope, it is generally recognized, is the awareness of foreign precedents and the willingness and ability to follow them" on uniformity in general." *Id.*

[290] Of the 87 cases analyzed for the present paper, there have been only two: the present one from Trib. Civile from Cueno and the above judgment from OLG Canton Luzern, 8 January 1997, <http://cisgw3.law.pace.edu/cases/970108s1.html> (Pace). Prof. Ferrari cites Trib. Civile of Cuneo, 31 January 1996 <http://cisgw3.law.pace.edu/cases/960131i3.html> (Pace), as the only one of nearly 300 CISG cases published by Michael Will which refers to international caselaw. *See* Franco Ferrari, *Remarks on the Autonomy and the Uniform Application of the CISG on the Occasion of its Tenth Anniversary, in* INTERNATIONAL CONTRACT ADVISOR, 41, n. 33 (1991).

[291] See JOSEPH M. LOOKOFSKY, TRANSNATIONAL LITIGATION AND COMMERCIAL ARBITRATION: A COMPARATIVE ANALYSIS OF AMERICAN, EUROPEAN, AND INTERNATIONAL LAW 560 (1992),

which is often (mistakenly) perceived as more confidential, faster, less expensive and more flexible than litigation.[292] It provides businessmen from different legal systems with the framework for a procedure that is mutually acceptable, and which avoids the potential pitfalls of unfamiliar procedures, laws, and mentalities.[293]

Regardless of where the case is physically heard (ICC in Paris or elsewhere, Commercial Chambers in Hungary, Vienna or Hamburg, etc.), the forum of arbitration is legally stateless, with no domestic law or domestic practice to guide or misguide its work.[294] It is therefore the ideal forum for the practice of the uniform CISG, as all precedents in caselaw from Courts applying this law (although not technically binding) are equal and will be considered under the uniformity of the Convention, in accordance with Article 7(1), in the determination of terms.

Since international commercial law often concerns the CISG, and since arbitration is a popular forum in this area of the law, there have been many Arbitral Awards concerning the CISG, which seems a popular Convention amongst commercial law arbitrators. There can even be said to be a slight "pro-CISG construction" in some arbitration regimes where the choice of law is concerned.[295] This is hardly surprising, as the CISG represents a regulation of trade law in its "purest" form, without any domestic

---

who states "[I]ndeed, the fact that many states enforce arbitral awards far more readily than foreign judgments is itself a very good reason for choosing the arbitration route." *Id.*

[292] Prof. Lookofsky criticizes this perception: "In actual fact, international arbitration is sometimes a slow-moving business, and it rarely comes cheap." *Id.* at 559.

[293] *See generally* Albert Jan Van Den Berg, The New York Arbitration Convention of 1958 — Towards a Uniform Judicial Interpretation 1 (1981).

[294] Although the Tribunal is technically stateless, the arbitrator or arbitrators are not; as such they may naturally be influenced by their cultural, legal and economic backgrounds.

[295] In the regime of the International Chamber of Commerce [hereinafter the ICC], the CISG is often taken as a reflection of trade usage and used directly even if neither buyer nor seller reside in countries which are party to the convention, as a reflection of *lex mercatoria. See e.g.,* ICC International Court of Arbitration 5713/1989 <http://cisgw3.law.pace.edu/cases/895713i1.html> (Pace) and 7331/1994 <http://cisgw3.law.pace.edu/cases/947331i1.html> (Pace), both of which concern Art. 39. Note also, that since the CISG is technically part of domestic law, reference in a choice-of-law clause in an international sales contract to the domestic laws of a specific country party to the Convention will mean a reference to the CISG, unless the Convention is explicitly exempted. *See, e.g.,* ICC International Court of Arbitration 7565/1994 <http://

compromises or taints while still representing internationally accepted provisions — it can be said to represent *lex mercatoria.*

Correspondingly, there are many CISG rulings reported from the Arbitration regime, and there are several rulings concerning Article 39. Surprisingly, however, not many of these reported cases have had the opportunity to examine or rule on the term "reasonable time."

The first reported ICC Award on Article 39(1) concerned a notice of lack of conformity given to the seller 8 days after the publication of an expert report commissioned before the goods were delivered.[296] The award does not identify the type of goods that were involved. The arbitrators found a period of eight days after discovery of the non-conformity to constitute reasonable time in accordance with Article 39(1),[297] and found that the lack of conformity could not have been discovered sooner.[298] They did not comment on what they would usually consider reasonable time, nor give any guidelines for their conclusions in the present case.

In a 1995 award from the Hungarian Chamber of Commerce,[299] the sole arbitrator assessed a time-frame of 32 days after discovery of non-conformity of waste containers in the light of Article 39(1). He considered "the speed in which the parties were used to carry on their relationship under the contract,"[300] and concluded that 32 days was not reasonable time as understood by Article 39(1). This approach is reminiscent of Schwenzer's noble month — the arbitrator did not dismiss a period of about a month, but used the individual circumstances of the case to determine that notice should reasonably have been given sooner. The factor introduced to reduce the acceptable period of time was an entirely applicable one. The parties' re-

cisgw3.law.pace.edu/cases/947565i1.html> (Pace) and 7660/JK of August 23, 1994 <http://cisgw3.law.pace.edu/cases/947660i1.html> (Pace), both concerning Art. 39.

296 See ICC Int. Ct. of Arb. 5713/1989 <http://cisgw3.law.pace.edu/cases/895713i1.html> (Pace), where the CISG applied as a reflection of trade usage although neither the buyer's nor the seller's countries were parties to the Convention.

297 In any event, the seller could not rely on Art. 39 as he could not have been unaware of the non-conformity in accordance with art. 40.

298 *See* ICC Int. Ct. of Arb. 5713/1989 <http://cisgw3.law.pace.edu/cases/895713i1.html> (Pace).

299 Hungarian Chamber of Commerce and Industry, Ct of Arb. Award of 5 December 1995 [VB/94131] <http://cisgw3.law.pace.edu/cases/951205h1.html> (Pace) (regarding the sale of waste containers from an Austrian seller to a Hungarian buyer).

300 Quoted from the abstract of the judgment printed in UNILEX 1996.

liance on previous speedy negotiations and communications was a valid concern when determining the reasonableness of a communicated notice, and thus should be considered in the light of Article 9(1).[301]

In a 1994 ICC Award concerning the sale of cowhides,[302] the Tribunal considered an agreed notice time-frame of one month after delivery, and pronounced that it would be upheld since it was reasonable.[303] The Tribunal did not pronounce on why it considered one month reasonable, nor on it's interpretation of Articles 38 and 39, nor did it mention any factors that may have influenced the assessment of reasonableness. Other awards mentioning Article 39(1) refer to notices the timeliness of which the seller has not disputed,[304] and also to a notice that is over the 2 year cut-off period in Article 39(2).[305]

Finally, it is interesting to note that in 1994 a Tribunal in Vienna[306] considered an agreement for the sale of two lots of rolled metal sheets,

---

301 Art. 9(1) provides: "The parties are bound by any usage to which they have agreed and by any practices which they have established between themselves."

302 See ICC Ct of Arb. 7331 (1994) <http://cisgw3.law.pace.edu/cases/947331i1.html> (Pace), concerning the sale of cowhides from Yugoslavia to Italy.

303 Regardless of the fact that the CISG applies in this case as a reflection of trade usage, it is peculiar that the Tribunal stated that it upheld the agreed notice time-frame since it considered it in accordance with arts. 38 and 39. Surely, even if it had not been considered reasonable by the tribunal, the agreed time-frame for notification would have had to be upheld in any event by way of art. 6 of the CISG which allows parties to derogate from the Convention, or by way of the general principle of *pacta sunt servanda.*

304 See ICC Ct of Arb.7565 (1994) <http://cisgw3.law.pace.edu/cases/947565i1.html> (Pace), which primarily concerned the contractual period of guarantee permitted in art. 39(2) and ICC Ct. of Arb. 7660/JK (1994) (Pace), which pronounced that a prescription period of commencement of legal action is not relevant to art. 39(2) or any other provision of the CISG, but is to be decided in accordance with otherwise applicable domestic law. Neither judgment discusses the reasonable time of the actual notices of non-conformity given.

305 See Schiedsgericht der Handelskammer Hamburg, Teilschiedsspruch of 21 March 1996 <http://cisgw3.law.pace.edu/cases/960321g1.html> (Pace), regarding the sale of Chinese goods from Hong Kong to Germany.

306 See Internationales Schiedsgericht der Bundeskammer der gewerblichen Wirtshaft, Wien SCH-4318 <http://cisgw3.law.pace.edu/cases/940615a4.html> (Pace) and SCH-4366 <http://cisgw3.law.pace.edu/cases/940615a3.html> (Pace) of 15 June 1994 regarding the sale of metal sheets from Austria to Germany. The former award concerns the notification and estoppel.

which derogated from Article 38 by prescribing that the goods must be examined "immediately upon delivery," and from Article 39 by prescribing that notice must be given "without delay" and within two months of delivery at the latest.[307] In the assessment of the two notices given (three and six months after delivery), the Arbitrator held the seller estopped from claiming that the notice was not timely given with regard to the first notice,[308] since the seller had given the buyer reason to believe that he considered the claim justified despite the untimely notice. With regard to the second notice, the Court did not find that there was sufficient evidence to conclude that the seller had intended to waive the right to rely on the untimeliness.[309]

All in all, on the basis of existing practice, it is difficult to pinpoint a specific trend before arbitral tribunals concerning reasonable time. The approaches to determining the notices are very much in keeping with Schwenzer's "noble month," with periods of one month generally being considered reasonable, and various factors influencing the individual time-frames, but no arbitrator has yet referred directly to this guideline of international compromise. Moreover, the factor of regular speed of communication applied by the arbitrator in the 1995 award from Hungary is a relevant one, and one that focused on the fact that the notice requirement concerned communication. This should ideally be taken into account by all practitioners considering "reasonable time," as it is a subjective element unique for each individual case and determines the appropriateness of the notice given in the light of trade usage between the parties.

---

[307] The comment by Ferrari, *supra* note 38, at 109-10, that these awards are overdoing it when stating that 2 months are "reasonable," seems puzzling since this was the agreed time-frame for notification.

[308] This conclusion with respect to the former notice would seem to contradict the earlier mentioned German practice, according to which the seller's right to rely on the timeliness of the notice could not be implied by taking back the goods (OLG Düsseldorf of 12 March 1993), <http://cisgw3.law.pace.edu/cases/930312g1.html> (Pace), but only by directly accepting the notice (Bundesgerichthof of 25 June 1997 <http://cisgw3.law.pace.edu/cases/970625g2.html> (Pace).

[309] It is surprising that the arbitrator reaches this conclusion by inference that the principle of estoppel is a general principle which applies to the Convention via art. 7(2), and not by way of art. 8(2) and 8(3), which together would grant the buyer a right to rely on the reasonable conclusions that the negotiations for settlement represented acceptance of the timeliness of the notice.

IV. Predictions of Interpretations

With the CISG still a fairly young convention, there are many Contracting States with legal systems that have not yet had an opportunity to contribute to the determination of "reasonable time" by applying Article 39(1) before their Courts. Two of these legal systems are of particular interest, because they both concern countries with experience in the field of uniform sales law, namely the Danish (Scandinavian) and American legal systems.[310] The rulings of their domestic Courts are eagerly awaited, but in the meantime it would be interesting to take a brief look at these two legal systems and attempt to predict an outcome of possible applications of Article 39(1).

A. *Danish Law*

The Scandinavian countries (Norway, Sweden and Denmark), Iceland and to a certain degree Finland,[311] previously had a generally uniform sales act from 1906/1905, which the countries applied virtually identically.[312] In 1962, a committee for the drafting of a new Nordic Sales Act began. However, work was delayed, and upon completion of the CISG, the drafters were quick to seize the opportunity to be influenced by the provisions of this Convention as a standard "blueprint"[313] for uniform provisions on sales.[314]

[310] *See* Honnold, *supra* note 16, at 3. "Scandinavia and my country of fifty states have had a century or more of experience with uniform laws. These laws operate within a relatively homogenous legal and economic background; we are now concerned with a uniform law that is going into force in each inhabited continent and in settings with different economic systems, legal tradition and judicial practices." *Id.*

[311] Finland did not, to begin with, adhere to the Sales Act due to the Czar-regime, but gradually developed regulations corresponding to the Scandinavian Sales Act.

[312] Consumer law regulations are an exception, as they were introduced differently, from 1979 onwards.

[313] *See* Schlechtriem, *supra* note 26, at 1. Prof. Schlechtriem refers to the CISG as the blueprint of the new Swedish Sales Law (which is the new Nordic Sales Act).

[314] For further information on the new Nordic Sales Act, see Leif Sevón, *The New Scandinavian Codification on the Sale of Goods and the 1980 United Nations Convention on Contracts for the International Sale of Goods, in* Einheitliches Kaufrecht und Nationales Obligationenrecht (Peter Schlechtriem ed., 1987).

The new Nordic Sales Act has become incorporated in Finland, Norway and Sweden almost uniformly,[315] whereas Denmark has not yet adopted it.

With regard to notification of non-conformity, Section 32(1) of the Nordic Sales Act is, essentially, a reflection of Article 39(1).[316] The Nordic Sales Act represents two major changes from the former Scandinavian Sales Act concerning the notification.[317] One is the fact that the latter does not distinguish between commercial and civil parties in trade, and the second is the wording of the commercial time-frame from immediately (*"straks"*/ *"genast"*) to within reasonable time (*"inden rimelig tid"*/*"inom skälig* [318] tid").[319]

The current Danish Sales Act, which is based upon the former Scandinavian Sales Act, imposes a duty in Section 52 for the commercial buyer to notify the seller immediately (*"straks"*) after he discovers or ought to have discovered the non-conformity. Despite its linguistic implications, this pe-

[315] The Nordic Sales Act became incorporated in Finland in 1987, Norway in 1988 and Sweden in 1989, respectively. Norwegian Law has incorporated provisions regarding consumer sales in the Sales Act, whereas Swedish and Finnish Law has a separate law for consumer sales.

[316] *See* OLE LANDO, UDENRIGSHANDELENS KONTRAKTER 353 (1991), which states "Den nye nordiske kbl. pålægger ligesom CISG art. 39(1) køberen at give meddelelse om mangelen inden rimelig tid efter, at han har eller burde have opdaget den. Køberen skal samtidig angive, hvori manglen består, § 32(1). Det er ligesom efter CISG ikke tilstrækkeligt at meddele at varen er dårlig. . . ." (The new Nordic Sales Act, like Art. 39(1) of the CISG, imposes a duty on the buyer to notify of non-conformity within reasonable time after he discovers it or ought to have discovered it. At the same time, the buyer must also specify the nature of the non-conformity. *See* § 32(1). Just like according to the CISG, it is not enough to communicate that the goods are bad).

[317] Other major changes throughout the Nordic Sales Act concern the abolition of the distinction between specific (Species) and generic (Genus) objects in sales, and the provisions on damages. *See* ANDERS VINDING KRUSE, KØBSRETTEN 135-41 (1992).

[318] The subtle nuance of the Swedish language in the difference between "skälig tid" (from the Nordic Sales Act) and "rimlig tid" (from the Swedish translation of art. 39(1) of the CISG) would not seem significant, albeit slightly puzzling.

[319] *See* CHRISTINA HULTMARK, REKLAMATION VID KONTRAKSBROTT 58-60 (1996). In the determination of "skälig tid," the author notes that the time-frame is influenced by the practical possibilities of the buyer for communication, any obstacles to notice giving, the seller's need for receiving swift notice, and whether a late notice has jeopardized a restriction of the consequences of a breach. *See id.*

riod of time is a flexible one, somewhat reminiscent of Section 377 from the HGB in German law. Danish caselaw indicates that the time-frame depends on the discernability of the non-conformity, any false information by the seller, trade usage and the possible processing of the goods,[320] and that it is usually interpreted to be a short period of time.[321]

All Scandinavian countries are signatories to the CISG in unison,[322] with reservations taken against Part II of the Convention (Formation of Contract) and application of the Convention to inter-Scandinavian sales.[323] The Norwegian ratification has been a unique approach of direct incorporation of the CISG into Norwegian law.[324]

---

[320] *See* Karnov Lovsamling på CD-Rom, note 334 to "Lovbekendtgørelse 1980.28 — Købelov."

[321] Pending the discernability of the defect, or other factors, the time-frame can be as brief as under four days after delivery (in a case of potatoes from 1946, *see* UfR 1946 p.719) where the goods are perishable. In a comparison between the examination and notification provisions of the CISG and Danish law, Prof. Lookofsky has stated that the CISG provisions seem less strict. *See* Joseph Lookofsky, *Nye Love: International Kobelov, in* 3 JURITSEN 106, 112 (1989), in which Lookofsky states "CISG-kravene til købers undersøgelsespligt, reklamation m.v. virker noget mildere end de tilsvarende KBL(I) krav." *Id.* [The CISG-requirements for the buyers examination, notification, etc., seem somewhat milder than the corresponding Sales Act requirements].

[322] All Nordic countries signed the Convention from 4-26 May 1981. Denmark acceded CISG on 14 February 1989, with entry into force on 1 March 1990. Sweden acceded on 15 December 1987, with entry into force on 1 January 1989. Finland acceded on 15 December 1987, with entry into force on 1 January 1989. Norway acceded on 20 July 1988 with entry into force in Norwegian law on 1 August 1989. *See Status of Conventions, supra* note 7.

[323] *See id.* "Upon ratifying the Convention, Denmark, Finland, Norway and Sweden declared in accordance with article 92(1) that they would not be bound by Part II of the Convention (Formation of the Contract). Upon ratifying the Convention, Denmark, Finland, Norway and Sweden declared, pursuant to article 94(1) and 94(2), that the Convention would not apply to contracts of sale where the parties have their places of business in Denmark, Finland, Sweden, Iceland or Norway." *Id.*

[324] The Norwegian implementation of the CISG is highly unorthodox, as it incorporates the Convention into the Norwegian Sales Act, creating some problems. For a critical analysis of the Norwegian incorporation of the CISG and the uniformity of the Convention, *see* Viggio Halstrøm, *Kjøpsretten Norsk Kjøpslov og Internasjonal Rettsenhetin, in* 4 TIDSSKRIFT FOR RETTSVITENSKAP 561 (1995). Halstrøm concludes with a hope that the Norwegian solution forms no precedents and is temporary. *Id.*

There is very little Danish practice of the CISG reported, and none regarding Article 39(1).[325] This lack of practice could easily fuel a suspicion that the CISG is being overlooked on a regular basis.[326] Any prediction on the outcome of a Danish Article 39(1) case is very uncertain. The judge's awareness of international precedents or international scholars will often be dependant on the claims of the parties. Even a CISG-conscious judge would have problems since there is currently no accepted international standard guideline for determining "reasonable time," it would be difficult for a judge to accept precedents cited by a party at face value, since they may be one-sided and taken out of context of other judgments which may not be easily obtainable. Again, the problem of accessibility of caselaw can prevent the congruency of international practice.

However, it would seem likely that a Danish judge assessing the time-frame for notice giving would look at the circumstances of the case and criteria such as the nature of the goods (i.e., Were they perishable or seasonal?), the commercial status of the parties (i.e., Who is to be protected most, if anyone?), deadlines or excuses for longer time-frames, and any indications that speedy notice was of the essence to the seller. These criteria have applied in domestic law as to the determination of the timeliness of notice of non-conformity, and may well apply to Article 39(1) as long as the Danish judge does not have the same (brief) vantage point.

When such a case surfaces, we can only hope that the judge will be aware of the need for uniformity, and that scholars may discern the judge's guidelines and reasoning for the determination of "reasonable time" in spite of the traditional (and lamentable) briefness of the Danish *ratio decidendi* in printed judgments.

---

[325] The Danish periodical of the judiciary, "Ugeskrift for Retsvæsen" (UfR), reports only one judgment concerning the CISG (UfR 1996, p. 616 regarding Article 57). This may in part be due to the fact that CISG cases are heard solely in the smaller District Courts (Byretterne), whose judgments are rarely reported.

[326] There are certainly some case which border on overlooking the CISG, see the Danish Supreme Court judgment in UfR 1989, p. 713, concerning the sale of tinned tomatoes from Germany to a Danish supermarket, via a Danish middleman. Although the case concerned the contract between the two Danish parties (the middleman and the supermarket), the contract between the German supplier and the middleman was also analyzed. The Supreme Court did not apply the CISG to this contract, or state any deliberations as to why it should not apply.

B. US Law

United States law varies between the different states, but with regard to sales law, the Uniform Commercial Code (UCC) establishes common ground that is applied equally in almost all states. UCC Article 2 concerns sales. According to Section 607(3)(a) of Article 2 of the UCC, a "buyer must within a reasonable time after he discovers or should have discovered any breach" communicate this to the seller or be barred from reliance hereupon, with two different provisions for rejection and revocation of acceptance requiring the same notification.[327] The duty to specify the defect is prescribed by UCC Section 2-605(1). The UCC is currently being revised and re-drafted, but the changes to the domestic duty to notify of non-conformity in the current draft from 1997 (which may not be indicative of the final draft) are not substantial as regards the time-frame.[328] Note,

[327] The two provisions are: UCC § 2-602(1), which prescribes a rejection of goods which have not yet been accepted "within a reasonable time" after delivery or tender, and UCC § 2-608(2), which prescribes that revocation of acceptance occurs "within a reasonable time after the buyer discovers or should have discovered the ground for it and before any substantial change in condition of the goods which is not caused by their own defects." The former notice would seem briefer as it commences sooner.

[328] The 1997 draft to art. 2 of the UCC (from the conference of Commissioner on Uniform Law on 25th July — 1st August 1997) provides:

§ 2-707(c): "If a tender has been accepted, the following rules apply: (1) The buyer, within a reasonable time after the buyer discovers or should have discovered a breach of contract, shall notify the party claimed against of the breach. However, a failure to give notice bars the buyer from a remedy only to the extent that the party entitled to notice establishes that it was prejudiced by the failure," and

§ 2-707(d): "A buyer has the burden of establishing a breach of contract with respect to goods accepted."

The 1997 draft has retained two provisions for rejection and revocation, § 2-703 and § 2-708 respectively. The only major difference in these to date is that § 2-703 amends the current § 2-602(1) so the time-frame commences from discovery (or when discovery ought to have taken place) instead of from delivery or tender. See draft articles:

§ 2-703(b): "A rejection under subsection (a) is not effective unless the buyer notifies the seller within a reasonable time after (tender of delivery) (the nonconformity was or should have been discovered)," and

§ 2-708(b): "To be effective, a buyer's acceptance must be revoked within a rea-

however, that the barring of remedies due to the lack of timely notice has been limited to cases where the seller establishes that he was "prejudiced by the failure" to give notice.[329]

The wording of the provision in the UCC is remarkably similar to that in Article 39(1) of the CISG. In the practice of the UCC, reasonable time has been interpreted to mean many things. The determination is influenced by such factors as the seller's opportunity for loss adjustment (which especially prompts the commercial buyer to be swift), the seller's opportunity to prepare for negotiation and litigation, and the reasonableness of a "limitation period" on reliance on non-conformity.[330] In some cases, notice has been deemed acceptable after a very long period of time,[331] but there are instances where circumstances prompt a swifter notice for consumers,[332] as well as for commercial traders.[333] Although similar criteria apply for the Article 39(1) determination of reasonable time, the time-frames allowed under the UCC would seem generally longer than those permitted under the CISG, but they fluctuate greatly.

The CISG entered into force in the United States in 1988,[334] and since then there have been several reported judgments on the CISG before US

---

sonable time after the buyer discovers or should have discovered the ground for it and before any substantial change in condition of the goods which is not caused by their own defects. The revocation is not effective until the buyer notifies the seller of it."

[329] *See* Draft § 2-207(c)(1), second full stop sentence, above. This proposition regarding art. 39 of the CISG was made by the US representative. *See* UN Doc. A/CN.9/WG.2/WP.10, ¶ 49, but was not drafted following objections from the Austrian representative.

[330] *See* J. White & R. Summers, Uniform Commercial Code 421-22, § 11-10 (2[d] ed. 1980).

[331] *See id.* at 421 n. 84 for examples of case law (notices held timely include periods of up to 60 weeks from time when underground gasoline tank began leaking 150 gallons per week, two and one-half years from delivery of non-additive oil which dealer knew was suspect, and six and one-half months after delivery of horse suffering from splints).

[332] *See, e.g.*, Hays Merchandise, Inc. v. Dale R. Dewey, 474 F.2d 270 (Wash. 1970), where a notice given after two months was held unreasonable since the goods were toys connected to the Christmas season. (This criteria of goods connected to a special season requiring swifter notice is well known from the regime of art. 39(1)).

[333] *See* A.C. Carter Inc. v. Boyer Potato Chips, 1969 WL 10993, where the seller's receipt of a letter notifying of non-conformity 12 days after delivery of non-conforming potatoes was untimely as the goods were perishable.

[334] The United States of America acceded the Convention on December 11, 1986, and it entered into force on January 1, 1988. *See Status of Conventions, supra* note 7.

courts. Sadly, however, there has been no practice to date on Article 39(1) of the CISG, and a definite answer to the question of whether the American Courts will apply the more generous UCC guidelines for this determination of reasonable time cannot be given.

However, although similar considerations as those applying to the Danish practitioner (above) apply for the US practitioner, there are certain indications that the uniformity of the CISG is in good hands before US courts. There is a general awareness of the CISG in US law,[335] and a recent judgment concerning parol evidence provided the first reported example of Internet source application to ensure thorough CISG research of caselaw from other jurisdictions.[336] Although previous US courts have not looked to international precedents when interpreting provisions of the CISG,[337] there are references to scholars who do, [338] and a precedent that states that domestic UCC caselaw is inapplicable in CISG cases.[339] Moreover, the courts have lengthy experience with uniform laws (through the practice of uniform state laws), which — along with the common-law roots of the legal system[340] — may in the long run prompt a judge applying Article 39(1) to look for international precedents.

---

335 For instance, the notes to the re-drafting of the UCC relate every article to the CISG and compares and equates the content.

336 *See* MCC Marble Ceramic Center, Inc. v. Ceramica Nuova D'Agostino, S.P.A., 144 F.3d 1384 (11th Cir. 1998), <http://cisgw3.law.pace.edu/cases/980629u1.html>, which refers to the Pace CISG database at <http:\www.cisg.law.pace.edu/> to ensure thorough research of International caselaw.

337 There has, as of yet, been no reported US CISG case in which the judge has referred directly to foreign caselaw. In Filanto S.p.A. v. Chilewich Int. Corp., 789 F. Supp. 1229 (1992); <http://cisgw3.law.pace.edu/cases/920414u1.html> (Pace), the judge observed the lack of US case law on the CISG, but did not consider turning to international precedents.

338 Reference to Prof. Honnold has been given in several cases, for instance in Delchi Carrier S.p.A v. Rotorex Corp., 71 F.3d 1024, 1028 (2d Cir. 1995). <http://cisgw3.law.pace.edu/cases/951206u1.html.> (Pace).

339 *See* Orbisphere Corp. v. United States, 13 Ct. Int.'l Trade 866 (1989). <http://cisgw3.law.pace.edu/cases/891024u1.html> (Pace).

340 With regard to the United Kingdom, the other principal common law country, note that the UK is not currently party to the Convention, and that there has been no reported practice on art. 39(1) through the application of the CISG via art. 1(1)(b). Although, as practitioners of common-law, the UK Courts might be expected to naturally

In other words, if there were an international guideline for the determination of reasonable time in the CISG, it would probably find its way into an American courtroom if Article 39(1) were at issue, especially if the Internet sources to the CISG are consulted, as in the above mentioned judgment. Unfortunately, with the variations in international practice (and theory) as plentiful as they are, even the most CISG-conscientious American judge would be stumped to find unified precedents or a perfect theory. The outcome of the deliberations would depend on which theory or caselaw is chosen. But it is highly probable that the more generous UCC guidelines for reasonable time will not apply in the CISG regime and will not unduly influence the determination.

V. Findings from Theory and Practice on "Reasonable Time"

A. *The Problems*

The problem of accessibility of international judgments and commentaries has, predictably, proven a significant one for the present paper. The determination of terms on an international scale and assessment of their uniformity is, at best, inaccurate without certainty that all interpretations of the terms in question have been analyzed. Furthermore, it will be impossible to be sure that all relevant caselaw has been included when it is uncertain whether all caselaw has been reported and made accessible.[341] Through necessity, the present paper has had to focus on the understanding of this provision in Europe.[342]

---

look for international precedents in the determination of "reasonable time," there may be a labeling problem in UK Law, due to art. 59 of the UK Sales of Goods Act of 1979, which provides: "Where a reference is made in this Act to a reasonable time the question what is a reasonable time is a question of fact." In other words, UK judges will presumably be conditioned to not looking to precedents in the determination of the timeframe, but solely applying the facts of the case. The practice of art. 39(1) from UK Courts is eagerly awaited, as is the accession of the UK to the Convention. *See supra* note 12.

341 The vastness of German practice has, moreover, tended to make the analysis of art. 39(1) very focused on this legal system

342 *See* Inta S.A. vs. MCS Officina Meccanica S.p.A. Cámera Nacional de Apelaciones en lo Commercial, 14 October 1993 (45626)(Argentina)(UNILEX) <http://cisgw3.law.pace.edu/cases/931014a1.html> (Pace). This is the only reported judgment

Additionally, there *must* be a multitude of cases throughout these jurisdictions that have overlooked the CISG, which have not been reported.[343] Even a perfect caselaw network could not prevent this "vicious circle:" if the CISG is not applied, the case is not reported as a CISG case, the mistake cannot be found and pointed out, and the practitioner will not be aware that a mistake has been made, and he will overlook the CISG in a similar case again. Nevertheless, some general conclusion on the available practice and theory of Article 39(1) can, at least, paint a picture of the provision.

B. The Vantage Point

Reported international practice has set different yardsticks for measuring the reasonableness of Article 39(1) time-frames. Some have been set at either a period of about one month (based on the "noble month" or traditional buyer-friendliness), or a more restrictive period of about a week (presumably based on the vantage point of more seller-friendly domestic law).

Regardless of the vantage point, however, it is the factors and considerations which determine the actual timeliness. Just like, in the realm of mathematics, the number five can be reached through subtracting five from ten or adding three to two, so the results of a determination of a reasonable time-frame can reach the same result regardless of the vantage point, through the assessment of the criteria. If the vantage point of the time-frame is already restrictive, then very few criteria should be permitted to restrict it even further, whereas a multitude of factors may advocate its extension. Opposite considerations apply to the generous vantage point. But the assessment of these factors can be tricky without a common vantage point in practice, and can easily result in arbitrary decisions. Moreover, it is especially difficult for buyer and seller alike to predict the notification time-frame where no set vantage point and evaluation of criteria has been established in caselaw.

---

concerning art. 39(1) which is not from Europe where the Court decided that there was no need to address the question of notice.

343 I find it especially hard to believe that throughout the now eight years that the CISG has applied in my country of study, Denmark, there have been only two interesting (report-worthy) cases concerning a contract for the international sale of goods.

C. *The Criteria*

There are numerous criteria for the determination of "reasonable time" that can be extrapolated from the available practice and theory. And countless more may surface — a multitude of factors may influence the determination of reasonable time, as long as it is a relevant and objective consideration which is not based on legal misconceptions.

1. The Contract and Customary Trade Usage

The contract and agreement between the parties is the most important aspect of their relations in the CISG regime, as the Convention serves only as a gap-filler. Furthermore, international trade usage and usage established between the parties is secondary only to the contract when gap-filling and interpreting provisions of the agreement.[344] In accordance with this, the nature of the contract between the parties is a deciding factor in the determination of notice giving, including not only instances where a time-frame is agreed, but also where it is implied. If, for example, the contract reflects a need for expediency, a swifter notice will be required. Moreover, the customary speed of communication between the parties helps determine when the seller is entitled to expect a notice, and the timeliness of the actual notice will be influenced by this, as this is considered a (binding) practice that the parties have established between themselves, in accordance with Article 9(1). Where neither the contract nor trade usage sheds any light on whether notice was given within reasonable time, other criteria may assist the practitioner in his determination, regardless of his vantage point.

2. Reducing the Generous Time-Frame

In reported practice, some of the more obvious factors to reduce a more generous time-frame have been the perishable nature of the goods (such as foodstuffs) and their affiliation with a particular season (such as fashion goods). Moreover, any knowledge that a buyer may have which would require a speedy notice to the seller (such as a deadline for publication) would require a speedier notice depending on the circumstances.

The factor suggested by scholars, that notice should be swifter where the buyer has chosen the remedy of avoidance, has not yet been mentioned

[344] The hierarchy of (1) Contract, (2) Trade usage, and (3) CISG gap-filling, is evidenced in arts. 6 and 9 of the Convention. *See also* LOOKOFSKY, *supra* note 14, at 48-9.

by the courts or tribunals as a deciding factor. Nonetheless, it is certainly a valid consideration that could have been taken into consideration. Surprisingly, closures and work-pressures in connection with seasonal holidays (such as Christmas) have been judged irrelevant in one case, but it could still be considered relevant in other circumstances. Although applied in one case, the factor of the parties commercial character should not be permitted to restrict the time-frame for notification. This would essentially apply to almost all CISG cases, as merchants are the rule and not the exception in CISG contracts. If this is to be taken into consideration, the factor of a "weaker" party's civil standing would be more suited to the extension of a restrictive time-frame vantage point.

3. Extending the Restrictive Time-Frame

In reported practice, there has been no evidence of any factors which have been pronounced as extending a restrictive vantage point. Moreover, there have not been many judgments that find the buyer's notice timely without applying a generous vantage point similar to the "noble month."

Where the buyer chooses a remedy of damages for the non-conformity, some scholarly writing states that the notice-period may be longer, whereas others disagree with this suggestion. There is as of yet no evidence that such a criteria has been decisive in caselaw.[345] Surprisingly, there are very few reported cases that speak on the question of whether an earlier notice would have made any *actual difference* to the seller's damage control and confirmation of the non-conformity, or if the time of notice has compromised the seller in any way. For courts choosing to prioritize the reasonableness of each case over the certainty of contracts stemming from a uniform guideline, without combining the two — such as the recent German courts rejection of the "noble month" — this is especially surprising. A duty for uniform application is sacrificed for individual fairness, which will be incomplete as long as the court does not examine the extent to which the notice actually compromised the seller. Moreover, there have not to date been any reported cases where the court stated that the behavior of

[345] However, there are indications that some Courts may have considered this. *See, e.g.*, LG Frankfurt, 9 December 1992 (3/3 O 37/92) (Germany)(UNILEX). <http://cisgw3.law.pace.edu/cases/921209g1.html.> (Pace). *See also* M. Caiato Roger v. La Societe francaise de factoring international factor France AS.F.F.C (SA), CA de Grenoble, 13 September 1995 (93/4126)(France)(UNILEX).

the seller was such that the buyer reasonably presumed the seller did not need a swift notice — although such a factor is entirely valid in the determination in accordance with Article 8(2).

All in all, the only criteria to date that have clearly influenced the timeframes set by the courts have been those which restrict the period of time. However, the courts do not always share the same yardstick for measuring reasonableness, and it would seem that uniform results in the application of Article 39(1) cannot be achieved.

VI. The Uniformity of Reasonable Time in Article 39(1) Caselaw

A. *Is Article 39(1) Applied Uniformly?*

In the quest for answers regarding legal science, the search for certainty may well prove futile — especially when attempting to determine the meaning of a term as flexible as "reasonable time." But there are, however, certain patterns and factors concerning the application of Article 39(1) that have been made clear. Although Article 7(1) prescribes uniformity, this is by no means perfectly reflected in the application of the provision as applied by the domestic courts and tribunals, since the application of "reasonable time" has varied greatly domestically as well as internationally.

There are no instances in international Article 39(1) caselaw that unequivocally demonstrate any undue influence of domestic law, although there are few examples of practice that disprove it, such as the judgment from Italy that not only ignores the domestic provision, but also looks to international precedents to insure uniformity, despite the subsidiary status of caselaw in Italian law. Although the German courts have been known to refer to their own domestic notification provisions, this has solely been done to equate the considerations behind this rule and Article 39(1), in order to explain the conclusions of the court. Although such reference has no place in the application of an international uniform provision, it does not actually demonstrate that domestic law has undue influence that will jeopardize the uniformity of the Convention. Similarly, although the French courts ruled in favor of a buyer concerning a notice that might not have been considered timely before courts of another nationality, this does not evidence the influence of French "buyer-friendly" domestic law, as the notice was such that it might conceivably be considered timely elsewhere. Nevertheless, this judgment does not disprove that French courts might have a tendency to be too lenient with the buyer's notices. But . . . *In Dubio pro Reo.*[346] We should not rush to criticize national courts for something of which they are not necessarily guilty.

Nevertheless, the fact still remains that there are significant variations in the practice of Article 39(1). Both internationally and nationally, Article 39(1) is not applied with perfect uniformity throughout the countries that have ratified the Convention. The severity of this lack of uniformity is difficult to assess. In 1961, Prof. Sundberg observed, about uniformity in general, that there is not always a need for perfect unification and identical meaning of legal terms in uniform law. He characterizes severe variations in uniform law thus: "A margin of imperfection is not necessarily an actual defect as long as it does not invite plaintiffs to go "shopping" for the most generous jurisdiction. Details therefore can be allowed to vary if the basic conceptualism is retained."[347] This timeless general observation might well apply to the determination of whether a lack of uniformity in the CISG is severe today.

Although the variations in practice are rather unpredictable in some cases (such as in German law), there are still certain trends. With these trends as they are today, forum shopping is a very real "invitation" in the regime of the Convention. I would certainly, if I were a buyer facing the threat of an Article 39(1) suit in my own jurisdiction from a French seller, rush to the courts of France, if at all possible, and hope for the best. Similarly, a seller might be well advised to chose a less buyer-friendly jurisdiction, and hope for a court that does not practice the "noble month," like Austria or Italy.

So regardless of whether these variations and the ensuing lack of uniformity is due to the influence of domestic law, they invite forum shopping and most certainly do not retain the basic conceptualism for uniformity in the CISG. This presents a problem that should be rectified. Although the provision must retain its flexibility for the sake of fairness, it should be more predictable for the sake of foreseeability in contracts. This age-old

[346] Doubt should benefit the accused.

[347] Referring to general problems of uniformity in the Warsaw Convention in "Air Charter" from 1963, *quoted in* GILES, *supra* note 245, at 23-4.

dilemma of conflict between individual reasonableness and predictability is not easily solved, but a solution may be obtained in the case of Article 39(1).

B. Recommended Approach for Future Practice

For a determination of a period of time such as "reasonable time" to be transnationally uniform, it would seem recommendable that there be a "uniform scale" that can be applied to fit every country and every set of facts in the determination. Such a "uniform scale" must have a benchmark setting or vantage point from which to begin the assessment, and an obligation upon courts and arbitral tribunals to move upward or downward from this vantage point when the specific circumstances of the case at hand support it.

The question is, of course, whether there really is a need for a "uniform scale" for the assessment of reasonable time. It may be argued that if such a scale or vantage point were intended by the drafters, then it would have been included in the Convention. On the other hand, when interpreting the Convention, regard is to be had to the need to promote uniformity in its application (Article 7), so that any interpretation of Article 39(1) that promotes uniformity to the extent that a uniform scale for measuring "reasonable" time does, would surely be in the spirit of the CISG and in accordance with the will of the drafters. Moreover, a uniform scale does not fix the time-frame to such a degree that it is no longer as flexible as intended; it is merely a question of agreeing on a yardstick with which to measure the reasonableness. And based on the caselaw illustrated above, there is certainly a need for agreeing on such a yardstick if Article 39(1) practice is to become more uniform.

It may also be argued that the drafters of the Convention never strove for such perfect uniformity as that which we may hope to obtain in the realm of Article 39(1) through a uniform scale. But, barring such a discussion, a uniform scale only serves to promote the goals and ideas of the Convention, as well as the harmonization of trade law, and will help take uniformity one step further. This is possible where Article 39(1) is concerned.

In this author's opinion, a uniform scale with a flexible vantage point is sorely needed, and the most suitable available international guideline is the "noble month" vantage point, which represents a compromise between acceptable time-frames in international domestic law. As a (flexible and not absolute) vantage point, the individual circumstances and considerations may reduce the period of notice to be "reasonable" for each specific case, and, in rare circumstances, adapt the time-frame to be even longer where needed. Since practice has proven reluctant to provide the restrictive period with any means of "growing" with the circumstances of the case, a more generous vantage point would seem recommendable, not only for the sake of more certainty in contracts and better predictability of the notice time-frame for both the buyer and the seller, but also for the sake of the uniformity of the Convention. All in all, the application of the "noble month" as a vantage point in a uniform scale for the determination of reasonable time would seem a sure step towards safeguarding the uniformity of Article 39(1).

C. *Overall Conclusion and Criteria*

The term "reasonable time," as it is defined today, has proven too imprecise due to its flexibility without a defined uniform scale to assist the practitioners in a uniform application of Article 39(1). Such a uniform scale, with a vantage point that permits the factors of each individual case to determine the precise notice time-frame, is a positive step towards an autonomous definition of "reasonable time" and still retains the flexibility of the provision.

The "noble month" guideline as a vantage point seems ideally suited, not only as it represents a compromise between acceptable time-frames in different domestic laws, but also since it already has gained a foothold in German practice, which represents the majority of Article 39(1) practice, as well as Swiss practice. Moreover, the "noble month" is not wholly inconsistent with existing international practice, and with the cementing of definite criteria for its expansion/reduction it remains flexible enough to allow for the "reasonableness" of the timeframe in individual cases while still protecting a certain predictability in contracts.

It is not, however, a firm reality in international practice yet — no matter how recommendable. However, there are factors that determine the timeliness of the notice which can be said to be internationally generally recognized, and which would also be suited to the application of a recognized vantage-point, such as the "noble month."

The present paper concludes with a list of these factors, and a hope that some day they will apply to a common guideline such as the "noble month," so that the uniformity of the CISG may be ensured by Article 39(1) taking on its own international autonomous meaning while retaining its flexibility. The factors currently influencing whether an Article 39(1) notice is given within reasonable time in international practice are:

- Any derogation from Article 39(1) (Is a notification time-frame agreed or perhaps implied? Agreed time-frames will apply regardless of reasonableness (Article 6), and implied time-frames will influence the court's/tribunal's decision of timeliness under Article 39(1));
- The speed of communication established by the parties (If the parties usually communicate quickly with one another, the seller will be entitled to expect a speedier notice, and this will be required of the buyer. Similarly, other trade usages established between the parties may influence the time-frame (Article 9(1));
- Any international trade usage that may influence the time-frame (Article 9(2));
- Considerations for the seller's reasonable expectations for when notice may be delivered (Article 8(2));
- The nature of the remedy chosen (If the buyer chooses to avoid the contract the seller will need more time to take care of his goods, whereas a remedy of damages places no such pressures on the buyer);
- The perishable physical nature of the goods, particularly foodstuffs (Such goods would call for a swifter notice, to stop them from "rotting away in a warehouse, unwanted," in the interests of the seller's loss adjustment);
- The affiliation of the goods to a particular season, and their economic perishability (Such goods would also require notice to be given sooner, to protect the sellers economic interests); and
- The nature of the contract between the parties, and the buyer's duty to limit the seller's loss (Is the seller facing a particular deadline which the buyer is aware of? This will require speedier notice within the framework of the deadline in question).

This list of factors is not exclusive. Any circumstances suitable for influencing the "reasonable time" of the notice may be applied by the court/tribunal hearing a case, as long as they are relevant to Article 39(1), objective, and not based on any legal misconception. Article 39(1) is essentially a flexible provision, and should remain so in the interest of fairness. The provision just requires a little clarification in the form of a guideline with some known criteria, in the interest of predictability in contracts and the uniformity of the Convention of which it is an important part.

APPENDIX A

List of Article 39 Caselaw

Note: The following caselaw is a reflection of all the decisions rendered, and is not restricted to the highest instance findings in individual cases. Cases marked with ~ have been reversed at a higher instance.

German Courts

Venue	Date	Docket. No.	Buyer/Seller/Goods	Notice within Reasonable Time?
Landgericht München	03.07.89	17 HKO 3726/89	German/Italian/ Fashion	No; notice not specific enough
Landgericht Stuttgar	31.08.89	3KfHO 97/89	German/Italian/ Shoes	No; telephone call not proven
Landgericht Aachen	03.04.90	41 O 198/89	German/Italian/ Shoes	Yes; 1 day after discovery
Amtsgericht Ludwigsberg	21.12.90	4 C 549/90	German/French/ Clothes	Article 39 overlooked
Landgericht Bielefeld	18.01.91	15 O 201/90	German/Italian/ Bacon	Yes/No; 3 days not specific
OLG Koblenz	27.09.91	2 U 1899/89	German/Italian/ Marble	Issue left unresolved by Court
Landgericht Stuttgart	13.08.91	16 S 40/91	German/French/ Clothes	No; 6 weeks not reasonable
LG Baden — Baden	14.08.91	4 O 113/90	German/Italian/ Tiles	No; outside time-limit agreed
Landgericht Krefeld	18.03.92	11 O 159/91	German/Turkish/ Gherkins	[CISG overlooked]
Landgericht Saarbrücken	23.03.92	9 O 4084/89	German/French/ Doors	No; Misunderstanding of 39

LG Mönchen-gladbach	22.05.92	7 O 80/91	German/Italian/ Textiles	No; 1 month (1 week OK)
Landgericht Berlin	16.09.92	99 O 29/93	German/Italian/ Shoes	No; over 2 months after delivery
Landgericht Berlin	30.09.92	99 O 123/92	German/Italian/ Shoes	No; 3 _ months after delivery
Landgericht Düsseldorf	04.12.92	40 O 91/91	German/French/ Textiles	[CISG over-looked]
Landgericht Frankfurt	09.12.92	3/3 O 37/92	German/Italian/ Shoes	Yes; tele-phone 19 days after del.
Landgericht Darmstadt	22.12.92	14 O 165/92	German/Swiss/ Mussels	Article 39 overlooked
OLG Düsseldorf	08.01.93	17 U 82/92	German/Turkish/ Gherkins	No; 7 days, implied agreement
OLG Saarbrücken	13.01.93	1 U 69/92 Doors	German/French/ after delivery	No; 2 months
OLG Düsseldorf	12.03.93	17 U 136/92	German/Italian/ Textiles	No; 25 days, analogy HGB §377
LG Düsseldorf	22.03.93	37 0 169/92	German/Italian/ Textiles	[CISG over-looked]
Landgericht Aachen~	28.07.93	42 O 68/93	German/Nigerian/ Wood	No; non-payment not enough
OLG Koblenz	17.09.93	2 U 1230/91	German/French/ Chip	No; none & defect not proven
Landgericht Köln	11.11.93	86 O 119/93	German/Swiss/ Research	No; 21 days, due to deadline
Landgericht Hannover	01.12.93	22 O 107/93	German/Italian/ Shoes	No; outside time-limit agreed
OLG Frankfurt	18.01.94	5 U 15/93	German/Italian/ Shoes	Article 39 not men-tioned

OLG Düsseldorf	10.02.94	6 U 32/93	German/French/ Textiles	No; 2 month, strict construction
OLG Düsseldorf	10.02.94	6 U 119/93	German/Italian/ Textiles	No; nachfrist duty imposed
OLG Köln	22.02.94	29 U 202/93	German/Nigerian/ Wood	Yes; 8 days after examination
Landgericht München	07.03.94	14 HKO 23317/93	German/Austrian/ Plastic	[CISG over looked]
OLG Frankfurt	20.04.94	13 U 51/93	German/Swiss/ Mussels	Article 39 overlooked
Amtsgericht Nordhorn	14.06.94	3 C 75/94	German/Italian/ Shoes	Yes; return of goods valid notice
Landgericht Düsseldorf	23.06.94	31 O 231/94	German/Turkish/ Presses	No;4&20 months after delivery
Landgericht Gießen	05.07.94	6 O 85/93	German/Italian/ Clothes	No; outside time-limit agreed
Landgericht Frankfurt	13.07.94	3/13 O 3/94	German/Italian/ Shoes	No; telephone call not proven
OLG Köln	26.08.94	19 U 282/93	German/Swiss/ Research	No; Art. 39 not in appeal
Landgericht Arnsberg	12.10.94	2 O 217/94	German/Italian/ Windows	[CISG overlooked]
Amtsgericht Riedlingen	21.10.94	2 C 395/93	German/Italian/ Ham	No; 20 days, despite holidays
Landgericht Oldenburg	09.11.94	12 O 674/93	German/Italian/ Lorry Parts	No; need new notice after repair
Landgericht München	08.02.95	8 HKO 24667/93	German/French/ Software	No; not specific to ask for help
OLG München	08.02.95	7 U 375/94	German/Austrian/ Plastic	No; 3 months (8 days OK)

Bundesger-Mussels	08.03.95	VIII ZR 159/94	German/Swiss/Mussels	No; 6 weeks (1 noble month OK)
Landgericht München	20.03.95	10 HKO 23750/94	German/Italian/Bacon	No; non-specific telex, 25 days
Landgericht Landshut	05.04.95	54 O 644/94	Swiss/German/Clothes	No/Yes; 19 days, many n.c's
OLG Frankfurt a.M.	23.05.95	5 U 209/94	German/Italian/Shoes	No; telephone call not proven
OLG Hamm	09.06.95	11 U 191/94	German/Italian/Windows	Yes; applied to Article 46
Landgericht Kassel	22.06.95	8 O 2391/93	German/Italian/Clothes	No; telephone call not proven
Landgericht München	09.08.95	7 U 7143/92	Italian/German/Chemicals	ULIS case, not CISG (Art.100)
LG Ellwangen	21.08.95	1 KfH 0 32/95	German/Spanish/Paprika	Article 39 issue overlooked
OLG Stuttgart	21.08.95	5 U 195/94	German/Italian/Machines	No; 1 month & not proven
LG Nürnberg-Fürth	26.07.94	5 HKO 10824/93	German/Austrian/Software	Yes; 1 day after discovery
OLG Software	20.09.95	12 U 2919/94	German/Austrian/Software	Yes; 1 day after discovery
Amtsgericht Kehl	06.10.95	3 C 925/93	German/Italian/Fashion	No; 6 weeks & call not proven
Landgericht Düsseldorf	11.10.95	2 O 506/94	Danish/German/Generator	Yes; 1 week, but not mentioned
Landgericht Trier	12.10.95	7 HO 78/95	Italian/German/Wine	Article 40 prevents Article 39

Landgericht Koblenz	29.11.95	3 HO 188/94	German/Dutch/ Blankets	No not specific enough
Landgericht Marburg	12.12.95	2 O 246/95	German/Italian/ Machines	No; notices not specific/ proven
Landgericht Bochum	24.01.96	Unavailable	German/Italian/ Truffles	No; not specific enough
Amtsgericht Augsburg	29.01.96	11 C 4004/95	German/Swiss/ Fashion	No; 18 months (1 month OK)
Landgericht Kassel	15.02.96	11 O 4187/95	German/Italian/ Marble	No; oral notice to third party
Landgericht Duisburg	17.04.96	45(19) O 80/94	German/Italian/ Textiles	None, and nachfrist imposed
Landgericht Aachen	19.04.96	43 O 70/95	Dutch/German/ Machines	No; notice not proven
Landgericht Paderborn	25.06.96	7 O 147/94	German/French/ Plastic	None, but fault too hard to spot
Landgericht Heidelberg	02.10.96	O 37/96 KfH II	Austrian/German/ St. Film	Yes; 24 days after delivery
Bundesgerichtshof	04.12.96	VIII ZR 306/95	German/Austrian/ Software	Yes; 1 day, undoubtedly timely
OLG Köln	08.01.97	27 U 58/96	Dutch/German/ Machines	No; notice not proven
OLG Koblenz	31.01.97	2 U 31/96	German/Dutch/ Blankets	No; not specific enough
OLG Karlsruhe	25.06.97	1 U 280/96	Austrian/German/ St. Film	No; 24 days after delivery
Bundesgerichtshof	25.06.97	VIII ZR 300/96	Swiss/German/ Kor. Steel	Yes; seller accepted the notice
OLG München	09.07.97	7 U 2070/97	German/Italian/ Leatherw.	No; no notice given
OLG Köln	21.08.97	18 U 121/96	French/German/ Aluminium	No; Noble month not apply

OLG München	11.03.98	7 U 4427/97	German/Italian/ Clothing	No; 1 month, 2 weeks agreed.

Austrian Courts

Venue	Date	Docket. No.	Buyer/Seller/Goods	Notice within Reasonable Time?
OLG Innsbruck	01.07.94	4 R 161/94	Austrian/Danish/ Flowers	No; 3 weeks from discovery
Landesgericht Feldkirch	29.03.94	5 Cg 176/92y-64	Austrian/Danish/	No; non-conf. not proven

French Courts

Venue	Date	Docket. No.	Buyer/Seller/Goods	Notice within Reasonable Time?
Cour d'appel de Grenoble	13.09.95	93/4126 Cheese	French/Italian/ after delivery	Yes; 30 days
Cour d'appel de Versailles	29.01.98	95/1222	French/Italian/ Machines	Yes; before and after delivery

Italian Courts

Venue	Date	Docket. No.	Buyer/Seller/Goods	Notice within Reasonable Time?
Tribunale Civ. di Cuneo	31.01.96	[45/96]	Italian/French/ Clothes	No; 23 days after delivery

Swiss Courts

Venue	Date	Docket. No.	Buyer/Seller/Goods	Notice within Reasonable Time?
Pretura di	27.04.92	6252	Swiss/Italian/	No; not rely

Locarno-Campagna			Furniture	on customers
Handelsgercht Zürich	09.09.93	HG 930138 U/H93	Swiss/Italian/ Furniture	No; notice not proven
Handelsgercht Zürich	26.04.95	HG 920670	German/Swiss/ Iso. Tank	No; four weeks after disc.
OG Kanton Luzern	08.01.97	11 95 123/357	Swiss/French/ Tubes	Yes;"noble month" applied

Dutch Courts

Venue	Date	Docket. No.	Buyer/Seller/Goods	Notice within Reasonable Time?
Arrondissementsrechtbank Dordrecht	21.11.90	2762/1989	Dutch/French/ Textiles	Interim; buyer must prove
Arrondissementsrechtbank Roermond	19.12.91	900366	Dutch/Italian/ Mozzarella	No; 2 months, perishables
Arrondissementsrechtbank Roermond	06.05.93	925159	Dutch/Italian/ Kettles	No; three months after disc.
Arrondissementsrechtbank Gravehage	07.06.95	94/0670	French/Dutch/ Apple Trees	No; none proven by buyer

Belgian Courts

Venue	Date	Docket. No.	Buyer/Seller/Goods	Notice within Reasonable Time?
Tribunal Commercial de Bruxelles	05.10.94	RR 1.205/93	Belgian/Italian/ Shoes	No; nine months after delivery

Arbitral Awards

	Date	Docket. No.	Buyer/Seller/Goods	Notice within Reasonable Time?
ICC International Court of Arbitration				
	1989	5713/1989	Unavailable	Yes; 8 days after discovery
ICC International Court of Arbitration				
	1994	7565/1994	U.S./Dutch/Coke	Yes; undisputed
ICC International Court of Arbitration				
	1994	7331/1994	Italian/Yugoslav/ Cowhides	Yes; agreed timeframe OK
Int. Schiedsgericht der Bundeskammer der gewerblichen Wirtshaft				
	15.06.94	SCH-4318	German/Austrian/ Metal	No; outside agreed timeframe
ICC International Court of Arbitration				
	23.08.94	7660/JK	Czech/Italian/ Machinery	Yes; not explained why
Hungarian Chamber of Commerce and Industry, Court of Arbitration				
	05.12.95	VB/94131	Austrian/Hung./ Containers	No; 32 days speedy affairs
Schiedsgericht der Handelskammer Hamburg				
	21.03.96	Unavailable	German/Hong Kong/Goods	No; over 2 years

APPENDIX B

History of the Current Article 39(1) as reflected by UN Documents

UN Document A/7618: **"Report of the United Nations Commission on International Trade Law on the works of its second session (1969),** ***Official Records of the General Assembly, Twenty-fourth Session, Supplement No. 18.*"** Herein the UNCITRAL established the "Working Group on the International Sale of Goods" to ascertain which modifications of the Hague Convention of 1964 (ULIS) might render it capable of wider acceptance by countries of different legal, social and economic systems, and to elaborate a new text reflecting such modifications.

UN Document A/CN.9/37: **"Analysis of replies and comments by governments on the Hague Conventions of 1964, report of the Secretary-General".** This report contains no replies or comments pertaining to Article 39 of the ULIS, which is the predecessor to Article 39 of the CISG. This is surprising, since this provision later became one of the more controversial and difficult to reach agreement on.

UN Document A/CN.9/35: **"Report of the Working Group on the International Sale of Goods, first session, 5th-16th January 1970."** No mention is made of the notification requirement, save to mention that the duty to examine is too strict considering the consequences in Article 39. ("Working Party IV" consequently proposed a new Article 38 in para. 109, which has been retained except for the substitution of the term "promptly").

UN Document A/CN.9/52: **"Working Group on the International Sale of Goods; report on the work of the second session, 7th-18th December 1970".** This session dealt with Articles 1-17 of the ULIS, and therefore did not deal with Article 39 directly. However, Article 11 of the ULIS was discussed and heavily criticised as being unnecessarily complex, and unclear and ambiguous in its definition of "promptly". It was decided that the term "promptly" was unsuitable for Article 39(1), as this Article had its own starting point. A new draft article was recommended, which defined promptly in the words of the current Article 38 ("within as short a period as practicable").

UN Document A/CN.9/62 add. 1 & add. 2: **"Progress report of the Working Group on the International Sale of Goods on the work of its third session, held in Geneva from 17th to 28th January 1972."** The Working Group decided to exchange the term "promptly" with the term "within reasonable time". This term is not, however, defined, and the remainder of the comments concerning Article 39 regard the two-year cut-off period and an additional period of guarantee.

UN Document A/CN.9/WG.2/WP.10: **"Analysis of comments and proposals relating to Articles 18-55 of the Uniform Law on the International Sale of Goods (ULIS): note by the Secretary-General."** The Working Party to Articles 38 — 40 of the ULIS consisted of Austrian, U.S. and Kenyan delegates. The U.S. representative found Articles 38 and 39 too inflexible, and suggested a redrafting to take latent defects into consideration, as well as the possibility that price reduction be exempt from the loss of remedy ensuing from a failure to give timely notice of non-conformity. The Austrian representative did not agree, and further objected to suggestions that time-limits within which the buyer had to notify the seller of the defects of the goods should vary according to the action of the buyer (e.g. rejection versus acceptance and claim for damages). Austria furthermore suggested that Article 39(1) be amended so that the second full-stop sentence become Article 39(2).

UN Document A/CN.9/WG.2/WP.16: **"Report of the Secretary General: obligations of the seller in an international sale of goods; consolidation of work done by the Working Group on the International Sale of Goods and suggested solutions for unresolved problems."** Article 39(1) has not yet been split up as suggested by the Austrian delegate. Para. 84 of this document explains the purpose of Article 39 as (i) giving the seller the opportunity to cure the defect or (ii) preserve evidence of the quality of the goods. Para. 85 explains why the substitution in terms took place. "Within reasonable time" was thought sufficiently flexible to adapt to the varying circumstances in which inspection might be required.

UN Document A/CN.9/75: **"Report of the Working Group on the International Sale of Goods on the work of its fourth session (New York, 22nd January–2nd February, 1973)."** All comments pertaining to Article 39 regard the period of guarantee.

UN Document A/CN.9/87: **"Report of the Working Group on the International Sale of Goods on the work of its fifth session (Geneva 21st Jan-**

uary — 1st February, 1974).” No comments on Article 39, as all comments restricted to Articles 58-70 of the ULIS.

UN Document A/CN.9/100, annex II): **“Text of comments and proposals of representatives on the revised text of a uniform law on the international sale of goods as approved or deferred for further consideration by the Working Group at its first five sessions.”** General comments and the comment from the Russian representative regard the additional period of guarantee (“different” or “longer”) mentioned in the two-year outside limit for notice. Comments from Norway include a restatement of the Austrian suggestion to split Article 39(1) up and form the current Article 39(2).

UN Document A/CN.9/100, annex III): **“Report of the Secretary General: pending questions with respect to the revised text of a Uniform Law on the International Sale of Goods.”** The Secretary-General observes that failure to comply with the notice requirement in Article 39(1) has drastic consequences (para. 102), but goes on to point out that the rigours of this requirement are mitigated by making the rules of Article 38 more flexible. The modification of the term “promptly” is also noted, but the term “reasonable time” is not explained or defined.

UN Document A/CN.9/100: **“Report of the Working Group on the International Sale of Goods on the work of its sixth session (New York, 27th January–7th February 1975).”** The Working Group considers the new Article 39(2), and the two year cut-off period.

UN Document A/CN.9/116: **“Report of the Working Group on the International Sale of Goods on the work of its seventh session (New York, 2nd-12th February 1976).”** The working group has completed a Draft Convention wherein Article 39(1) of the ULIS has been restated as Article 23 in a new section dealing exclusively with non-conformity of goods. The wording of Article 39(1) as it appeared at the previous session has not been altered.

UN Document A/CN.9/116, annex I: **“Draft Convention on the International Sale of Goods.”** Article 39(1), in the shape of Article 23(1), is submitted with its current wording for comments from Governments and international organisations. The duty to specify the non-conformity is now included in ¶ 1.

UN Document A/CN.9/116, annex II: **“Commentary on the draft Convention on the International Sale of Goods.”** This commentary to Article 23 of the draft Convention explains the purpose of the provision, the relationship with the duty to examine the goods (the current Article 38, then Article 22), and the two-year cut-off period and contractual periods of guarantee. But the term "reasonable time" is not explained or defined.

UN Document A/CN.9/125: **"Comments by Governments and International Organisations on the draft Convention on the International Sale of Goods."** Comments on the draft Convention where Article 39(1) was drafted as Article 23. Czechoslovakia proposed that the loss of remedy ensuing from the non-compliance with the duty to notify be limited to non-recovery. Pakistan stated that the term "reasonable time" needed definition.

UN Document A/CN.9/126: **"Report of the Secretary-General: Analysis of Comments by Governments and International Organisations on the draft Convention on the international sale of goods as adopted by the Working Group on the international sale of goods."** The request from Pakistan on determination of "reasonable time" is re-printed but not commented. The proposal from Czechoslovakia is not mentioned.

UN Document A/CN.9/128: **"Report of the Working Group on the International Sale of Goods on the work of its eight session (New York, 4th-14th January, 1977)."** The Working Group has begun revising the Uniform Law on the Formation of Contracts for the International Sale of Goods as a separate Convention.

UN Document A/CN.9/142: **"Report of the Working Group on the International Sale of Goods on the work of its ninth session (Geneva, 19th-30th September 1977)."** German proposal to speed up the work on the ULF and include it in the Uniform Law for International Sales made. New draft for the Uniform Law on Formation of Contracts for the International Sales completed.

UN Document A/CN.9/145: **"Report of the Secretary General: incorporation of the provisions of the draft Convention on the Formation of Contracts for the International Sale of Goods into the draft Convention for the International Sale of Goods."** German proposition for integration of revised laws on formation and sales adopted, meaning shift in numbers of provisions. Article 23 becomes Article 37 in the new draft on Uniform law on Contracts for the International sale of Goods.

UN Document A/CONF. 97/5: **"Commentary on the Draft Convention on Contracts for the International Sale of Goods, prepared by the Secretariat."** Integration and improvements on the former commentaries on "sales" and "formation" draft conventions. The commentary to Article 37 is very similar to the commentary to Article 23 in UN Doc. A/CN.9/116, annex II, and there is still no reference to the determination of "reasonable time."

***UN Document A/33/17:* "Report of the United Nations Commission on Trade Law on the works of its eleventh session."** A unanimous approval of the Draft Convention on Contracts for the International Sale of Goods, and recommendation for the UN General Assembly to convene an international conference.

***UN Document A/CN.9/183:* "United Nations Conference on Contracts for the International Sale of Goods."** The conference was held on 10th March–11th April 1980, and the CISG (A/CONF.97/18, annex I) was adopted with protocol (A/CONF.97/18, annex II) by a final act of the General Assembly (A/CONF.9/18). After final changes to the incorporation of the Draft Convention, Article 37 is now Article 39.

***UN Document A/CN.9/SER.C/GUIDE/1 English 12 September 1995:* "UNCITRAL Outline of the CISG [The UNCITRAL Thesaurus]."** In 1995, the United Nations Commission on International Trade Law commissioned Professor John O. Honnold (working in conjunction with Professor Michael Joachim Bonell and Ambassador Mahmoud Soliman) to devise a classification of each of the provisions of the CISG. The issues under 39(1) were classified as: 39A1: Specification of nature of non-conformity. 39A11: Degree of specificity required 39A2: Within reasonable time.

CHAPTER FIVE

The Concept of Fundamental Breach of Contract under the United Nations Convention on Contracts for the International Sale of Goods (CISG)

By Robert Koch*

* Dr. jur., Georg-August University Göttingen (Germany), 1994; associate in the law firm Graf von Westphalen, Fritze & Modest, Cologne (Germany); LL.M. (Dean's Honor List) McGill University, Montréal (Canada), 1996/97; Visiting Lecturer at Ural State Law Academy in Yekaterinburg (Russian Federation) 1997/98

This paper has been submitted to the McGill University Faculty of Graduate Studies and Research in partial fulfillment of the requirements of the degree Master of Laws. The author would like to express his gratitude to Albert Kritzer, the Executive Secretary, Institute of International Commercial Law, Pace University School of Law for his valuable comments on this paper. This work is dedicated to my wife, Olga Sosnovskaja.

C. The Concept of "Fundamental Breach" in Context
  1. Remedial System of the Convention
    a. Uniform Concept of Breach and the Notion of Fundamental Breach
    b. The Concept of Fundamental Breach and Party Autonomy (Article 6)
  2. Cross-References to the Concept of Fundamental Breach
    a. Fundamental Breach and Avoidance of the Contract
      (1) Seller's Fundamental Breach: Articles 49(1)(a) and 51(2
      (2) Buyer's Fundamental Breach: Article 64(1)(a)
      (3) Anticipatory Fundamental Breach: Article 72
      (4) Fundamental Breach and Installment Sales: Article 73(1)(2)
    b. The Concept of Fundamental Breach and the Duty to Deliver Substitute Goods (Article 46(2))
      (1) Fundamental Breach in the Light of the Text of Article 46(2)
      (2) Fundamental Breach and the Legislative History of Article 46(2)
        (a) Deliberations within the UNCITRAL
        (b) First Committee Deliberations and the Decisions by Plenary Conference
        (c) Conclusion
  3. Avoidance Situations Where No Fundamental Breach Is Required
    a. Non-Performance within Time Fixed by *Nachfrist* Notice: Articles 49(1)(b), 64(1)(b)
    b. Avoidance of Installments Based on Interdependence with a Defective Installment: Article 73(3)
  4. Limitations on the Concept of Fundamental Breach
    a. Foreseeability of the Consequences of the Breach
    b. Seller's Right to Cure: Article 48
    c. Duty to Mitigate Losses
  5. Fundamental Breach in the Light of the Regime Governing the Seller's Obligations under the Convention
  6. Conclusion (The Concept of "Fundamental Breach" in Context)

D. Underlying Purposes and Policies of the Term "Fundamental Breach" within the Remedial System of the Convention

E. The Concept of Fundamental Breach and the Observance of Good Faith

I. Introduction

Judging by the number of states that have adopted it, there is no doubt that the United Nations Convention on Contracts for the International Sale of Goods[1] is one of the most successful examples of unification in the area of international commercial law.[2] The Convention was unanimously adopted in 1980 at a diplomatic Conference with representatives from 62 states and 8 international organizations. Since then, 54 states from five continents, including almost all of the major trading nations, have approved, ratified, accepted, or acceded to the Convention.[3]

---

[1] United Nations Convention on Contracts for the International Sale of Goods, Apr. 11, 1980, U.N. Doc. A/CONF. 97/18, Annex I, reprinted in 19 I.L.M. 668 [hereinafter CISG]. Articles without any further designation refer to "the Convention." The English, French and Spanish versions are available at <http://www.un.or.at/uncitral/[english][french][spanish]/texts/sales/salescon. htm#top>.

[2] *See* Michael J. Bonell, *The UNIDROIT Principles of International Commercial Contracts and thePrinciples of European Contract Law: Similar Rules for the Same Purpose?*, 26 Uniform L. Rev 26 (1996); Franco Ferrari, *Specific Topics of the CISG in the Light of Doctrinal Writings and Judicial Applications*, 15 J.L. & Com. 1, 13 (1995); Frank Diedrich, *Lückenfüllung im Internationalen Einheitsrecht. Möglichkeiten und Grenzen richterlicher Rechtsfortbildung, im* Wiener Kaufrecht 353, 353 RIW (1995); and Ronald A. Brand & Harry M. Flechtner, *Arbitration and Contract Formation in International Trade: First Interpretation of the U.N. Sales Convention*, 12 J.L. & Com. 239 (1993).

[3] These countries and the date the Convention has or will come into force for them are: Argentina, Jan. 1, 1988; Australia, Apr. 1, 1989; Austria, Jan. 1, 1989; Belarus, Aug. 1, 1991; Belgium, Nov. 1, 1997; Bosnia-Herzegovina, Mar. 6, 1992; Bulgaria, Aug. 1, 1991; Burundi, Oct. 1, 1998; Canada, May 1, 1992; Chile, Mar. 1, 1991; China, Jan. 1, 1988; Croatia, Oct. 8, 1991; Cuba, Dec. 1, 1995; Czech Republic, Jan. 1, 1993; Denmark, Mar. 1, 1991; Ecuador, Feb. 1, 1993; Egypt, Jan. 1, 1988; Estonia, Oct. 1, 1994; Finland, Jan. 1, 1989; France, Jan. 1, 1988; Georgia, Sep. 1, 1995; Germany, Jan. 1, 1991; Greece, Feb. 1, 1999; Guinea, Feb. 1, 1992; Hungary, Jan. 1, 1988; Iraq, Apr. 1, 1991; Italy, Jan. 1, 1988; Latvia, Aug. 1, 1998; Lesotho, Jan. 1, 1988; Lithuania, Feb. 1, 1996; Luxembourg, Febr. 1, 1998; Mexico, Jan. 1, 1988; Moldova, Nov. 1, 1995; Mongolia, Jan. 1, 1999; Netherlands, Jan. 1, 1992; New Zealand, Oct. 1, 1995; Norway, Aug. 1, 1989; Poland, Jun. 1, 1996; Romania, Jun. 1, 1992; Russian Federation, Sept. 1, 1991; Singapore, Mar. 1, 1996; Slovakia, Jan. 1, 1993; Slovenia, June 25, 1991; Spain, Aug. 1, 1991; Sweden, Jan. 1, 1989; Switzerland, Mar. 1, 1991; Syrian Arabian Republic, Jan. 1, 1988; Uganda, Mar. 1, 1993; Ukraine, Jan. 1, 1991; United States of America, Jan. 1, 1988; Uruguay, Feb. 1, 2000; Uzbekistan, Dec. 1, 1997; Yugoslavia, Jan. 1, 1988; Zambia, Jan. 1, 1988.

Ghana and Venezuela have each signed, but have yet to officially ratify, approve or accept the Convention. For relevant information on the status of the Convention, see

While important, the extent of adoption by nations is not the only criteria by which to evaluate the Convention's success. Of equal importance is the level of acceptance of uniform commercial law by the business world whose interest it is primarily meant to serve.[4] In the business world, however, the Convention lacks the wide acceptance it enjoys in the political arena; this can best be seen by the limited number of published decisions interpreting the Convention.[5] Even if one considers that not all decisions have been published or reported and that arbitration awards are often not published at all, in relation to the actual number of sales transactions since the Convention entered into force in 1988, the number of reported Convention cases nonetheless remains very small. This gives rise to the assumption that the Convention has often been excluded by the parties.[6]

Any attempt to explain this exclusion of the Convention, in the absence of empirical data, remains a rather speculative exercise. From the present writer's own personal and professional experience as a practicing

---

United Nations Dept. of Public Information (visited March 15, 1999) <http://www.un.or.at/UNCITRAL/english/status/index.htm>.

[4] The Convention does not apply to consumer sales. *See* Art. 2(a). *See also* V. Suzanne Cook, *The U.N. Convention of Contracts for the International Sale of Goods, A Mandate to Abandon Legal Ethnocentricity*, 16 J.L. & COM. 257, 258 (1997)(emphasizing that "the business community and legal practitioners however will cast the final decisive votes by either embracing, or opting out of, the Convention"); Albert Kritzer, *The Convention on Contracts for the International Sale of Goods: Scope, Interpretation, and Resources, in* CORNELL CISG REVIEW 147 (1995) (stating that the Convention "is designed to foster world trade by acting as a bridge to improved understanding in business dealings between persons from different countries and cultures").

[5] In the database of the University of Freiburg, 353 cases on the Convention has been registered. *See University of Freiburg CISG Guide*, (visited Aug. 18, 1998) <http://www.jura.uni-freiburg.de/ipr1/cisg/guide/8-2.htm>. According to Professor Michael R. Will of the University of Geneva, who has established a network of correspondents for the purpose to share knowledge on citations to scholarly writings and case law on the CISG, courts and arbitral tribunals have rendered approximately 444 decisions. *See* MICHAEL WILL, THE FIRST 555 OR SO DECISIONS (8th ed., 1999).

[6] For similar statements, see Burghard Piltz, *Voices of International Practice, in* Uniform Commercial Law in the Twenty First Century: Proceedings of the Congress of the United Nations Commission on International Trade Law, U.N. GAOR Comm. on Int'l Trade L., 25th Sess., at 85, U.N. Doc. A/CN.9/SER.D/1 (1992) (stating that "surprisingly, only a very limited number of Sales Convention cases — in Germany as elsewhere — has been reported now"). *See also* Cook, *supra* note 4, at 257 (calling the fact that only two U.S. cases interpreting the Convention have been reported yet as "a stunning result considering the broad scope of the Convention's application").

attorney in Germany, however, parties often exclude the Convention for two main reasons: First, simply because the parties, as well as their lawyers, neither know the Convention nor are interested in becoming acquainted with it.[7] It is more convenient for such persons to confine themselves to well-known domestic rules than to learn a completely new set of rules.[8] Second, some very important provisions of the Convention contain vague language and terminology that cause uncertainty and unpredictability.[9]

---

[7] *See* Kritzer, *supra* note 4, at 148 (stating that "there are many attorneys who are not aware of the CISG"); Stewart F. Hancock, *A Uniform Commercial Code for International Sales? We Have it Now,* 67 N.Y. St. Bar J. 20, 21 (1995)(emphasizing that on the one hand all lawyers appreciate the significance of such widely acclaimed achievements in international economic cooperation such as GATT and NAFTA but know little if anything of the Convention); and Claude Witz, *La Convention de Vienne sur la vente internationale de marchandises a l'epreuve de la jurisprudence naissante,* Rec. Dall. Sir. 143, 144 (1995) (stating that "les juges et avocats . . . n'aient pas encore suffisamment pris conscience de ce que les contrats dont ils ont à connaître sont régis par la Convention de Vienne").

[8] *See also* R.M. Lavers, *CISG, To Use or Not to Use?,* Int'l Bus.L. 10 (1993) (stating that "many lawyers tend to opt out of the CISG, according to the maxim the devil you know is better than the devil you do not know"); Willem Vis, *Process of Preparing Universally Acceptable Uniform Legal Rules, in* Uniform Commercial Law in the Twenty First Century: Proceedings of the Congress of the United Nations Commission on International Trade Law, U.N. GAOR Comm. on Int'l Trade L., 25th Sess., at 16, U.N. Doc. A/CN.9/SER.D/1 (1992) (pointing out that "[t]raders, merchants, bankers and lawyers will accept UNCITRAL texts only if they conclude that it is to their advantage to have their international transactions governed by such rules"); Martin Karollus, *Der Anwendungsbereich des UN-Kaufrechts im Uberblick,* 378 JuS (1993); Willibald Posch, *On the Law of International Zsale of Goods: An Introduction, in* International Sale of Goods, 8-9 (Lafili et al. eds., 1986).

[9] For similar conclusions see Jacob Ziegel, *Canada Prepares to Adopt the International Sales Convention,* 18 Can.Bus.L.J. 1, 15 (1991) (stating that some lawyers will treat the uncertainties and untested Convention provisions as sufficient reason to exclude the Convention entirely). *See also* Cook, *supra* note 4, at 258; Note, *Unification and Certainty: The United Nations Convention on Contracts for the International Sale of Goods,* 97 Harv. L. R. 1984, 1986 (1984).

See Michael Sher, *Voices of International Practice, in* Uniform Commercial Law in the Twenty First Century: Proceedings of the Congress of the United Nations Commission on International Trade Law, U.N. GAOR Comm. on Int'l Trade L., 25th Sess., at 95, U.N. Doc. A/CN.9/SER.D/1 (1992) where the author comments on the practical implications of the Convention for the practice of law in New York, from the perspective of members of the New York Bar: "The uncertainty of the interpretation, and hence of the application, of the Sales Convention makes the New York practitioner wary, and thus reluctant to utilize the Sales Convention. The New York practitioner elects to opt out of

This thesis explores one of those vague provisions, namely, the concept of fundamental breach of contract in Article 25. Fundamental breach plays a crucial role within the remedial system of the Convention because the remedies available to the buyer and the seller depend on the characterization of the breach. Generally speaking, only if one of the party's failure to perform his contractual obligations amounts to a fundamental breach will the other party be entitled to avoid the contract as of right (*de pleno jure*).[10] Moreover, fundamental breach is a prerequisite for the right of the buyer to demand substitute delivery if the goods delivered do not conform to the contract.[11] Finally, fundamental breach is important in the transfer of risk.[12]

Article 25 provides that a breach is fundamental if:

> it results in such detriment to the other party as substantially to deprive him of what he is entitled to expect under the contract, unless the party in breach did not foresee and a reasonable person of the same kind in the same circumstances would not have foreseen such result.[13]

Article 25 does not provide any examples of events that constitute such a fundamental breach.[14] Instead, general terms and phrases are used to define fundamental breach, such as "detriment," "substantial deprivation,"

---

the utilization of the Sales Convention in favor of a law with which he or she is more familiar, and therefore more comfortable. There is a tendency of the New York practitioners to opt out even in those situations where the likely outcome under the unsettled law of the Convention may be more favourable to the position of the practitioner and his or her client than the likely outcome under the settled law of the familiar Uniform Commercial Code." *Id.*

[10] *See* Arts. 49(1)(a), 51(2), 64(1)(a), 72(1), 73 (1)(2).

[11] *See* Art. 46(2).

[12] *See* Art. 70.

[13] A similar emphasis on the actual effect of the breach was given in *Hong Kong Fir Shipping Co. Ltd. v. Kawasaki Kisen Kaisha Ltd.*, [1962] 2 Q. B. 26; [1962] All E.R. 474, where a similar formula to article 25 was established: "Does the occurrence of the event deprive the party. . . of substantially the whole benefit which it was the intention of the parties as expressed in the contract that he should obtain . . .?" *Id.*

The formula was applied to contracts of the sale of goods in *Cehave N.V. v. Bremer Handels-gesellschaft m.b.H.*, [1976] Q.B. 44, [1975] All E.R. 739, at 747, 755-57, 765. *See also* Kenneth C. Sutton, *The Draft Convention on the International Sale of Goods*, AUSTR. BUS. L.R. 269, 287 (1976)(commenting on an early draft of art. 25).

[14] For a determination of the term "breach of contract," see *infra* Part III, A. 1.

and "foreseeability."[15] These terms hardly allow the parties to a sales contract, in case of dispute, to determine *ex ante* (before one of the parties deems the contract avoided) whether a breach was fundamental.[16]

In such a situation, there is a need for certainty and predictability since parties must use different measures to effect either a contract avoidance or continuance.[17] For example, in the case of a fundamental breach of a seller's obligation, once the buyer avoids the contract, the seller must immediately

---

[15] *See* ALBERT KRITZER, GUIDE TO PRACTICAL APPLICATIONS OF THE UNITED NATIONS CONVENTION ON CONTRACTS FOR THE INTERNATIONAL SALE OF GOODS 211 (1992).

[16] For a similar statement, see Michael Will, *Art. 48, in* COMMENTARY ON THE INTERNATIONAL SALES LAW, THE 1980 VIENNA SALES CONVENTION 3.2.2 (C. Bianca & M. Bonell eds., 1987), (emphasizing that the buyer bears the risk of evaluating the degree of nonconformity); Antonio Boggiano, *Uniform Law and Its Introduction into National Law — The Experience of Latin American States, in* INTERNATIONAL UNIFORM LAW IN PRACTICE 35 (UNIDROIT ed., 1988); ROF HERBER & BRIGITTE CZERWENKA, INTERNATIONALES KAUFRECHT, KOMMENTAR ZU DEM ÜBEREINKOMMEN DER VEREINTEN NATIONEN VOM 11 APRIL 1980 ÜBER VERTRÄGE ÜBER DEN INTERNATIONALEN WARENKAUF Art. 49, n. 6 (1991); *Bernd v. Hoffman, Gewährleistungsansprüche im UN-Kaufrecht — verglichen mit dem EKG und BGB, in* EINHEITLICHES KAUFRECHT UND NATIONALES OBLIGATIONENRECHT 293, 300 (Peter Schlechtriem ed., 1987) (all emphasizing that in the absence of an express agreement, it will be very often not clear whether or not a breach amounts to a fundamental one; and that the seller runs the risk to commit a fundamental breach himself if he declares the contract avoided and a court later does not find for fundamental breach.); Jelena Vilus, *Common Law Institutions in the United Nations Sales Convention, in* ESTUDIOS EN HOMENAGE A JORGE ARRERA GRAF 1431, 1450 (Universidad Nacional Autonoma de Mexico, ed., 1989) (stating that businessmen, legal profession and judges of the civil law system will face difficulties in that the principle according to which liability is to be assessed in relation to the contract is unknown to them).

See also Commentary on the Draft Convention on Contracts for the International Sale of Goods prepared by the Secretariat, Document A/CONF.97/5, ¶ 2, art. 45 (antecedent to art. 49), United Nations Conference on Contracts for the International Sale of Goods, Official Records, New York, 1981 (A/CONF 97/19) [hereinafter Secretariat Commentary] (pointing out that uncertainty still exists as to whether the conditions for contract avoidance had been met). For a harsh criticism on the 1978 Draft art. 23 (antecedent to article 25 of the Official Text), see Ulrich Huber, *Der UNCITRAL-Entwurf eines Ubereinkommens uber internationale Warenkaufvertrage,* 43 RABELSZ 413, 524 (1979) (stating that the definition of fundamental breach is "meaningless, ambiguous and imprecise" and therefore "in general useless for practitioners").

[17] The mercantile need for predictability and certainty is emphasized by Kenneth C. Randall & John E. Norris, *A New Paradigm for International Business Transactions,* 71 WASH. U.L.Q. 599, 609 (1993).

take back the goods supplied. This necessarily involves risk of damage or loss and expenses such as transportation and storage.[18]

It is true, however, that the uncertainty created by the definition of fundamental breach can be avoided through a more specific avoidance regime negotiated by the parties[19] or by making use of the "*Nachfrist*-type" avoidance mechanism provided for under articles 49(1)(b) and 64(1)(b).[20] These opportunities, however, do not resolve the uncertainty inherent in the definition of fundamental breach. Moreover, the buyer and the seller cannot anticipate every problem that might arise. Thus, the circumstances which give rise to fundamental breach still must be determined.[21]

---

[18] *See* Robert Koch, *Zum Begriff der wesentlichen Vertragsverltezung im Falle der Lieferung nicht vertragsgemaser Ware*, RIW 98, 99 (1996) (pointing out that the seller has practically no choice but to take immediate possession of the goods delivered and/or try to sell them to a third party once the buyer has avoided the contract).

[19] For a similar statement, see Jacob Ziegel, *Analysis from a Provincial Common Law Perspective, in* REPORT TO THE UNIFORM LAW CONFERENCE OF CANADA ON CONVENTION ON CONTRACTS FOR THE INTERNATIONAL SALE OF GOODS 33, Comment on Art. 25, (Jacob Ziegel & Claude Samson, eds., 1981) (emphasizing that the parties are always free to make arrangements with respect to the consequences of a breach); Steven J. Stein, *Sales Contracts and the Impact of the UN Convention on the International Sale of Goods on U.S. Business, in* INTERNATIONAL COMMERCIAL AGREEMENTS 49, 79 (Practicing Law Institute, ed. 1990) (stating the parties are advised to specify performance characteristics or testing procedures that "enable each side to make a more objective determination of whether a breach has occurred").

[20] See Arts. 49(1)(b) and 64(1)(b), which enable the aggrieved party to declare the contract avoided if there is a delay in performance and if this breach of contract is not remedied within a reasonable time after notice in accordance with articles 47(1) or 63(1), respectively, has been given. The procedure authorized by these particular articles has a certain parentage in the German procedure of "*Nachfrist*" and the French procedure of a "*mise en demure,*" although in its current form, as emphasized in ¶ 7 of the Secretariat Commentary on 1978 Draft Art. 43 [antecedent to Art. 47 of the Official Text] (Original Records, at 39; Doc. History, at 429), it does not partake of either one. In the commentaries on the Convention the procedure is usually referred to as *Nachfrist*. *See, e.g.*, Will, *supra* note 16, at Art. 49, 2.1.3; and JOHN O. HONNOLD, UNIFORM LAW FOR INTERNATIONAL SALES UNDER THE 1980 UNITED NATIONS CONVENTION § 305 (2d ed. 1991). *See also infra* note 27.

[21] *See* Ziegel, *supra* note 19, at 3 (comment on art. 25).

Purpose

This paper attempts to elucidate the concept of fundamental breach. Its purpose is to replace the various approaches previously introduced by the courts and scholars with a methodology that provides more assistance to parties to determine whether a fundamental breach has occurred in a sales transaction governed by the Convention. To that end, the different approaches taken by scholars and the courts in defining fundamental breach will be critically examined. As mentioned above, article 25 was drafted in general terms and must be interpreted. Therefore, before examining the different approaches, it is necessary to identify the methods of interpretation provided by the Convention.

- Part I deals with the Convention's rules of interpretation. These rules require first and foremost an autonomous interpretation of the terms of the Convention in order to ensure its uniform application. They also provide that the traditional domestic rules of interpretation serve this goal.
- Part II analyzes legal writing and the reported case law on fundamental breach based on the premise that uniform application, in the absence of a supranational court endowed with the exclusive jurisdiction to interpret the Convention, requires consideration of case law and doctrine. It will become clear that both legal writers and courts basically employ the same approaches in determining whether a fundamental breach has been committed.
- Part III examines whether the employment of the different approaches can be justified by means of the Convention's rules of interpretation. Special emphasis will be given to the Convention's legislative history and the context of fundamental breach within the Convention.
- Part IV critiques the different approaches of the Convention's rules of interpretation. The following will be shown: First, the approaches cannot be applied to all situations of fundamental breach, past, present and future; second, that some of them are not applicable to the remedy of substitute delivery; and third, that their concurrent application is likely to produce conflicting results.
- Part V introduces a new methodology to determine fundamental breach, which further elaborates an approach that has recently been

employed by the German Supreme Court. This new methodology is based on a single concept and incorporates a test that asks whether the purpose of the contract is frustrated due to the breach, and determines whether the aggrieved party needs the remedy of avoidance or substitute delivery.

Part I — Rules of Interpretation and Construction under the Convention

The objective of Part I is to identify the rules of interpretation and construction under the Convention.

A. Interpretation Autonomous to the CISG

When interpreting the meaning of a certain work, term, or phrase under uniform international law, which is subject to various interpretations, it is first necessary to determine whether that term or phrase must be interpreted "autonomously" or as interpreted in domestic law.[22] Within the scope of the Convention and except for those cases where express reference is made to the *lex fori,* such as under articles 1(1)(b) and 28, it follows from article 7(1), that an "autonomous" interpretation is required. According to the latter provision, "regard is to be had to its international character and to

[22] *See* Peter Schlechtriem, *Unification of the Law for the International Sale of Goods, National Report: Germany, in* INTERNATIONALER KONGRESS FÜR RECHTSVERGLEICHNG 1986, DEUTSCHER LAENDERBERICHTE 121,136 (Schlechtriem, ed., 1987). A good example of the co-existence of both theories — interpretation autonomous to the Convention and interpretation in the light of domestic law — can be found in a decision of the European Court of Justice, Oct. 6, 1976, 12/76, Tessili/Dunlop, E.C.R. 1976, 1485, regarding the interpretation of the 1968 Brussels "Convention on Jurisdiction and the Enforcement of Judgements in Civil and Commercial Matters." The Court stated: "The Convention frequently uses expressions and terms from the field of Civil, Commercial and Civil Procedure Law whose meaning may differ in the several member states. Consequently, the question arises as to whether these expressions and terms must be seen as autonomous — and thus common to all member states —, or as reference to the substantive provisions of that law which is applicable on the basis of conflict-of-laws rules of the court at first concerned with the matter." *Id.*

the need to promote uniformity in its application and the observance of good faith in international trade."[23]

Respecting the "international character" of the Convention and "the need to promote uniformity" requires an autonomous interpretation of its terms and concepts in the context of the Convention itself, without reference to any meaning under a particular domestic legal system.[24] The articles and concepts of the Convention cannot be regarded as a species of domestic legislation, even after its incorporation or implementation into domestic law.[25] To do otherwise would not only lead to a breakdown of uniformity but would also promote forum shopping.[26]

---

[23] Art. 7 (1) provides:

> In the interpretation of this Convention, regard is to be had to its international character and to the need to promote uniformity in its application and the observance of good faith in international trade.

[24] This point has been emphasized by Michael J. Bonell, *Methodology in Applying Uniform Law for International Sales Under the U.N. Convention, in* Italian National Reports to the 12th International Congress of Comparatice Law, 45 (1986); Schlechtriem, *supra* note 23, at 137; Frank Diedrich, *Maintaining Uniformity in International Uniform Law via Autonomous Interpretation: Software Contracts and the* CISG, 8 PACE INT'L L.REV. 303, 313 (1996); Helen Elizabeth Hartnell, *Rousing the Sleeping Dog: The Validity to the Convention on Contracts for the International Sale of Goods,* 18 Y. J. INT'L L. 1, 47 (1993).

[25] *See* Michael Bonell, *Art. 7,*COMMENTARY ON THE INTERNATIONAL SALES LAW, THE 1980 VIENNA SALES CONVENTION, 2.2.1 (C. Bianca & M. Bonell eds., 1987); Amy H. Kastely, *Unification and Community: A Rhetorical Analysis of the United Nations Sales Convention,* 8 N.W. J.INT'L L. & BUS. 574, 601-2 (1988); Zhang Yuqing, *Principles of Interpretation of a Uniform Law and Functions of Travauz Preparatories, Commentaries and Case Collections for Interpretation of a Uniform Law, in* Uniform Commercial Law in the Twenty First Century: Proceedings of the Congress of the United Nations Commission on International Trade Law, U.N. GAOR Comm. on Int'l Trade L., 25th Sess., at 43, U.N. Doc. A/CN.9/SER.D/1 (1992).

[26] This point has been emphasized by Ferarri. *See* Franco Ferarri, *Uniform Interpretation of the 1980 Uniform Sales Law,* 24 GA. J. INT'L & COMP.L. 183, at 199 (1994), and Franco Ferarri, *Recent Development: CISG: Specific Topics of the CISG in Light of Judicial Application and Scholarly Writing,* 15 J.L. & COM. 1, at 9 (1995). The danger of forum shopping as a result of divergent interpretations has also been pointed out by Honnold. *See* JOHN HONNOLD, UNIFORM LAW FOR INTERNATIONAL SALES UNDER THE 1980 UNITED NATIONS CONVENTION § 92 (2d ed. 1991). The author states that "(t)he settlement of disputes would be complicated and litigants would be encouraged to engage in forum shopping if the courts of different countries persist in divergent interpretations of the Convention." *Id.*

However, where a term in the Convention has been taken from one or several legal systems, such as the "*Nachfrist*-type" requirement,[27] an analysis of its domestic meaning does not necessarily diminish the international character of the Convention and its primary aim of promoting uniformity.[28] Nor can one conclude that domestic interpretive techniques are excluded by that reference, provided that their application leads to results

---

[27] The "*Nachfrist*-type" requirement has its origin in German law and requires the creditor to give the debtor a notice requiring him to perform within a stated time. This principle is stated with regard to obligation to make reparation in BGB § 250; with regard to cases where a decision for performance has been rendered against the debtor in BGB § 283; and with regard to reciprocal contracts in BGB § 326. *See* GUENTER HEINZ TREITEL, REMEDIES FOR BREACH OF CONTRACT, A COMPARATIVE ACCOUNT 16-149 (1988).

[28] For similar conclusions, *see, e.g.*, Frans J.A. van der Velden, *The Law of International Sales, National Report: Netherlands, in* NETHERLAND REPORTS TO THE TWELFTH INTERNATIONAL CONGRESS OF COMPARATIVE LAW 21, 31-34 (Gerver et al. eds., 1986) (stating that where a source of uniform law is a specific provision of national law recourse to its domestic interpretation is a logical aid to interpretation of the uniform law). *See also* F.A. Mann, *Uniform Statutes in English Law*, 99 L.Q.R. 376, 383 (1983) (stating that "[i]t is simply common sense that if the Convention adopts a phrase which appears to have been taken from one legal system . . . where it is used in a specific sense, the international legislators are likely to have had that sense in mind and to intend its introduction into the Convention"); Paul Volken, *The Vienna Convention: Scope, Interpretation and Gap-Filling, in* DUBROVNIK LECTURES 40 (Sarcevic & Volken eds. 1986) (emphasizing that recourse to domestic interpretation theories is admissible as long as the ultimate goal of uniform application remains unchallenged); Franco Ferarri, *Uniform Interpretation of the 1980 Uniform Sales Law*, 24 GA. J. INT'L & COMP.L. 183, 209 (1994) (stating that recourse to the study of foreign concepts is admissible when "either the legislative history or the Convention itself leads to the conclusion that the drafters referred to concepts peculiar to a specific domestic legal system"); Ulrich Magnus, *UN-Kaufrecht, in* JULIUS VON STAUDINGERS KOMMENTAR ZUM BÜRGERLICHEN GESETZBUCH MIT EINFÜHRUNGSGESETZ UND NEBENGESETZEN Art. 7 n. 13 (13th ed. 1995) (stating with regard to the foreseeability requirement under article 74 that recourse to its English roots is admissible).

For somewhat different conclusions, *see* Bonell, *supra* note 25, at 2.2.1 (stating that "[t]o have regard to the 'international character' of the Convention means first of all to avoid relying on the rules and techniques traditionally followed in interpreting ordinary domestic legislation"); Bernard Audit, *The Vienna Sales Convention and the Lex Mercatoria, in* LEX MERCATORIA AND ARBITRATION 154 (Carbonneau ed., 1990); Gyula Eörsi, *General Provisions, in* INTERNATIONAL SALES 5-6 (1984); Franco Ferarri, *Uniform Interpretation of the 1980 Uniform Sales Law*, 24 GA. J. INT'L & COMP.L. 183, at 201-202 (1994); Nives Povrzenic, *Interpretation and Gap-Filling under the United Nations Convention on Contracts for the International Sale of Goods*, at 3(A) *Pace CISG Database* (visited April 1997) <http://www.cisg.law.pace.edu/cisg/biblio/gap-fill.html>.

which are persuasive and conform to the goals of the Convention in general, as well as those of the specific provision.[29] Domestic interpretation is compatible with article 7(1)[30] only if it is critically analyzed before application.

For example, interpretation under the English law "doctrine of fundamental breach"[31] is not permissible, since that concept was developed to enable an aggrieved buyer to escape contractual provisions when goods are defective.[32] It would be equally inconsistent with the Convention's objec-

---

[29] For similar affirmations, see Fritz Enderlein, *Uniform Law and its Application by Judges and Arbrators, in* INTERNATIONAL UNIFORM LAW IN PRACTICE 331-333 (UNIDROIT ed. 1988).

[30] The need for *critical* consideration of domestic legal concepts when interpreting uniform law has been pointed out by a decision of the German Supreme Court, BGH 14 July 1983, RIW 1984, 153, on art. 29 CMR (Convention on the Contract for the International Carriage of Goods by Road), where the carrier's liability depends on how the words "willful misconduct" in the English version and "faute . . . qui . . . est consideré comme equivalent au dol" in the French version were construed. After exhaustive consideration of foreign cases and analyses, the court came to the conclusion that in view of the linguistic ambiguities, regard should be had to "the Convention's legislative history as well as to its underlying policy and objective; in doing so, one must take care not to borrow domestic legal concepts *without closer inspection* as this might endanger the intended unification". [emphasis added]. *See id.*

A translated summary of the decision is reprinted in Peter Schlechtriem, *Unification of the Law for the International Sale of Goods, National Report: Germany, in* INTERNATIONALER KONGRESS FUER RECHTSVERGLEICHNG 1986, DEUTSCHER LAENDERBERICHTE 139 n.34 (Peter Schlechtriem ed., 1987).

[31] The doctrine of fundamental breach was introduced in Smeaton Hanscomb v. Sassoon I Setty [1953] 2 All E.R. 1471; Spurling v. Bradsbau [1956] 2 All E.R. 121; Karsales (Harrow) Ltd. v. Wallis [1956] 2 All E.R. 866. These decisions established the principle that it was a rule of law that a party to a contract could not be allowed to rely on an exclusion or exemption clause if he was guilty of a fundamental breach of that contract. This doctrine was put to rest by the House of Lords in Suisse Atlantique Sociétié d'Armement Maritime S.A. v. Rotterdamsche Kolen Centrale, [1967] A.C. 361, where the rule of law concept was rejected in favor of an approach based on the true construction of the contract. See *also* Photo Production Ltd. v. Securicor Transport Ltd., [1980] A.C. 827.

[32] For a similar conclusion, *see* New Zealand Law Commission, Report, at ¶ 56; *see also* John O. Honnold, UNIFORM LAW FOR INTERNATIONAL SALES UNDER THE 1980 UNITED NATIONS CONVENTION § 181.1 (2d ed. 1991).

tives to interpret its provisions according to a common law standard, in which a narrow statutory interpretation is utilized to limit the effect of a particular court decision.[33] Moreover, in contrast to common law legislation,[34] reference to (equitable) rules previously governing matters within the Convention's scope, whether derived from statute or case law, is also excluded by article 7(1).[35]

Traditional rules of interpretation in civilian legal systems, such as literal, historical, systematical and teleological rules, on the other hand, make allowances for the Convention's international character and its primary goal of uniform application.[36] If the meaning of a word or term in a statute

---

[33] For a similar affirmation, *see* Bonell, *supra* note 25, at 2.2.1 (stating that "there is no valid reason to adopt a narrow interpretation"). *See also* Audit, *supra* note 28, at 153. Historically, much of the common law world adhered to the doctrine of English courts that statutes must be given a literal reading, whereas in most civil law countries the judge may examine the preparatory works (*travaux préparatoires*) in pursuit of the subjective intention of the legislature. As for the interpretation of international conventions, however, the *House of Lords* in 1980 made a significant departure from the strict English approach with respect to treaty interpretation (see Fothergill v. Monarch Airlines, [1980] 2 All ER 696, where four of five law lords made reference to the legislative history in order to interpret a provision of the Warsaw Convention on the liability of air carriers). Recently, the *House of Lords* has further relaxed the traditional approach in respect of domestic legislation (§ 63(1) of the Finance Act 1976). It held that:

> The rule prohibiting courts from referring to parliamentary material as aid to statutory construction should, subject to any question of parliamentary privilege, be relaxed so as to permit reference to parliamentary materials where (a) the legislation was ambiguous or obscure or the literal meaning led to an absurdity, (b) the material relied on consisted of statements by a minister or other promoter of the Bill which lead to the enactment of the legislation together if necessary with such other parliamentary material as was necessary to understand such statements and their effect and (c) the statements relied on were clear. *See* Pepper v. Hart, [1993] 1 All ER 42, at 43; [1992] 3 W.L.R. 1032, at 1033.

[34] *See, e.g.*, UCC § 1-103 which provides:

> "Unless displaced by the particular provision of this Act, the principles of [common] law and equity, including the law merchant . . . shall supplement its provisions." *Id.*

[35] *See* Frank Diedrich, *Voraussetzungen einer Vertragsaufhebung wegen Sachmängeln nach dem Wiener Kaufrecht,* 11, 13, RIW (1995). *See also* Diedrich, *supra* note 24, at 319 (stating that recourse to common law rules is not admissible).

[36] For similar affirmation, see ENDERLEIN, *supra* note 26, at 331-33; Joanne M. Darkey, *Recent Developments: CISG: A U.S. Court's Interpretation of Damage Provisions under the U.N. Convention on Contracts for the International Sale of Goods: A Preliminary Step Towards an International Jurisprudence of CISG or Missed Opportunity?* 15 J.L. & Com. 138,

is clear, literal interpretation best serves both requirements.[37] The same is generally true with historical, systematical or teleological interpretation. Such applications require no reference to domestic law, but only to the provisions, legislative history, and goals of the Convention as a whole, and to the particular provision.[38] If the meaning of a statute is ambiguous, article 7(1) requires the application of these methods of interpretation.[39]

In the following section, the suitability of these traditional methods of interpretation of the Convention will be examined in greater detail.

---

141 (1995) (stating that "since the CISG is a code, it is a logical assumption that a civil law approach to interpretation is favored"); Schlechtriem, *supra* note 22, at 149 (stating that in "the interpretation of uniform law of sales just as in the interpretation of domestic law, the grammatical/verbal, the systematic, the historical and the teleological methods are distinguished").

[37] *See, e.g.*, Van der Velden, *supra* note 28, at 24 and Diedrich, *supra* note 24, at 328.

[38] Though concerned with the interpretation of treaties between states, the 1969 Vienna Convention on the Law of Treaties, U.N. Doc. A/CONF. 39/27, *reprinted* in 289 I.L.M. 679 (1969), confirms this point. Art. 31 of that Convention provides that a treaty shall be interpreted in good faith in accordance with the ordinary meaning to be given to the terms of the treaty in their context and in the light of its object and purpose. Art. 32 of that Convention further provides that recourse may be had to supplementary means of interpretation, including the preparatory work of the treaty and the circumstances of its conclusion, in order to confirm the meaning resulting from the application of art. 31, or to determine the meaning when the interpretation according to art. 31 leaves the meaning ambiguous or obscure or leads to a result which is manifestly absurd or unreasonable.

[39] For similar conclusions, see, e.g., Diedrich, *supra* note 24, at 321; ENDERLEIN, *supra* note 26, at 333-34; Frans J.A. van der Velden, *The Law of international Sales: The Hague Conventions 1964 and the UNCITRAL Uniform Sales Code 1980 — Some Main Items Compared, in* HAGUE-ZAGREB ESSAYS 4 58 (Voskuil & Wade eds., 1983). *See also* Peter Schlechtriem, *From The Hague to Vienna-Progress in Unification of the Law of International Sale Contracts, in* THE TRANSNATIONAL LAW OF INTERNATIONAL COMMERCIAL TRANSACTIONS: STUDIES IN TRANSNATIONAL ECONOMIC LAW 125, 134 (Horn & Schmitthoff eds., 1982) (stressing with regard to the teleological interpretation the importance of the teleological method to preserve and further uniformity).

B. The Four Classical Methods of Interpretation

1. Literal Interpretation

With regard to the Convention's overriding objective of uniformity, the primary guide to interpretation is the ordinary meaning of the words.[40] If a word's meaning is evident, either in its ordinary connotation or within a unique context, no further interpretation is required. In the event of ambiguity in one of the several language versions of the Convention, the various versions must be compared to determine whether each presents the same linguistic uncertainty.[41] If, after such comparison the exact meaning cannot be ascertained, or if it reveals disparities between the authentic texts,[42] then the literal interpretation must be supported by other methods of interpretation, since no single language may prevail.[43]

---

[40] *See* ENDERLEIN, *supra* note 26, at 331; Van der Velden, *supra* note 28, at 24; and Diedrich, *supra* note 24, at 328.

[41] *See* Schlechtriem, *supra* note 22, at 138 (observing that "numerous volumes [of decisions by German Courts] could be filled with similar decisions on uniform law created by international conventions: all of these decisions attempt to find a solution by analyzing the wording with regard to the several original languages. . . ."); and ENDERLEIN, *supra* note 26, at 331.

The UNIDROIT Principles art. 4.7, see *infra* note 67, provides that preference should be given to the version in the language in which the contract was originally drawn up.

[42] Several disparities in wording and content between the various language texts, mostly between the English and the French version, have been reported. *See, e.g.*, Vivian Curran, *Book Review: The Interpretive Challenge to Uniformity by Claude Witz,* 15 J.L. & COM. 175, 180 (1995) (referring to differences in terminology between the French and the English version of arts. 3(1), 71 and 72); Audit, *supra* note 28, at 154 (referring to the differences between the English and the French version of art. 39 which refers to the "non-conformity of the goods" whereas the French text speaks of "*défault de conformité*" in general terms); van der Velden, *supra* note 28, at 25 (asserting that the English and French enumerations under art. 2(d) are not identical in all details); and Arthur Rosett, *Critical Relections on the United Nations Convention on Contracts for the International Sale of Goods,* 45 OHIO ST. L.J. 265, 302 (1984) (analyzing the problems of translation when drafting and interpreting multilingual legal texts with reference to article 46).

[43] *See, e.g.*, Suzanne V. Cook, *The Need for Uniform Interpretation of the 1980 United Nations Convention on Contracts for the International Sale of Goods,* 50 U.PITT.L.REV. 197, (1988); and van der Velden, *supra* note 28, at 25. For somewhat different conclusions, see

2. Legislative History

Interpretation by way of legislative history seeks to resolve inherent ambiguities by considering the drafters' motives and deliberations, as evidenced in the officially published *travaux préparatoires.*[44] At the national level, materials connected with the preparation of the law are parliamentary debates, minutes of meetings of commissions etc. At the international level, such materials include the records of diplomatic conferences, documents that formed the basis for the work of the conferences, commentaries, drafts proposed by working groups, and comments of governments that participated in the drafting process.[45] Consequently, one should not only refer to the acts and proceedings of the Vienna Conference and the summary records of the previous deliberations within UNCITRAL. One must also examine the Convention's predecessor, the 1964 Hague Sales Conventions,[46] since the deliberations in UNCITRAL started with an analysis of the 1964 text.[47]

Diedrich, *supra* note 24, at 328 (asserting that in case of disparities article 33 of the Vienna Convention on the Law of Treaties has to be applied, which provides that the real or normative intention of the final diplomatic conference is decisive, and concluding that only the French and English texts have to examined).

[44] In the eyes of some scholars interpretation by means of legislative history is only one way of historical interpretation. *See, e.g.*, ENDERLEIN, *supra* note 26, at 333 and van der Velden, *supra* note 28, at 28. They contrast between interpretation by means of *legal* history and by means of *legislative* history. They are apparently of the opinion that the latter method does not allow consideration and analysis of the law as it was before the enactment of a statute. This is not true as far as the previous law was subject of the drafters' deliberations and the starting point for amendments. Besides, reference to previous provisions is not allowed if such reference is aimed at justifying an interpretation different from the one that can be found in the officially published preparatory works. Thus only when these works are silent on the reasons for amendments or the drafters expressly referred to previous provisions reference to them is admissible.

[45] *See* PETER SCHLECHTRIEM, UNIFORM SALES LAW: THE UN CONVENTION ON CONTRACTS FOR THE INTERNATIONAL SALE OF GOODS 19 (1986) and Yuqing, *supra* note 25, at 45.

[46] Convention Relating to a Uniform Law on the International Sale of Goods ("ULIS"), July 1, 1964, 834 U.N.T.S. 107 (1972); 3 I.L.M. 854; also available in full text at http://www.cisg.law.pace. edu/cisg/text/ulis.html; and Convention Relating to a Uniform Law on the Formation of Contracts for the International Sale of Goods ("ULFC"), July 1, 1964, 834 U.N.T.S. 169 (1972); 3 I.L.M. 864; also available in full text at http://www.cisg.law.pace.edu/cisg/text /ulf.html.

[47] *See* HONNOLD, *supra* note 20, at § 88. *See also* John O. Honnold, *Uniform Words and Uniform Application. The 1980 Sales Convention and International Juridicial Practice, in*

The unofficial commentary prepared by the UNCITRAL Secretariat for the 1980 Vienna Diplomatic Conference on the Convention must also be considered.[48] This commentary summarizes relevant conclusions derived from the legislative history of the Convention prior to the Conference and was used extensively by the delegates as a guide to the meaning of certain 1978 Draft Convention provisions. Where the Official Text of a provision is typically close to or identical with the 1978 Draft version of the same provision, it is said that the Secretariat Commentary is nevertheless the most persuasive citation.[49]

The interpretation of an international convention through legislative history presents some difficulties.[50] First, unlike those at the national level, preparatory materials of a diplomatic conference are often neither widely known nor available.[51] This, however, is not true for the Convention, because the deliberations of the Vienna Diplomatic Conference are well documented.[52]

EINHEITLICHES KAUFRECHT UND NATIONALES OBLIGATIONENRECHT 115, 130 (Peter Schlechtriem ed., 1987) (stating that where the Hague text was retained, modified, or rejected the discussions shed light on the common understanding of the Hague solution and the reasons for its retention or for the change); Claude Samson, *La vente: Convention des Nations Unies sur les contrats de vente internationale de marchandises, in* CONFÉRENCES SUR LE NOUVEAU CODE CIVIL DU QUÉBEC 269, 283 (Yvon Blais ed., 1992) ("Pour s'assurer que l'interprète devra prendre connaissance de l'historique du mouvement d'uniformisation du droit de la vente internationale de marchandises qui constitute le contexte dans lequel la C.V.I.M. a été adoptée").

[48] *See generally* Secretariat Commentary, *supra* note 16.

[49] To the same effect, see database of the University of Freiburg, http://www.jura.uni-freiburg. de/ipr1/cisg/guide/8-2.htm (explaining the function of the Secretariat Commentary).

However, it is important to keep in mind that the Secretariat Commentary is a commentary on the 1978 Draft Convention, not on the official text that was eventually adopted by the 1980 Diplomatic Conference.

[50] *See, e.g.*, van der Velden, *supra* note 28, at 28.

[51] *See* ENDERLEIN, *supra* note 26, at 333.

[52] The documents embodying this legislative history are reproduced in Volumes I-X of the UNCITRAL Yearbooks and in the Official Records of the 1980 Diplomatic Conference. *See* United Nations Conference on Contracts for the International Sale of Goods, Official Records, UN Document No. A/CONF. 97/19, (Vienna, 10 March-11 April 1980) [hereinafter Official Records].

Furthermore, the relevant documents are reproduced and introduced and references in the documents' margins to the final articles of the Convention for which the

Second, it is difficult to determine the opinion of a diplomatic conference.[53] Like other international agreements, the Convention was not established unilaterally but was negotiated. One of the features of negotiation is that the negotiating parties do not always reveal their true intentions.[54] An agreement is typically reached without respect to the individual intentions of the contracting parties, but instead, through compromise. Accordingly, agreement on a text does not necessarily imply agreement as to the intentions of the delegates to a conference.[55] Divergent or even conflicting intentions may well underlie a final text.[56]

These concerns, however, may also be raised in the context of national legislation. It is therefore evident that caution is needed in approaching legislative history in general. In this author's opinion, where a proposal has been rejected by a clear majority and, provided that official records reveal the prevalent understanding of the delegates, legislative history creates a binding interpretation of the Convention, i.e. those proposals should never be admissible evidence in a dispute.[57]

---

legislative deliberations were relevant are provided by Honnold's excellent Documentary History of Uniform Law for International Sales. *See generally* JOHN O. HONNOLD, DOCUMENTARY HISTORY OF THE UNIFORM LAW FOR INTERNATIONAL SALES (1989) [hereinafter Documentary History].

[53] *See* ENDERLEIN, *supra* note 26, at 333.

[54] *See* Note, *supra* note 5, at 1989 (criticizing the negotiation procedure at the Vienna Conference and stating that "[t]he delegates may have accepted compromises simply because they regarded the portions reflecting their own national laws to be the essence of the new formulations"); Leif Sevón, *Method of Unification of Law for the International Sale of Goods, in* THE FINNISH NATIONAL REPORTS TO THE TWELFH CONGRESS OF THE INTERNATIONAL ACADEMY OF COMPARATIVE LAW 22 (Burre-Hägglund eds., 1986) (stating that the reasons for introducing or supporting a provision do not necessarily reveal the background of that provision).

[55] *See* Bonell, *supra* note 25, at 3.1.3. (stating that even when the arguments put forward in favor of the adoption of a given provision were not controversial they are not necessarily decisive).

[56] For a similar statement, see Sevón, *supra* note 54, at 22 (stating that the reasons for introducing or supporting a provision given by one or a few delegates does not necessarily reveal the background of that provision).

[57] For a similar conclusion, see ENDERLEIN, *supra* note 26, at 333. But see, for a somewhat different conclusion, Dietrich Maskow, *On the Interpretation of the Uniform Rulse of the 1980 UN Convention on Contracts for the International Sale of Goods, in* NATIONALES KOMITEE FÜR RECHTSWISSENSCHAFT DER DDR 14 (1986).

3. Systematic Interpretation

There are two ways of interpreting law systematically.[58] One seeks to discover the meaning of a statutory provision by looking at its context and interpreting it in relation to other provisions of a given instrument.[59] This approach, both at the domestic and the international level, is important to avoid conflicting interpretations of identical or similar terms within a complex legal text, especially where each provision is to be understood as part of a broader analytic system.[60] Even though international conventions sometimes lack the coherent structure that exists in a national code,[61] in general, this variant of systematic interpretation promotes the uniform application of rules within a single statute, such as the Convention.[62]

---

[58] *See* van der Velden, *supra* note 28, at 27 and ENDERLEIN, *supra* note 26, at 332 (stating that systematic interpretation has two aspects). Sometimes systematic interpretation is also called logical interpretation. It seems that these terms are used interchangeably when used to describe interpretive techniques and do not in fact differ.

[59] *See* van der Velden, *supra* note 28, at 27 and ENDERLEIN, *supra* note 26, at 332.

[60] The importance of the systematic approach to interpretation within the Convention is emphasized by Schlechtriem, *supra* note 22, at 139. *See also* Kastely, *supra* note 25, at 604 (stating with regard to the systematical interpretation that it follows from Art. 7 (1) that the Convention is to be interpreted as a "complex legal text, in which each detailed provision is to be understood as a part of a larger analytic system, given coherence by an underlying set of values"); HONNOLD, *supra* note 20, at § 186 (as to the term "fundamental breach" in context); Andrew Babiak, *Defining "Fundamental Breach" under the United Nations Convention on Contracts for the International Sale of Goods*, 6 TEMPLE INT'L & COMP. L.J. 113, 117 (1992); Mann, *supra* note 28, at 382; Magnus, *supra* note 28, at Art. 7 n. 34; and GERHARD DANNEMANN, AN INTRODUCTION TO GERMAN CIVIL AND COMMERCIAL LAW 4 (1993) (stressing that the unified structure of [German] law requires that legal provisions must be interpreted in such a way that they do not contradict each other).

[61] For a similar statement, see J. S. Hobhouse, *International Conventions and Commercial Law: The Pursuit of Uniformity*, 106 L. Q. R. 530, 534 (1990).

[62] The controversy over whether the lack of a definite price term in an offer leads to the failure of the offer shows the practical significance of the systematic interpretation under the Convention. To determine the validity of an offer that neither fixes the price nor makes provision for determining the price, the relationship between Article 14 and Article 55 needs to be examined to avoid discrepancy. For an overview and detailed discussion of the controversy, see generally Paul Amato, *Recent Developments: CISG. U.N. Convention on Contracts for the International Sale of Goods — The Open Price Term and Uniform Application: an Early Interpretation by the Hungarian Courts*, 13 J.L. & COM. 1

The second approach to systematic interpretation is to look at a certain provision within a legal system as a whole.[63] Unlike at the domestic level, however, at the international level there exists no international legislator and thus no legal order, which requires consideration of one statute's relationship to other statutes and interpretation of similar provisions in such a way to avoid contradiction.[64] In addition, the purpose of each convention usually differs, as with special statutes for particular issues under domestic law. For these reasons, as long as a general system of uniform laws has not been established, it would be arbitrary and therefore contrary to the purpose of unification to compare international conventions with each other in order to systematically interpret their provisions.[65] Only when a convention expressly refers to another convention should reference to the latter be permissible. Under the Convention, however, there is no such reference and, therefore, other international conventions should not generally act as a source for its systematic interpretation.[66]

(1993) (commenting on early interpretations of the open price term by Hungarian Courts) and Gyula Eörsi, *Art. 55, in* COMMENTARY ON THE INTERNATIONAL SALES LAW, THE 1980 VIENNA SALES CONVENTION 2.2.2 (C. Bianca & M. Bonell eds., 1987).

[63] *See* van der Velden, *supra* note 28, at 27 and ENDERLEIN, *supra* note 26, at 332.

[64] *See* Diedrich, *supra* note 24, at 335 (stating that systematic comparison with other conventions is dogmatically inadmissible since there is no international uniform law that could serve as justification for the principle of legal unity within one system of law that presupposes a methodical and dogmatic consistency of its laws). *See also* van der Velden, *supra* note 28, at 27.

[65] *See* Diedrich, *supra* note 24, at 335 (stating that as long as the international legislator is generally not identical it would be questionable to "transplant definitions or legal maxims from one convention to another unless these were explicitly or obviously adopted by the international legislator with the same specific meaning for the convention in question"). *See also* van der Velden, *supra* note 28, at 27, where the author points out as follows: "[O]nce we try to interpret a provision by considering its relation to other statutes, we are on a slippery slope. Then we have to decide the question, what relationship exists between the various uniform statutes. Are they to be considered part of a general system of uniform law that is still in *statu nascendi*, part of a *lex mercatoria moderna*?" *Id.*

[66] For somewhat different conclusions, without further explanation, however, see ENDERLEIN, *supra* note 26, at 332; (asserting that different uniform laws, such as the 1974 Limitation Convention for International Sale of Goods, should be compared and used for systematic interpretation).

It has recently been suggested that the UNIDROIT Principles of International Commercial Contracts[67] should be used as a means of interpreting the Convention, provided that the relevant provision of the UNIDROIT Principles serves the same purpose as its corresponding provision in the Convention.[68] The objections to reliance on other international conventions, however, also apply in this context. In addition, there is another argument against the employment of the UNIDROIT Principles, namely the

---

[67] International Institute for the Unification of Private Law, Principles of International Commercial Contracts (Rome 1994) [hereinafter UNIDROIT Principles]. The UNIDROIT Principles were approved in May 1994 by the UNIDROIT Governing Council of the International Institute for the Unification of Private Law. They do not have the force of law and can be best compared to Restatements of the law published in the United States. To an extent, the Principles are modeled on the Convention. The Principles are, however, far broader in scope since they are, unlike the Convention, not limited to contracts for the sale of goods and furthermore also deal with the question of contract validity. The UNIDROIT Principles are divided into seven chapters ("General Provisions," "Formation," "Validity," "Interpretation," "Content," "Performance," and "Non-Performance") and preceded by a Preamble defining their scope of application.

For an overview of the UNIDROIT Principles, see generally, Joseph M. Perillo, *UNIDROIT Principles of Internationale Commercial Contracts: The Black Letter Text and a Review,* 63 Fordham L. Rev. 281 (1994) and Franco Ferrari, *Defining the Sphere of Application of the 1994 "UNIDROIT Principles of International Commercial Contracts,"* 69 Tul.L.Rev. 1225 (1995). The text of the Black Letter Rules of the UNIDROIT Principles is also available at <http://www.unidroit.org/english/principles/princ.html>.

[68] *See* Michael J.Bonell, *The UNIDROIT Principles of International Commercial Contracts: Why? What? How?,* 69 Tul.L.Rev. 1121, 1142-1143 (1995); Perillo, *supra* note 67, at 283; Ferrari, *supra* note 67, at 1232-35; Alejandro M. Garro, *The Gap Filling Role of the UNIDROIT Principles in International Sales Law: Some Comments on the Interplay between the Principles and the CISG,* 69 Tul.L.Rev. 1149, 1152-55 (1995); Luiz Olavo Baptista, *The UNIDROIT Principles for International Commercial Law Project: Aspects of International Private Law,* 69 Tul. L.Rev. 1209, 1218 (1995); Ulrich Magnus, *The General Principles of the CISG,* 3 Int'l Trade & Bus. L. A. (Austr.) 33-56, at 6(b) (1997); Ralph Amissah, The Autonomous Contract, in Seminar on Legal Information 10, 33 (1997) (at <http://itl.irv.uit.no/trade_law/papers/The.Autonomous.Contract.18.08.1997.Amissah.c.html>; and Maskow, *supra* note 57, at 11 (all stating that the UNIDROIT Principles could play a role in interpreting and supplementing international instruments). As to the relationship between the UNIDROIT Principles and the Convention in general, see A.S. Hartkamp, *The UNIDROIT Principles for International Commercial Contracts and the United Nations Convention on Contracts for the International Sale of Goods, in*

very existence of another uniform law project within the framework of the Commission on European Contract Law; the Principles of European Contract Law.[69]

Although the European Principles address basically the same issues of general contract law and are very similar to the UNIDROIT Principles in terms of formal presentation,[70] the existence of competing instruments to interpret the Convention *per se* contradicts the purpose of the Convention to unify international sales law. More important than this theoretical argument, however, is the fact that the two intruments do not entirely coincide as to their content.[71] Since the territorial scope of the European Principles

---

COMPARABILITY AND EVALUATION. ESSAYS ON COMPARATIVE LAW, PRIVATE INTERNATIONAL LAW AND INTERNATIONAL COMMERCIAL ARBITRATION 95 (1994).

[69] *See generally* COMMISSION ON EUROPEAN CONTRACT LAW, THE PRINCIPLES OF EUROPEAN CONTRACT LAW (Ole Lando & Hugh Beale eds., 1995) [hereinafter European Principles]. Like the UNIDROIT Principles, the European Principles do not have the force of law. To date, the European Community has no legislative competence in the area of sales law. This lack of jurisdiction, however, does not exclude that, at a future date, the European Principles may be set in place as an instrument that has the force of law in the European Community, such as the Rome Convention on the Law Applicable to Contractual Obligations, June 19, 1980, O.J. (L.266); *reprinted* in 8 I.L.M. 1492 (1980) [hereinafter Rome Convention]. Referring to the desirability of "a common European Code of Private Law," this goal is set forth in the Resolution of 6 May 1994 of the European Parliament that set in place the Commission on European Contract Law that authored the Principles of European Contract Law. *See Cross Reference and Editorial Analysis of CISG Article 7, in* Pace CISG Database, <*http://www.cisg.law.pace.edu/cisg/biblio/hillman.htm*> fn.18 (Sept. 1997). For an account of the efforts made in order to create the "European Contract Law," see Ole Lando, *European Contract Law,* 31 AM.J.COMP.L. 653, 653-55 (1983). As for the relationship between the UNIDROIT Principles, the Convention and the European Principles, see Bonell, *supra* note 2, at 229-46.

There are two versions of the European Principles. The English text of the first version is available at <http://www.ufsia.be/ ~estorme/PECL1en.html>. The completed and revised English text of the second version is available at <http://www.ufsia.be/ ~estorme/PECL2en.html>.[/FN]

[70] To this effect, see Bonell, *supra* note 69, at 245.

[71] The practically most important example for a significant divergence in the remedial system between the two instruments concerns the non-performing party's right to cure. While the UNIDROIT Principles grant the non-performing party such right even if the aggrieved party has rightfully terminated the contract (see art. 7.1.4), according to the European Principles, the non-performing party may cure only where the time of performance has not yet arrived or the delay would not be such as to constitute a funda-

is formally limited to the Member States of the European Union, while the UNIDROIT Principles are universal, it is to be expected that the courts and tribunals outside of Europe or in commercial transactions involving non-Europeans would apply the UNIDROIT Principles to interpret the Convention, while within the European Union or in purely intra-European contracts, the European Principles would be applied.[72]

Such a scenario clearly jeopardizes the objectives of the Convention and, therefore, courts and arbitral tribunals should not apply either instrument as a means of interpreting ambiguous terms.[73] Critical consideration

---

mental non-performance. *See* European Principes, *supra* note 69, at art. 8:104 (ex art. 3.104).

For further examples of divergences, see Bonell, *supra* note 69, at 236-41.

[72] *See id.* at 245 (envisaging that "outside Europe or in commercial transactions involving non-Europeans, it will be the UNIDROIT Principles that apply, while within the European Union or in purely intra-European contracts, especially between merchants and consumers, it will be the European Principles that prevail"). *Id.*

[73] The future existence of two similar sets of "Principles" has led some commentators to make "doomsday" predictions. Parties and arbitrators, it is argued, will be faced with two competing instruments and the need to choose between them is seen as a veritable "nightmare scenario." *See, e.g.,* H. Raeschke-Kessler, *Should an Arbitrator in an International Arbitration Procedure Apply the UNIDROIT Principles?, in* UNIDROIT PRINCIPLES FOR INTERNATIONAL COMMERCIAL CONTRACTS, A NEW LEX MERCATORIA? 167, 174–75 (Inst. Of Int'l Bus. Law ed., 1995). *See also* C. Kessedian, *Un exercise de rénovation des sources du droit des contrats du commerce international: Les Principes proposés par l'Unidroit, in* RCDIP 641, 669 (1995).

The few reported cases where courts have applied the UNIDROIT Principles do not concern the interpretation of the Convention but the filling of gaps in the Convention, namely three arbitration awards — two rendered by the International Court of Arbitration of the Federal Chamber of Commerce of Vienna, [Award No. 4318 and Award No. 4366 of 15 June 1994] (for an English translation see UNILEX, third release (1997), E.1994-13 and E.1994-14; for extracts of the original German version, see RIW 1995, 590 et seq.) and one by the Court of Arbitration of the International Chamber of Commerce [ICC Award No. 8128 of 1995] (an abstract of which has been published in J.D.I. 1996, 1024). They all deal with the determination of interest rates, the amount of which is not fixed under the Convention.

There is also a national court decision, which applied the UNIDROIT Principles in order to confirm a result already reached under the Convention. In determining the place of performance of the seller's obligation to return part of the price unduly paid by the buyer, a Swiss court stated that monetary obligations are to be performed at the promisee's place of business, which could be extracted not only from art. 57(1), but also

of concepts and criteria used in properly interpreting the Convention offered by those instruments, however, should be permissible. In this respect, the same restrictions pertinent to the use of the domestic interpretation of a given Convention term apply to those instruments.[74] In other words, resorting to the principles and criteria under the UNIDROIT Principles or any other uniform law project should only be permissible when their application can be justified by the legislative history and the underlying purposes of a given provision in the context of the Convention itself.

4. Teleological Method of Interpretation

The teleological method of interpretation attempts to resolve uncertainties and bridge lacunae in legislation by looking at the objectives and underlying policies of the text in question.[75] There are two different aspects to teleological interpretation; the object and purpose of the particular provision or terms which require interpretation, and the object and purpose of the statute as a whole.[76] Determining the legislator's intent requires the use of *travaux préparatoires*.[77] As far as it concerns the interpretation of a single provision, the teleological approach thus faces the same problems as interpretation by legislative history. In regard to the object of the Convention as a whole, however, the drafting parties' intent is more easily discernible. That intent is laid out in the Convention's preamble[78] and reinforced by the directive in Article 7(1) for regard to be had to its "international character" and the need to "promote uniformity."[79] In practice, this means that at-

---

from art. 6.1.6 of the UNIDROIT Principles. *See* Cour d'appel de Grenoble, 23 October 1996, unpublished; a summary is published in 1 UNIFORM L.REV. (1997).

[74] *See supra* Part I, B. 1.

[75] *See* Schlechtriem, *supra* note 22, at 141 and Lisa M. Ryan, *The Convention on Contracts for the International Sale of Goods: Divergent Interpretations,* 4 TUL.J.INT'L & COMP.L. 99, 117 (both emphasizing the importance of the interpretation of the Convention by way of the teleological method).

[76] *See* Mann, *supra* note 28, at 383.

[77] *See, e.g.*, Honnold, Uniform Words, *supra* note 47, at § 88 (underlining the link of legislative materials to realize the purpose of the legislation).

[78] See The Vienna Convention on the Law of Treaties, *supra* note 38, art 31(2), which specifically mentions the preamble of a treaty as being part of the context for the purpose of the interpretation of a treaty.

[79] See the third clause of the Convention's preamble which reads:

> *Being of the opinion* that the adoption of uniform rules which govern contracts for the inter-

tention must be given to the way the Convention is interpreted in other countries by the courts, scholars, and practitioners.[80]

5. Prevailing Method in Case of Conflicting Results

Although there is much scholarly writing on the Convention's interpretive techniques, the problem of which technique prevails in the event of conflicting results has not yet been discussed. As discussed later in this Paper, this question becomes pertinent in determining fundamental breach in the context of the seller's right to cure a defect under article 48(1) and the buyer's right to avoid the contract under article 49(1)(a). The point at issue is whether it is permissible to replace the literal, historical, and contextual interpretation by a teleological approach.[81]

In the absence of a supranational tribunal endowed with exclusive jurisdiction to interpret the Convention's provisions, it seems to be contrary to the principle of uniform application, as embodied in the Convention, to allow national courts to disregard the plain wording in order to give effect to what it deems the overriding purpose of a single provision.[82] Only where the plain meaning of one provision contradicts that of another, as with articles 14 and 55,[83] is recourse to other interpretive methods permissible,

---

national sale of goods and take into account the different social, economic and legal systems would contribute to the removal of legal barriers in international trade and promote the development of international trade.

See *Official Records,* supra *note 52.*

[80] For similar conclusions, see Audit, *supra* note 28, at 154; Bonell, *supra* note 25, at 3.1.3; Mann, *supra* note 28, at 383-84; Diedrich, *supra* note 24, at 321; Yuqing, *supra* note 25, at 45-6; and Babiak, *supra* note 60, at 117.

For a discussion of the role of doctrinal writing in the unification of law, see Edgar Bodenheimer, *Doctrine as Source of the International Unification of Law,* 43 AM. J. COMP. L. 67 (1986).

[81] *See infra* Part II, B. 1. f.

[82] For a similar reasoning and conclusion, see Magnus, *supra* note 28, at art. 7, n.32. For a somewhat different conclusion, see Bonell, *supra* note 25, at 2.2.1 (stating that courts are expected to look whenever it is possible to the underlying purposes and policies of individual provisions as well as the Convention as a whole instead of sticking to their grammatical meaning).

[83] According to art. 14 a proposal "is sufficiently definite if it . . . expressly or implicitly fixes or makes provision for determining . . . the price. On the other hand, art. 55 provides that "where a contract has been validly concluded but does not expressly or implicitly fix or make provision for determining the price, the parties are considered, in the

since such contradictions endanger the Convention's overall goal to promote uniformity.

C. Observance of Good Faith in International Trade

Article 7(1) requires that, in the application of the Convention, attention be paid not only to the need to promote uniformity but also to "the observance of good faith in international trade." The Convention does not provide a definition or the scope that should be given to "good faith" as an aid to interpretation, and there are as yet no published decisions which apply that principle.[84] With regard to its scope, scholars find themselves in disaccord as to whether good faith operates simply as an additional criterion in interpreting the Convention or if it is also governs the conduct of the parties to a contract.[85] There is, however, a general consensus of opin-

---

absence of any indication to the contrary, to have impliedly made reference to the price generally charged at the time of the conclusion of the contract for such goods sold under comparable circumstances in the trade concerned". To resolve this controversy it has been argued that art. 55, in Part III of the Convention dealing with the obligations of the buyer, was designed for use only where a Contracting State made a declaration under art. 92(1) that it will not be bound by Part II of the Convention on contract formation. For an overview on and detailed discussion of the controversy, see Amato, *supra* note 62, at 8 (commenting on early interpretations of the open price term by Hungarian Courts). *See also* E. Allan Farnsworth, *Formation of Contract, in* INTERNATIONAL SALES 1, ch.3, 8-9 (Galston & Smit eds., 1984).

[84] *See* Yuqing, *supra* note 25, at 43. The vagueness of the concept of good faith has been criticized, for instance, by Rosett, *supra* note 42, at 289, where the author points out "the multiple meanings of good faith and the differing connotations the doctrine possesses in different legal systems." *See also* E. Allan Farnsworth, *Problems of the Unification of Sales Law from the Standpoint of the Common Law Countries,* 7 DIG. COM. L. 3, 18 (1980) (where the author draws attention to the disadvantages of the good faith term due to its vagueness).

Its incorporation into the Convention has been welcomed, *inter alia*, by Muna Ndulo, *The Vienna Sales Convention 1980 and the Hague Uniform Laws on International Sale of Goods 1964: A Comparative Analysis,* 38 INT'L & COMP. L.Q. 1, 9 (1989)(asserting that the good faith principle gives the courts the flexibility which is needed by any code to make it work in practice since it allows courts to avoid an over-literal interpretation which would provide inequitable results not intended by the drafters, and could prevent a too hasty resort to domestic law).

[85] See Bonell, *supra* note 25, at 2.4, who points out that the "good faith" requirement represents a compromise between the views of those representatives "who would have preferred a provision imposing directly on the parties the duty to act in good faith, and

ion that the use of domestic definitions and concepts is barred by the reference to "international trade," which reinforces the Convention's goal "to promote uniformity."[86]

The controversy over the scope of the concept of "good faith" seems to be of purely academic character. In practice, it appears to be nearly impossible to apply this principle to the interpretation of the Convention without also applying it to the parties' conduct.[87] Moreover, there are several provisions in the Convention that are directed at the parties' conduct and which

---

those who in the contrary were opposed to any explicit reference to the principle of good faith in the Convention." *Id.*

However, the compromise did not end the controversy between the divergent views and it is now in dispute how the reference to the interpretation of the Convention is to be understood. Some authors insist on the literal meaning of art. 7(1) and conclude that the principle of good faith is just an additional criterion to which judges must make reference in the interpretation of the Convention. *See, e.g.*, Hillman, *supra* note 69, at ¶ 3; E. Allan Farnsworth, *The Vienna Convention: History and Scope,* 18 Int'l Law 17, 18 (1984); Peter Winship, *International Sales Contracts Under the 1980 Vienna Covention,* 17 U.C.C. L.J. 55, 67 (1984); and Gyula Eörsi, *A Propos for the 1980 Vienna Convention on Contracts for the International Sale of Goods,* 27 AM.J.COMP.L 333, 349 (1983). Others take the view that "the need to promote. . .the observance of good faith in international trade" is also necessarily directed to the parties to each individual contract of sale. *See, e.g.*, Bonell, *supra* note 25, at 84; Rosett, *supra* note 42, at 290. In substance, see also SCHLECHTRIEM, *supra* note 45, at 39; Dietrich Maskow, *The Convention on Contracts for the International Sale of Goods from the Perspective of the Socialist Countries, in* La Vendita Internazionale 39, 54-57 (Giuffre ed., 1981); Alejando M. Garro, *Reconciliation of Legal Traditions in the U.N. Convention on Contracts for the International Sale of Goods,* 23 INT'L LAW. 443, 467-68 (1989); and Glower W. Jones, *Warranties in International Sale of Goods Compared to the U.S. Uniform Commercial Code on Sales,* 17 INT'L BUS. LAW. 497, 499 (1989).

[86] For similar statements, see, *e.g.*, Bianca, *supra* note 25, at 2.4.2.; Yuqing, *supra* note 25, at 43; and Maskow, *supra* note 57, at 18.

[87] For similar affirmations, see Maskow, *supra* note 57, at 18 (pointing out that the dispute is of no practical relevance because "in the relationship between the parties the principle of good faith must be observed because in case of a subsequent examination of their conduct by an arbitration board this principle would be revoked anyhow in interpreting the Convention"); Eörsi, *supra* note 28, at 2-9 (arguing that interpretation of the contract and the Convention cannot be separated "since the Convention is also necessarily interpreted by the parties"); and Rolf Herber, *Art. 7, in* COMMENTARY ON THE UN CONVENTION ON THE INTERNATIONAL SALE OF GOODS 59, n.16 (Peter Schlechtriem ed., 1998) (stating that any differentiation is impossible because the interpretation of the Convention is to promote conduct that accords with good commercial practice).

undeniably represent a particular application of the good faith principle.[88] Hence, the requirement of good faith can be considered as one of the "general principles" upon which the Convention is based. As such, it is not limited to the interpretation of the Convention itself, but also governs the parties' conduct.[89] The reference to general principles underlying the Con-

---

[88] For a list of applications of the good faith principle in particular provisions of the Convention, see the Secretariat Commentary, *supra* note 16, at art. 6 [antecedent to art. 7 of the Official Text] or the Official Records, *supra* note 52, at 18, where it is stated that

> [a]mong the manifestations of the requirement of good faith are the rules contained in the following articles:
>
> - Art. 14(2)(b) [antecedent to art. 16(2)(b) of the Official Text] on the non-revocability of an offer where it was reasonable for the offeree to rely upon the offer being held open and the offeree acted in reliance on the offer;
> - Art. 19(2) [antecedent to art. 21(2) of the Official Text] on the status of late acceptance which was sent in such circumstances that if its transmission had been normal it would have reached the offeror in due time;
> - Art. 27(2) [antecedent to art. 29(2) of the Official Text] in relation to the preclusion of a party from relying on a provision in a contract that modification or abrogation of the contract must be in writing;
> - Arts. 35 and 44 [antecedent to arts. 37 and 48 of the Official Text] on the rights of a seller to remedy non-conformities in the goods;
> - Art. 38 [antecedent to art. 40 of the Official Text] which precludes the seller from relying on the fact that notice of non-conformity has been given by the buyer in accordance with articles [antecedent to articles 38 and 39 of the Official Text] if the lack of conformity relates to facts of which the seller knew or could not have been unaware and which he did not disclose to the buyer;
> - Arts. 45(2), 60(2) and 67 [antecedent to arts. 49(2), 64(2) and 82 of the Official Text] on the loss of the right to declare the contract avoided;
> - articles 74 to 77 [antecedent to articles 85 to 88 of the Official Text] which impose on the parties obligations to take steps to preserve the goods."

See also Secretariat Commentary, *supra* note 16, at ¶ 4, art. 73 [antecedent to art. 77 of the Official Text], Official Records, *supra* note 52, at 61, which reads in part:

> The duty to mitigate applies to an anticipatory breach of contract under article 63 as well as to a breach in respect of an obligation the performance of which is currently due. If it is clear that one party will commit a fundamental breach a fundamental breach of the contract, the other party cannot await the contract date of performance before he declares the contract avoided and take measures to reduce the loss arising out of the breach by making a cover purchase, reselling the goods or otherwise.

[89] Similar statements can be found in SCHLECHTRIEM, *supra* note 45, at 39; HONNOLD, *supra* note 20, at § 95 (asserting that this approach is analogous to and supported by art. 9, which provides that contractual obligations include "practices established by the par-

vention as a whole best ensures the uniform interpretation of the good faith requirement, since this reference secures an interpretation based on principles found *within* the Convention, such as the concepts of reasonableness[90]

---

ties and usages. . . in the particular trade"); Phanesh Koneru, *The International Interpretation of the UN Convention on Contracts for the International Sale of Goods: An Approach Based on General Principles,* 6 MINN.J. GLOBAL TRADE 105, III.A (1997) (stating that "a general-principles analysis of the various provisions of the Convention makes it clear that 'good faith' is so pervasive a concept that it must be a general principle of the Convention").

A similar linkage can be found in UCC § 1-203 (1978) ("Every contract or duty within this Act imposes an obligation of good faith in its performance or enforcement"). *See also* Issak Dore and James E. Defranco, *A Comparison of the Non-Substantive Provisions of the UNCITRAL Convention on the International Sale of Goods and the Uniform Commercial Code,* 23 HARV. INT'L L.J. 49, 61 (1982) (where the authors state that the good faith requirement provision does not constitute a mere instrument of interpretation, but rather, it "appears to be a pervasive norm analogous to the good faith provision of the U.C.C").

[90] For similar conclusions, see Maskow, *supra* note 57, at 18 (asserting that "[i]n determining what observance of good faith means, one has to proceed, from the Convention itself, i.e. its individual principles and rules, being an expression of this principle" and concluding that "the principles of the Convention concretize each other"); HONNOLD, *supra* note 20, at § 95 (stating that interpreting the Convention to promote the observance of good faith is related to the general principles on which the Convention is based); SCHLECHTRIEM, *supra* note 45, at 39 (stating that "good faith in international trade" is of the general principles and should be construed in the light of the Convention's many references to standards of reasonableness).

For references to reasonableness or the reasonable person, see the following overview in HONNOLD, *supra* note 20, at § 95, n. 28: Arts. 8(2) (reasonable person), 8(3) (same), 16(b) (reasonable reliance), 18(2) (reasonable time), 34 (unreasonable inconvenience or expense), 35(2)(b) (unreasonable to rely), 37 (unreasonable inconvenience or expense), 38(3) (reasonable opportunity for examination), 39(1) (reasonable time), 48(1) (unreasonable delay, inconvenience), 48(2) (reasonable time), 49(2) (reasonable notice), 60(a) (acts reasonably expected), 63(1) (reasonable time), 72 (reasonable time for notice), 75 (reasonable time and manner), 76(2) (reasonable substitute), 79(1) (reasonable expectations), 79(4) (reasonable time), 85 (reasonable steps), 86(1) (same), 86(2) (unreasonable inconvenience or expense), 88(1) (unreasonable delay), 88(2) (unreasonable expense; reasonable measures to sell). Honnold suggests determining what is "reasonable" by "ascertaining what is normal and acceptable in the relevant trade." *Id.* *See also* Maskow, *supra* note 57, at 87, who refers to "a conduct as is normal among tradesmen."

and the principle of mitigation.[91] The latter, for example, is contained in article 50. This provision limits the availability of the buyers remedy of price reduction if he does not permit the seller to remedy any failure of obligations under the contract.[92]

It should be noted, however, that the Convention's good faith principle does not permit the courts to introduce a general principle of fairness and equity. In other words, a national court may not replace the effects of a *statutory provision*, contrary to its plain wording and the legislative intent, by an outcome, which it believes to be more fair and equitable.[93] Any other reading of the good faith principle cannot be justified by the legislative his-

---

[91] This principle is also considered one of the general principles of the Convention by Honnold. *See* HONNOLD, *supra* note 20, at § 101; Samson, *supra* note 47, at 247; Ferrari, *supra* note 26, at 225; and Mark N. Rosenberg, *The Vienna Convention: Uniformity in Interpretation for Gap-Filling — An Analysis and Application,* 20 AUSTR. BUS. L. REV. 442, 452 (1992).

[92] *See* Secretariat Commentary, *supra* note 16, at art. 73, ¶ 3, fn.2, Official Records, *supra* note 52, at 61; Eric E. Bergsten and Anthony J. Miller, *The Remedy of Reduction of Price,* 27 AM. J. COMP.L. 255, 265 (1979)(stating that although the mitigation principle of Draft article 73 [antecedent to art. 77 of the Official Text] does not directly apply to the reduction of price the same result is achieved by Draft article 46 [antecedent to art. 50 of the Official Text]; Magnus, *supra* note 68, at 5(b)(3), takes the view that the limitation under art. 50 is an expression of the Convention's general principle of the prohibition of *venire contra factum proprium* (actions contrary to prior conduct).

[93] There is a considerable difference between the legal systems as to how extensive and how powerful the penetration of the principle of good faith has been. At the one end of the spectrum figures a system where the principle has revolutionized the contract law and added a special feature to the style of that system (Germany). At the other end we find systems, which do not recognize a general obligation of the parties to conform to good faith in the performance of a contract, but which in many cases by specific rules reach the results that the other systems reach by the principle of good faith (the Common Law of England). However, even in those systems where the principle of good faith is recognized, the courts are not generally permitted to establish a general principle of fairness and equity. *See* Lando & Beale, *supra* note 69, at 56-58. Only the new Dutch civil code (*BW* articles 6:2 and 6:248(2)) goes further and, under exceptional circumstances, allows a court to replace the effects of a contract or statutory provision by an outcome which it believes to be more fair and equitable. *See* INTRODUCTION TO DUTCH LAW 95-97(Chorus, et.al. eds., 2d. ed. 1993) (emphasizing that these new provisions adopt the view that statutory provisions and even express terms of contract can be set aside whenever their application or enforcement would be grossly unjust).

tory and would endanger the uniform application of the Convention.[94] If, and to what extent this principle may take precedence over a *contract provision* will be discussed later in this Paper.[95]

D. Filing Gaps in the Provisions of the Convention

It is hardly possible at both the national and international level to draft a lengthy and complicated piece of legislation without any gaps. Paragraph (2) of article 7 thus provides that questions which

> are not expressly settled in [the Convention] are to be settled in conformity with the general principles on which [the Convention] is based, or in the absence of such principles, in conformity with the law applicable by virtue of the rules of private international law.

The concept of fundamental breach, however, is expressly settled in article 25 and, consequently, its interpretation is restricted to the rules under paragraph (1) of article 7.[96]

E. Conclusion (Part I)

The objective of Part I was to identify the rules of interpretation under the Convention. It was shown that the Convention's rules of interpretation require first and foremost an autonomous interpretation of the terms of the Convention in order to ensure their uniform application. We examined different methods of interpretation and reached the conclusion that the traditional rules of interpretation in civilian legal systems best serves that goal. We argued that in cases where the application of different methods leads to conflicting results, the courts are not allowed to disregard the plain wording or the clear legislative intent in order to give effect to what they deem the over-

[94] See the discussion of the inclusion of a provision on good faith within the Official Records, *supra* note 52, at 35. It is reported that the retention of the good faith requirement was criticized on the basis that the Draft Convention did not specify the consequences of a failure to observe the principles which were made binding on the parties, and consequently, no uniformity of sanctions would be achieved.

[95] *See infra* Part III, C.1.b., and E.2.a.

[96] For a similar conclusion, see Babiak, *supra* note 60, at 116-17.

riding purpose of a single provision. With regard to the Convention's principle of good faith, we hold the view that it is not limited to the interpretation of the Convention itself, but also governs the parties' conduct. Finally, we argued that this principle does not permit the courts to modify or replace the effects of a statutory provision, contrary to its plain wording and the legislative intent, by an outcome that they believe to be more fair and equitable.

Part II — Case Law and Scholarly Writing on Fundamental Breach

The principal objective of Part II is to identify the various factors employed by scholars and courts in determining when a breach of contract is fundamental.

A. The Role of Case Law and Scholarly Writing (Doctrine) under the Convention

Unlike the Members of the European Union, the states participating in the drafting of the Convention were unwilling to transfer any of their sovereignty in order to establish a supranational court, such as the European Court of Justice, to ensure a unified interpretation of the Convention.[97] Furthermore, decisions of foreign courts are not binding on domestic courts,[98] nor are domestic courts required to consider foreign scholarly

[97] Within the European Union it is the European Court of Justice (ECJ) which has been given the jurisdiction to render, at the request of national courts, binding decisions on questions of interpretation relating to EU-law in the narrow sense, as well as to international conventions adopted by the member states, such as the Brussels Convention on Jurisdiction and the Enforcement of Judgments in Civil and Commercial Matters, Sept. 27, 1968, 1990 O.J. (C 189) [hereinafter Brussels Convention] and the Rome Convention, *supra* note 69. In theory, European national courts, in tune with civil law systems' rejection of *stare decisis*, are not bound by decisions rendered by the ECJ. In practice, however, courts follow the ECJ's rulings. *See* P.S.R.F. MATHIJSEN, A GUIDE TO EUROPEAN UNION LAW 98-99 (1995).

[98] *See* Diedrich, *supra* note 24, at 338 (stating that there is no internationally binding rule that foreign judgements have the force of "binding precedents"); Enderlein, *supra* note 26, at 348 (emphasizing that "the only force foreign decisions have is their persuasive effect"); Boggiano, *supra* note 16, at 47 (stating that domestic courts should consider academic writings, *obiter dicta*, and decisions in previous cases, and the probability considered that other courts will follow such decisions).

writing.[99] On the other hand, the Convention's requirement of having regard for "uniformity in its application" calls for courts to consider interpretations of the Convention in other countries.[100] Therefore, we will next canvas scholarly commentary (A) and case law (B) on fundamental breach.[101]

But see Ferrari, *supra* note 2, at 11-12 (asserting that if "the same-or analogous-issues have already been examined by other States' courts such decisions should have either the value of precedent 'if there is already a body of international case law', or a persuasive value").

[99] Like foreign decisions, scholarly writings have persuasive authority only. *See* Honnold's review, in Uniform Words, *supra* note 47, 125-27, for the role of legal writing in different common and civil law jurisdictions. *See also* Michael Bonell, *The UNIDROIT Principles of International Commercial Contracts and the CISG, in* Uniform Commercial Law in the Twenty First Century: Proceedings of the Congress of the United Nations Commission on International Trade Law, U.N. GAOR Comm. on Int'l Trade L., 25th Sess., at 37, U.N. Doc. A/CN.9/SER.D/1 (1992) (emphasizing the interaction between case law and comments by legal writing in the attempt to constantly improve the understanding of the legislative texts).

[100] *See* Bonell, *supra* note 99, at 35 (stating that the most effective way of ensuring uniformity in the interpretation of uniform law is to have regard to the way in which the single convention or uniform law is interpreted in the other countries); Maskow, *supra* note 85, at 54 (stating that the interpreter must consider "what others have already done"); VOLKEN, *supra* note 28, at 45 (emphasizing that "[i]n order to achieve uniform application of the Convention, in addition to applying basically similar interpretation theories and taking other linguistic versions of the same provision into account, the courts of one country should be able to consult the judicial decisions and doctrine of another country").

For similar statements, see *inter alia*, John O. Honnold, *The Sales Convention in Action — Uniform International Words: Uniform Application,* 8 J.L. & COM. 207, § III (1988); Yuqing, *supra* note 25, at 45; Audit, *supra* note 28, at 154-55; Cook, *supra* note 50, at 226; BURGHARD PILTZ, INTERNATIONALES KAUFRECHT 66 (1993); Michael Kabik, *Through the Looking Glass: International Trade in the "Wonderland" of the United Nations Convention on the Contracts for the International Sale of Goods,* 9 INT'L TAX & BUS. LAW. 408, 429 (1992); Elizabeth Hayes Patterson, *United Nations Convention on Contracts for the International Sale of Goods: Unification Between Compromise and Domination,* 22 STAN.J.INT'L L. 263, 283 (1986).

[101] A variety of guides to and sources of information about the Convention are available. Based on a decision by the United Nations Commission on International Trade Law (UNCITRAL) at its twenty-first session, U.N. Doc. A/43/17, at 98-109, the Secretariat has established a system of collecting and disseminating information on court decisions and arbitral awards relating to Conventions and Model Laws that have emanated from the work of the UNCITRAL. The acronym for the system is "CLOUT" (Case law on

B. Scholarly Writing on Fundamental Breach

According to the statement of the unofficial secretariat commentary on the 1978 Draft Convention,[102]scholars from different legal systems debated on standards for determining whether a breach is fundamental. A consensus was reached that the determination must be made in the light of the circumstances of each case.[103] There is no such agreement, however, as

---

UNCITRAL texts). *See* U.N. DOC. A/CN.9/SER.C/ ABSTRACTS/1 et seq. (1993 and later). The case abstracts are available as hard copy and on the Internet at http:// www.un.or.at./uncitral/clout. Cites to CISG commentary and case law from around the world are also available through UNILEX, a commercial case collection system on CISG, published in paper and electronic form by Transnational Juris Publications, Inc., Irvington-on-Hudson, New York, Copyright: Italian National Research Council-Center for Comparative and Foreign Law Studies.

For comprehensive Internet databases devoted exclusively to the CISG, see the website of the *Pace University School of Law <http://www.cisg.law.pace.edu>*, created by the Pace Institute of International Commercial Law, Albert H. Kritzer/Nicholas Triffin eds.; the CISG online website *<http://www.jura.uni-freiburg.de/ipr1/cisg>*, created by the Institut für ausländisches und internationales Privatrecht (Director: Peter Schlechtriem, Albert-Ludwigs-Universität Freiburg) [special attention to German case law on the CISG]; the CISG — France website <http://www.jura.uni-sb.de/FB/LS/Witz/cisg.htm>, Claude Witz ed. [special attention to French case law on the CISG].

Examples of other particularly valuable Internet databases containing information on the CISG or related to the CISG: the International Trade Law website of the Faculty of Law of Norway's University of Tromsø <http://itl.irv.uit.no/trade_law/>: Ralph Amissah ed. [the first WWW site dedicated to a given area of law on the Internet: international trade law (an important site for international trade law materials and links to related information on the "net")]; CISG Finland <http://www.utn.fi/oik/fdk/cisg/cisg/ htm>; CISG W3 Database de CISG Brazil <http://www.cisg3.law. pace.edu /galiudo-da-fouseca/brasil-uff/>; for texts of Italian and Spanish-language cases see the website of the Centre for Comparative and Foreign Law Studies in Rome <http://soi.cnr.it/~crdcs/ crdcs/index.htm> and of the CISG — Spain and Latin America database <http:// www.uc3m.es/cisg>. Currently in process are the CISG — Arabic, CISG — Belgium, CISG — Canada, CISG — Iran, and CISG — Israel databases.

[102] *See* Secretariat Commentary, *supra* note 16, at ¶ 3, Draft art. 23 [antecedent to article 25 of the Official Text], Official Records, *supra* note 52, at 26 (stating that "the determination whether the injury is substantial must be made in the light of the circumstances of each case. . . .").

[103] *See* HONNOLD, *supra* note 20, at § 181.2; Babiak, *supra* note 60, at 12; Gyula Eörsi, *supra* note 103, at 336 (emphasizing that "[i]n applying such concepts [fundamental breach] the judge forms an opinion, taking all circumstances into consideration

to which factors are decisive in determining whether an injury is substantial enough to amount to a fundamental breach and the point in time from which foreseeability is measured.

The section below first illustrates the different approaches and the relevant factors used for determining fundamental breach and then addresses the relevant point in time. Reference will be made to a very recent approach that involves the UNIDROIT Principles concerning non-performance in order to determine fundamental breach under the Convention.

1. Relevant Factors in Determining Fundamental Breach

Because of its practical importance within the Convention's remedial system and its vagueness, the concept of fundamental breach has generated much commentary by scholars and practitioners. They have employed several factors in determining whether a breach is fundamental; which may be roughly categorized under the following headings: (a) nature of the contractual obligation; (b) gravity of the circumstances of breach; (c) remedy-oriented approach; (d) (in)ability of performance; (e) (un)willingness to perform; (f) lack of reliance on the other party's future performance; (g) offer to cure; and (h) possible cure.

a. Nature of the Contractual Obligation

The nature of the contractual obligation is one factor in the determination of fundamental breach. Where the parties have expressly or implicitly agreed that in the case of a breach by one party the other party may

whether (in this case) the breach of contract is so significant as to justify avoidance or not"); Sutton, *supra* note 13, at 286; Jaska Barbic, *Uniform Law on the International Sale of Goods, Uniform Law on the Formation of Contracts for the International Sale of Goods (1964) and United Nations Convention on Contracts for the International Sale of Goods, in* HAGUE-ZAGREB ESSAYS 4 19 (Voskuil & Wade eds., 1983); Magnus, *supra* note 28, at art. 25 n.3 (stating that the concept is as vague as flexible and that, in practice, its determination will depend on the context of each case where the distinction between a fundamental and a non-fundamental breach is relevant); Horacio A. Grigera Naón, *The U.N. Convention on Contracts for the International Sale of Goods, in* THE TRANSNATIONAL LAW OF INTERNATIONAL COMMERCIAL TRANSACTIONS: STUDIES IN TRANSNATIONAL ECONOMIC LAW 89, (Horn & Schmitthof eds., 1982); and L.W. Melville, *The Nature of Fundamental Breach,* New L. J., 307, 308 (Mar. 27, 1980).

terminate the contract, strict compliance with the contract is essential and any deviation from the obligation is to be regarded as a fundamental breach.[104] Absent such an express provision, the duty of strict compliance may also be inferred from the language of the contract, the surrounding circumstances, custom, usage, or a course of dealing between the parties.[105]

For example, it has been argued that the time of delivery is of the essence and consequently late performance amounts to a fundamental breach where the parties have stipulated that performance should be effected at an exact time ("*Fixgeschäft*")[106]and the importance of timely performance flows from the nature of the goods,[107] the circumstances

---

[104] The right of the parties to indicate the circumstances under which an act or omission by one party entitles the other to avoid the contract follows from art. 6, which reinforces the supremacy of the parties' agreement over the language of art. 25. *See* Secretariat Commentary, *supra* note 16, at ¶ 1, art. 5 of the 1978 Draft Convention (antecedent to art. 6 of the Official Text), Official Records, *supra* note 52, at 17(stating that the parties "may derogate or vary the effect of any of its provisions by adopting provisions in their contract providing solutions different from those in the Convention").

[105] *See* Rudolf Welser, *Die Vertragsverletzung des Verkäufers und ihre Sanktion, in* DAS UNCITRAL-KAUFRECHT IM VERGLEICH ZUM ÖSTERREICHISCHEN RECHT 120 (Doralt ed., 1985); HERBER & CZERWENKA, *supra* note 16, at art. 47, n.4; Rüdiger Holthausen, *Die wesentliche Vertragsverletzung nach,* RIW 101, 105 (1990); Martin Karollus, *Art. 25, in* KOMMENTAR ZUM UN-KAUFRECHT Art. 25, n. 32 (Heinrich Honsell ed., 1997); Olaf Clausson, *Avoidance in Nonpayment Situations and Fundamental Breach under the 1980 U.N. Convention on Contracts for the International Sale of Goods, 6* N.Y.L.SCH.J.INT. & COMP.L 93, 113 (1984); Schnyder & Straub, *Art. 49, in* KOMMENTAR ZUM UN-KAUFRECHT Art. 49, n.26 (Heinrich Honsell ed., 1997); and Magnus, *supra* note 28, at art. 46 n.42.

[106] *See* FRITZ ENDERLEIN AND DIETRICH MASKOW, INTERNATIONAL SALES LAW, Art. 25, at 3.4 (stating that the use of customary terms as "fixed," "absolutely," "precisely," "at the latest," indicates that late delivery is to be regarded as a fundamental breach of contract). *See also* Ulrich Huber, *Art. 49, in* Commentary on the U.N. Convention on the International Sale of Goods Art. 49, n.5 (Peter Schlechtriem ed., 1998); Welser, *supra* note 105, at 120; Magnus,*supra* note 28, at art. 49 n.10 (stating that the Incoterms CIF, FOB give the buyer the right to avoid the contract in the event of late delivery); Holthausen, *supra* note 105, at 105; and HERBER & CZERWENKA, *supra* note 16, at art. 47 n.4.

Where the buyer has informed the seller that he needs the goods at a certain date to fulfill his own obligations towards third parties, late delivery is to be considered fundamental breach. *See, e.g.*, Peter Schlechtriem, *Art. 25, in* COMMENTARY ON THE U.N. CONVENTION ON THE INTERNATIONAL SALE OF GOODS Art. 25, n.18 (Peter Schlechtriem ed., 1998).

[107] Where the goods in question are of fashionable or seasonable character, or where they have a stock or market price, or where the prices are subject to sharp fluctuations, late

of payment,[108]or from the time the taking of the goods was to be effected.[109]

Where the parties have expressly specified the quality of the goods, *e.g.* in case of an express warranty, any defect in quality constitutes a fundamental breach. Likewise, where the buyer has insisted that goods be fit for a

---

delivery has been viewed as fundamental breach. *See, e.g.*, Schlechtriem, *supra* note 106, at Art. 25 n.18; SCHLECHTRIEM, *supra* note 45, at 60 (stating that defaulted delivery of goods with a quoted market price is considered a fundamental breach); Magnus, *supra* note 28, at art. 49, n.11 (stating that late delivery of fashionable or seasonable goods generally constitutes fundamental breach); ENDERLEIN & MASKOW, *supra* note 106, at 3, art. 25 (stating that in "the case of goods which have a stock or market price, untimely-delivery certainly constitutes a fundamental breach"). *But see* Huber, *supra* note 106, at Art. 49, n.5 (stating that late delivery of goods with a quoted stock or market price do not generally constitute a fundamental breach, but that a longer delay can turn into a fundamental breach even if no additional period of time has been fixed).

[108] The buyer's obligation to pay the price includes all of the measures required by the contract, such as the duties to provide a letter of credit, and to comply with relevant domestic laws to enable payment to be made. *See* SCHLECHTRIEM, *supra* note 45, at 81; HONNOLD, *supra* note 20, at § 354; and the Secretariat Commentary, *supra* note 16, at ¶ 7, art. 60 of the 1978 Draft Convention [antecedent to art. 64 of the Official Text], Official Records, *supra* note 52, at 50.

Whether the failure to open a documentary credit within a fixed time constitutes a fundamental breach is disputed. While one author argues that the seller should always be allowed to declare the contract avoided if the buyer does not open a credit within a fixed time (*see* Jan Hellner, *The Vienna Convention and Standard Form Contracts, in* DUBROVNIK LECTURERS 335, 353 (Sarcevic & Volken eds., 1986)), others take the view that a delay in opening a credit constitutes a fundamental breach only in such cases where payment was to be made by letter of credit against delivery of shipping documents (*See* Günter Hager, *Art. 64, in* COMMENTARY ON THE UN CONVENTION ON THE INTERNATIONAL SALE OF GOODS art 64, n.5 (Peter Schlechtriem ed., 1998) and ENDERLEIN & MASKOW, *supra* note 106, at 244).

[109] For example, a delay in taking delivery is to be regarded as fundamental breach in "just-in-time" contracts, when the goods are of perishable nature or where the goods cannot be stored. *See* Hager, *supra* note 108, at art. 64, n.5, Magnus, *supra* note 28, at art. 64, n.17; Willibald Posch, *Die Pflichten des Kaüfers und die Rechtsbehelfe des Verkäufers, in* Das Einheitliche Wiener Kaufrecht 143, 159 (Hans Hoyer & Willibald Posch eds., 1992); Magnus, *supra* note 28,at Art. 64, n.17.

For further examples where timely performance is essential, see SCHLECHTRIEM, *supra* note 45, at 84 (stating that seller's need to clear his warehouse can make timely taking delivery an essential duty); Hager, *supra* note 108, at Art. 64, n.6; and ENDERLEIN & MASKOW, *supra* note 106, Art. 64, at 3, where the authors state that "time for performance can, for instance, in regard to fulfillment of the obligation to participate in the

particular purpose,[110] or where he has notified the seller for what purposes he would need the goods (expressing his special interest that the goods be fit for that purpose), then any defect affecting this particular use is to also be regarded as a fundamental breach.[111]

b. Gravity of the Consequences of Breach

The gravity of the consequences of the breach is another factor in determining fundamental breach. Whether or not the consequences of the breach actually deprive the aggrieved party of the expectation under the contract is discussed under the following headings:[112] the contract's overall value plus the monetary loss suffered by the aggrieved party, frustration of the purpose of the contract, and the remedy oriented approach.

---

manufacture of goods, supply of drawings or sub-supply of material, be agreed as an essential date for the goods cannot be finished at another time because of different use of the facilities, planned changes in production, shutting-down of plant etc." *Id.*

[110] *See* SCHLECHTRIEM, *supra* note 45, at 59-60 (stating that delivery of defective goods entitles buyer to avoid the contract only if the contract indicates that non-conformity is of special importance to him "such as in the case of an express warranty"). For a similar statement see Magnus, *supra* note 28, at Art. 46, n.42. *See also* Schlechtriem's example: "[I]f the buyer has unmistakenly insisted on, but not received, chips suitable for the tropics, then the breach is fundamental and the buyer retains the right to demand substitute goods, even if the buyer can otherwise use the non-performing transistors without great loss." *Id.* at 77.

[111] *See, e.g.*, Schlechtriem, *supra* note 106, at Art. 25, n.21 and Andreas Kappus, *Rechtsvergleichende Aspekte zur Vertragsaufhebung wegen Sachmangels nach UN-Kaufrecht,* 985 NJW (1994).

[112] Where no detriment whatsoever has been caused or is expected to be caused by the breach of contract, it is undisputed among scholars that there is no right of avoidance:

See SCHLECHTRIEM, *supra* note 45, at 60 n.210 (stating that there is no fundamental breach where, despite the seller's failure to properly pack and insure the goods, they nonetheless arrived in good order and condition; if, however, the buyer has lost a chance to resell the goods, there would be a detriment). *See also* Will, *supra* note 16, at Art. 25, at 2.1.1.2.; Magnus, *supra* note 28, at Art. 25 n.12; Karollus, *supra* note 105, at Art. 25 n.14; and Schnyder & Straub, *supra* note 105, at Art. 49 n.23.

(1) *Contract's Overall Value and the Monetary Loss Suffered by the Aggrieved Party*

There is some debate among scholars as to whether the monetary loss suffered by the injured party is a decisive factor in determining fundamental breach. Based upon the Secretariat Commentary on the fundemental breach governing provision under the 1978 Draft Convention,[113] some authors conclude that the contract's overall value and the loss suffered by the buyer as a result of the non-performance are to be considered in determining fundamental breach.[114] Most authors, however, take the view that damages are not the decisive factor. Rather, the aggrieved party's special interest in the performance of the particular obligation as fixed by the terms of the contract is the decisive factor in determining fundamental breach.[115]

[113] *See* Secretariat Commentary, *supra* note 16, at ¶ 3 of art. 23 [antecedent to art. 25 of the Official Text], Official Records, *supra* note 52, at 25, where it is stated that "[t]he determination whether the injury is substantial must be made in the light of the circumstance of each case, e.g., *the monetary value of the contract, the monetary harm caused by the breach,* or the extent to which the breach interferes with other activities of the injured party." [emphasis added]

[114] *See* Babiak, *supra* note 60, at 118 and Sutton, *supra* note 13, at 286. A similar notion seems to be supported by Magnus, *supra* note 28, at Art. 25, n.11 (stating that the term "detriment" draws one's attention to the fact that the extent of the damages is a relevant factor in determining fundamental breach).

[115] *See* SCHLECHTRIEM, *supra* note 45, at 77 (stating that the objective damages will not be the decisive factor in determining fundamental breach but "whether the risk of the particular non-conformity was considered so serious by the parties that its existence would eliminate the buyer's interest in the performance of the contract concerning these goods"); ENDERLEIN & MASKOW, *supra* note 106, at 3, Art. 25 (stressing that "[t]hough in commercial relations most things can be reduced to a damage, this is not the central issue"). For similar statements, see Will, *supra* note 16, at Art. 25, 2.1.1.2. (stating that detriment does not equal damages); Barry Nicholas, *The Vienna Convention on Contracts for the International Sale of Goods,* 15 L.Q.R. 201, 218 (1989); Karollus, *supra* note 105, at Art. 25, n.16; Gert Reinhart, UN-Kaufrecht, KOMMERNTAR ZUM ÜBEREINKOMMEN DER VEREINTEN NATIONEN VOM 11 APRIL 1980 ÜBER VERTRÄGE ÜBER DEN INTERNATIONALEN WARENKAUF, Art. 25, n.5, 6; HERBER & CZERWENKA, *supra* note 16, at Art. 25 n.3, 8. *See also* Jacob Ziegel, *The Remedial Provisions in the Vienna Sales Convention: Some Common Law Prespectives, in* INTERNATIONAL SALES 16, ch. 9 (1984).

(2) *Frustration of the Purpose of the Contract*

To determine fundamental breach, many authors focus on whether or not the purpose of the contract has been frustrated by the breach.[116] They argue that the buyer has purchased the goods for some purpose and consider those breaches that make the intended use of the goods impossible as fundamental.[117] In their view, when the goods do not possess the features necessary for the purpose,[118] or when a third party claims a right to possession or prohibits the use by virtue of a patent or other industrial or intellectual property right, a fundamental breach has been committed.[119] For example, the buyer's interest in reselling the goods is not protected if it was evident that he bought the goods for manufacturing purposes, but his interest in selling the proceeds is protected. Accordingly, only if the sale of the latter is not possible due to the defective delivery is there a fundamental breach.[120]

Where documents are necessary in order to dispose of the goods or take delivery of the goods at their place of destination, *e.g.* a bill of lading, the delivery of defective and incomplete documents constitutes a fundamental breach.[121] Delivery of short or damaged goods entitles the buyer to

[116] *See* ENDERLEIN & MASKOW, *supra* note 106, at Art. 25, 3.4, where the authors state that to what extent non-fulfillment of an obligation is fundamental "depends on its relevance for the achievement of the *purpose of the contract.*" [emphasis added]. *See also*, Karollus, *supra* note 105, at Art. 25, n.22 (stating that the detriment is only relevant under the condition that the violated obligation is important and the terms of the contract are aimed at protecting the aggrieved party from the consequences of breach).

[117] *See, e.g.*, Karollus, *supra* note 105, at Art. 25, n.21; KARL NEUMAYER & CATHERINE MING, CONVENTION DE VIENE SUR LES CONTRATS DE VENTE INTERNATIONALE DE MARCHANDISES Art. 25, n.3 (1993); ENDERLEIN & MASKOW, *supra* note 106, at Art. 25, 3.4; and Schnyder & Straub, *supra* note 105, at Art. 46, n.59.

[118] *See* Karollus, *supra* note 105, at Art. 25, n.21.

[119] *See* Schlechtriem, *supra* note 106, at Art. 25, n.20; ENDERLEIN & MASKOW, *supra* note 106, at Art. 25, 3.4; Magnus, *supra* note 28, at Art. 49, n.16; and Holthausen, *supra* note 105, at 107.

[120] *See* Karollus, *supra* note 105, at Art. 25, n.21.

[121] *See* Huber, *supra* note 106, at Art. 49, n.16. For the same conclusion see Schnyder & Straub, *supra* note 105, at Art. 49, n.27 and ENDERLEIN & MASKOW, *supra* note 106, at Art. 49, 3 (stating that failure to hand over negotiable documents constitutes a fundamental breach).

avoid the contract where complete and/or non-defective delivery was necessary for the use intended by the buyer.[122] Delivery of an *aliud* constitutes a fundamental breach where the merchandise delivered deviates so substantially from that ordered that the seller must view the buyer's acceptance as impossible.[123]

(3) Remedy-Oriented Approach

Concerning the delivery of non-conforming goods, the case-by-case approach, which looks at whether the purpose of the contract has been frustrated, has been challenged by a more comprehensive one. Inspired by some recent German court rulings[124] on fundamental breach, this new approach asks whether it is reasonable for the buyer to retain the defective goods, make use of them and to then claim for damages for any loss suffered as a result of the breach.[125] In answering this question, the new approach considers the nature of the goods, the extent of the deviation from

[122] *See* SCHLECHTRIEM, *supra* note 106, Art. 25, n.19; ENDERLEIN & MASKOW, *supra* note 106, at Art. 25, 3.4 (regarding non-conforming delivery). As or partial non-delivery see Huber, *supra* note 106, at Art. 51 n.5, where the author with respect to art. 51(2) holds the buyer to be entitled to avoid a contract to deliver computer systems, if the seller delivered only the hardware but not the software necessary to work with the computer. *See also* HONNOLD, *supra* note 20, at § 317 (emphasizing that one factor of special significance with respect to avoidance as to the entire contract is "whether the non-conformity of some goods interferes with the *use* or *salability* of the remainder")[emphasis added].

[123] *See, e.g.*, Michael Will, *supra* note 16, at Art. 46, 2.2.1.2 (stating that "[r]eceiving apples instead of pineapples satisfies the criteria of Article 25"). For somewhat different conclusions, see Schlechtriem, *supra* note 106, at Art. 25, n.21 (stating that even the delivery of a totally different *aliud* not always impairs the fundamental contractual expectations of the buyer); Magnus, *supra* note 28, at Art. 46, n.39 (stating that an *aliud* delivery does not constitute *per se* a fundamental breach except when it is of no use for the buyer and it would demand unreasonable measures to sell them); and ENDERLEIN & MASKOW, *supra* note 106, at Art. 25, 3.4 (stating that the right to immediate avoidance in any case of an *aliud* delivery cannot be justified).

[124] *See infra* Part II, C.2.c.

[125] *See* Huber, *supra* note 106, at Art. 46, n.35 and Burghard Piltz, *Neue Entwicklungen im UN-Kaufrecht,* 2768, 2772 NJW (1996).

the agreed quality, the purpose for which the buyer purchased the goods, and the size of the buyer's business.[126]

According to this somewhat remedy-oriented approach, it is generally unreasonable for the buyer to run the risk of engaging in a dispute with the seller as to whether he had sold the goods for a reasonable price and thereby observed his duty to mitigate losses.[127] Consequently, defective delivery generally constitutes a fundamental breach when the goods would not be marketable or a reasonable price could not be realized.[128] Moreover, where the buyer is only a retailer, it is generally unreasonable for him to sell defective goods to his customers.[129]

If the defective goods were not purchased for resale but for other purposes, such as processing, it would also be unreasonable for the buyer to use the goods unless there were a market where the goods could be easily sold.[130] "*Aliud*" deliveries always constitute a fundamental breach where the goods in question are of a specific character, irrespective of whether they are unique or fungible.[131] Where the goods are generic, "*aliud*" deliveries are to be considered a fundamental breach when it is unreasonable for the buyer to resell them and to claim damages.[132] In determining unreasonableness, the extent to which the delivered goods deviate from the stipulated description must be considered.[133]

---

[126] *See* Huber, *supra* note 106, at Art. 46, n.35, 42 and Schlechtriem, *supra* note 106, at Art. 25, n.20.

[127] *See* Huber, *supra* note 106, at Art. 46 n.36 (stating that it is unreasonable to expect a buyer to resell the goods if there is a danger that, when calculating the loss, there will be a dispute with the seller regarding the reasonableness of the resale price or where there was a breach of the duty to mitigate loss).

[128] *See id.* (stating that the goods must be marketable despite their lack of conformity and it must be foreseeable that the buyer will receive a reasonable price).

[129] *See id.* at n.37 (arguing that a retailer can generally never be expected to sell goods outside his normal course of business).

[130] *See id.* at n.38 (arguing that a commercial buyer may be expected to resell the goods if there is a market on which the goods may be sold without great difficulties, that market is easily accessible for the buyer and likely to produce reasonable price).

[131] *See id.*at n.40.

[132] *See* Huber, *supra* note 106, at Art. 46, n.39 (stating that the question is whether it is reasonable to expect the buyer to dispose of the goods himself and to content himself with price reduction or damages).

[133] *See id.* (stating that the "more blatant the discrepancy, the less it can be expected of the buyer to dispose of the goods"). *See also* Schnyder & Straub, *supra* note 105, at Art. 46, n.59 (without differentiation between generic or specific goods).

c. (In)ability of Performance

Another consideration in the determination of fundamental breach is the party's (in)ability to perform at all, that is to say either to deliver the ordered goods or to pay the purchase price and to take delivery. Regardless of whether or not performance is due, non-performance is considered a fundamental breach where performance is objectively impossible, namely where the object of the transaction is unique and has been destroyed.[134] For example, if a party contracts to sell his Kandinsky and it has perished, performance is objectively impossible since no one could deliver the painting.[135] A fundamental breach has also been committed where only the party, which has yet to fulfill its obligation, is unable to perform the contract (subjective impossibility).[136] If, in the foregoing example, the Kandinsky were not destroyed but stolen, the seller would only be subjectively prevented from performing, since the thief or any other person having bought the stolen painting from him would be able to deliver it to the buyer, if only theoretically.[137]

---

[134] *See* Magnus, *supra* note 28, at Art. 49, n.13; Schlechtriem, *supra* note 106, at Art. 25, n.17; and Huber, *supra* note 16, at 504.

[135] For a similar example, see J. Baronage Marcantonio, *Unifying the Law of Impossibility*, 8 HAST. INT'L & COMP. L. R. 41, 53 (1984) (commenting on the German concept of objective impossibility).

[136] *See* Schlechtriem, *supra* note 106, at Art. 25, n.17; Sutton, *supra* note 13, at 93 (stating that failure to perform at all constitutes fundamental breach); Magnus, *supra* note 28, at Art. 72, n.11 (stating that insolvency of the buyer entitles seller to avoid the contract). For a somewhat different conclusion, see Huber, *supra* note 106, at Art. 49, n.7 (stating that subjective impossibility only constitutes fundamental breach if the seller does not cure the defect within a reasonable time).

See also Secretariat Commentary, *supra* note 16, at ¶ 2, art. 63 [antecedent to art. 72 of the Official Text], Official Records, *supra* note 52, at 53 (stating that a future fundamental breach "may be clear either because of the *words* or *actions* of the party which constitutes a repudiation of the contract or because of an *objective fact*, such as the destruction of the seller's plant by fire or the imposition of an embargo or monetary control which will render impossible future performance")[emphasis added].

[137] For further examples, see Marcantanio, *supra* note 135, at 53 (commenting on the German concept of subjective impossibility).

d. (Un)willingness to Perform

The parties' (un)willingness to perform is another factor in the determination of fundamental breach. For example, one party's express refusal to perform his obligation, such as to pay for the goods or to take delivery of them, constitutes fundamental breach, except where the promisor is entitled to refuse to perform.[138] Making performance dependent on an unjustified counter-performance or additional guarantees also constitutes fundamental breach.[139]

e. Lack of Reliance on the Other Party's Future Performance

In determining fundamental breach, consideration is also given to whether the breach gives the aggrieved party reason to believe that he may not rely on the other party's future performance. It has been argued, for example, that even where the contractual term broken is minor and the consequences of the breach do not substantially deprive the aggrieved party of his expectations under the contract, he can nonetheless treat the breach as fundamental if it was intentional.[140] In addition, where one party can rea-

[138] *See, e.g.*, Schlechtriem, *supra* note 106, at Art. 25, n.17 (stating that seller's refusal to deliver before or at the time when performance is due constitutes fundamental breach); Hager, *supra* note 108, at Art. 64, n.6; Hans Stoll, *Zur Haftung bei Erfüllungsverweigerung im Einheitlichen Kaufrecht*, 52 RabelsZ 617, 624 (1988); and Magnus, *supra* note 28, at Art. 64, n.17 (stating that buyer's refusal to pay for the goods or to take delivery is to be considered a fundamental breach).

See also Huber, *supra* note 106, at Art. 49, n.6 (emphasizing that in practice, when the seller is not willing to perform, he often argues that the contract is not valid; the contract is avoided due to an alleged fundamental breach of contract on the side of the buyer; or invokes *force majeure* or article 71).

[139] *See* Magnus, *supra* note 28, at Art. 72, n.11 and Stoll, *supra* note 138, at 625. Schlechtriem notes that "the frequent cases in which a demand for new terms or alleged contract violations by the other side are used as a pretext for not performing one's own obligations" provide in most cases a basis for immediate avoidance. *See* SCHLECHTRIEM, *supra* note 45, at 95.

For a somewhat different view, see HONNOLD, *supra* note 20, at § 396 (stating that avoidance should not be "triggered" if one party informs the other one of the need to negotiate a modification of their agreement).

[140] *See, e.g.*, Karollus, *supra* note 105, at Art. 25, n.2.

sonably conclude from the other party's conduct that he will not perform a substantial part of his obligation, the former may ask the latter for an adequate assurance of performance, and failure to provide an additional guarantee is regarded as a fundamental breach.[141]

f. Offer to Cure

When one reads academic commentary on the drafting history of the Convention,[142] there is much controversy among scholars as to whether fundamental breach should be determined in the light of an offer to cure. Many authors favor the consideration of such an offer in determining whether or not a fundamental breach has occurred.[143] Their position is that a breach is not fundamental as long as the requirements of article 48(1) are met, namely, that repair is possible within a reasonable time and without causing the aggrieved party unreasonable inconvenience or uncertainty of reimbursement by the seller of expenses advanced by the buyer. Consequently, the seller's refusal or failure to cure the defect within a reasonable time con-

---

[141] *See, e.g.*, Trevor Bennet, *Anticipatory Breach and Installment Contracts, Art. 71, in* COMMENTARY ON THE INTERNATIONAL SALES LAW, THE 1980 VIENNA SALES CONVENTION 513, Art. 71, 3.7 (C. Bianca & M. Bonell eds., 1987); HONNOLD, *supra* note 20, at § 394; and Magnus, *supra* note 28, at Art. 72, n.12.

See also Secretariat Commentary, *supra* note 16, at ¶ 2, art. 63 [antecedent to art. 72 of the Official Text], Official Records, *supra* note 52, at 53 (stating that "failure by a party to give adequate assurances that he will perform when properly requested to do so under art. 62(3) [antecedent to art. 72 of Official Text of the Convention] may help make it 'clear' that he will commit a fundamental breach").

[142] For the drafting history, see *infra* Part III, B.

[143] *See* Schlechtriem, *supra* note 106, at Art. 25, 21; HONNOLD, *supra* note 20, at § 296; Ziegel, *supra* note 115, at 9-22/3; Shinichiro Michida, *Cancellation of Contracts*, 27 AM.J.COMP.L. 279, 288 (1979); E. Allan Farnsworth, *Rights and Obligations of the Seller, in* LAUSANNER KOLLOQUIM 83, 88 (Schweizerisches Institut für Rechtsvergleichung ed. 1985); Eric C. Schneider, *The Seller's Right to Cure under the Uniform Commercial Code and the United Nations Convention on Contracts for the International Sale of Goods*, 7 ARIZ.J.INT'L & COMP. L. 69, 102 (1989); Huber, *supra* note 106, at Art. 48, n.23; HERBER & CZERWENKA, *supra* note 16, at Art. 48, n.9; Kastely, *supra* note 25, at 599; W. Mapp & C. Nicoll, *The Vienna Convention on International Sale of Goods: Obligations under the Contract and Remedies for Breach*, N.Z.L.J. 316, 319 (1993); Martin Karollus, *Un-Kaufrecht: Vertragsaufhebung und Nacherfüllungsrecht bei Lieferung mangelhafter Ware*, ZIP 490, 493-94 (1993); and Diedrich, *supra* note 35, at 13.

stitutes a fundamental breach.[144] The same is true where timely delivery is an essential term of the contract.[145] Moreover, a fundamental breach has been committed where it is unreasonable for the buyer to keep the repaired merchandise,[146] or where the buyer reasonably cannot rely on the seller's ability[147] or willingness[148] to cure the defect within a reasonable time.

Some authors, on the other hand, believe that an offer to cure should not be considered in determining fundamental breach.[149] They are of the opinion that taking into account an offer to cure and the curability of a defect contradicts the opening words of article 48(1), according to which the seller's right to cure is "subject to article 49."[150] They conclude from that wording that the buyer's right to avoid the contract always prevails over the seller's right to cure and, thus, the question of whether the breach was fun-

---

[144] *See* Huber, *supra* note 106, at Art. 49, n.12; Magnus, *supra* note 28, at Art. 46, n.40; and Karollus, *supra* note 143, at 496.

[145] *See* Karollus, *supra* note 143, at 496.

[146] *See* Huber, *supra* note 106, at Art. 49, n.12 and Karollus, *supra* note 143, at 496 (stating that where a car has been seriously damaged a fundamental breach is given since it is unreasonable for the buyer to keep such car even if repaired).

[147] *See* Huber, *supra* note 106, at Art. 49, n.12; Karollus, *supra* note 143, at 496; and Magnus, *supra* note 28, at Art. 46, n.41 (stating that failure to remedy a defect often gives rise to doubt seller's general ability to cure and thus constitutes a fundamental breach).

[148] *See* Huber, *supra* note 106, at Art. 49, n.12 and Karollus, *supra* note 143, at 496 (both stating that fraudulent behavior on the part of the seller constitutes fundamental breach).

[149] *See, e.g.*, Will, *supra* note 16, at Art. 48, 3.2.1., 3.2.2.; Magnus, *supra* note 28, at Art. 48, n.30; PILTZ, *supra* note 100, at § 4, n.66; ENDERLEIN & MASKOW, *supra* note 106, at 10; Klaus Detzer & Manfred Thamm, *Überblich über das neue UN-Kaufrecht*, BB 2369, 2373 (1992); Holthausen, *supra* note 105, at 103; REINHART, *supra* note 115, at Art. 48, n.2; Welser, *supra* note 105, at 125; Fritz Enderlein, *Rights and Obligations of the Seller Under the U.N. Convention on Contracts for the International Sale of Goods, in* DUBROVNIK LECTURES 133, 193 (Sarcevic & Volken eds., 1986); Babiak, *supra* note 60, at 127, fn.92; and Rolf Herber, *The Rules of the Convention Relating to the Buyer's Remedies in Case of Breach of Contract, in* PROBLEMS OF UNIFICATION 104, 123 (1980).

To protect the seller's right to cure, some authors suggest suspending the buyer's right to avoid "when a rightful offer to cure arrives" (*See* Will, *supra* note 16, at 3.2.2; W. Bitter & G. Bitter, *Wandlungsmöglichkeit des professionellen Käufers und Nachlieferungsrecht des Verkäufers bei aliud-Lieferung. Eine Untersuchung zum ceutschen und UN-Kaufrecht,* BB 2315, 2323 (1993); and BERNARD AUDIT, LA VENTE INTERNATIONALE DE MARCHANDISES, CONVENTION DES NATIONS UNIES DU 11 AVRIL 1980 133 (1990).

[150] *See* Holthausen, *supra* note 105, at 103.

damental for the purpose of avoidance cannot be answered in the light of an offer to cure.[151] Another argument advanced is that such an approach is incompatible with article 46(2), according to which the buyer can request substitute delivery if the lack of conformity constitutes a fundamental breach.[152] Defining fundamental breach in light of a feasible repair would practically bar the buyer from requiring substitute performance whenever the seller offers a cure.[153] The buyer's right to require substitute goods would be limited to those situations where repair is impossible.[154] Moreover, it has been argued, that consideration of a possible repair contributes to the further weakening of the concept of fundamental breach since it is not clear under what circumstances the buyer's right to cure would prevail.[155]

Those authors favoring consideration of an offer to cure in determining fundamental breach, with reference to the legislative history of article 48(1), defend their position on the ground that the opening words of that article do not clarify the exact relationship between the seller's right to cure and the buyer's right to avoid.[156] It could not, therefore, be answered with certainty whether avoidance or cure should prevail.[157] Furthermore, they argue that the purpose of article 48(1) would be frustrated if the buyer were

---

[151] *See id.*

[152] *See* Will, *supra* note 16, at Art. 48, 3.2.1 and Schnyder & Straub, *supra* note 105, at Art. 49, n.20.

[153] *See* Will, *supra* note 16, at Art. 48, 3.2.1 and Schnyder & Straub, *supra* note 105, at Art. 49, n.20 (the latter arguing that determining fundamental breach in light of an offer to cure contradicts arts. 48(1), 49, 72 and 73(2)).

[154] *See* Will, *supra* note 16, at Art. 48, 3.2.1 and Schnyder & Straub, *supra* note 106, at Art. 49, n.20.

[155] *See* Will, *supra* note 16, at Art. 48, 3.2.2, where the author argues that it is not clear what elements qualify a rightful offer and that leads to further burdening the buyer who already bears the risk of evaluating the degree of non-conformity.

[156] *See id.* At 1.3. (referring to the legislative history of article 48 and stating that the cross-reference to art. 49 in art. 48(1) is "enigmatic" and leaves the relationship to avoidance "open to interpretation"). *See also* Karollus, *supra* note 143, at 495 (arguing that art. 48(1) represents a compromise between those delegates at the Vienna Conference who feared that the seller's right to cure might be frustrated and those who preferred the priority of avoidance, and that the delegates wanted to leave the relationship of cure and avoidance open to interpretation)

[157] *See* Will, *supra* note 16, at Art. 48, 1.3 and Karollus, *supra* note 143, at 495.

HONNOLD, *supra* note 20, at § 296, goes even further. He takes the view that the legislative history of art. 48(1) "leaves little room for doubt" that the right to cure prevails

allowed to avoid the contract before giving the seller an opportunity to cure the defect.[158] As to the compatibility with article 46(2), they argue that the term fundamental breach must be interpreted differently, depending on whether the avoidance or the substitute delivery remedy is sought,[159] or if, for policy reasons, the seller's right to cure should prevail over the buyer's right to request substitute delivery.[160]

g. Possible Cure

In an attempt to overcome some of the doctrinal concerns about the approach focusing on the existence of an offer to cure, some legal writers look exclusively at the curability of a given breach.[161] They determine fundamental breach not in the light of an offer to cure by the seller, but by looking at whether cure is possible at all. In their view, there is no fundamental breach when the breach is curable.[162]

2. Foreseeability of Consequences of Breach

Most authors conclude from the wording and legislative history of article 25 that there is a presumption that the party in breach foresaw the far-reaching consequences of the breach for the other party.[163] Consequently, they take the view that whether a breach is fundamental depends not only on its consequences but also on the foreseeability of those consequences to the other party.[164] For them, the foreseeability element has two functions:

---

and that the cure provision of art. 48(1) could be frustrated "by an unqualified application of art. 49(1)."*Id.*

[158] *See* HONNOLD, *supra* note 20, at § 296.

[159] *See* Karollus, *supra* note 105, at Art. 25, n.11.

[160] According to Huber, *supra* note 106, at Art. 48, n.23, only the consideration of an offer to cure "does justice to the legal policy concerns underlying art. 48, namely that the seller should be given a 'right to cure' which is efficient and does not merely exist on the paper."*Id.*

[161] *See e.g.*, Huber, *supra* note 106, at Art. 46, n.42; Karollus, *supra* note 143, at 493-94; and HERBER & CZERWENKA, *supra* note 16, at Art. 48, n.9.

[162] *See* Huber, *supra* note 106, at Art. 46, n.42 and Karollus, *supra* note 143, at 494.

[163] *See, e.g.*, ENDERLEIN & MASKOW, *supra* note 106, at Art. 25, 4.1; Will, *supra* note 16, at Art. 25, 2.2.2; and Schlechtriem, *supra* note 106, at Art. 25, n.11.

[164] *See, e.g.*, Schlechtriem, *supra* note 106, at Art. 25, n.11 (stating that knowledge or foreseeability of the aggrieved party's expectations are relevant for interpreting and assess-

first, a substantive function, i.e. the breaching party's knowledge or foreseeability of the harsh consequences of the breach;[165] secondly, a procedural function, since the element of foreseeability shifts the burden of proof to the party in breach when that party claims that neither he nor any reasonable person of a similar class[166] and in the same circumstances[167] could have foreseen the result.[168]

The actual foreseeability of a substantial detriment caused by the breach depends on all relevant circumstances of the case, including the negotiations and any practices, established between the parties.[169] Where the parties, for instance, expressly or implicitly agreed that strict compliance with the contract terms is essential and any deviation from those terms is to be regarded as fundamental, the party in breach cannot invoke non-foreseeability. Under such circumstances, substantial detriment is foreseeable to a reasonable person of the same kind and in the same circumstances.[170] The same is true where the importance of the obligation breached follows from

---

ing the importance of the obligation breached and its significance for the aggrieved party) and ENDERLEIN & MASKOW, *supra* note 106, at Art. 25, 4.1.

[165] For a somewhat different conclusion, see Babiak, *supra* note 60, at 118 (stating that the detriment/expectation component is what makes a breach "fundamental").

[166] It has been suggested that one should construe a "reasonable person" as a reasonable merchant encompassing all merchants that satisfy the standards of their trade and that are not intellectually or professionally sub-standard. *See id.* at 122 (stating that the phrase "of the same kind" refers to the standard merchant in the same business). *See also* Will, *supra* note 16, at Art. 25, 2.2.2.2.1 & 2.2.2.2.3 (stating that not only must it be examined how a "man with due diligence" must act in a certain sector of trade, but also the socio-economic background in which this party operates, including the language, religion and professional status).

[167] It has been argued that the requirement "in the same circumstances" refers to the market conditions, both regional and worldwide. *See* Babiak, *supra* note 60, at 122 and Will, *supra* note 16, at Art. 25, 2.2.2.2.2. (stating that this element refers to all circumstances such as legislation, political situation, climate, and also previous contracts and negotiations between the parties).

[168] For similar conclusions, see, *e.g.*, Will, *supra* note 16, at Art. 25, 2.2; Schlechtriem, *supra* note 106, at Art. 25, n.11; ENDERLEIN & MASKOW, *supra* note 106, at Art. 25, 4.1; HONNOLD, *supra* note 20, at § 183; and Ziegel, *supra* note 115, at 9-18 & 19.

[169] *See* Will, *supra* note 16, at Art. 25, 2.2.2.1 (suggesting that whether a breaching party actually failed to foresee the substantial detriment caused to the non-breaching party will be evaluated in light of art. 74).

[170] For this conclusion, see Schlechtriem, *supra* note 106, at Art. 25, n.12.

the terms of contract or from the negotiations between the parties, which preceded the formation of the contract.[171] For example, where the parties stipulated that performance should be effected at an exact time, or where the buyer had made known to the seller that he needed the goods by a certain date in order to fulfill his own obligations *vis-à-vis* third parties, the seller cannot argue in defense that he was unaware of the fact that his failure to deliver on time would result in substantial detriment to the seller.[172] Only when the particular importance of the violated duty has neither been established in the contract itself nor discussed during the contract negotiations, can foreseeability be relevant.[173]

With regard to the relevant point at which foreseeability is measured there are basically two different positions.[174] Relying on the fact that the definition of fundamental breach is focused on the injured party's expectations under the contract, some authors take the view that the time of the conclusion of the contract is relevant.[175] In their view, a contract in which the delivery time is not binding cannot be turned into a transaction where time is of the essence merely because the seller subsequently learns that the buyer needs the goods at a particular time.[176]

Furthermore, they argue that the relevant point at which foreseeability is measured must be evaluated in conjunction with article 74, which deals with monetary damages for breach of contract and limits the recovery of damages to cases where the breach is foreseeable "at the time of the conclusion of the contract."[177] They point out that it would be anomalous if a

---

[171] *See id.* at n.13.
[172] *See id.*
[173] *See id.* at Art. 25, n.14.
[174] *See* Babiak, *supra* note 60, at 118; Michida, *supra* note 143, at 284-85; Schlechtriem, *supra* note 106, at Art. 25, n.3 & n.15; HONNOLD, *supra* note 20, at § 183; Will, *supra* note 16, at Art. 25, 2.2; and Ziegel, *supra* note 115, at 9-18 & 19.
[175] *See* SCHLECHTRIEM, *supra* note 45, at 60; van der Velden, *supra* note 39, at 64; Ziegel, *supra* note 115, at 9-20; Holthausen, *supra* note 105, at 105; and Magnus, *supra* note 28, at Art. 25, n.19.
[176] *See, e.g.*, SCHLECHTRIEM, *supa* note 45, at 60.
[177] Art. 74 provides:

> Damages for breach of contract by one party consist of a sum equal to the loss, including loss of profit, suffered by the other party as a consequence of the breach. Such damages may not exceed the loss which the party in breach foresaw or ought to have foreseen at the time of the conclusion of the contract, in the light of the facts and matters of which he then knew or ought to have known, as a possible consequence of the breach of the contract.

buyer were allowed to avoid the contract because of the seller's breach while the grounds justifying avoidance were regarded as being too remote for the recovery of damages.[178]

This approach is opposed by those authors who want more protection for the aggrieved party. While some of them favor the time of the breach[179] or the period "before the time of the breach"[180] approach, most of them consider these interpretations as too far-reaching. They generally hold the time of the conclusion of the contract as the decisive point and will permit consideration of subsequent knowledge only in exceptional cases, e.g. in cases where preparations in view of performance have not yet started so that the other party can still adapt itself to the new situation.[181]

3. UNIDROIT Principles

As mentioned above, some renowned scholars advocate making use of the UNIDROIT Principles as a means of interpreting ambiguous terms of the Convention.[182] They suggest employing them in the determination of

---

[178] This point, in particular, has been emphasized by Ziegel, *supra* note 115, at 9-20.

[179] *See, e.g.*, Bento Soarez & Moura Ramos, CONTRATOS INTERNACIONAIS. COMPRA E VENDA 128, fn.83 (1986).

[180] *See, e.g.*, J.D. Feltham, *The United Nations Convention on Contracts for the International Sale of Goods,* J.BUS.L. 346, 353 (1981); and Olga Gonzalez, *Remedies Under the U.N. Convention for the International Sale of Goods,* 2 INT'L TAX & BUS. LAW. 79, 87 (1984) (stating that "a breach which becomes foreseeable after the conclusion of the contract, but before the time of delivery of the goods, may fall within the definition of fundamental breach"). A similar notion seems to be supported by Honnold, who believes that information received after formation but prior to performance can be relevant for the determining fundamental breach. *See* HONNOLD, *supra* note 20, at § 183 (giving example of situation where information sent by buyer to seller after formation but prior to performance allowed for conclusion that seller's noncompliance with contract terms amounted to fundamental breach).

[181] *See* Will, *supra* note 16, at Art. 25, 2.2.2.2.5; ENDERLEIN & MASKOW, *supra* note 106, at 112; HERBER & CZERWENKA, *supra* note 106, at Art. 25, n.9; Karollus, *supra* note 105, at Art. 25, n.27; Josef Aicher, *Leistungsstörungen aus der Verkäufersphäre, in* DAS EINHEITLICHE WIENDER KAUFRECHT 133 (Hoyer & Posch eds., 1992); NEUMAYER & MING, *supra* note 117, at Art. 25, n.8.

The Commentary on art. 23 of the 1978 Draft Convention [antecedent to art. 25 of the Official Text], however, seems to admit only the alternative "time of conclusion" or "time of breach." *See* Secretariat Commentary, *supra* note 16, at ¶ 5, art. 23, Official Records, *supra* note 52, at 26.

[182] *See supra* Part I B. 4.

fundamental breach of contract, arguing that both the UNIDROIT Principles and the Convention follow the same policy, namely to preserve the enforceability of the contract whenever feasible.[183] This approach would be reflected by offering the breaching party the possibility to cure,[184] requiring the non-breaching party to provide an additional period of performance,[185] and most importantly, by allowing the termination of the contract only when the breach or non-performance qualifies as "fundamental."[186]

The UNIDROIT Principles provide a more express guideline than does the Convention as to which factors are relevant in determining fundamental non-performance, the counterpart of the Convention's fundamental breach.[187] In determining fundamental non-performance, the UNIDROIT Principles state that regard shall be had to whether the non-performance substantially deprives the aggrieved party of what it was entitled to expect under the contract.[188] Other factors to be taken into account in each case are: whether strict compliance with the unfulfilled obligation is

---

[183] *See* Garro, *supra* note 68, at 1157 & 1185 (stating that "the UNIDROIT principles may be resorted to in order to determine whether or not there has been a fundamental breach of contract"); Perillo, *supra* note 68, at 308-9; Michael Bonell, *The Unidroit Principles of International Commercial Contracts and CISG, in* Uniform Commercial Law in the Twenty First Century: Proceedings of the Congress of the United Nations Commission on International Trade Law, U.N. GAOR Comm. on Int'l Trade L., 25th Sess., at 11, U.N. Doc. A/CN.9/SER.D/1 (1992) (he suggests that the criteria laid down in art. 7.3.1 of the UNIDROIT Principles may be used for a better understanding of art. 25).

[184] Compare arts. 37, 48 with UNIDROIT Principles, *supra* note 68, at art. 7.1.4.

[185] *See* UNIDROIT Principles, *supra* note 68, at art. 7.1.5 (requiring the aggrieved party to provide an additional period of time to perform upon expiration of which the aggrieved party may proceed with any of the remedial provisions available under the UNIDROIT Principles).

[186] Compare art. 25 with UNIDROIT Principles, *supra* note 68, at art. 7.1.3. *See also* Garro, *supra* note 68, at 1185.

[187] UNIDROIT Principles, *supra* note 68, at art. 7.1.1, defines non-performance as a failure to perform any obligation under the contract, and it includes defective performance or late performance. Non-performance under UNIDROIT Principles has thus the same meaning as "breach of contract" under the Convention. The difference between the two instruments is that the UNIDROIT Principles, unlike the Convention, do not refer to the remedies available to one party in case of a breach by the other, but provide a set of rules applicable to non-performance in general.

For the meaning of breach of contract under the Convention, see *infra* Part III, A.1.

[188] *See* UNIDROIT Principles, *supra* note 68, at art. 7.3.1, ¶ 2(a).

of essence under the contract;[189] whether the aggrieved party has reason to believe that it cannot rely on the other's party's future performance;[190] whether the non-performance is intentional or reckless;[191] and finally, whether the non-performing party would suffer a disproportionate loss as a result of the preparation or performance if the contract is terminated.[192]

With the exception of the last two enumerated factors, those applied by the UNIDROIT Principles in determining fundamental non-performance do not differ substantially from those employed by scholars and practitioners in defining fundamental breach under the Convention.[193] There is, however, a significant difference. Unlike under the Convention, the relationship between the seller's right to cure and the buyer's right to terminate is clear under the UNIDROIT Principles. The buyer's right to terminate is suspended provided that the seller's offer to cure is appropriate and the buyer has no "legitimate interest" in refusing an offer to cure.[194] Moreover, the seller's right to cure is not precluded by notice of termination.[195] In other words, the buyer cannot exercise his right of termination for the purpose of denying the seller an opportunity to cure. Under the UNIDROIT Principles, therefore, curability is, *de facto*, a relevant factor in determining whether or not non-performance is fundamental.

---

[189] *See id.* at art. 7.3.1, ¶ 2(b).

[190] *See id.* at ¶ 2 (d).

[191] *See id.* at ¶ 2(c).

[192] *See id.* at ¶ 2(e).

[193] The reason for this parallel seems to be that many of the same individuals who labored to produce the Convention and later commented on it, such as Michael Joachim Bonell and Alan Farnsworth, continued under UNIDROIT auspices to produce the UNIDROIT Principles. For a list of the members of the working group who drafted the UNIDROIT Principles, see Bonell, *supra* note 68, at 1126.

[194] *See* UNIDROIT Principles, *supra* note 68, at art. 7.1.4., which states in part:

> (1) The non-performing party may, at its own expense, cure any non-performance, provided that
>
> (a) without undue delay, it gives notice indicating the proposed manner and timing of the cure;
>
> (b) cure is appropriate in the circumstances;
>
> (c) the aggrieved party has no legitimate interest in refusing cure, and
>
> (d) cure is effected promptly.
>
> (2) The right to cure is not precluded by notice of termination.
>
> (3) Upon effective notice of cure, rights of the aggrieved party that are inconsistent with the non-performing party's performance are suspended until the time for cure has expired.

[195] *See id.* at art. 7.1.4(2).

C. Case Law on Fundamental Breach

As of April 1999, there have been 54 reported decisions dealing with fundamental breach in its various settings.[196] As discussed in greater depth below, in most cases the courts and tribunals do not provide a detailed analysis as to the definition of fundamental breach.[197] Their reasoning, however, gives some insight as to why the courts considered a given non-performance as being fundamental or not. The factors enumerated by the courts in determining fundamental breach are similar to those employed by the scholars and practitioners as mentioned above. There are two principal reasons that account for this convergence.

First, all but three of the reported decisions dealing with fundamental breach[198] were rendered by courts in civil law jurisdictions, where the influence of legal writing on the interpretation and development of law is tradi-

[196] The number of reported decisions dealing with fundamental breach differs between the databases set up by the Institute of International Commercial Law, Pace University School of Law, and by the University of Freiburg. As of April 5, 1999, 37 decisions dealing with art. 25 were cited in the Freiburg database, while 54 decisions were listed in the Pace University database. Different methods of reporting seem to be the reason for that difference. As for most of these decisions, a cross-reference to the buyer's remedies in arts. 46(2), 49(1)(a) and 51(2), very few of those of the seller which reference art. 64(1)(a) can be found. Hence, fundamental breach was invoked more frequently by buyers than by sellers.

[197] In many cases the issue of fundamental breach was not decisive, since the buyer did not observe the notice requirements under arts. 38 and 39. *See, e.g., Landgericht* Berlin, 16 September 1992, 99 O 29/92, the full text of the decision is published in German. *See Database of the University of Freiburg*, <http://www.jura.uni-freiburg.de/ipr1/cisg/text/49.htm>; *Oberlandesgericht* München, 8 February 1995, 7 U 1720/94; the full text of the decision is published in German. *See Database of the University of Freiburg*, <http://www.jura.uni-freiburg.de/ipr1/cisg/text/143.htm>; *Handelsgericht des Kantons* Zürich, 26 April 1995; HG 920670; an abstract of the decision is published in German in SZIER/RSDIE 1996, 51-52.

[198] See Delchi Carrier, SpA v. Rotorex Corp., 71 F.3d 1024, 1027 (2nd Cir. 1995). The full text is also available in the *Pace University Database*, <http://www.cisg.law.pace.edu/cisg/ wais/db/cases2/951206u1.html>; an English abstract is available as CLOUT Case 85. Roder Zelt- und Hallenkonstruktionen v. Rosedown Park Pty Ltd and Reginald R Eustace, 1995 Fed. Ct. Rep. (Australia) 216-40; also available in full text at the *Pace University Database* <http://www.cisg.law.pace.edu/cisg/wais/db/cases2/950428a2.html> and the *University of Freiburg*,<http://www.jura.uni-freiburg.de/ipr1 /cisg/urteile/ text/218.htm>.

tionally much greater than in most common law countries.[199] Second, many articles and some of the standard commentaries on the Convention were published before the Convention entered into force and thus were the only source of interpretation for the courts in the absence of any case law on the Convention.[200]

Scholars and practitioners, however, could not anticipate all of the problems arising out of the application of the Convention. It is necessary, therefore, to more closely examine the reported decisions on fundamental breach.

1. Nature of the Contractual Obligation

The courts often looked at the nature of the contractual obligation in considering whether strict performance is of the essence of the contract. In the absence of express terms stipulating that any failure to perform strictly in compliance with the contractual obligations is considered a fundamental breach, the courts have tried to infer from the language of the contract, whether there was a duty of strict compliance, and if so, its nature and the surrounding circumstances.

a. Quality of the Goods

In two cases, buyers invoked fundamental breach, claiming that the quality of the goods did not meet the stipulated requirements. In the first case, the Innsbruck Court of Appeals heard a dispute between a Danish exporter and an Austrian buyer. The buyer refused to pay the price and argued that the seller committed a fundamental breach of the contract because the flowers he purchased did not bloom throughout the entire summer. The Court denied that there was a fundamental breach on the grounds that the

---

[199] *See* Dannemann, *supra* note 60, at 5; and Eric C. Schneider, *Consequential Damages in the International Sale of Goods: Analysis of Two Decisions*, 16 U.PA.J.INT'L BUS.L. 615, 668 (1995).

The fact that most of the reported decisions on the Convention were rendered by European (civil law jurisdiction) courts gave one author reason to warn against regionalized interpretations. *See* Harry M. Flechtner, *Recent Development: CISG: Another CISG Case in the U.S. Courts: Pitfalls for the Practitioners and the Potential for Regionalized Interpretations*, 15 J.L. & COM. 127, 135 (1995).

[200] *See, e.g.*, the commentaries by HONNOLD, *supra* note 20; SCHLECHTRIEM, *supra* note 45; and Bianca & Bonell, *supra* note 16.

buyer failed to prove that the seller had guaranteed that the flowers would bloom through the entire summer.[201]

The second case involved litigation between German and Spanish parties over the delivery of a shipment of pepper. The pepper contained approximately 150% of the maximum concentration of ethyl oxide admissible under German food and drug law. Here the buyer was more successful, proving it had an express agreement with the seller that the goods must be fit for human consumption in Germany. Consequently, the Ellwangen District Court held the seller was in a fundamental breach.[202]

b. Timely Delivery

In many cases where the seller has effected late delivery, the buyer, alleging that the time of the delivery was an essential term of the contract, declared the contract avoided and refused payment. To date, however, in only one reported case did a court hold that timely delivery was essential. In a dispute between a British seller and a German buyer over the non-delivery of iron-molybdenum ("CIF Rotterdam"), the Hamburg Court of Appeals held that in CIF contracts timely delivery is *per definitionem* an essential term of the contract.[203] In all other cases, however, the buyer failed to show

---

[201] *See* OLG Innsbruck, 1 July 1994, 4 R 161/94 (affirming LG Feldkirch, 29 March 1994, 5 Cg 176/92y — 64, holding); the full text of the decision is published in German. *See University of Freiburg Database, <http://www.jura.uni-freiburg.de/ipr1/cisg/urteile/text/107.htm>* and the English abstract available as CLOUT Case 107.

The appellate court further held that, even if the buyer had been able to establish lack of conformity of the goods, he would have lost his right to avoid the contract, since he had failed to give the seller notice within a reasonable period of time after discovery of the defect in accordance with art. 39(1).

The decision of LG Feldkirch is available at *Pace University Database*, <http://www. cisg.law.pace.edu/cisg/wais/db/cases2/940329a3.html>.

[202] *See* LG Ellwangen, 21 August 1995, 1 KfH O 32/95. The full text of the decision is published in German at *University of Freiburg Database*, <http://www.jura.uni-freiburg.de/ipr1/cisg/urteile/ text/279.htm>.

[203] *See Hanseatisches* OLG Hamburg, 28 February 1997, 1 U 167/95 (affirming LG Hamburg, 2 October 1995, 419 O 85/95). The text of the decision is published in German. *See University of Freiburg Database*, <http://www.jura.uni-freiburg.de/ipr1/cisg/text/261.htm>.

The Hamburg Court of Appeal stated as follows: "[translation] The untimely delivery constitutes a fundamental breach according to art. 49(1)(a), 25 CISG. Untimely delivery, it is true, does not always constitute a fundamental breach. This general rule

that time was significant for the buyer in the sense that the contract stands or falls with timely delivery.[204]

The Oldenburg District Court, for example, denied fundamental breach in a dispute between a German buyer and an Italian seller, where the seller had dispatched summer clothes one day later than the stipulated time.[205] The Court concluded from the fact that the buyer took delivery of the goods instead of rejecting them that time was not of the essence of the contract.

In another case involving the sale of women's wear, where the French seller dispatched the goods two days after the stipulated time, the Ludwigsburg Petty District Court held that the inconvenience caused by the delay was only of minor importance to the German buyer and thus did not amount to fundamental breach.[206]

c. Disregard of the Seller's Distribution System

In a French case, the Grenoble Court of Appeals held that a buyer breached by reselling goods to an unexpected third party. The seller ex-

---

under the Convention, however, does not apply to cases where, at the time of the formation of the contract, it was obvious to the seller that the buyer had a special interest in punctual delivery. . . . In the pertinent case such special interest of the buyer follows from the reference to the Incoterm "CIF" in the contract."

For the factual background, see *infra* note 245.

[204] Very often the buyer could not even show that the parties had established the terms of delivery. *See, e.g.,* Arbitration Court attached to the Hungarian Chamber of Commerce and Industry Arbitral award in case No. VB/94131 of 5 December 1995. The original German full text of the decision is published in the *University of Freiburg Database,<http://www.jura.uni-freiburg.de/ipr1/cisg/urteile/text/134.htm>*. The English abstract is available as CLOUT Case 164. *See also* OLG München, 8 February 1995, 7 U 1720/94. The full text of the decision is published in German. *See University of Freiburg Database, <http://www.jura.uni-freiburg.de/ipr1/cisg/urteile/text/143.htm>*. The English abstract is available as CLOUT Case 133.

[205] *See* LG Oldenburg, 27 March 1996, 12 O 2541/95. The full text of the decision is published in German. *See University of Freiburg Database*, <http://www.jura.uni-freiburg.de/ipr1/ cisg/urteile/text/188.htm>.

[206] *See* Amtsgericht Ludwigsburg, 21 December 1990, 4 C 549/90; the full text of the decision is published in German. *See University of Freiburg Database*, <http:// www.jura.uni-freiburg.de/ ipr1/cisg /urteile/text/134.htm> (affirmed by LG Stuttgart, 30 August 1991, 16 S 14/91); for comments on the decision of the Amtsgericht Ludwigsburg, see Burghard Piltz, *Neue Entwicklungen im UN-Kaufrecht,* NJW 1101 (1994).

pected the buyer to resell in South America or Africa but the buyer instead resold in Spain, where the seller also resold.[207] The Court found that the parties clearly understood that resale was to be in South America or Africa and that seller's expectations under the contract were substantially impaired, because sale of its products in Spain had been seriously hampered by the parallel distribution caused when the buyer resold the goods in Spain.

2. Gravity of the Consequences of the Breach

In some cases, courts determining fundamental breach have in particular looked at the gravity of the consequences of the breach in the light of: (a) the contract's overall value and the monetary loss suffered by the aggrieved party; (b) the fitness of the goods for the intended purpose and (c) whether or not an award of damages would adequately protect the aggrieved party.

a. Contract's Overall Value and the Monetary Loss Suffered by the Aggrieved Party

In none of the following cases, has a court expressly held that there was a fundamental breach due to the monetary loss suffered by the aggrieved party as a consequence of the breach. Nor have the courts denied the occurrence of such a breach on the grounds that the breach did not cause the aggrieved party any damages. The *ratio decendi* of these cases, however, leads one to believe that the courts were focusing on the monetary loss suf-

---

[207] *See* CA Grenoble, Chambre commerciale; S.A.R.L. Bri Production "Bonaventure" v. Société Pan Africa Export; 22 February 1995; original in French; the text of the decision is published in French. *See University of Freiburg Database*, <*http://www.jura.uni-freiburg.de/ipr1/cisg/urteile/text/ 151.htm*>. An English abstract is available as CLOUT Case 154. An English translation of the text of the decision is available in this issue of the 1998 CISG Review.

In this case, a U.S. export company had entered into contractual relations with a French manufacturer of "*Bonaventure*" jeans and had declared to restrict resale to South America and Africa. In fact, the U.S. company had sold the jeans to a fashion store in Madrid and subsequently not only refused to reveal their true destination but even provided the seller's lawyers with misleading information. The appellate court found for fundamental breach, justifying avoidance of this particular contract according to art. 64(1)(a) on the grounds that the final destination of the merchandise was an essential condition of the contract.

fered by the aggrieved party in relation to the contract's overall value for the determination of fundamental breach.

For example, in *Delchi v. Rotorex*, a U.S. District Court admitted fundamental breach where 93% of the air condition compressors delivered were rejected in quality control checks because they had lower cooling capacity and consumed more energy than the sample model and specifications.[208] The U.S. Court of Appeals for the Second Circuit affirmed the District court's conclusion "because the cooling power and energy consumption of an air conditioner compressor are important determinants of the *product's value.*"[209]

In a dispute between a German seller and a Swiss buyer where fundamental breach was alleged, the Landshut District Court emphasized that the buyer would suffer considerable detriment because all of the sportswear delivered had shrunk about 10 to 15% after being washed.[210] The Court held that there was a fundamental breach since the buyer's customers would have either returned the merchandise or would not have bought any more from the buyer.[211]

The delivery of 80,000 scaffolding fittings, which did not entirely conform to the sample, was the subject of an arbitration award in a Chinese-

---

[208] *See Delchi Carrier, SpA,* 71 F.3d 1024, at 1027.

The defendant, a Maryland manufacturer of compressors for air conditioners, agreed to sell 10,800 compressors to the plaintiff, an Italian manufacturer of air conditioners. The sales contract provided for delivery in three shipments. The defendant made the first shipment. While the second shipment was in transit, the plaintiff discovered that the compressors contained in the first shipment did not conform with the contract specifications. The plaintiff rejected the second shipment, stored it at the port of delivery and, after having tried unsuccessfully to cure the defects, sued claiming damages for breach of contract pursuant to article 74 CISG. The court held that the defendant's breach was fundamental and granted the plaintiff damages to cover.

[209] *See* Delchi Carrier SpA, *supra* note 198.

[210] *See* LG Landshut, 5 April 1995, 54 O 644/94. The full text of the decision is published in German. *See University of Freiburg Database*, <http://www.jura.uni-freiburg.de/ipr1/cisg/text/193.htm>.

[211] See LG Landshut, <http://www.jura.uni-freiburg.de/ipr1/cisg/text/193.htm>, at 4, where it states that as a result of being washed the sportswear shrunk one or two sizes. Accordingly, the customers could not wear the sportswear anymore after having washed them for the first time. As a result, the court concluded, the customers would either complain to the buyer (later a retail seller) or would not buy clothes offered by this seller anymore which would cause substantial detriment to the buyer.

Austrian dispute. Stating that the estimated costs of sorting out the bad fittings from the good would have amounted to more than one third of the purchase price, the tribunal found a fundamental breach on the grounds that "an important part" of 80,000 scaffold fittings did not conform to the sample.[212]

The Hamm Court of Appeals found fundamental breach in a German case where the German buyer refused to take delivery of more than half of the ordered bacon.[213] In this case, the Italian seller had contracted with the buyer to deliver 200 tons of bacon in 10 installments. The seller delivered 4 installments, totaling 83.4 tons. Due to the way the bacon was packaged and claiming that 420 kilograms out of 22.4 tons of the fourth installment were dirty, the buyer refused to take delivery of the remaining installments. The Court found that even if 420 kg of the bacon were contaminated, the buyer would not have been entitled to refuse to take delivery according to article 71(1),[214] since such an amount could not be considered a "substantial part" as required under this provision.

In two other cases, the courts have denied fundamental breach since the aggrieved parties did not suffer any loss due to the alleged breach by the other party. In a Russian case, a Russian buyer failed to pay for the delivered goods and objected to the seller's claim for the stipulated price, arguing, *inter alia*, that the seller had breached the contract by dispatching the goods before the buyer had transmitted the bank's guarantee. Emphasizing that

---

[212] *See* Court of Arbitration of the International Chamber of Commerce, ICC Arbitration Case No. 7531 of 1994; See also the editorial remarks by Kritzer, in the Institute of International Commercial Law, *Pace University School of Law Database,* <http://www.cisg.law.pace.edu/cisg/wais/db/cases2/947531i1.html>, according to which the tribunal elaborated that the "[Buyer] has estimated the cost of sorting out bad fittings at USD 17,000,which may be compared with the invoiced price of the supplies, USD 46,397. The estimate has been communicated to [seller] and has not been disputed."

[213] *See* OLG Hamm, 22 September 1992, 19 U 97/91 (partially reversing LG Bielefeld, 18 January 1991, 15 O 201/90); full text of the decision is published in German: see database of the *University of Freiburg Database,*<http://www.jura.uni-freiburg.de/ipr1/cisg/urteile/text/57.htm>.

[214] Art. 71 provides:

> (1) A party may suspend the performance of his obligations if, after the conclusion of the contract, it becomes apparent that the other party will not perform a substantial part of his obligations as a result of:
>
> (a) a serious deficiency in his ability to perform or in his creditworthiness; or his conduct in preparing to perform or in performing the contract.

the buyer did not suffer any damage, the Russian tribunal held that such a violation by the seller of the terms specified for dispatch of the goods (delivery in the absence of a banker's guarantee) could not be termed a fundamental breach of contract.[215]

In another case, the plaintiff, a Swedish seller of coke delivered to a company in the former Yugoslavia, sued a German buyer for the purchase price. The defendant objected that the coke was of inferior quality and that the seller had sold the coke in his own name directly to the buyer's client in Yugoslavia. The Munich Court of Appeals held that, if proven, such interference might be regarded as a violation by the seller of his "post-contractual" obligations. The court, however, found that such a breach of contract would not result in any objectively significant detriment to the buyer since he would not have lost his claim under the Convention to be paid the price.[216]

b. Frustration of the Purpose of the Contract

In two cases the buyer has invoked fundamental breach on the grounds that the goods delivered could not be used for their intended purpose and were therefore not merchantable. In the first case, the German Supreme Court held that, as a general rule, the merchantability of the goods (New Zealand mussels) in the importer's country was not an essential term of the contract.[217] According to the court, in the absence of an agreement as

---

[215] *See* Tribunal of International Commercial Arbitration at the Russian Federation Chamber of Commerce and Industry, Arbitral award in case No. 200/1994 of 25 April 1995. The original is in Russian, but it is unpublished. An abstract is available as CLOUT Case 141. The tribunal further noted that under the CISG, if the violation of the contract on the part of the seller caused the buyer to suffer any damage, it would be entitled to compensation, but that in this particular case the buyer had not brought any such claim.

[216] See OLG München, 2 March 1994, 7 U 4419/93 (affirming Landgericht München I, 8 November 1993, 15 HKO 12117/93). The text of the decision is in part published in German. *See University of Freiburg Database*, *<http://www.jura.uni-freiburg.de/ipr1/cisg/urteile/ text/108.htm>*. An English abstract is available as CLOUT Case 83.

[217] Michida, *supra* note 143, at 288; and Farnsworth, *supra* note 115, at 88.

See also OLG Frankfurt a.m., 20 April 1994, 13 U 51/93 (affirming LG Darmstadt, 22 December 1992, 14 O 165/92); the full text of the decision is published in German. *See University of Freiburg Database*, <http://www.jura.uni-freiburg.de/ipr1/cisg/urteile/

to the merchantability of the goods, unmerchantability arising from the failure to observe special statutory provisions of the importer's country only constitutes a fundamental breach if one of the following conditions are met: (i) the same provision existed in the seller's state; (ii) the buyer had informed the seller and relied on the latter's expert knowledge; or (iii) the seller had or could have had knowledge of such provisions due to the particular circumstances of the case.[218]

In another case, the French Supreme Court reached what at first glance appears to be a somewhat different conclusion in a French-Italian controversy over the delivery of Italian wine that did not conform to the French wine law due to the addition of sugar by the Italian seller.[219] The French Supreme Court found a fundamental breach on the ground that the wine was not merchantable in France.[220] Unlike in the New Zealand mussels case, here the unmerchantability was the result of manipulations by the seller. For that reason it seems justifiable to impose on the seller the duty to verify whether such manipulations affect the merchantability of the goods sold, thereby shifting the risk of unmerchantability to the seller, and to treat his failure to do so as fundamental breach.[221]

---

text/125.htm>. An English abstract is available as CLOUT Case 84. For comments on that decision, see Ulrich Magnus, *Aktuelle Fragen des UN-Kaufrechts,* ZEuP 202, 210 (1995), (criticizing the decision on the grounds that the appellate court apparently views food only then not fit for human consumption when it actually harms the health of the consumers).

The decision of the LG Darmstadt is published in German. *See University of Freiburg Database*, <http://www.jura.uni-freiburg.de/ipr1/cisg/urteile/text/177.htm>.

[218] *See* BGH, 8 March 1995, VIII ZR 159/94. The full text of the decision is published in German. *See University of Freiburg Database,* <http://www.jura.uni-freiburg.de/ipr1/cisg/urteile/text/ 144.htm>.

[219] *See* Cour de Cassation, 23 January 1996, *1re chambre civile,* published in French in IPRax 126 (1997); commented on by Peter Schlechtriem, *Wesentlicher Vertragsbruch durch Lieferung gezuckerten Weins,* IPRax 132 (1997); Witz, *supra* note 7, at 334; and Claude Witz & Gerhard Wolter, *Die neuere Rechtsprechung französischer Gerichte zum Einheitlichen UN-Kaufrecht,* RIW 278, 279-81 (1998).

[220] *See Cour de Cassation,* 23 January 1996.

[221] For a somewhat different conclusion, see Schlechtriem, *supra* note 219, at 132 (stating that the French approach in treating "unmerchantability" in the buyer's country as fundamental breach differs from the German one).

c. Remedy-Oriented Approach

Recently, a new approach to determine fundamental breach has been introduced by the Frankfurt Court of Appeals and the German Supreme Court. Both the Frankfurt Court of Appeals[222] and the German Supreme Court[223] focused on whether it was reasonable for the aggrieved party to make use of the goods delivered, in particular to resell them, and to claim damages to compensate for the loss.[224]

In the case decided by the Frankfurt Court of Appeals, the plaintiff, an Italian shoe manufacturer, had delivered shoes to the defendant, located in

---

[222] See OLG Frankfurt a.M., 18 January 1994, 5 U 15/93 (reversing LG Frankfurt a.M., 9 December 1992, 3/3 O 37/92). The text of the decision is in part published in German. *See University of Freiburg Database*, <http://www.jura.uni-freiburg.de/ipr1/cisg/urteile/text/123.htm>; RIW 240-41 (1994); NJW 1013-14 (1994). An English abstract is available as CLOUT Case 79. For comments on that decision, see Eva Diederichsen, *Recent Developments: CISG: Commentary to Journal of Law and Commerce Case I: Oberlandesgericht Frankfurt a.M.,* 14 J.L. & Com, 177-80 (1995); Andreas Kappus, *Vertragsaufhebengsrecht nach UN-Kaufrecht in der Praxis,* NJW 984, 85 (1994); Diedrich, *supra* note 35, at 11-16; and Koch, *supra* note 18, at 98-100.

[223] *See* BGH, 3 April 1996, VIII ZR 51/95. The full text of the decision is published in German. *See University of Freiburg Database*, <http://www.jura.uni-freiburg.de/ipr1/cisg/urteile/text/ 135.htm>; RIW 594-97 (1996); NJW 2364, 67 (1996). For comments on that decision, see Burghard Piltz, *Anmerkung zu Bundesgerichtshof,* EuZW 448 (1996); Peter Schlechtriem, *Anmerkung zu Bundesgerichtshof,* EWiR 597-98 (1996). An English abstract is available as CLOUT Case 171.

[224] For a similar conception, see LG Heidelberg, 3 July 1992, O 42/92. The full text of the decision is published in German. *See University of Freiburg Database*, <http://www.jura.uni-freiburg.de/ipr1/cisg/urteile/text/38.htm>.

In that case the German buyer concluded a contract for the sale of computer components with an U.S. seller. After delivery of 5 parts had been carried out, the buyer refused payment and declared the contract avoided on the grounds that the delivery of 11 parts had been agreed. The Berlin District Court held that even if delivery of 11 parts had been agreed the dispatch of only five parts would not entitle the buyer to declare the contract in its entirety avoided according to art. 51(2). The Court further held that, in determining fundamental breach, regard must be had whether it was reasonable for the buyer to make a substitute purchase and claim damages for any extra costs arising out of that substitute transaction. Since it turned out that the buyer had purchased the missing parts already before the delivery became due in order to satisfy his own client in Vienna, the Court found that no fundamental breach was committed.

Germany, and issued invoices for the purchase price. The defendant paid only a portion of the price and denied any further obligation to pay the balance by asserting that the contract was avoided due to the late delivery and non-conformity of the shoes. The court held that the defendant was not entitled to declare the contract avoided because it had not set a time limit within which the seller had to deliver and had failed to establish that a fundamental breach of contract was committed.[225] The court noted that the evidence produced by the defendant proved neither specific defects nor the unfeasibility of further use of the goods and was therefore insufficient to determine whether or not the buyer could be reasonably expected to make use of the shoes.

In the case decided by the German Supreme Court, a Dutch company had entered into four separate sales agreements for the delivery of cobalt sulfate with the buyer, a German company. It was agreed that the goods should be of British origin and that the seller should supply certificates of origin and quality. After the receipt of the documents, the buyer discovered that the sulfate came from South Africa, that the certificate of origin was wrong, and that the quality fell short of the description in the contract. The buyer several times declared the contract avoided. Both the Hamburg District Court and the Hamburg Court of Appeals held that there were no grounds for contract avoidance.[226]

Affirming the lower courts' holdings, the German Supreme Court held that there was no fundamental breach justifying contract avoidance since the buyer could not show that the sale of the South African cobalt sulfate in Germany or abroad was not reasonably possible.[227] The defendant therefore failed to demonstrate that it was substantially deprived of what it was entitled to expect under the contract. The Supreme Court expressly rejected

---

[225] *See* OLG Frankfurt a.M., 18 January 1994, 5 U 15/93, *University of Freiburg Database*, <http://www.jura.uni-freiburg.de/ipr1/cisg/urteile/text/123.htm>.

[226] See *Hanseatisches* OLG Hamburg, 14 December 1994, 5 U 224/93 (affirming LG Hamburg, 5 November 1993, 404 O 175/92). The full text of the decision is published in German. *See University of Freiburg Database*, <http://www.jura.uni-freiburg.de/ipr1/cisg/urteile/text/216.htm>.

[227] According to the German Supreme Court, the delivery of goods, which do not conform to the contract either because they are of lesser quality or of different origin, does not constitute non-delivery. Thus, the declaration of avoidance could not be based on art. 49(1)(b) CISG since the plaintiff had effected delivery. *See* BGH, 3 April 1996, VIII ZR 51/95, *supra* note 223, at II.2.b.

the buyer's argument on appeal that the feasibility to cure a defect is the only decisive factor in determining fundamental breach and held that unfeasibility to cure does not necessarily constitute a fundamental breach.[228]

In the absence of express terms in the contract, the Supreme Court argued that in determining fundamental breach, the remedial system of the Convention and its underlying purposes, namely to preserve the enforceability of the contract and to restrain avoidance in favor of the damage or price reduction remedies, must be taken into account. The avoidance remedy, therefore, should only be allowed as a last resort in response to a breach so serious that the non-breaching party would have lost his interest in performing the contract.[229] Finally, the Court held that the delivery of wrong certificates of origin and of quality did not amount to a fundamental breach of contract since the defendant could have obtained correct documents from other sources.[230]

3. (In)ability of Performance

The Düsseldorf Court of Appeals, in a German-Swiss dispute, held that the inability to perform constituted a fundamental breach. A Swiss buyer declared avoided a contract with a German seller to deliver a machine designed to press keys after having been informed by the manufacturer of the ordered machine that the manufacturer had terminated the distribution agreement with the seller and would not carry out delivery of the machine in question unless payments were made directly to him. The buyer then made payments directly to the manufacturer. When the seller sued the buyer for the purchase price, the buyer objected that the seller was not able to deliver the machine and therefore he — the buyer — was entitled to declare the contract avoided. The Düsseldorf Court of Appeals rejected the buyer's arguments and held that mere non- or late delivery does not constitute a fundamental breach under article 25 provided that delivery is *objectively possible* and the seller was willing to deliver.[231] The Court continued that where delivery was objectively possible, but where it was obvious that

---

[228] *See id.* at II.2.c.dd.

[229] *See id.* at II.2.c.dd.

[230] *See id.* at II.2.d.

[231] *See* OLG Düsseldorf, 18 November 1993, 6 U 228/92 (partly reversing LG Düsseldorf, 9 July 1992, 31 O 223/91). The text of the decision is published in German. *See University of Freiburg Database,* <http://www.jura.uni-freiburg.de/ipr1/cisg/urteile/text/

the seller for idiosyncratic reasons would not be able to deliver the goods in question (*subjective impossibility*), the buyer would be entitled to avoid the contract. Since none of the requirements were pertinent the Court denied that any fundamental breach had been committed by seller.[232]

The insolvency of the buyer and the subsequent appointment of an administrator were found to have been a fundamental breach in an Australian case.[233] A German company sold tent hall structures to an Australian firm specializing in major events, such as the Australian Grand Prix and other large festivals. The buyer agreed to pay for the goods according to a set schedule but fell behind in its payments and, having encountered other financial difficulties, was placed under administration. The seller demanded that the administrator deliver up possession of the goods on the grounds that the contract of sales contained a retention of title clause, whereby title to the goods did not pass to the purchaser until the purchase price had been paid in full.[234] The administrator denied the existence of such a clause and refused to return the goods. The Court held that the fact that the company was insolvent or was likely to become so and the placement of the company

---

92.htm>. The decision of the LG Düsseldorf is published in German. *See University of Freiburg Database*, <http://www.jura.uni-freiburg.de/ipr1/cisg/urteile/ text/92.htm>.

232 On appeal, the German Supreme Court affirmed the decision of the appellate court insofar as it concerned the buyer's right to avoid the contract. The Court held that art. 72 applies only where future performance is still due. Where the non-performance occurred after the performance had become due, the right to declare the contract avoided would be governed by art. 49. Since in the case at issue the buyer declared the contract only avoided after delivery had been made and payment had become due, the Court thus held that the buyer could not invoke art. 72. As for the buyer's right to declare the contract avoided under art. 49 the Court held that he lost his right according to art. 49(2)(b).

See BGH, 15 November 1995; VIII ZR 18/94 (partly reversing OLG Düsseldorf, see *supra* note 231. The full text of the decision is published in German. *See University of Freiburg Database*, <http://www.jura.uni-freiburg.de/ipr1/cisg/urteile/text/149.htm>. For a German abstract, see NJW 2101-103 (1995).

233 *See* Roder Zelt- und Hallenkonstruktionen v. Rosedown Park Pty Ltd and Reginald R Eustace; 1995 Fed. Ct. Rep. (Australia) 216-40. The full text of the decision is published in English. *See University of Freiburg Database*, <http://www.jura.uni-freiburg.de/ipr1/cisg/urteile/text/218.htm>.

234 *See University of Freiburg Database*, <http://www.jura.uni-freiburg.de/ipr1/cisg/urteile/text/92.htm>, at ¶ 58.

under administration resulted in such a detriment to the seller so as to substantially to deprive it of what it was entitled to expect under the contract. The denial by the administrator of a retention of title term in the contract also amounted to fundamental breach within the meaning of article 25.[235]

4. (Un)willingness of Performance

A party's unwillingness to perform was the subject of an Italian-German dispute over the delivery of textiles, some of which were of a different color from that specified in the contract. After being informed by the Italian seller that he could not at that time deliver the remaining textiles of the ordered color, the German buyer declared the contract avoided. The Düsseldorf Court of Appeals held that a fundamental breach occurs if the seller declares seriously and definitely that he will not deliver substitute goods, but does not occur if he only declares that he cannot deliver at the moment.[236]

5. No-Reliance on the Other's Party Future Performance

Where a party has legitimately lost his faith and confidence in the other party's future performance and cannot be reasonably expected to continue the contractual relationship, courts have frequently found for fundamental breach. The reasons for the courts' findings can be best classified under the following headings:

a. Violation of Exclusive Rights By the Seller or the Buyer

The buyer's exclusive right to market and sell shoes under a certain brand name through an Italian manufacturer was the subject of a decision

---

[235] *See id.*

[236] *See* OLG Düsseldorf, 10 February 1994, 6 U 119/93 (affirming *Landgericht* Düsseldorf, 22 March 1993, 37 O 169/92; not published). The full text of the decision is published in German. *See University of Freiburg Database*, <http://www.jura.uni-freiburg.de/ipr1/cisg/urteile/text/187.htm>. An English abstract is also available as CLOUT Case 82 and commented on by Ulrich Magnus, *Probleme der Vertragsaufhebung nach dem UN-Kaufrecht (CISG) — Anmerkung zu OLG Düsseldorf*, Jus 870 (1995). (criticizing the decision on the grounds that the appellate court did not apply art. 51(2)).

by the Frankfurt Court of Appeals.[237] The seller contracted to manufacture shoes with a trademark ("Marlboro") to be used as a basis for further orders. The manufacturer produced the shoes and subsequently displayed them with the trademark at a fair without the buyer's prior consent. Despite the buyer's urgent requests, the seller refused to remove the shoes from the exhibit. The buyer, after the fair, advised the manufacturer that he was severing the relationship and would not pay for the sample shoes, which were no longer of any value to the buyer. The court found for fundamental breach on the grounds that the seller exhibited the shoes without the buyer's consent and under circumstances indicating that they could also be ordered directly from the manufacturer. It held that, in particular, the seller's refusal to remove the shoes at the buyer's request gave rise to the conclusion that the seller would breach the agreement again in the future. Therefore, the buyer could not reasonably be expected to further cooperate with the manufacturer.

In three cases fundamental breach was invoked by the buyer due to an alleged violation on the part of the seller of an exclusive distribution system. The first case was decided by the Frankfurt District Court and involved another German-Italian shoe dispute where a German retailer had ordered from an Italian manufacturer through a commercial agent 120 pairs of shoes "Exclusiva su B."[238] After delivery was effected and 20 pairs were resold, the buyer learned that identical shoes supplied by the Italian manufacturer were offered for sale by a competing retailer at a considerably lower price, in violation of his exclusive right of distribution in his home district. The buyer then returned the unsold 100 pairs. The Frankfurt District Court

---

[237] *See* OLG Frankfurt a.M., 17 September 1991, 5 U 164/90. The text of the decision is in part published in German. *See University of Freiburg Database*, <http://www.jura.uni-freiburg.de/ipr1/cisg/urteile/text/28.htm>. A translation of the decision is published in English at 12 J.L.& COM. 261-70 (1993) and an English abstract is available as CLOUT Case 2. For comments on that decision, see Babiak, *supra* note 60, at 126; Volker Behr, *Interpretive Decisions Applying CISG: Commentary to Journal of Law and Commerce Case I; Oberlandesgericht Frankfurt a.M.*, 12 J.L. & COM. 271 (1993); and Martin Karollus, *Judicial Interpretation and Application of the CISG in Germany 1988-1994, in* CISG REVIEW 51, 63 (Cornell Int'l L.J. ed., 1995).

[238] See LG Frankfurt a.M., 16 September 1991, 3/11 O 3/91. The text of the decision is in part published in German. *See University of Freiburg Database*, <http:/www.jura.uni-freiburg.de/ipr1/cisg/text/26.htm>. An English abstract is available as CLOUT Case 6.

did not have to decide the issue of fundamental breach since it held that there was no express declaration of avoidance of the contract. Nevertheless, the District Court noted in *obiter dictum* that even if the buyer was substantially deprived of what he was entitled to expect under the contract, the seller could not have foreseen such result.[239]

An alleged violation of an exclusive distribution agreement was also the subject of a recent decision rendered by the Koblenz Court of Appeals in a German-Dutch dispute over the delivery of acrylic blankets where the buyer refused any payment, *inter alia*, on the grounds that the seller had breached an exclusive distribution agreement.[240] The court held that the buyer lost his right to declare the contract avoided under article 49(2)(b)(i)[241] and that in fact, the buyer had never declared the contract avoided for the alleged violation. Nevertheless, the court stated in *obiter* that, if proven, such a violation could constitute a fundamental breach.[242]

In the above mentioned "*Bonaventure*" jeans case where the U.S. buyer disregarded the seller's exclusive distribution system, the Grenoble Court of Appeals held with reference to article 73(2)[243] that the buyer's fundamental

---

[239] This reasoning has been criticized by Karollus, *supra* note 237, at 63 (remarking that a seller who promises exclusive delivery must organize his distribution in such a way that he can meet his contractual obligations).

[240] See OLG Koblenz, 31 January 1997, 2 U 31/96 (affirming LG Koblenz, 29 November 1995, 3 HO 188/94). The buyer's appeal from the appellate court's decision to the BGH (BGH, VIII ZR 64/97) is pending. The full text of the appellate court's decision is published in German. *See University of Freiburg Database*, <http:/www.jura.uni-freiburg.de/ipr1/ cisg/text/ 256.htm>.

[241] Art. 49(2)(b)(i) provides:

> (2) However, in cases where the seller has delivered the goods, the buyer loses the right to declare the contract avoided unless he does so:
>
> (a) . . .
>
> (b) in respect of any breach other than late delivery, within a reasonable time:
>
> (i) after he knew or ought to have known of the breach;

[242] *See* OLG Koblenz, *University of Freiburg Database,* <http:/www.jura.uni-freiburg.de/ipr1/cisg/text/256.htm>.[/FN]

[243] Art. 73(2) provides:

> If one party's failure to perform any of his obligations in respect of any installment gives the other party good grounds to conclude that a fundamental breach of contract will occur with respect to future installments, he may declare the contract avoided for the future, provided that he does so within a reasonable time.

breach of the particular contract in question gave the seller sufficient grounds to conclude that the buyer would also fundamentally breach the contract in respect to further deliveries.[244]

b. Uncertainty as to the Seller's Future Performance

In two reported cases, uncertainty as to the seller's future performance seems to have been the decisive factor in finding fundamental breach. The Hamburg Court of Appeals, in the above mentioned Chinese iron-molybdenum case, found a fundamental breach was indeed committed where the seller, after not having been able to deliver the goods within the stipulated time, asked for more time due to ongoing negotiations with his supplier either for delivery of the goods or indemnification. Such a declaration, the court held, constituted a fundamental breach since it remained uncertain for the buyer if and when seller would fulfil his obligation to deliver the goods.[245]

---

[244] *See* Cour d'appel de Grenoble, S.A.R.L. Bri Production "Bonaventure" v. Société Pan Africa Export, 22 February 1995.

[245] *See Hanseatisches* OLG Hamburg, 28 February 1997, 1 U 167/95, *supra* note 203.

In this case the German buyer contracted with the British seller to deliver iron-molybdenum (65 % molybdenum) from China for a price of $9.70 /kg, CIF Rotterdam, time of delivery: October 1994 "from Chinaport to Rotterdam." The seller later informed the buyer that his supplier, due to a raise of the market price for molybdenum, demanded $10.50 /kg. The buyer denied any adjustment of the contract price. The seller then offered the buyer iron-molybdenum with a lower percentage of molybdenum (60%) for 10,20 US $/kg to be shipped in November/early December 1994 from China to Rotterdam. The buyer accepted the lower percentage but insisted on the agreed price and shipment of the goods no later than November 30, 1994, otherwise he would make a substitute purchase and claim damages for all loss suffered thereby. Following an inquiry by the buyer on November 15, the seller ensured that he would make all efforts to fulfil the contract in November. On December 2, the seller informed the buyer of the shipment of the molybdenum form Tianjin to Rotterdam. On December 13, however, he admitted that his Chinese supplier would not have delivered the molybdenum and asked for more time to fulfil the contract. The buyer replied on the same day that he needed the molybdenum and stressed again that he would make a substitute purchase and claim the difference between the current market price of $31 /kg and the agreed price as damages. The buyer, however, indicated that he would accept an indemnity. In his response on December 14, the seller again asked for more time due to ongoing negotiations with his supplier either for delivery of the goods or indemnification. He also

In the second case, a Swiss buyer had placed an order with an Italian seller requesting that the goods be delivered within the next 10 to 15 days. Almost two months later, the seller, after asking the buyer to confirm its order, specified the purchase price and assured the buyer that all the goods would be dispatched within a week. Two months after that, the buyer had not yet received the goods. The buyer then sent the seller a notice canceling the order and demanding a refund of the price. After receiving this notice the seller delivered part of the goods. The buyer refused to accept the late and short delivery and, as the seller did not refund the purchase price, commenced legal action, claiming avoidance of the contract for breach by the seller and asked for a refund of the purchase price with interest and damages. The Italian court found that there was a fundamental breach on the grounds that, two months after ordering and paying the price, the buyer was still waiting for two thirds of the goods.[246]

---

offered the buyer payment of $10,088 as indemnity. The buyer turned down that offer, made a substitute purchase, and sued the seller for the difference between the contract price and the price in the substitute transaction.

[246] *See* Pretura circondariale di Parma, sez.di Fidenza; 77/89; 24 November 1989; Foliopack Ag v. Daniplast S.p.A.; The original text of the decision is published in Italian. *See University of Freiburg Database,* <http://www.jura.uni-freiburg.de/ipr1/cisg/urteile/text/316.htm>. An English abstract is also available as CLOUT Case 90.

See, on the other hand, the case decided by the Court of Arbitration of the International Chamber of Commerce, where a Finnish buyer of machinery for a production line of foamed boards failed to make the third payment to his Italian seller. *See* ICC case n. 7585 of 1992. Although the tribunal stated that it was absolutely clear that the defendant did not have the financial resources, it did not find for fundamental breach and, thus, based the seller's right of avoidance on art. 64(1)(b) thereby regarding the three-and-a-half months' waiting time as an "additional period of time" pursuant to art. 63(1). A French abstract is available in: Bulletin de la Cour Internationale d'Arbitrage de la Chambre de Commerce Internationale 59 (November 1995). See also the editorial remarks by Kritzer, *Pace University Database,* <http://www.cisg.law.edu/cisg/wais/db/cases2/947858i1.html>, where the author states that "[w]ithout reference to arts. 63(1) and 64(1)(b), another provision of the CISG that could have been relevant to the results reached is art. 64(1)(a) on the theory that delay of over three months in providing the required letter of credit is a 'fundamental breach' of contract."

c. Failure to Provide Security for the Purchase Price

In one of the many German-Italian disputes regarding the delivery of shoes, the Italian manufacturer demanded security for the sales price because the German buyer had still not paid the manufacturer for a previous delivery. After the buyer failed to furnish security, the seller declared the contract avoided and resold the shoes to other retailers. The seller demanded compensation for various damages caused by the breach. The Düsseldorf Court of Appeals held that the Italian seller was entitled to avoid the contract under article 72[247] due to the German buyer's failure to furnish security for the sales price.[248]

Similarly, and again in a German-Italian shoe dispute, the Berlin District Court found the Italian seller to be entitled to avoid the contract.[249] Here the Italian seller had already manufactured the 212 pairs of shoes ordered by a German buyer. Shortly before handing them over to the carrier, however, the seller noticed that two out of three checks concerning an earlier sale had not been honored and payment had been made only after the courts rendered respectively judgements of consent and default. The seller requested security for the payment, but the buyer refused to honor this request. Highlighting the buyer's previous experience with the seller's unwillingness to pay, the Court held that, prior to the date fixed for the delivery of the shoes, it was "clear"[250] that the buyer would not pay the price. The court

[247] Art. 72 provides:

(1) If prior to the date for performance of the contract it is clear that one of the parties will commit a fundamental breach of contract, the other party may declare the contract avoided.

(2) If time allows, the party intending to declare the contract avoided must give reasonable notice to the other party in order to permit him to provide adequate assurance of his performance.

(3) The requirements of the preceding paragraph do not apply if the other party has declared that he will not perform his obligations.

[248] See OLG Düsseldorf, 14 January 1994, 17 U 146/93 (affirming LG Krefeld, 28 April 1993, 11 O 210/92). The text of the decision is published in German. *See University of Freiburg Database*, <http://www.jura.uni-freiburg.de/ipr1/cisg/urteile/text/119.htm>; an English abstract is available as CLOUT Case 130. The decision of the LG Krefeld is published in German. *See University of Freiburg Database*, <http://www.jura.uni-freiburg.de/ipr1/cisg/urteile/text/101.htm>.

[249] *See* LG Berlin, 30 September 1992, 99 O 123/92. The text of the decision is published in German. *See University of Freiburg Database*, <http://www.jura.uni-freiburg.de/ipr1/cisg/ urteile/text/70.htm>.

[250] "Clear" in the — unofficial — German version of article 72 reads "offensichtlich" (obvious).

defined "clear," in the sense of article 72, in terms of probability. "Clear" requires that a fact be obvious to anyone. Probability close to certainty, however, is not required.[251]

d. Making Delivery Dependent on an Unjustified Condition

A dispute between a German buyer and a Hong Kong seller was the subject of a decision by the Hamburg Chamber of Commerce Arbitration Tribunal.[252] The Hong Kong claimant and the German defendant concluded a general agreement for the exclusive delivery and distribution of Chinese goods, under which the claimant was responsible for business relations with Chinese manufacturers while the defendant was responsible for distribution of the goods in Europe. On this basis, the parties regularly concluded successive contracts of sale. In 1993, the German buyer ordered goods from the Hong Kong seller. Following prepayment and confirmation by the Hong Kong seller, the latter, owing to financial difficulties of his Chinese supplier, made delivery dependent on the payment of unpaid invoices from previous sales contracts. The tribunal found that both parties had committed a fundamental breach. It held that making delivery dependent on payment of arrears from previous sales contracts, where the parties had agreed upon prepayment of a specific order and the total sum for that had been paid, entitled the German company to avoid that order. On the other hand, the tribunal also held that the Hong Kong seller was entitled to avoid the general agreement due to the unpaid invoices, which had been due for many months.

6. Offer to Cure/Possible Cure

Whether or not a breach is curable without causing the buyer unreasonable inconvenience appears to be the decisive factor in a number of decisions rendered by German, French, and Swiss courts.

The Koblenz Court of Appeals, in the above mentioned dispute over the delivery of acrylic blankets, expressly held that there is no fundamental

---

[251] *See* LG Berlin, <http://www.jura.uni-freiburg.de/ipr1/cisg/urteile/text/70.htm.>

[252] *See* Schiedsgericht der Handelskammer Hamburg; 21 March 1996 (award on substantive issues). The text of the decision is published in German. *See University of Freiburg Database*, <http://www.jura.uni-freiburg.de/ipr1/cisg/urteile/text/187.htm>. An English abstract is available as CLOUT Case 166.

breach if there is a serious offer to cure the defect.[253] In that case, the buyer refused payment of the purchase price not only on the grounds that the seller had broken an exclusive distribution agreement, but also because the goods delivered were defective and 5 acrylic blankets' rolls were missing. Attempts to settle the dispute in the presence of the Spanish manufacturer of the goods, who had offered to make a substitute delivery against payment of the purchase price, were unsuccessful. The Koblenz District Court[254] found for the seller and the appellate court affirmed the decision.[255]

With regard to the alleged non-conformity of the goods, the court held that, even if proven, such a breach of contract would not be fundamental, since the seller's supplier had offered substitute delivery. The appellate court stated that, according to article 49(1)(a), the buyer's right to avoid the contract generally prevailed over the seller's right to cure under article 48(1).[256] However, referring to its underlying purposes, the court held that article 49(1)(a) only prevails if the delivery of non-conforming goods amounted to a fundamental breach. In determining fundamental breach, the court stated that regard must be had not only to the gravity of the breach, but also to the willingness of the seller to cure the defect. Where the seller is willing to make substitute delivery and such delivery would not cause the buyer unreasonable inconvenience even non-conformity of major significance does not constitute a fundamental breach.[257]

The existence of a fundamental breach was denied by the Grenoble Court of Appeals in a Franco-Portuguese dispute as to whether the Portuguese buyer was entitled to refuse partial payment of the purchase

---

[253] *See* OLG Koblenz, 31 January 1997, 2 U 31/96.

[254] *See* LG Koblenz, 29 November 1995, 3 HO 188/94 (not published).

[255] *See* OLG Koblenz, 31 January 1997, 2 U 31/96.

Art. 39(1) provides:

> The buyer loses the right to rely on a lack of conformity of the goods if he does not give notice to the seller specifying the nature of the lack of conformity within a reasonable time after he has discovered it or ought to have discovered it.

[256] *See* OLG Koblenz, 31 January 1997, 2 U 31/96.

Art. 48(1) provides:

> Subject to art. 49, the seller may, even after the date for delivery, remedy on his own expense any failure to perform his obligations, if he can do so without unreasonable inconvenience or uncertainty of reimbursement by the seller of expenses advanced by the buyer. However, the buyer retains any right to claim damages as provided for in this Convention.

[257] *See* OLG Koblenz, 31 January 1997, 2 U 31/96.

price.[258] A French company had sold a second hand metallic hangar to a Portuguese buyer, the purchase price including the cost of dismantling and delivery. Following the buyer's refusal to pay the last installment of the price on the grounds that the dismantled metal elements were defective, the court found that a certain quantity of the goods were not fit to be exactly re-assembled, a fact expressly made known to the seller. Since that defect related to only part of the hangar and concerned metal elements, which could be repaired, the court held, however, that it did not constitute a fundamental breach justifying avoidance of the contract pursuant to article 49(1)(a).[259]

The possibility of repair was also taken into account by the Munich Court of Appeals in the above mentioned case of Polish coke sold from Sweden to Germany to be shipped to Yugoslavia, which was found to be of inferior quality.[260] The court denied fundamental breach on the ground that the deviation from the description was objectively of minor significance and could be compensated for by adapting the firing process.

The Commercial Court of Zürich did not need to decide whether or not a fundamental occurred, since the buyer failed to notify the seller about the lack of conformity of the goods within a reasonable time.[261] The Swiss plaintiff had sold a "floating centre," a container filled with salt water for weightless floating, to the German defendant. The buyer alleged that the container leaked, declared the contract avoided and refused to pay the outstanding balance. The seller then sued to recover the outstanding balance and the court ruled in favor of the plaintiff. After stating that the buyer had

---

[258] *See* Cour d'appel de Grenoble, 26 April 1995, Marques Roque, Joaquim v. S.A.R.L. Holding Manin Riviegravere; original in French. The full text of the decision is published in French. *See University of Freiburg Database*, <http://www.jura.uni-freiburg.de/iprl/cisg/urteile/text/154.htm>. An English abstract is available as CLOUT Case 152.

The Court held that the disputed contract covered the sale of a used hangar together with its dismantling and that it was apparent from the invoices submitted that the supply of services did not constitute the significant part [of the contractual obligations]. The Court concluded that the contract therefore fell within the scope of application of CISG in accordance with art. 3(2).

[259] *See* Marques Roque, Joaquim.

[260] *See* OLG München, 2 March 1994, 7 U 4419/93.

[261] *See* Handelsgericht des Kantons Zürich, 26 April 1995, HG 920670. A German abstract of the decision is published in German in SZIER/RSDIE 51-52 (1996). An English abstract is available as CLOUT Case 191.

lost its right to declare the contract avoided under article 39, the court held in *obiter dictum* that there would not have been a fundamental breach because the non-conformity could have been easily cured.[262]

Fundamental breach was found in a case based on how a seller tried to cure a defect and also in a case of an unsuccessful cure. In the first case, the plaintiff, an Italian tile manufacturer, had supplied the defendant, a German company, with basic tiles and corresponding decorative tiles. After it was discovered that the basic tiles were defective, the manufacturer made a second delivery, of both basic and decorative tiles, in a larger number than had been ordered, to ensure that there would be enough tiles for the buyer to complete its work. When the seller demanded payment, the buyer declared the contract avoided. The Baden-Baden District Court held that the buyer cannot reasonably be expected to open all the packages, to sort out the tiles, to examine them and see whether a sufficient number of one kind were supplied, and then to repackage them.[263] It further held that the buyer had the right to avoid the contract in its entirety because the decorative tiles were of no interest for him without the basic tiles.[264]

In the second case, the Oldenburg Court of Appeals viewed the unsuccessful attempt of an Austrian seller to repair furniture, which did not conform to the contract, as a fundamental breach, and thus held that the German buyer was entitled to avoid the contract.[265]

---

[262] *See* Handelsgericht des Kantons, SZIER/RSDIE 52 (1996).

[263] *See* LG Baden-Baden, 14 August 1991, 4 0 113/90. The text of the decision is in part published in German. *See University of Freiburg Database*, <http://www.jura.uni-freiburg.de/ipr1 /cisg/urteile/text/24.htm>; RIW 62 (1992). An English abstract is available as CLOUT Case 50. For comments on that decision, see Karollus, *supra* note 237, at 63 (agreeing with the court's finding).

[264] *See* LG Baden-Baden.

[265] *See* OLG Oldenburg, 1 February 1995, 11 U 64/94. Original in German; unpublished. An English abstract is available as CLOUT Case 165.

The Austrian seller, a furniture manufacturer, agreed to manufacture a leather seating arrangement for the German buyer. The buyer sold the furniture to one of its clients, who discovered that the furniture did not conform with the contract. The buyer required the plaintiff to remedy the lack of conformity by repair. Even after the furniture had been repaired, the buyer still found that the furniture did not conform with the contract and declared the contract avoided. The seller demanded payment. The Court held that the seller did not have a payment claim against the buyer since the repaired furniture did not conform with the contract and this amounted to a fundamental breach of the contract giving the buyer the right to declare the contract avoided.

D. Conclusion (Part II)

The principle objective of this Part has been to identify the various factors employed by scholars and the courts in determining when a breach of contract is fundamental. We have seen that both employ, with some minor variations, the following criteria in determining fundamental breach:

- the nature of the contractual obligation violated, namely whether the non-performed obligation was an essential term of the contract;
- in case of the delivery of non-conforming goods, the gravity of the consequences of the breach in the light of
  - the contract's overall value and the monetary loss suffered by the aggrieved party;
  - the fitness of the goods for their intended purpose; and
  - whether it is reasonable for the aggrieved party to retain the defective goods, make use of them, and then claim damages for any loss suffered as a result of the breach ("remedy-oriented"-approach);
- the existence of an offer to cure, when the requirements of article 48(1) are met;
- the possibility of cure;
- the parties' (in)ability to perform;
- the parties' (un)willingness to perform; and
- whether a breach or conduct of one party gives the other party reason to believe that it cannot rely on the other party's future performance.[266]

[266] The concept of fundamental breach as set out by scholars and courts also corresponds closely to the position in English law. In particular, it seems that there is a direct correspondence to the four following cases: (1) where the term broken was a condition (*e.g.*, Bunge Corp. v. Tradax S.A. [1981] 1 W.L.R. 711.); (2) where the breach deprived the aggrieved party of the substance of what he was contracting for (*e.g.*, Hong Kong Fir Shipping Co.Ltd. v. Kawasaki Kisen Kaisha Ltd. [1962] 2 Q. B. 26; [1962] All E.R. 474); (3) where the breach evidences an intention not to perform the remainder of the contract (*e.g.*, *Sale of Goods Act* 1979, U.K. 1979, c.54, s. 31(2)) and (4) that even an unintentional breach may give rise to an anticipatory repudiation of the rest of the contract (cf. Universal Cargo Carriers Corp. v. Citati [1957] 2 Q.B. 401, at 438).

Moreover, the criteria employed to determine fundamental breach under the Convention do not differ significantly from the American approach according to which

With regard to these different factors, the following points should be noted:

(1) While factors (2) through (4) basically concern situations where non-conforming goods were delivered, factors (5) and (6) respectively apply to non-delivery and non-payment or failure to take delivery situations. The scope of factors (1) and (7) is wider and applies to all forms of breach. The latter even covers situations where no breach has occurred at all but is to be expected.

(2) As for the *remedy-oriented* approach, at first glance it appears as if the courts are more concerned with whether the goods are reasonably (re)salable, while scholars also take into account other forms of making use of the goods, such as processing, and the buyer's risk of getting involved in a dispute over whether he observed his duty to mitigate. Since scholars, however, deny a fundamental breach when the goods, even if they cannot be used for processing, are reasonably resalable, it seems that there is, in fact, no material difference from the jurisprudence.

(3) With regard to the approaches, which look at the existence of an *offer to cure* or a *possible cure*, it should be noted that only in one of the reported cases, in which the courts denied the occurrence of a fundamental breach, was an offer to cure made. In all other cases, the courts denied fundamental breach on the grounds that the breach was curable without stating whether an offer to cure was made and the reported facts did not reveal such an offer. On the other hand, courts never found for fundamental breach on the grounds that the non-conformity could not be cured, and it

---

a failure to render or offer performance must be *material*. The Restatement (Second) of Contracts (1979) § 241 provides:

In determining whether a failure to render or offer performance is material, the following circumstances are significant:

(a) the extent to which the injured party will be deprived of the benefit which he reasonably expected;

(b) the extent to which the injured party can be adequately compensated for the part of that benefit of which he will be deprived;

(c) the extent to which the party failing to perform or to offer to perform will suffer forfeiture;

(d) the likelihood that the party failing to perform or to offer to perform will cure his failure, taking into account all of the circumstances including any reasonable any reasonable assurances; [and]

(e) the extent to which the behavior of the other party failing to perform or to offer to perform comports with standards of good faith and fair dealing.

should be noted that the German Supreme Court, in the above mentioned South African cobalt sulfate case, held that unfeasibility to cure does not necessarily constitute a fundamental breach.[267] It seems therefore possible to conclude from the case law that while the possibility to cure usually means that the non-conformity does not constitute fundamental breach, the contrary situation, namely that the non-conformity cannot be cured, does not in itself indicate a fundamental breach.

(4) Courts never made express reference to the UNIDROIT Principles in any of the reported cases. Nor did the courts discuss whether the fact that the breaching party would suffer disproportionate loss as a result of the avoidance, or that the breach was intentional or reckless, as relevant in determining fundamental breach.

(5) In no case did the breaching party successfully invoke unforeseeability of the consequences of the breach and, consequently, the courts did not need to decide the relevant point in time at which foreseeability is measured.[268] In other words, whenever the courts concluded that the injured party was substantially deprived of what he was entitled to expect under the contract and the notice requirements according to articles 38 and 39 were met, they found that a fundamental breach had been committed.

This is hardly surprising since unforeseeability can be successfully invoked only when the aggrieved party's special interest in the performance of the violated duty does not follow from the terms of the contract or from the negotiations between the parties prior to the conclusion. In most of the reported cases in which the courts found for fundamental breach, however, the aggrieved party's special interest was obvious from the terms of the contract, or the aggrieved party was able to prove that it had made clear its special interest during the contract negotiations.[269]

[267] *See* BGH, 3 April 1996, VIII ZR 51/95.

[268] In the "esclusiva su B" case, the Frankfurt District Court noted only *obiter* that the seller could not have foreseen such result. *See* LG Frankfurt, 16.09.1991, 3/11 O 3/91.

[269] *See, e.g.*, the Chinese iron-molybdenum case, where the Hamburg Court of Appeal stated as follows: "[Translation] The untimely delivery constitutes a fundamental breach according to arts. 49(1)(a) and 25. Untimely delivery, it is true, does not always constitute a fundamental breach. This general rule under the Convention, however, does not apply to cases where, at the time of the contract formation, it was obvious to the seller, that the buyer had a special interest in punctual delivery. In the pertinent case *such special interest of the buyer follows from the reference to the Incoterm 'CIF' in the contract.*" See *Hanseatisches* OLG Hamburg, 28 February 1997, 1 U 167/95 [emphasis added].

Part III — The Meaning of the Concept of Fundamental Breach in Light of the Text of Article 25, the Convention's Legislative History, Context within the Convention, Underlying Purposes and the Observance of Good Faith

The success of any uniform law depends on its uniform application and, consequently, article 7(1) calls for consideration of interpretations by judges, arbitrators, and scholars in all contracting states. Uniform application, however, is not an end in itself. Consideration of foreign decisions or scholarly writing is only permissible to the extent the foreign courts or scholars arrived at their conclusions by following the Convention's interpretation guidelines outlined above.[270] Part III examines whether the various factors employed by scholars and the courts in determining fundamental breach can be justified by means of the Convention's interpretive techniques. The question of whether the criteria of the UNIDROIT Principles regarding the determination of fundamental non-performance can be involved in determining fundamental breach, insofar as they deviate from the approaches employed under the Convention, is also addressed

A. Elements Constituting "Fundamental Breach"

The primary guide to interpretation is the ordinary meaning of the words used in the Convention. Therefore, this section examines the definition of fundamental breach under article 25. Subsection 1 determines the term "breach of contract" and the elements which transforms a "simple breach of contract" into a fundamental breach. Subsection 2 focuses on the detriment suffered by one of the parties. Subsection 3 defines substantial deprivation; and subsection 4 determines the meaning of foreseeability.

[270] For somewhat similar conclusions, see Amato, *supra* note 62, at 27 (stating that promoting uniformity does not mean "a slavish deference"). *See also* Yuqing, *supra* note 25, at 45-46; Boggiano, *supra* note 16, at 47 (emphasizing that "court should take into account all available foreign precedents and academic writings in a comparative and *critical* manner"); and Sevon, *supra* note 54, at 18.

1. Breach of a Contractual Obligation

Breach of a contractual obligation, as a precondition to a finding of fundamental breach of contract, is not defined in article 25 for the purpose of the Convention. However, one can conclude from the Convention's remedial regime[271] and article 79(1)[272] that "breach of contract" includes all forms of defective performance, as well as a complete failure to perform. It also includes both excusable and inexcusable non-performance. The contractual obligation may either be one expressly defined in the Convention (*e.g.* delivery at the right time,[273] at the right place[274] and of the correct goods[275] etc.) or one created and defined by the parties as a *sui generis* obligation.[276] Where a transaction cannot be considered a "contract of sale," domestic law governs the legal consequences of the breach, unless the parties have agreed that the transaction is subject to the Convention's rules.[277] Fi-

---

[271] Art. 45, which enumerates the remedies available to the buyer, provides in part:

> (1) If the seller fails to perform *any of his obligations under the contract or this Convention*, the buyer may:
>
> (a) exercise the rights provided in arts. 46 to 52;
>
> (b) claim damages as provided in arts. 74 to 77.

Art. 61, which enumerates the remedies available to the seller, provides in part:

> (1) If the buyer fails to perform *any of his obligations under the contract or this Convention*, the seller may:
>
> (a) exercise the rights provided in arts. 62 to 65;
>
> (b) claim damages as provided in arts. 74 to 77.

[emphasis added]

[272] Art. 79(1) provides:

> A party is not liable for a failure to perform *any of his obligations* if he proves that the failure was due to an impediment beyond his control and that he could not reasonably be expected to have taken the impediment into account at the time of the conclusion of the contract. [emphasis added]

[273] *See* art. 33 (time of delivery).

[274] *See* art. 31 (place of delivery).

[275] *See* art. 35 (conformity of the goods).

[276] *See* Schlechtriem, *supra* note 106, at Art. 25, n.8.

[277] There is no definition of "contract of sale" in the Convention. However, it is possible to reconstruct a definition from the articles defining the obligations of the parties. Art. 30 requires the seller "[t]o deliver the goods, hand over any documents relating to them and transfer the property in the goods;" while art. 53 requires the buyer "[t]o pay the price for the goods and to take delivery of them." For this conclusion, see Peter Winship,

nally, there is no breach of contract if the promisor's refusal to perform[278]is authorized by the convention.

2. Detriment

The CISG does not contain any definitions for the term 'detriment.' It also does not give any examples of a detriment that rises to the level of a fundemental breach.[279] It is unclear whether the detriment requires actual injury, damage or loss, and whether it refers only to material losses or to intangible losses as well. It is also unclear whether a legal detriment, as distinguished from a detriment in fact, is required.[280] Neither the French, Spanish or Russian versions of detriment,[281] nor the Secretariat Commentary on the 1978 Draft Convention, provides any greater assistance in this respect. The latter states that:

> The determination whether the injury is substantial must be made in the light of the circumstances of each case, e.g., the monetary value of the contract, the monetary harm caused by the breach, or the extent to which the breach interferes with other activities of the injured party.[282]

The Scope of the Vienna Convention on International Sales Contracts, in INTERNATIONAL SALES 1, 1-22 (Galston & Smith eds., 1984).

[278] *See* Schlechtriem, *supra* note 106, at Art. 25, n.8 (stating that if the seller suspends performance under art. 71 because of the buyer's economic circumstances have deteriorated, the buyer is not entitled to avoid the contract for fundamental breach of contract).

[279] This point has been stressed by Babiak, *supra* note 60, at 119.

[280] Van der Velden, *supra* note 39, at 64-65, suggests the employment of the detriment definition given by the *Corpus Iuris Secundum*, according to which "the detriment need not be real and involve actual loss, nor does it necessarily refer to material disadvantage to the party suffering it, but means a legal detriment as distinguished from a detriment in fact. It has also been defined as giving up something which one had the right to keep, or doing something which one had the right to do."*Id.* Will, *supra* note 16, at Art. 25, 2.1.1, has opposed this suggestion "because of the difference in context (*i.e.*, the doctrine of consideration)" and "the need for autonomous and uniform interpretation."

[281] The French version uses the word "*préjudice*," the Spanish "*perjuicio*" and the Russian "*bpeg.*" For the text of the different language versions, see *supra* note 1 and *infra* note 296.

[282] *See* Secretariat Commentary, *supra* note 16, at ¶ 2, art. 23 of the 1978 Draft Convention [antecedent to article 25 of the Official Text], Official Records, *supra* note 52, at 26.

Confronted with such vagueness, it is tempting to resort to domestic interpretation of detriment. However, that would not shed any greater light on the matter, putting aside the fact that any uncritical reference would contradict the Convention's need for an autonomous and uniform interpretation.[283] Detriment is unfamiliar as a technical term anywhere in the common law world.[284] The same is not true with regard to the French, Spanish or Russian version. *Préjudice, perjuicio, bpeg* — each of these words in its domestic setting represents a common legal terminology indicating injury, damage and loss.[285] Unfortunately, these terms are obscure and offer no help in determining the elements of detriment.[286] The most persuasive approach is to view the detriment element as a mere filter for those cases in which breach of a fundamental obligation occurred but has caused no injury. For example, where the seller fails in his duty to package or insure the goods but they arrive safely, there is no detriment. If on the other hand the buyer lost a customer or the opportunity to resell the goods, there would be a detriment.[287]

3. Substantial Deprivation

A breach must cause a detriment that "substantially deprives" the aggrieved party of what he is "entitled to expect under the contract" in order for it to be fundamental.[288] The reference to the expectation *under the con-*

[283] *See* Will, *supra* note 16, at Art. 25, 2.1.1.
[284] *See id.*and Van der Velden, *supra* note 39, at 64.
[285] *See* Will, *supra* note 16, at Art. 25, 2.1.1.
[286] *See* Will, *supra* note 16, at Art. 25, 2.1.1 (emphasizing that the meaning attached to the French, Spanish and Russian version of detriment in their domestic contexts indicates injury, damage, and loss in "a rather large and vague sense").
[287] *See id.* at 2.1.1.2. For a similar notion, see Gonzalez, *supra* note 180, at 86 (stating that the "Convention's definition of fundamental breach makes it possible to reconcile the interests of the parties in cases where an insignificant deviation from the contract produces surprising and serious consequences"); Mark L. Ziontz, *A New Uniform Law for the International Sale of Godds: Is it Compatible with American Interests?,* NW. J.INT'L.L. & BUS. 129, 173 (1980) (stating that "[a]voidance of an international sales contract is a remedy reserved for serious breaches by one of the parties"); Grigera Naón, *supra* note 103, at 105 (emphasizing that the notion of fundamental breach is consequently linked to the idea that no minor default shall give recourse to the extreme remedy of contract avoidance); Kastely, *supra* note 25, at 599; and Ndulo, *supra* note 84, at 16.
[288] *See* CISG Art. 25

tract makes clear that the yardstick for breach of contract is first and foremost to be found in the express and implied terms of the contract itself. This reference leaves open the question of whether other circumstances of the case, including the negotiations, trade practices established between the parties, usages, and any subsequent conduct of the parties should also be taken into account. Moreover, it is unclear when a breach substantially deprives the aggrieved party of his expectations. Is a party, for instance, substantially deprived when he has completely lost his interest in the performance? Or does substantial deprivation require that the aggrieved party's purpose in entering the contract be "frustrated" or the benefit of the bargain be lost due to the breach? Is the monetary injury or harm suffered by the non-breaching party decisive? Literal interpretation does not provide answers to any of these questions.

4. Foreseeability

The element of foreseeability sheds no further light on the concept of fundamental breach. First, the function of the foreseeability requirement itself is unclear. From the wording of the conditional clause "unless the party in breach did not foresee and a reasonable person of the same kind in the same circumstances would not have foreseen such result,"[289] one may infer that there is a presumption of foreseeability of the consequences of the breach. It thus confirms the opinion of many scholars that foreseeability is not only a burden of proof rule, but also requires taking into account the breaching party's knowledge or foreseeability of the harsh consequences of the breach in determining whether or not it is fundamental.[290] On the other hand, the foreseeability requirement under article 25 has a similar effect as the foreseeability requirement under the general rule for calculation of damages in article 74, since it limits the rights of the aggrieved party in the event the other party did not foresee the far-reaching consequences and helps determine the severity of the breach.[291] It therefore seems plausible to conclude that only the detriment/substantial deprivation component is what makes a breach "fundamental," and that the foreseeability element

---

[289] *See* CISG Art. 25

[290] *See supra* Part II, B. 2, note 164.

[291] *See* ENDERLEIN & MASKOW, *supra* note 106, at Art. 25, 4.1 (emphasizing that the special circumstances make up the severity of the breach).

serves solely to exempt the breaching party from his liability for breach of the contract.[292]

Another ambiguity results from the phrase "*and* a reasonable person of the same kind in the same circumstances."[293] In order to determine "foreseeability," the subjective and objective perspective of the party in breach must be considered. Additionally, the objective perspective of the reasonable merchant in the breaching party's position is relevant.[294] In other words, the party in breach is considered to have been able to foresee the consequences of the breach if, when objectively viewed, it is determined that he could or should have known them. But what happens when the breaching party had special knowledge and thus could have foreseen more than the average merchant? The conjunction "and," makes it possible to conclude that such special knowledge cannot be taken into account, allowing the breaching party to escape a finding of fundamental breach by hiding behind the paradigm of the reasonable person of the same kind in the same circumstances.[295]

Finally, the text of article 25 does not expressly address the point in time at which the foreseeability standard is to be applied. The use of the present tense "[a] breach of contract committed. . . is fundamental if it results" in depriving the other party "of what he is entitled to expect under the contract" makes it possible to conclude that a judge should place himself at the time the breach of contract has occurred.[296] Likewise, where article 25 states "unless the party in breach did not foresee. . . such a result" it would

---

[292] For this conclusion, see Babiak, *supra* note 60, at 118.

[293] Emphasis added.

[294] *See id.* at 121 for the same conclusion. *See also* Grigera Naón, *supra* note 103, at 105 (stating that the decisive test can only be an objective one and that the judge will therefore have to analyze objectively the position of the non-performing party); Will, *supra* note 16, at Art. 25, 2.2.2.2.4; ENDERLEIN & MASKOW, *supra* note 106, at Art. 25, at 4.2; and Magnus, *supra* note 28, at Art. 25, n.14.

[295] For a different conclusion, see ENDERLEIN & MASKOW, *supra* note 106, at Art. 25, 4.2; Will, *supra* note 16, at Art. 25, 2.2.2.2.4 (stating that "an overly astute merchant [who] in fact knew and foresaw more than his peers should not be allowed to hide the reasonable person of the same kind in the same circumstances").

[296] This point has been emphasized by Alain A. Levasseur, *The Civil Code of Quebec and the Vienna Convention on International Contracts for the Sale of Goods: some Commetns, in* CONFÉRENCES SUR LE NOUVEAU CODE CIVIL DU QUÉBEC 269, 282 (Yvon Blais ed., 1992).

appear that one should be placed at the time of the breach.[297] The French, Spanish and Russian text of article 25, however, gives rise to a different conclusion.[298] The use of the past tense "*était*" instead of "*est*," "*tenia*" instead of "*tiene*," and "*byla*" instead of "*yest*" in the French, Spanish and Russian texts, respectively, conveys the impression that the formation of the contract is the relevant point in time to determine foreseeability.[299] This view is confirmed by the reference to the rights which the aggrieved party was entitled to expect *under the contract*.[300]

5. Conclusion (Elements Constituting "Fundamental Breach")

This section illustrates that the meaning of the elements constituting fundamental breach is not evident. The same is true for other official texts of the Convention, namely the French, Spanish and Russian versions. Therefore, the literal method of interpretation does not offer much guidance in answering the question of which of the various factors enumerated

---

[297] *See* Levasseur, *supra* note 296, at 282.

[298] The French text of art. 25 reads:

> Une contravention au contrat commise par l'une des parties est essentielle lorsqu'elle cause à l'autre partie un préjudice tel qu'elle la prive substantiellement de ce que celle-ci *était* en droit d'attendre du contrat, à moins que la partie en défault n'ait pas prévu un tel résultat et qu'une personne raisonnable de même qualité placeé dans la même situation ne l'aurait pas prévu non plus. [emphasis added]

The Spanish text of art. 25 reads:

> El incumplimiento del contrato por une de las partes será esecial cuando cause a la otra parte un perjuicio tal que la prive sustancialmente de lo que *tenia* derecho a esperar en virtud del contrato, salvo que la parte que ha incumplido no haya previsto tal resultado y que una persona razonable de la misma condición no lo hubiera previsto en igual situación. [emphasis added]

[299] With regard to the French text of art. 25, this point has been emphasized by Levasseur, *supra* note 296, at 282.

[300] For the same conclusion, see, *e.g.* SCHLECHTRIEM, *supra* note 45, at 60.

For a different conclusion, see Harry M. Flechtner, *Remedies Under the New International Sales Convention: The Perspective from Article 2 of the U.C.C.*, 8 J.L. & COM. 53-108, fn. 114 (1988). He argues that if, after the formation of the contract, it becomes clear that a failure to perform will cause substantial detriment, nothing in the text of art. 25 prevents such failure to perform up to this expectation from being a fundamental breach.

above can be employed in determining fundamental breach. However, with regard to these factors, the following conclusions seem possible:

(1) Reference to the expectations under the contract support the employment of those factors which focus on the terms of the contract itself in determining fundamental breach; the *nature of the contractual obligation*.

(2) When one considers that a buyer purchases goods for some purpose, the severity of a breach may be evaluated in the light of whether the *purpose of the contract* is frustrated or whether the aggrieved party lost his *interest* due to the fact that the goods do not possess the features necessary for the intended use.

(3) The *remedy-oriented approach* is not excluded by the wording of article 25. Here one could argue that businessmen generally enter into commercial contracts for purely economic reasons and can therefore be fully compensated by damages for any loss resulting from the breach. They are only substantially deprived of their expectations if they can not be fully compensated with damages. By the same token, employment of an *offer to cure* or the *possibility of cure* is not excluded by the wording of article 25. Where the requirements of article 48(1) are met, the repair is possible within a reasonable time without causing the aggrieved party unreasonable inconvenience or uncertainty of reimbursement of expenses, the aggrieved party is not substantially deprived of his expectations.

(4) Demonstration of a *monetary loss suffered by the aggrieved party* cannot be used to justify the remedy-oriented approach. Employing this factor would impose a heavy burden on the aggrieved party to prove his substantial deprivation. Any determination of fundamental breach by reference to monetary loss would seem to be arbitrary since it is unclear when the loss amounts to a substantial deprivation. Is it required that the loss caused by the breach result in 50% or more of the monetary value of the contract? Or could a lesser percentage suffice? On the other hand, to require that the aggrieved party must have suffered a loss of more than 50% of the monetary value of the contract could not be justified etymologically.[301]

---

[301] For a similar argument where the seller delivers less of a quantity of goods than he had agreed to deliver, see Ziegel, *supra* note 115, at 9-16, where the author argues that to require that the buyer must have been deprived by 50% or more of what he was entitled to receive before it can be said that there has been a fundamental breach cannot be "justified etymologically and would lead to startling results that could

(5) The wording of article 25 does not prohibit consideration of the parties' ability or willingness to perform because total non-performance can be considered a breach which strikes at the root of the contract. A contract of sale is generally concluded for the very purpose of exchanging goods in return for consideration and if such exchange does not take place then the purpose of the contract is frustrated.

(6) The employment of the *no-reliance* factor also seems permissible where the breach or conduct creates uncertainty as to one party's future performance and where, as a consequence, the other party loses his interest in the contract. For the same reason, the UNCITRAL factor focusing on whether the breach was committed *intentionally* seems legitimate.[302] The other UNCITRAL factor looks to whether the breaching party would suffer disproportionate loss when the breach is treated as fundamental. This factor cannot be supported by the wording of article 25. The concerns expressed in respect to the approach focusing on the monetary loss suffered by the aggrieved party also apply to this approach. It is not clear under which circumstances a breaching party's loss becomes significant, and therefore any determination of fundamental breach would be arbitrary. In addition, the UNIDROIT factor is aimed at limiting the exercise of the right of avoidance, not at determining fundamental breach. In other words, it limits the availability of the avoidance remedy in spite of the existence of a fundamental breach but it does not prevent a breach from being fundamental. It therefore is inappropriate to use it as a factor in determining fundamental breach.

B. The Meaning of the Concept of Fundamental Breach in Light of the Convention's Legislative History

Interpretation by way of legislative history seeks to resolve inherent ambiguities in a provision by considering the drafter's motives and deliberations as evidenced in the officially published preparatory works. To that end,

---

not have been intended by the delegates voting in support of the amendment of [Draft] art. 23."

[302] See comment d. on UNIDROIT art. 7.3.1 (stating that "[s]ometimes an intentional breach may show that a party cannot be trusted").

this section looks briefly at the history of the concept of fundamental breach as a principle of uniform sales law. Subsection 1 deals with the deliberations within the UN Commission on International Trade Law (UNCITRAL) based on an analysis of the corresponding concept under the Convention Relating to a Uniform Law on the International Sale of Goods (ULIS).[303] Subsection 2 examines the Official Records of the Vienna Diplomatic Conference proceedings and the preliminary discussions within UNCITRAL and its Working Group, reproduced in the UNCITRAL yearbooks.

1. Pre-Convention Period

The notion of making the parties' right to terminate a contract dependent on the seriousness of the breach can be traced back to 1930 when the International Institute for the Unification of Private Law in Rome (UNIDROIT) appointed a committee to prepare a uniform law on international sales.[304] The early draft of 1939, however, did not contain a single concept of breach of contract applicable to violation of an obligation by any party to the contract. Instead, breach of contract was conceived as being a breach of a particular contractual obligation, such as the obligation to deliver or to take delivery.[305] Moreover, the remedial system resembled that of traditional English common law in that it gave the aggrieved party the right

---

[303] *See* Uniform Law on the International Sale of Goods (1964), reprinted in 3 I.L.M. 855 (1964) [hereinafter ULIS]. The text of ULIS also appears in The Hague I, at 333-354. The English text is also available at the Pace University database, <http://www.cisg.law.pace.edu/cisg/text/ulis.html>.

[304] The Council of UNIDROIT resolved on April 29, 1930, to appoint a Committee, for the purpose of preparing a draft of an international uniform law of sale. The Committee met eleven times, from 1930 to 1934, and submitted a preliminary draft, which was adopted by the Council of UNIDROIT and forwarded to the Council of the League of Nations. The draft was then transmitted to the Governments for comments. On receiving the remarks of the governments, the Committee prepared a new revised draft, which was adopted by the Council of UNIDROIT in 1939. The French text of the 1934 Draft (*Projet d'une loi internationale sur la vente*) is *reprinted* in 9 RabelsZ 8-40 (1935). The governments' comments on the 1934 Draft are reprinted in 10 RabelsZ 651-65 (1936). The English and French texts of the revised 1939 Draft are *reprinted* in UNIDROIT, Unification of Law, at 101-59 (1948).

[305] *See, e.g,* arts. 53-55 (Remedies for non-compliance with the duty to deliver) and art. 66 (Sanctions in the event of failure to take delivery).

to avoid the contract only in cases where the term violated could be classified as a condition.[306] The notion of fundamental breach of contract as an all-embracing concept was first introduced during the preparatory work for ULIS and was included in the Drafts of 1956 and 1963.[307]

The ULIS text adopted at the 1964 Hague Conference was further developed. ULIS Article 10 provided the following definition of a fundamental breach:[308]

> For the purposes of the present Law, a breach of contract shall be deemed to be fundamental wherever a party in breach knew, or

---

[306] *See* art. 55(3) of the 1939 Draft:

> An obligation of the seller is an essential *condition* of the contract where it appears from the circumstances that the buyer would not have concluded the contract without such undertaking. [emphasis added]

[307] In 1951 an international conference convened by the Government of the Netherlands in The Hague and attended by the representatives of 20 governments examined the 1939 draft and appointed a Special Commission with the task to further elaborate its text. By 1956 this commission had prepared a new draft which introduced at art. 15 the principle of fundamental breach and defined it as follows:

> "A breach of contract shall be deemed fundamental wherever the party in breach knew or ought have known, at the time the contract was made, that the other party would not have contracted had he foreseen that such breach would occur."

The 1956 Draft was circulated to governments and other interested international bodies for comment. On the basis of these comments the commission completed a final draft in 1963 for submission to an international conference. The text of art. 15, however, was unchanged.

The English and French text of the 1956 Draft is *reprinted* in UNIDROIT, Unification of Law, at 70-115 (1956).

For a brief summary of the early efforts to unify the law of international sales, see Bonell, *supra* note 25, at 3-5; Winship, *supra* note 277, at 1-3/9. For a summary of the early efforts to define fundamental breach, see Eörsi, *supra* note 103, at 336-39.

[308] The text presented to the 1964 Hague Conference by the Text Committee contains only minor changes compared with the definition of fundamental breach under the 1956/1963 draft. These were: "From the point of view of this statute" — an introduction; instead of "party," "party in breach," instead of "contracted," "entered into the contract;" instead of "breach of contract," "breach of contract and its consequences." Finally, the place of the "other party" is taken by the "reasonable person;" this reasonable person must be in the same position as the other party. See the ironic comment on the amendments by Eörsi, *supra* note 103, at 339, where the author states that the "number of words was increased from 31 to 64; for those who believe in the possibility of a definition of fundamental breach this was a quite useful change."

ought to have known, at the time of the conclusion of the contract, that a reasonable person in the same situation as the other party would not have entered into the contract if he had foreseen the breach and its effects.

2. Preparatory Work for the Convention

The review of the preparatory works of the Convention is structured as follows. Section "a" looks at the attempts within UNCITRAL and at the Diplomatic Conference to define the concept of fundamental breach. Section "b" focuses on the existence of an offer to cure. This section discusses the relationship between the fundamental nature of a breach and the seller's right to cure.

a. Definition of Fundamental Breach

(1) Deliberations within the UNCITRAL

Already at the Hague Conference, the concept of fundamental breach under ULIS Article 10 was criticized on the grounds that it was too subjective, in that it relied on a test that required the breaching party to anticipate whether or not the non-breaching party would have entered into the contract had he foreseen the breach.[309]

[309] *See, e.g.*, observations of the Austrian government (The Hague II, at 108), Dutch government (The Hague II, at 138), U.K. government (The Hague II, at 169); in the course of the debate: Loewe (Austria), Yadin (Israel), Davis (U.K.); only Tunc (France) and O'-Keefe (Ireland) held the subjective notion appropriate (The Hague I, at 35-36).

To overcome the *ex post facto* reasoning necessary in the ULIS art. 10 definition, the British and Dutch Governments, at the Hague conference proposed a new formula, in which objective criteria were to be judged at the time of the occurrence of the breach of contract (The Hague II, at 274). Their proposal read:

> A breach of contract shall be deemed fundamental, wherever the performance of the contract is, by reason of the breach, rendered radically different from that for which the parties contracted.

See also Van der Velden, *supra* note 39, at 63 (stating that the defect in the definition resulted from the reference to the reasonable man's mind at the time of the conclusion of the contract). For a similar statement, see R.H. GRAVESON ET AL., THE UNIFORM LAWS OF INTERNATIONAL SALES ACT (1967) 55(1968).

During the preparatory work for the Convention, ULIS article 10 was once again the object of criticism. States and organizations objected to the ULIS definition on the grounds that it was too complex, and its subjective standards would be difficult to apply.[310] As a result, the UNCITRAL Working Group, based on a Mexican proposal, eliminated the subjective test as well as the related speculative element as to whether a "*reasonable* person" would have "entered into the contract *if* he had foreseen the breach and its effects."[311] Instead, the Working Group proposed a single objective criterion of whether the breach substantially impaired the value of the performance

---

[310] After it became evident that ULIS would not be widely adopted, the United Nations Commission on International Trade Law (UNCITRAL), established in 1966 with the task to promote "the progressive harmonization and unification of the law of international trade," decided at its first session in 1968 to inquire into the intentions of all Member States of the United Nations. Based on the comments of the 36 States that replied, UNCITRAL decided to set up a Working Group to determine whether ULIS could be modified to increase their acceptability or whether completely new texts should be drafted. The Working Group, composed of 14 States representing the different regions and legal traditions of the world, held nine sessions and produced two Draft Conventions, namely the 1976 Draft Convention on Sales, setting forth the rights and obligations of the seller and buyer under the sales contract, and the 1977 Draft Convention on Formation of the Sales Contract. At the second stage, the full Commission reviewed the two Draft Conventions, decided to consolidate the texts into one document — the 1978 Draft Convention on Contracts for the International Sale of Goods — and recommended to the U.N. General Assembly that it convene a diplomatic conference to review the Draft and finalize the Convention.

The General Assembly adopted this recommendation and convened a diplomatic conference in March-April, 1980 at UNCITRAL's headquarters in Vienna. At the Conference, attended by 62 States, most of the work was done in two "Committees," each of which included all of the States that attended the Conference. The larger task was assigned to the First Committee, which prepared Parts I-III (Arts. 1-88) of the Convention. The Second Committee prepared Part IV, Final Provisions (Arts. 89-101). The Committees could take action by majority vote, whereas significant action by the Conference Plenary required approval by a two-thirds majority. For the history of the drafting within UNCITRAL, see John O. Honnold, *The Draft Convention on Contracts for the International Sale of Goods: An Overview*, 27 AM.J.COMP.L. 223 (1979); Farnsworth, *supra* note 85, at 17-19; and Winship, *supra* note 277, at 1-1 to 1-15.

[311] Emphasis in the original. The Mexican proposal employs as a criterion "whether the breach of contract substantially alters the scope or contents of the rights of the other party" (*see* UNCITRAL Yearbook VI (1975), at 95; Doc. History, at 220).

required by the contract.[312] This purely objective test was further developed and led to the following definition of fundamental breach:

> Article 9
> A breach committed by one of the parties to the contract is fundamental if it results in substantial detriment to the other party and the party in breach foresaw or had reason to foresee such a result .[313]

In its comment on article 9, the government of the Philippines expressed dissatisfaction with the idea that the breaching party had to foresee the substantial detriment.[314] In case of litigation, the burden of proof would thus be on the non-breaching party. This was not considered a proper solution because it would be extremely difficult for the non-breaching party to prove that the party in breach "foresaw or had reason to foresee such a result."[315] The United States echoed this criticism, and both the Philippines' and the United States' delegates to UNCITRAL suggested that the final phrase of article 9 should be reworded to read "unless the party in breach did not foresee and had no reason to foresee such a result."[316] This suggestion was approved by a majority of the members of UNCITRAL and the definition of "fundamental breach," as embodied under article 23 in the 1978 Draft Convention, thus reads:

---

[312] The proposed revision of ULIS art. 10 reads as follows (*see* UNCITRAL Yearbook VI (1975), at 95; Doc. History, at 220):

> For the purpose of the present Law, a breach of contract shall be regarded as fundamental wherever such breach substantially [to a significant extent] impairs the value of the contract and the present law.

As negotiations over fundamental breach continued, the text adopted by the Working Group read as follows (see Report of the Working Group on its sixth session, UNCITRAL Yearbook VI (1975), at 53; Doc. History, at 244):

> A breach committed by one of the parties to the contract shall be regarded as fundamental if it results in substantial detriment to the other party and the party in breach had reason to foresee such a result.

[313] ULIS art. 10 was replaced by Draft art. 9. *See* Working Group, Report on its Seventh Session, UNCITRAL Yearbook, VII (1976), at 90.

[314] See UNCITRAL Yearbook VIII (1977), at 127.

[315] *See id.* For fuller review of the discussion, see Michida, *supra* note 143, at 284-86.

[316] *See* Michida, *supra* note 143, at 285.

Article 23
A breach committed by one of the parties is fundamental if it results in substantial detriment to the other party unless the party in breach did not foresee and had no reason to foresee such a result.[317]

Unlike ULIS article 10, the proposed text did not deal with the issue of the relevant time at which it was possible to foresee the result and UNCITRAL did not consider it necessary to specify at what moment the party in breach should have foreseen or had reason to foresee the consequences of the breach.[318]

(2) *First Committee Deliberations and the Decisions by Plenary Conference*

(a) Amendments

At the Vienna Conference, the Federal Republic of Germany,[319] Czechoslovakia,[320] Pakistan,[321] the United Kingdom,[322] Egypt,[323] Turkey,[324]

---

[317] *See* Official Records, *supra* note 52, at 26; Documentary History, *supra* note 52, at 416.

[318] *See* UNCITRAL Yearbook VIII (1977), at 31. UNCITRAL did not accept a proposal that the criterion of fundamental breach should be a "loss of interest in the contract" on the part of the innocent party. This proposal was opposed on the ground that it brought in the question of motive of contract and this was too subjective an element. *See* UNCITRAL Yearbook VIII (1977), at 31.

[319] *See* U.N. DOC. A/CONF.97/C.1/L.63; *reprinted* in Official Records, *supra* note 52, at 99; Documentary History, *supra* note 52, at 671.

[320] *See* U.N. DOC. A/CONF.97/C.1/L.81; *reprinted* in Official Records, *supra* note 52, at 99; Documentary History, *supra* note 52, at 671.

[321] *See* U.N. DOC. A/CONF.97/C.1/L.99; *reprinted* in Official Records, *supra* note 52, at 99; Documentary History, *supra* note 52, at 671.

[322] *See* U.N. DOC. A/CONF.97/C.1/L.104; *reprinted* in Official Records, *supra* note 52, at 99; Documentary History, *supra* note 52, at 671.

[323] *See* U.N. DOC. A/CONF.97/C.1/L.106; *reprinted* in Official Records, *supra* note 52, at 99; Documentary History, *supra* note 52, at 671.

[324] *See* U.N. DOC. A/CONF.97/C.1/L.121; *reprinted* in Official Records, *supra* note 52, at 99; Documentary History, *supra* note 52, at 671.

and India[325] submitted amendments to Draft article 23. What follows is a summary of those proposed amendments.

(i) Proposal of the former Czechoslovakia

The Czechoslovak delegation criticized Draft article 23 for two reasons. First, they asserted that the substantial detriment element lacked precision. Secondly, they stated that the foreseeability requirement introduced a subjective element, which could create difficulties, particularly in relation to the buyer's right to require substitute delivery, where it was important to have objective criteria to define fundamental breach. Had the existing definition of fundamental breach been accepted, they argued, the buyer would have to wait until he had suffered substantial detriment in order to avail himself of this right, and that was contrary to the requirements of international trade.[326] They proposed that the existing text be replaced with the following:

> A breach of contract is fundamental if the party in breach knew or ought to have known, in the light of the reasons for the conclusion of the contract, or any information disclosed at any time before or at the conclusion of the contract, that the other party would not be interested in performance in case of such a breach.[327]

This proposal was criticized by the Mexican delegation as too narrow in specifying that the party in breach ought to have known "that the other party would not be interested in performance in case of such a breach."[328] Similarly, the French delegation viewed the requirement that the non-breaching party must lose interest in the contract as a result of the breach as

---

[325] *See* U.N. DOC. A/CONF.97/C.1/L.126; reprinted in Official Records, *supra* note 52, at 99; Documentary History, *supra* note 52, at 671.

[326] See comments by the representative of the former Czechoslovakia (Kopac, ¶ 4), Official Records, *supra* note 52, at 295-96; Documentary History, *supra* note 52, at 516-17.

[327] *See* U.N. DOC. A/CONF.97/C.1/L.81; *reprinted* in Official Records, *supra* note 52, at 99; Documentary History, *supra* note 52, at 671.

[328] See comments by the representative of Mexico (Mantilla-Molina, ¶ 12), Official Records, *supra* note 52, at 296; Documentary History, *supra* note 52, at 517.

too severely limiting its right to terminate the contract.[329] The Danish delegation objected to the proposal on the ground that the proposed criteria were very difficult to apply in practice.[330] Later, the proposal of the former Czechoslovakia was rejected by the First Committee.[331]

(ii) Proposal of Egypt

The Egyptian delegation criticized Draft article 23 as being too subjective in nature, since the circumstances of the party in breach were taken as a basis for appreciating when this same party claimed that it had not foreseen and had no reason to foresee that substantial detriment to the other party would result.[332] The Egyptian amendment to Draft article 23 sought to introduce a more objective principle by indicating that the party in breach ought to provide proof that it had not foreseen such a result and that a reasonable person of the same kind in the same circumstances would not have foreseen it. It read as follows:

> A breach committed by one of the parties is fundamental if it results in substantial detriment to the other party unless the party in breach *proves that he did not foresee such a result and that a reasonable person of the same kind in the same circumstances would not have foreseen it.*[333] *[emphasis in the original]*

The introduction of the criterion of what a reasonable person of the same kind in the same circumstances could have foreseen in determining fundamental breach was welcomed by many delegations. Although there was consensus among the delegations that the burden of proof should lay on the party in breach, they did not, however, wish to include language in

---

329 See comments by the representative of France (Ghestin, ¶ 32), Official Records, *supra* note 52, at 298; Documentary History, *supra* note 52, at 519.

330 See comments by the representative of Denmark (Trönning, ¶ 22), Official Records, *supra* note 52, at 297; Documentary History, *supra* note 52, at 518.

331 *See* Official Records, *supra* note 52, at 298; Documentary History, *supra* note 52, at 519.

332 See comments by the representative of Egypt (Shafik, ¶ 3), Official Records, *supra* note 52, at 295; Documentary History, *supra* note 52, at 515.

333 *See* U.N. DOC. A/CONF.97/C.1/L.106; *reprinted* in Official Records, *supra* note 52, at 99; Documentary History, *supra* note 52, at 671.

the definition which would raise questions of civil procedure.[334] As a result, the Egyptian delegation deleted the reference to proof ("proves that he") from their amendment and suggested amending the corresponding part of his text.[335] The revised amendment was adopted.[336]

(iii) Proposal of Pakistan

In the view of the Pakistani delegation, the expression "substantial detriment" was imprecise.[337] It proposed replacing the words "if it results in substantial detriment to the other party" with the words "if it results in such detriment to the other party as would basically change the terms of the transaction."[338] Opinions as to this proposal were divided, but a majority of the delegations supported it,[339] and an *ad hoc* working group was established to redraft Draft article 23 on the basis of the Pakistani proposal.[340]

---

[334] See, *e.g.*, comments by the representative of Austria (Reishofer, ¶ 6); Norway (Rognlien, ¶ 9); Mexico (Mantilla-Molina, ¶ 12); Greece (Krispis, ¶ 13); Denmark (Trönning, ¶ 21); Szasz (Hungary, ¶ 34), Official Records, at 296-298; Doc. History, at 517-519.

[335] See the reply of the representative of Egypt (Shafik, ¶¶ 41-42), Official Records, *supra* note 52, at 298; Documentary History, at 519, to the comments by the various delegations.

[336] *See* Official Records, *supra* note 52, at 299; Documentary History, *supra* note 52, at 520.

[337] See comments by the representative of Pakistan (Inaamullah, ¶ 45), Official Records, *supra* note 52, at 299; Documentary History, *supra* note 52, at 520.

[338] *See* U.N. DOC. A/CONF 97/C.1/L.99; *reprinted* in Official Records, *supra* note 52, at 99; Documentary History, *supra* note 52, at 671.

[339] The delegations of Romania (Popescu, ¶ 46), the former Czechoslovakia (Kopac, ¶ 46), India (Kuchibhotla, ¶ 46) and Egypt (Shafik, ¶ 46) supported this amendment on the ground that it made the provision clearer and more precise; China (Wang, ¶ 53), Spain (Olivencia Ruiz, ¶ 50) and Kenya (Waititu, ¶ 59) also supported the Pakistan proposal. *See* Official Records, *supra* note 52, at 299-300; Documentary History, *supra* 52, at 520-21.

The delegations of Sweden (Hjerner, ¶ 47), Greece (Krispis, ¶ 49), the former USSR (Lebedev, ¶ 51), Hungary (Szasz, ¶ 54), Norway (Rognlien, ¶ 58) and the United States (Farnsworth, ¶ 55) criticized this amendment since they did not consider that it made the idea of substantial detriment more precise. *See* Official Records, *supra* note 52, at 299-300; Documentary History, *supra* note 52, at 520-21.

[340] The *ad hoc* working group consisted of the representatives of Argentina, Czechoslovakia, the Federal Republic of Germany, Ghana, Hungary, Norway, Pakistan, Romania and Spain. *See* Official Records, *supra* note, at 300, ¶ 65-66; Documentary History, *supra* note 52, at 521.

(iv) Proposal of the Federal Republic of Germany

The delegation of the Federal Republic of Germany took the view that it was impossible to determine whether a breach was fundamental without referring to the terms of the contract.[341] Accordingly, it suggested phrasing Draft article 23 as follows:

> A breach committed by one of the parties is fundamental if, *having regard to all express and implied terms of the contract*, the breach results in substantial detriment to the other party unless the party in breach did not foresee and had no reason to foresee such result.[342]
> [emphasis in the original]

This proposal was criticized by the delegations of the United Kingdom, Australia, the former USSR, and Sweden as too narrow because it would have limited the courts' authority to consider the express and implied terms of the contract, without also allowing them to take into account other relevant circumstances.[343] The German representative responded that the expectations of the parties as found in the contract provided an objective test for measuring substantial detriment and that this amendment would not bar an examination of the circumstances of the case.[344] Other delegations supported the amendment as a good basis for determining fundamental breach.[345]The First Committee decided to refer it to the *ad hoc* working group set up to consider the Pakistani proposal.[346]

---

[341] See comments by the representative of the Federal Republic of Germany (Klingsporn, ¶ 68), Official Records, *supra* note 52, at 300; Documentary History, *supra* note 52, at 521.
[342] *See* U.N. DOC. A/CONF.97/C.1/L.63; *reprinted* in Official Records, *supra* note 52, at 99; Documentary History, *supra* note 52, at 671.
[343] See comments by the representatives of the United Kingdom (Feltham, ¶ 70), Australia (Bennett, ¶ 74), the former USSR (Lebedev, ¶ 75) and Sweden (Hjerner, ¶ 77), Official Records, *supra* note 52, at 300-301; Documentary History, *supra* note 52, at 521-22.
[344] See comments by the German representative (Herber, ¶ 78); Official Records, *supra* note 52, at 301; Documentary History, *supra* note 52, at 522.
[345] See comments by the delegations of Finland (Sevon, ¶ 71), Belgium (Dabin, ¶ 69), Argentina (Boggiano, ¶ 72), Republic of Korea (Kim, ¶ 73) and Ireland (Plunkett, ¶ 76), Official Records, *supra* note 52, at 299-300; Documentary History, *supra* note 52, at 521-22.
[346] *See* Official Records, *supra* note 52, at 301 (¶ 79-80); Documentary History, *supra* note 52, at 522.

(v) Proposal of the United Kingdom

The amendment put forth by the delegation of the United Kingdom was comprised of two proposals. The first concerned the point in time at which foreseeability should be measured. The delegation was of the opinion that the article itself should be more specific and suggested that the moment when the contract was concluded was the relevant point, since it was at that point when the scope of the contract was defined by the parties.[347] The second proposal dealt with the definition of substantial detriment. The British delegation expressed its concern that a party adversely affected by an unfavorable shift in market prices could too easily escape from a detrimental situation by simply seeking all possible grounds to allege breach by the other party in order to avoid the contract.[348] To avert the extreme measure of avoidance in such cases, they suggested specifying that "a breach does not result in substantial detriment to the other party if damages would be an adequate remedy for him."[349] Their proposal read as follows:

> A breach committed by one of the parties is fundamental if it results in substantial detriment to the other party unless *at the time when the contract was concluded* the party in breach did not foresee and had no reason to foresee such result. *A breach does not result in substantial detriment to the other party if damages would be an adequate remedy for him.*[350] *[emphasis in the original]*

Both proposals were opposed by several delegations. The delegations of Norway, Finland, and Hungary voiced their opposition to the first proposal. They took the view that information provided after the conclusion of a contract could modify the situation with regard to both substantial detriment and foreseeability and, for that reason, the wording of Draft article 23

---

[347] *See* Official Records, *supra* note 52, at 302 (¶ 1); Documentary History, *supra* note 52, at 523.

[348] *See* Official Records, *supra* note 52, at 302 (¶ 4); Documentary History, *supra* note 52, at 523.

[349] *Id.*

[350] U.N. DOC. A/CONF.97/C.1/L.104; *reprinted* in Official Records, *supra* note 52, at 99; Documentary History, *supra* note 52, at 671.

should be flexible.[351] With regard to the second proposal, the Bulgarian delegation emphasized that the non-breaching party, as a matter of principle, should have the right to decide whether to sue for damages or to avoid the contract as a consequence of substantial detriment.[352] The delegations of Ghana and Ireland pointed out that the very use of the notion of adequacy of damages was likely to lead to the remedy of avoidance being available in too narrow a range of circumstances.[353] They felt that it might not only be unfair to oblige the non-breaching party to accept damages, but that there was also the question as to what constituted adequate damages.[354] The United Kingdom withdrew their proposals in light of those comments.[355]

(vi) Proposals of Turkey and India

The Turkish delegation suggested inserting the words "a breach" after the words "of the contract."[356] Due to the purely formal character of the proposal the Committee decided to transmit it without comment to the Drafting Committee.[357]

The delegation from India suggested inserting the words "as a reasonable person" after the words "had no reason" in the third line of article 23.[358] Since this idea was already incorporated in the Egyptian proposal, the Committee decided not further to discuss this amendment.[359]

---

[351] See comments by the delegations of Norway (Rognlien, ¶ 2), Finland (Sevon, ¶ 2) and Hungary (Szasz, ¶ 2), Official Records, *supra* note 52, at 302; Documentary History, *supra* note 52, at 523.

[352] See the comments of the Bulgarian representative (Stalev, ¶ 6), Official Records, *supra* note 52, at 302; Documentary History, *supra* note 52, at 523.

[353] See the comments by the delegations of Ghana (Date-Bah, ¶ 8) and Ireland (Plunkett, ¶ 9), Official Records, *supra* note 52, at 302-03; Documentary History, *supra* note 52, at 523-24.

[354] See the comments of the Irish representative (Plunkett, ¶ 9), Official Records, *supra* note 52, at 302-03; Documentary History, *supra* note 52, at 523-24.

[355] *See* Official Records, *supra* note 52, at 302, 303 (¶¶ 3, 11); Documentary History, *supra* note 52, at 523, 524.

[356] U.N. DOC. A/CONF.97/C.1/L.121; *reprinted* in Official Records, *supra* note 52, at 99; Documentary History, *supra* note 52, at 671.

[357] *See* Official Records, *supra* note 52, at 303 (¶¶12, 13); Documentary History, *supra* note 52, at 524.

[358] U.N. DOC. A/CONF.97/C.1/L.126; *reprinted* in Official Records, at 99; Doc. History, at 671.

[359] *See* Official Records, at 303 (¶ 15, 16); Doc. History, at 524.

(b) Proposal of the ad hoc Working Group

Having taken into account the amendments of the delegations of Pakistan and the Federal Republic of Germany, the *ad hoc* working group, Hungary dissenting, submitted the following text:

> A breach of contract committed by one of the parties is fundamental *if it results in such detriment to the other party as will substantially impair his expectations under the contract,* unless the party in breach did not foresee and had no reason to foresee such a result.[360]
> [emphasis in the original]

The text of the *ad hoc* working group was hotly debated. Many delegations were of the opinion that the text was no clearer than the existing formula "substantial detriment to the other party."[361] Moreover, some of them criticized the new text as being more subjective than the previous one.[362] The majority of delegations, however, took the exact opposite view. They argued that the reference to the expectations of the non-breaching party under the contract was an additional element of objectivity and, thus, some of the previous definition's vagueness was eliminated.[363] The proposal of the *ad hoc* working group was finally adopted by 22 votes in favor and 18

---

[360] U.N. DOC. A/CONF.97/C.1/L.176; *reprinted* in Official Records, *supra* note 52, at 99; Documentary History, *supra* note 52, at 671.

[361] See comments by the delegations of Iraq (Sami, ¶ 22), France (Ghestin, ¶ 21), the former USSR (Lebedev, ¶ 26), China (Li Chih-min, ¶ 29), Official Records, *supra* note 52, at 329-330; Documentary History, *supra* note 52, at 550-51.

[362] See comments of the representatives of France (Ghestin, ¶ 21), the former USSR (Lebedev, ¶ 26), China (Li Chih-min, ¶ 29), Official Records, *supra* note 52, at 329-30; Documentary History, *supra* note 52, at 550-51.

[363] See comments by the delegations of Bulgaria (Stalev, ¶ 16); Austria (Reishofer, ¶ 17); Federal Republic of Germany (Schlechtriem, ¶ 23); Italy (Bonell, ¶ 24); Norway (Rognlien, ¶ 23); Spain (Olivencia Ruiz, ¶ 31); the former Czechoslovakia (Kopac, ¶ 32-34); Ghana (Sam, ¶ 35); Argentina (Boggiano, ¶ 36); Ireland (Plunkett, ¶ 37), Official Records, *supra* note 52, at 329-30; Documentary History, *supra* note 52, at 550-51.

The delegations of the United Kingdom (Feltham, ¶ 15); German Democratic Republic (Wagner, ¶ 20) sought to replace the words "substantially impair his expectations" by "substantially disappoint his expectations." *See* Official Records, *supra* note 52, at 329-30; Documentary History, *supra* note 52, at 550-51.

against, and, together with the amendment by Egypt, was referred to the Drafting Committee.[364]

In the Drafting Committee, the wording "substantially impair his expectations" under the contract proved unacceptable to the representatives of the civil law countries.[365] Their representatives had suggested, that, rather than referring to expectations under the contract, the article should speak of the interests of one of the parties. However, that proposal was not acceptable to the representatives of the common law countries.[366] The Drafting Committee finally arrived at the present definition of fundamental breach, which represented a compromise acceptable to every one.[367] This definition was adopted at Plenary Conference by 42 votes to 2, with two abstentions.[368]

b. Relationship to the Seller's Right to Cure

(1) Deliberations within the UNCITRAL

During the preparatory work for the Convention several proposals to clarify the relationship between the seller's right to cure and the buyer's right to avoid a contract were made.[369] The central issue in discussing these pro-

[364] *See* Official Records, *supra* note 52, at 329-30 (¶ 39); Documentary History, *supra* note 52, at 550-51.

[365] See comments by the Executive Secretary of the Convention (Vis, ¶ 13) explaining the text finally adopted by the Drafting Committee, Official Records, *supra* note 52, at 425; Documentary History, *supra* note 52, at 646.

[366] *Id.*

[367] *Id.*

[368] *See* Official Records, *supra* note 52, at 206; Documentary History, *supra* note 52, at 741.

The Swedish delegate (Hjerner, ¶ 13) voted against it on the grounds that the new formulation "could lend itself to several different interpretations and lead to confusion." And for the Spanish delegate (Garrigues, ¶ 15), "the idea embodied in art. 23 that a breach would be taken into account only if it were 'fundamental' was totally unacceptable. The Canadian delegate (Ziegel, ¶ 12) explained in his abstention that the new definition of fundamental breach imposed an unduly heavy onus on the aggrieved party since it would be difficult for him, particularly in the case of delivery of defective goods, to establish fundamental breach. *See* Official Records, *supra* note 52, at 206; Documentary History, *supra* note 52, at 741.

[369] The seller's right to cure appeared in ULIS as art. 44 (1), which read:

The seller shall retain, even after the date fixed for the delivery of the goods, the right to deliver any missing part or quantity of the goods or to deliver other goods which

posals was whether the buyer may preclude the seller from curing any failure to perform his obligations where cure can be effected without causing the buyer unreasonable inconvenience or unreasonable expense. This issue was discussed in the context of a defect in the goods which, in the absence of repair, was so serious as to constitute a fundamental breach, but where the delay in remedying that defect would neither contribute a fundamental breach, nor even cause the buyer unreasonable inconvenience or expense.[370]

None of these proposals, however, was adopted. The first unsuccessful attempt was made at the Sixth Session of the Working Group. The Working Group rejected the proposal to add to proposed article [43 bis] [antecedent to article 25 of the Official Text] the words "on account of delay" following the words "unless the buyer."[371] The effect would have been that the buyer could have avoided the contract and thereby cut off the seller's right only if delivery was late.[372]

The second unsuccessful attempt to curtail the buyer's right of avoidance was made within UNCITRAL. In the discussion of the various proposals[373] to amend article [43 bis], then renumbered as article 29 [antecedent to article 48 of the Official Text], some delegates took the view

---

are in conformity with the contract or to remedy any defect in the goods handed over, provided that the exercise of this right does not cause the buyer either unreasonable inconvenience or unreasonable expense.

[370] *See* UNCITRAL Yearbook VIII (1977), at 45 (¶ 273); Documentary History, *supra* note 52, at 338.

[371] The amended text of ULIS art. 44(1) adopted by Working Group as art. [43 bis] (1) stated (see UNCITRAL Yearbook VI (1973), at 70, Documentary History, *supra* note 52, at 148):

The seller may, even after the date for delivery, cure any failure to perform his obligations, if he can do so without such delay as will amount to a fundamental breach of contract and without causing the buyer unreasonable inconvenience or unreasonable expense, unless the buyer has declared the contract avoided in accordance with art. 44 [antecedent to art. 49 of the Official Text] or the price reduced in accordance with article 45 [antecedent to art. 50 of the Official Text][or has notified the seller that he will himself cure the lack of conformity].

[372] *See* UNCITRAL Yearbook VI (1975), at 56; Documentary History, *supra* note 52, at 247.

[373] These proposals were as follows (*see* UNCITRALYearbook VIII (1977), at 44 (¶¶ 271, 272; Documentary History, *supra* note 52, at 337):

That the words "unless the buyer has declared the contract avoided in accordance with art. 30 [antecedent to art. 49 of the Official Text] or has declared the price to be reduced in accordance with art. 31[antecedent to art. 50 of the Official Text]" be deleted.

that the seller's right to cure should take precedence over the buyer's right to avoid. Such a rule would promote the upholding of contracts and prevent the unnecessary expense to the seller of avoidance where the defect could be quickly cured. The buyer would be protected by the fact that the seller's right would only operate where cure could be effected without such delay as would constitute a fundamental breach and only where the cure did not cause the buyer unreasonable inconvenience or expense.[374]

Another view was that if the defect could be cured easily there would be no fundamental breach of contract, since the notion of fundamental breach must be considered both in light of the defect itself as well as the possibility to cure.[375] It was pointed out that this result, however, would not be evident in many common law jurisdictions if the words "unless the buyer has declared the contract avoided in accordance with article 30 [antecedent to article 49 of the Official Text]" were retained in article 29(1).[376]

There was considerable opposition within UNCITRAL, however, to the idea that the buyer's right to declare the contract avoided could be affected by an offer to cure the defect. Any possibility to cure was viewed as a privilege, which should depend upon the consent of the buyer, who always has the right to declare the contract avoided. UNCITRAL, after considerable deliberations, adopted in principle the following proposal:

> Article 29(1)
> The seller may, at his own expense, cure, even after the date for delivery, any failure to perform his obligations, if he can do so without such delay as will amount to a fundamental breach of contract and without causing the buyer unreasonable inconvenience including any uncertainty in reimbursement by the seller of expenses advanced by the buyer, unless the buyer has declared the contract avoided in accordance with article 30.[377]

(i) That the words "or has declared the price to be reduced in accordance with article 31" be deleted. In addition, art. 31 should be amended to make it clear that the seller's right to cure his failure to perform takes precedence over the buyer's right to have the price reduced.
(ii) That the following sentence be added to paragraph (1): "The seller is, however, obliged to compensate the buyer for any expense caused by the seller in exercising his right to cure the failure to perform.

[374] *See* UNCITRAL Yearbook VIII (1977), at 44 (¶¶ 271, 272); Documentary History, *supra* note 52, at 337.
[375] *See id.*
[376] *See id.*
[377] *See* UNCITRAL Yearbook VIII (1977), at 44 (¶¶ 271, 272); Documentary History, *supra* note 52, at 337.

In light of the foregoing discussion, UNCITRAL reconsidered the definition of fundamental breach contained in article 9 [antecedent to article 25 of the Official Text] and the U.S. delegation proposed that article 9 read as follows (new language in italics):

> A breach committed by one of the parties to the contract is fundamental, if, *under all the circumstances, including a reasonable offer to cure,* it results in substantial detriment to the other party and the party in breach foresaw or had reason to foresee such a result.[378]
> [emphasis in the original]

In support of this proposal, the U.S. delegation argued that the proposed addition to article 9 would protect against a technical avoidance of the contract when there had been an offer to cure under article 29.[379] However, others took the view that this change was unnecessary because the conditions governing an offer by the seller to cure were governed by article 29 and, if there was no offer to cure, the situation was governed by article 9.[380] Accordingly, the proposal was found to be superfluous.[381] The UNCITRAL did not retain the proposal and finally arrived at the following text, then renumbered as 1978 Draft article 44(1):

> Unless the buyer has declared the contract avoided in accordance with [Draft] article 45, the seller may, even after the date for delivery, remedy

---

In the light of its deliberations the UNCITRAL considered the following proposals:

(i) That article 29(1) read as follows:

The seller may, at his own expense, cure, even after the date of delivery, any failure to perform his obligations, if he can do so within a reasonable time and without causing the buyer unreasonable inconvenience, unless the buyer has declared the contract avoided in accordance with article 30.

(ii) That article 29(1) read as follows:

The seller may, at his own expense, cure, even after the date of delivery, any failure to perform his obligations, if he can do so without such delay as will amount to fundamental breach of contract and without causing the buyer unreasonable inconvenience, including any uncertainty in reimbursement by the seller of expenses advanced by the buyer, unless the buyer has declared the contract avoided in accordance with article 30.

[378] UNCITRAL Yearbook VIII (1977), at 31 (¶ 93); Documentary History, *supra* note 52, at 324.

[379] *Id.*

[380] *Id.*

[381] For fuller review of the discussion, see Michida, *supra* note 143, at 286-88.

> at his own expense any failure to perform his obligations, if he can do so without such delay as will amount to a fundamental breach of contract and without causing the buyer unreasonable inconvenience or uncertainty of reimbursement by the seller of expenses advanced by the buyer. The buyer retains any right to claim damages as provided for in this Convention.[382]

(2) *First Committee Deliberations and the Decisions by Plenary Conference*

(a) Amendments

The controversy over the relationship between the buyer's right to avoid and the seller's right to cure continued at the Vienna Diplomatic Conference, where amendments were submitted to Draft article 44(1) by the Federal Republic of Germany,[383] Singapore,[384] Bulgaria,[385] Japan,[386] and the United States of America.[387] These amendments were to the following effect:

(i) Proposals of the Federal Republic of Germany, Bulgaria and Japan

In the view of the delegations of Bulgaria, the Federal Republic of Germany and Japan, the existing text of Draft article 44(1) did not achieve a

---

382 UNCITRAL Yearbook VIII (1977), at 31 (¶ 94); Documentary History, *supra* note 52, at 324.

383 *See* U.N. DOC. A/CONF.97/C.1/L.140; *reprinted* in Official Records, at 114; Doc. History, at 686.

384 *See id.* at U.N. DOC. A/CONF.97/C.1/L.148.

385 *See id.* at U.N. DOC. A/CONF.97/C.1/L.160.

386 *See id.* at U.N. DOC. A/CONF.97/C.1/L.164.

387 *See id.* at U.N. DOC. A/CONF.97/C.1/L.203. *See also* Pre-Conference Proposals, Official Records, *supra* note 52, at 78-79; Documentary History, *supra* note 52, at 399-400, made by the International Chamber of Commerce (proposing a rewording of Draft art. 44(1), which would have made it clear that there was no fundamental breach of contract if the defect, although serious in itself, could be easily cured); the Federal Republic of Germany (suggesting that the words "unless the buyer has declared the contract avoided in accordance with [Draft] article 45" be deleted from paragraph (1)) and Portugal (recommending the deletion of the second sentence of paragraph (1) since it already follows from [Draft] art. 41).

proper balance between the seller's interests and those of the buyer. They criticized that Draft article 44(1) would permit the buyer to immediately declare the contract avoided in the event of non-conformity amounting to fundamental breach of contract, without giving the seller an opportunity to remedy his failure to perform.[388] Explaining its position, the German delegation gave the example of a machine, which had been delivered but did not work. If the seller was prepared to remedy the fault within a reasonable time, the German delegate argued that the seller's right to remedy his failure to perform should prevail over the buyer's rights to avoid the contract.[389] The delegations of Bulgaria,[390] the Federal Republic of Germany,[391] and Japan[392] then, in separate proposals, proposed deleting the words "[u]nless the buyer has declared the contract avoided in accordance with Draft article 45."[393]

These proposals were opposed by several delegations. Most of them objected that they would unjustly deprive the buyer of the right to declare the contract avoided.[394] The Swedish delegation criticized the proposal for its ambiguity. In its opinion, it was not sufficient to delete the first phrase of Draft article 44(1) in order to clarify that the seller's right to remedy prevail over the buyer's right of avoidance. To achieve that end, it would be further necessary to precisely define what constituted a fundamental breach.[395]

The Canadian delegation then suggested setting up an *ad hoc* working group. However, at the request of the German delegation, the Commission first took an indicative vote on the principle behind the identical proposals,

---

388 See comments of the representatives of Germany (Klingsporn, ¶ 38); Bulgaria (Stalev, ¶ 37) and Japan (Hosokawa¶ 46); Documentary History, *supra* note 52, at 562-63; Official Records, *supra* note 52, at 341-42.

389 See comments of the representative of Germany (Klingsporn, ¶ 38); Official Records, *supra* note 52, at 341; Documentary History, *supra* note 52, at 562.

390 *See* U.N. DOC. A/CONF.97/C.1/L.160; *reprinted* in Official Records, at 114; Doc. History, at 686.

391 *See id.* at U.N. DOC. A/CONF.97/C.1/L.140.

392 *See id.* at U.N. DOC. A/CONF.97/C.1/L.164.

393 For the text of the Draft art. 45 [antecedent to art. 49 of the Official Text], see Official Records, *supra* note 52, at 41; Documentary History, *supra* note 52, at 431.

394 See the comments of the delegations of Iraq (Sami, ¶ 42), India (Kuchibhotla, ¶ 51); Argentinia (Boggiano, ¶ 55); Chile (Eyzaguirre, ¶ 56); Australia (Bennett, ¶ 43), United Kingdom (Feltham, ¶ 44); Official Records, *supra* note 52, at 341-43; Documetnary History, *supra* note 52, at 562-64.

395 *See* Official Records, *supra* note 52, at 341-43 (¶ 48); Documentary History, *supra* note 52, at 562-64.

namely, whether in Draft article 44 the seller's right to cure should prevail over the buyer's right of avoidance on the understanding that the vote would not affect the proposals themselves.[396] The principle behind the proposals was supported by 14 delegations and opposed by 18.[397]

(ii) Proposal of the United States of America

The U.S. delegation emphasized the close link between Draft article 42,[398] under which the buyer could require the seller to either remedy a lack of conformity or deliver substitute goods, and Draft article 44 under which the seller could remedy failure to perform or deliver substitute goods. It took the view that if the buyer, invoking his rights under Draft article 42, demanded substitute goods, and the seller, based on Draft article 44, offered to remedy, it would be reasonable to allow the seller to do so, and that was the purpose of their amendment.[399] The U.S. delegation proposed revising the first sentence of paragraph (1) of Draft article 44 as follows (new language in italics):

> Unless the buyer has declared the contract avoided in accordance with [Draft] article 45 *and regardless of any right of the buyer under* [Draft] *article 42,* the seller may, even after the date for delivery, remedy at his own expense any failure to perform his obligations, if he can do so without such delay as will amount to a fundamental breach of contract and without causing the buyer unreasonable inconvenience or uncertainty of reimbursement by the seller of expenses advanced by the buyer.[400] [emphasis in the original]

Alternatively, *the first sentence of paragraph (1) may commence as follows:*

---

[396] See the comments of the delegation of Canada (Ziegel, ¶ 52) and the Federal Republic of Germany (Klingsporn, ¶ 58), Official Records, *supra* note 52, at 342-43; Documentary History, *supra* note 52, at 563-64.
[397] *See* Official Records, *supra* note 52, at 343; Documentary History, *supra* note 52, at 564.
[398] For the text of the Draft art. 42 [antecedent to art. 46 of the Official Text], see Official Records, *supra* note 52, at 38; Documentary History, *supra* note 52, at 428.
[399] See comments of the U.S. delegation (Farnsworth, ¶ 32); Official Records, at 352; Doc. History, at 573.
[400] U.N. DOC. A/CONF.97/C.1/L.203; *reprinted* in Official Records, *supra* note 52, at 114; Documentary History, *supra* note 52, at 686.

> Unless the buyer has declared the contract avoided in accordance with [Draft] article 45, the seller may, even after the date of delivery *and regardless of any right of the buyer under* [Draft] *article 42*, remedy at his own expense . . .[401] [emphasis in the original]

The U.S. proposal was rejected without further discussion by 10 votes in favor and 10 against.[402]

(iii) Proposal of Singapore

The delegation of Singapore proposed that the words "without such delay as will amount to a fundamental breach of contract" in the first sentence of paragraph (1) be replaced by the words "without unreasonable delay."[403] It explained that its proposal was intended to make it easier to understand the principle espoused in Draft article 44(1). According to the existing text, a seller who committed a breach of contract could not remedy until the consequences of the delay in performance had been assessed.[404] As the paragraph did not make clear how to assess delay or how to determine whether that delay represented a fundamental breach of contract, it would be simpler to allow the seller to remedy, provided he could do so without unreasonable delay.[405]

(b) Joint Proposal of the Member of the ad hoc Working Group

The Working Group, consisting of the representatives of Bulgaria, Canada, the German Democratic Republic, the Federal Republic of Germany, the Netherlands, Norway, and the United States of America submitted the following joint proposal:

---

[401] *Id.*

[402] *See* Official Records, *supra* note 52, at 352 (¶ 34); Documentary History, *supra* note 52, at 573.

[403] U.N. DOC. A/CONF.97/C.1/L.148; *reprinted* in Official Records, *supra* note 52, at 114; Documentary History, *supra* note 52, at 686.

[404] See the comments by the delegation of Singapore (Khoo, ¶ 82), Official Records, at 344; Doc. History, at 565.

[405] *Id.*

(i) Alternative I:

Revise paragraph (1) of Draft article 44 to read as follows:

The seller may remedy at his own expense the failure to perform his obligations only if this is consistent with the reasonable interests of the buyer, does not cause him unreasonable inconvenience and the resulting delay does not amount to a fundamental breach of contract. *The buyer retains any right to claim damages as provided for in this Convention.*[406] [emphasis in the original]

At the end of Draft article 45(1)(a) [antecedent to article 49(1)(a) of the Official Text], add the following words:

. . . and the seller does not remedy the failure in accordance with article 44.[407] *[emphasis in the original]*

(ii) Alternative II:

Revise paragraph (1) of Draft article 44 to read as follows:

Subject to [Draft] article 45 the seller may, even after the date for delivery, remedy at his own expense any failure to perform his obligations, if he can do so *without unreasonable delay* and without causing the buyer unreasonable inconvenience or uncertainty of reimbursement by the seller of expenses advanced by the buyer. The buyer retains any right to claim damages as provided for in this Convention.[408]
[emphasis in the original]

The delegations of Bulgaria and Norway explained the joint proposal. The representative of the Bulgarian delegation emphasized that it was in-

---

[406] U.N. DOC. A/CONF.97/C.1/L.213; *reprinted* in Official Records, *supra* note 52, at 115; Documentary History, *supra* note 52, at 687.

The Federal Republic of Germany and Bulgaria withdrew their amendments in favor of the joint proposal. *See* Official Records, *supra* note 52, at 352 (¶ 12); Documentary History, *supra* note 52, at 573.

[407] U.N. DOC. A/CONF.97/C.1/L.213; *reprinted* in Official Records, *supra* note 52, at 115; Documentary History, *supra* note 52, at 687.

[408] U.N. DOC. A/CONF.97/C.1/L.213; *reprinted* in Official Records, *supra* note 52, at 115; Documentary History, *supra* note 52, at 687.

tended to guarantee the seller's right to remedy a failure to perform while at the same time safeguarding the legitimate interests of the buyer, who must be assured that the contract would be executed.[409] Explaining the different alternatives, the Norwegian delegation stressed that Alternative II deleted the reference to fundamental breach. It also made Draft article 44 subject to Draft article 45, since the buyer must preserve his right to declare the contract avoided. The formula of unreasonable delay replaced that of delay "not amounting to a fundamental breach," since the new formula was more flexible and offered a remedy which suspended the buyer's actual avoidance of the contract under Draft article 45.[410]

Having been criticized for introducing new conditions and elements,[411] alternative I of the joint proposal was rejected by 7 votes in favor and 17 against.[412] Paragraph (1) of Alternative II of the joint proposal was adopted in place of paragraph (1) as adopted by the Commission by 19 votes in favor and 7 against.[413] A Greek proposal to replace the words "[s]ubject to [Draft] article 45" at the beginning of paragraph (1) of alternative II with the words "[s]ubject to the contract not having been declared avoided in accordance with [Draft} article 45" found no support.[414] At the Plenary Conference Draft article 44 was adopted *in toto* by 42 votes to 2, with two abstentions.[415]

---

[409] See the comments by the delegation of Bulgaria (Stalev, ¶ 6), Official Records, *supra* note 52, at 351; Documentary History, *supra* note 52, at 572.

[410] See the comments by the delegation of Norway (Rognlien, ¶ 9), Official Records, *supra* note 52, at 351; Documentary History, *supra* note 52, at 572.

[411] See the comments of the Swedish delegation, see Official Records, *supra* note 52, at 352 (Hjerner, ¶ 17); Documentary History, *supra* note 52, at 573.

[412] *See* Official Records, *supra* note 52, at 352 (¶ 19); Documentary History, *supra* note 52, at 573.

[413] *Id.* After the adoption of ¶ 1 of Alternative II of the joint proposal, Singapore's own proposal became superfluous and was withdrawn accordingly. *See* Official Records, *supra* note 52, at 352 (¶ 36); Documentary History, *supra* note 52, at 573.

[414] *See* Official Records, *supra* note 52, at 352 (¶¶ 29, 30); Documentary History, *supra* note 52, at 573.

Only the delegation of the former Czechoslovakia (Cuker, ¶ 27) shared the Greek delegation's opinion. In the Czech delegation's view, the new wording of ¶ 1 was open to a number of interpretations and it was therefore desirable to refer the text to the Drafting Committee to make the necessary modifications. *See* Official Records, *supra* note 52, at 352; Documentary History, *supra* note 52, at 573 fn.3.

[415] *See* Official Records, at 211; Doc. History, at 746.

3. Conclusion (The Meaning of the Concept of Fundamental Breach in Light of the Convention's Legislative History)

The examination of the legislative history has demonstrated that the drafters of the Convention were primarily concerned with formulating a text which would provide a more objective test in determining fundamental breach, as under ULIS article 10.[416] To that end they introduced a "reasonable person" as standard and made express reference to the aggrieved party's "expectation under the contract." With regard to the various factors employed in determining the fundamental nature of a breach, the Convention's legislative history gives rise to the following analysis:

(1) The debate over the German proposal which, together with the Pakistani proposal, formed the basis for reference to the aggrieved party's "expectation under the contract" makes clear that not only are terms of the contract relevant in the determination of fundamental breach, but so too are the surrounding circumstances. The *travaux préparatoires* of article 25 thus confirms the approach which employs the *nature of the contractual obligation* as a relevant factor in the determination of fundamental breach.

(2) One must ask whether the *remedy-oriented* approach is excluded by the fierce criticism of the United Kingdom's proposal and its subsequent withdrawal. In the present writer's view, this question cannot be answered in the affirmative. The proposal of the United Kingdom was intended to introduce the notion of adequacy of damages to the Convention. This principle is applied under Common Law to determine the availability of specific performance, whereas the Convention's remedies depend on a fundamental breach, namely avoidance or substitute delivery.[417] The basic approach under the Common Law is that specific performance is a discretionary remedy available only when damages are inadequate.[418] Such inadequacy is present, for example, where the object of a contract is unique and cannot be

---

[416] For similar conclusions, see Michida, *supra* note 143, at 285-86; SCHLECHTRIEM, *supra* note 45, at 58-59; and Gonzalez, *supra* note 180, at 86 (stating that the new definition under the Convention shifts the burden of proving foreseeability to the party in breach, thereby alleviating the significant burden of proof which ULIS placed on the buyer).

[417] See the critical comments by the delegations of Ghana (Date-Bah, ¶ 8), Official Records, *supra* note 52, at 302; Documentary History, *supra* note 52, at 523.

[418] *See* Guenter Heinz Treitel, *Remedies for Breah of Contracts, in* INTERNATIONAL ENCYCLOPEDIA OF COMPARATIVE LAW 16-30 (Mouton & Mohr eds., 1988).

duplicated, or where obtaining a substantial equivalent involves difficulty, delay, or inconvenience.[419] Another factor taken into account is the difficulty of assessing and recovering damages.[420] Even where there is no difficulty in qualifying the loss, damages may be inadequate as a remedy because the aggrieved party's loss is difficult to prove,[421] certain items of loss may not be legally recoverable,[422] only nominal damages would be claimable,[423] or simply because the debtor may not be "good for the money."[424]

Ignoring the fact that not all of these factors are applicable in connection with the remedies of avoidance and substitute delivery,[425] the remedy-oriented approach as introduced by (civilian) scholars and (civilian) courts cannot be compared with the Common Law doctrine of adequacy of damages. It does not introduce any test of adequacy of damages in the sense that avoidance or substitute delivery could only be required if damages were an inadequate remedy. The emphasis is instead on whether the aggrieved party, under the circumstances, needs this remedy — as opposed to damages — to compensate for the detriment.[426]

It is true that some factors, such as difficulty in assessing damages, are significant under both the Common Law damage remedy and the remedy-oriented approach.[427] The Common Law remedy, however, does not make specific performance available on the grounds that it is unreasonable for the buyer to run the risk of engaging in a dispute with the seller as to whether goods sold for a reasonable price and in compliance with the duty to mitigate. On the contrary, under the Common Law one argument to support the existing doctrine is that the breaching party would lose the

---

[419] *See id.* at 16-31. *See also* Anthony T. Kronman, *Specific Performance,* 45 U.CHI.L.REV. 351, 358 (1978).

[420] *See* G.H. TREITEL, THE LAW OF CONTRACT 920 (8th ed. 1991).

[421] *See* Decro-Wall International S.A. v. Practitioners in Marketing Ltd. [1971] 1 W.L.R. 361.

[422] *See* Hill v. C.A. Parsons Ltd. [1972] 1 Ch. 305 and Evans Marshall & Co. Ltd. v. Bertola S.A. [1973] 1 W.L.R. 349.

[423] *See* Beswick v. Beswick, [1968] A.C. 58.

[424] *See Evans Marshall* at 380; The Oakworth [1975] 1 Lloyd's Rep. 531, at 583; The Oro Chef [1983] 2 Lloyd's Rep. 509, at 521.

[425] For example, where the subject matter is unique substitute delivery is impossible.

[426] For a similar conclusion, see Diederichsen, *supra* note 222, at 180.

[427] *See supra* Part II, B.1.b (3).

benefit of the mitigation rule if specific performance were the primary remedy.[428]

Moreover, the doctrinal basis and rationale for the remedy-oriented approach is completely different than the Common Law notion of adequacy of damages. The Common Law doctrine is rooted in the historical and jurisdictional conflict between Common Law courts and the Courts of Equity and the reluctance to use the process of contempt of court to redress private wrongs where less drastic methods of enforcement could provide adequate justice for the plaintiff.[429] At present, based on the notion of contract law as a means of promoting economic efficiency, scholars increasingly justify this doctrine on economic grounds. They argue that that the total cost of a breach is minimized by recognizing a right to break contracts, so long as the breaching party is able to fully compensate and reinstate the innocent party to their pre-contract position.[430] The remedy-oriented approach introduced by scholars and courts, on the other hand, is primarily based on the notion that avoidance and substitute delivery should be last-resort remedies used to preserve the contract, if at all feasible, and to avoid economic waste in international trade.[431]

Aside from these theoretical arguments, one must also consider that the United Kingdom proposal was not formally put to vote. Admittedly, it was apparent that the proposal would not receive the necessary support of the delegates at the Diplomatic Conference and that the United Kingdom's delegation withdrew it for that reason. The lack of support, however, does not mean that the adequacy of damages factor cannot at all be employed in determining fundamental breach. What one can conclude from the opposition to this proposal is that the adequacy of damages should not be the exclusive relevant factor. The remedy-oriented approach is therefore not excluded by the legislative history of the concept of fundamental breach.

---

[428] *See* Treitel, *supra* note 420, at 919 (stating that where, in a rising market, the buyer fails to make a substitute purchase, awarding him specific performance in such case would conflict with the principles of mitigation).

[429] *See* Treitel, *supra* note 418, at 16-30 to 16-31.

[430] *See* Alan Schwartz, *The Case for Specific Performance*, 89 YALE L.J. 271 (1979); Peter Linzer, *On the Amorality of Contract Remedies — Efficiency, Equity, and the Second Restatement*, 81 COLUM.L.REV. 111, 134-38 (1982); Kronman, *supra* note 419, at 351; RICHARD A. POSNER, ECONOMIC ANALYSIS OF THE LAW § 4.11 (4th ed. 1992); and S.M. WADDAMS, THE LAW OF CONTRACTS § 663 (3d ed. 1993).

[431] *See* BGF, 3 April 1996, VIII ZR 51/95, *supra* note 223, Part II, C.2.c.

(3) The discussion of the relationship between the seller's right to cure and the buyer's right to avoidance during the deliberations within UNCITRAL and at the Diplomatic Conference does preclude an approach which determines fundamental breach in the light of an *offer to cure*. No proposal aimed at precluding the buyer's right to avoidance in favor of the seller's right to cure was adopted. It might be true, as some authors argue, that the rejection of the U.S. proposal to amend the definition of fundamental breach within UNCITRAL was partly based on misunderstandings.[432] This argument, however, does not apply to the rejection of various proposals made at the Diplomatic Conference where the controversy over the effect of an offer to cure continued.

Moreover, the majority of the delegations to the Diplomatic Conference expressed that the right to cure should not prevail over the right to avoidance, although admittedly only in a preliminary vote. On the other hand, this vote becomes conclusive if viewed in conjunction with the failure to incorporate language into the cure provision which would have given the buyer's right to cure priority. Therefore, any recourse to an existing offer to cure could only be considered a distortion of the Convention's legislative history.

(4) The question remains, however, if the *possibility to cure* approach is also excluded by the *travaux préparatoires*. Whether the mere possibility of cure prevents a breach from being fundamental was not discussed. The controversies within UNCITRAL and at the Diplomatic Conference arose primarily out of the fact that article 48(1) gives only the seller the right to cure and, therefore, an offer must be made by him. The approach focusing on whether cure is possible, however, only looks at the curability of the breach in general. It requires neither an offer to cure by the seller nor a guarantee that the he will carry it out. Rather, the buyer can charge another

---

[432] *See* Michida, *supra* note 143, at 288, where the author comments on the discussion of the U.S. proposal as follows:

> After an hour's discussion it appeared that a majority did not support this proposal. Opposition was partly based upon misunderstanding: one argument, for example, emphasized that the problem was fully covered by the specific provision dealing with the right to cure. This was plainly an error; as was clearly explained during the discussion, the specific provision on cure (now art. 44 of the Draft Convention) is limited to cure by the seller while the new language was designed to extend similar protection to the buyer. But, as we have seen, there was no opportunity to consider the draft in the plenary session of UNCITRAL. [footnotes omitted] *Id.*

person to remedy the defect or remedy it himself and claim damages. Thus, it seems possible to argue that this approach is not excluded by the Convention's legislative history.

(5) In considereing the *relevant time* when the party in breach had to foresee or should have foreseen the detrimental consequences to the other party, the legislative history, at first glance, seems to oppose the approach which focuses on the formation of the contract. One might follow from the deliberations within UNCITRAL and the subsequent withdrawal of the United Kingdom proposal at the Diplomatic Conference (which would have made the formation of the contract the determining point in time), that information must be taken into account if it refers to the other party's special interest and is received by the breaching party after the conclusion of the contract. On the other hand, as rightly pointed out by one author, the opposing viewpoints in the discussion at the Diplomatic Conference were still based on the objective fundamental breach definition in article 23 of the 1978 Draft Convention, which stated that the extent of the detriment was the only determinative factor.[433] It is therefore possible to conclude that the present version, in which the decisive factor is the interest of the party concerned, as fixed by the terms of the contract, also permits the conclusion of the contract as the relevant time to evaluate foreseeability.[434]

(6) The Convention's legislative history provides no assistance concerning the permissibility of using the other approaches for the purpose of determining fundamental breach. Whether the legislative history of the various cross-references to fundamental breach in other provions offers any help will be examined in the next section.

C. The Concept of "Fundamental Breach" in Context

The method of systematic interpretation requires analysis of a provision within its context and in relation to other provisions. This method is primarily aimed at avoiding conflicting interpretations within a given instrument, and in most cases it can only confirm the correctness of a possible interpretation already achieved through analysis of wording and the legislative history of the provision in question. The following analysis thus focuses on whether the different factors (including the additional criteria

[433] *See* SCHLECHTRIEM, *supra* note 45, at 60.
[434] *See id.*

provided by the UNIDROIT Principles) employed to determine fundamental breach conform to the structure of the Convention's remedial system. This section will analyze: (1) the various cross-references to fundamental breach; (2) the few provisions under the Convention which give parties the right to avoidance without requiring a fundamental breach (3); possible limitations on the concept of fundamental breach; (4) whether the regime of the seller's obligations under the Convention may influence the definition of fundamental breach (5).

1. Remedial System of the Convention

a. Uniform Concept of Breach and the Notion of Fundamental Breach

The Convention provides a section on remedies available to each of the parties. Article 45(1) gives an overview of the remedies available to the buyer in the event of breach, namely specific performance (in the form of the right to delivery, substitute delivery and repair), avoidance, compensatory damages, and reduction in price.[435] The seller's remedies are enumerated at article 61(1).[436] They differ from the remedies available to the buyer for obvious reasons in two respects. First, the remedy of claiming a reduction in price is not available to the seller. Second, there is no need for substitutional performance or the requirement that the buyer cure a defect in his performance.[437]

[435] For the text of art. 45(1), see *supra* note 271.

[436] For the text of art. 61(1), see *supra* note 271.

[437] Although arts. 46 and 62 are phrased in terms of the "rights" of the parties, the Secretariat Commentary clearly indicates that they were intended to act as directives to a court in the event of litigation. The commentary on Draft art. 42 [antecedent to art. 46 of the Official Text], ¶ 8, Official Records, *supra* note 52, at 38; Documentary History, *supra* note 52, at 428, states:

> The style in which [Draft] article 42 in particular and Section III on the buyer's remedies in general is drafted should be noted. That style conforms to the view in many legal systems that a legislative text on the law of sales governs the rights and obligations between the parties and does not consist of directives to a tribunal. In other legal systems the remedies available to one party on the other party's failure to perform are stated in terms of the injured party's right to the judgement of a court granting the requested relief. However, these two different styles of legislative drafting are intended to achieve the same result. Therefore, when article 42(1) provides that "the buyer may require performance by the seller", it anticipates that, if the seller does not perform, a court will order such performance and will enforce that order by the means available to it under its procedural law. [footnote omitted]

Under the Convention, the notion of breach of contract covers all failures of a party to perform any obligation, without regard for whether the obligation has its origin in the contract, in usage, or in the Convention itself. Moreover, there is no distinction between "main" and "subordinate" obligations.[438]

Unlike under ULIS, the remedies available under the Convention are not effected by a particular type of breach.[439] In general, the type of the breach is of no importance in determining which remedies are available under the Convention. This principle is subject to two exceptions. First, substitute delivery and reduction in price are only available in case of the delivery of non-conforming goods. It is disputed whether goods, which are not free of third party rights (in the sense of articles 41 and 42), can be considered non-conforming.[440] Secondly, in cases of non-delivery and non-payment or failure to take delivery, the buyer's or the seller's right of avoidance, respectively, is subject to a "*Nachfrist*-type procedure," which allows avoidance only after having fixed a reasonable length of time for the defaulting party to remedy his non-performance.[441]

See also Secretariat Commentary, *supra* note 16, at Draft art. 58 [antecedent to art. 62 of the Official Text], ¶ 5, Official Records, *supra* note 52, at 48 (similar discussion of the drafting style of art. 62).

[438] *See* Enderlein, *supra* note 149, at 187.

[439] ULIS differentiated between remedies for the seller's failure to perform his obligations regarding the date and place of delivery (ULIS arts. 24-32), remedies for lack of conformity (ULIS arts. 41-49), remedies for non-payment (ULIS arts. 61-64). For the text of ULIS, see *supra* note 46.

[440] This question was not raised at the Vienna Diplomatic Conference when art. 46 was discussed. Since the debates were concerned with physical defects, some authors view the scope of the provision as being limited to physical defects. *See, e.g.*, Huber, *supra* note 106, at Art. 46, n.27 (stating that though it may seem permissible to regard goods encumbered with third party rights or claims as being in "conformity with the contract," the Convention uses the terms "conformity of the goods" and goods that "do not conform with the contract" in a technical sense, covering only cases falling under art. 35). For a similar view, see Piltz, *supra* note 100, at § 5, n.147.

For a different view, see Will, *supra* note 16, at Art. 46, 3.1 (arguing that the wording and the purpose of art. 46(1) allows the conclusion that the obligation to deliver goods free of any rights or claims by third parties is included). *See also* ENDERLEIN & MASKOW, *supra* note 106, Art. 46, 3; and AUDIT, *supra* note 149, at n.128.

[441] *See infra* Part III, C.3.a.

Under the Convention, apart from the damages remedy, avoidance and substitute delivery are only available when a fundamental breach occurs. Thus, it seems plausible to conclude that the starting point of the Convention's remedial system is that damages are adequate to compensate the aggrieved party, and that avoidance and substitute delivery are last-resort remedies available only when damages are inadequate. The structure of the Convention's remedial system, therefore, supports the *remedy-oriented* approach introduced by scholars and the courts,[442] which applies to situations where non-conforming goods were delivered. By the same token, it allows the conclusion that the *amount of damages* suffered is not decisive in the determination of fundamental breach.

It should also be noted that under the Convention, "fault" is not generally a prerequisite to a finding of contractual liability and that this principle is as true with respect to the right to avoid the contract as it is to the right to require substitute delivery or to claim damages. Neither remedy depends on "fault" in the sense of deliberate or negligent wrongdoing. Consequently, there is no room for the application of the approach found in the UNIDROIT Principles treating intentional non-performance as fundamental.[443]

b. The Concept of Fundamental Breach and Party Autonomy (Article 6)

The principle of freedom of contract as set out in article 6 is one of the cornerstone principles of the Convention.[444] According to article 6,

> [t]he parties may exclude the application of this Convention or, subject to article 12, derogate or vary from any of its provisions.

The debates of the Vienna Diplomatic Conference confirm that article 6 is to be interpreted at face value and that parties may indeed derogate from or vary the effect of any provision of the Convention with the exception of article 12, article 28, and the final provisions (articles 89 to 101).[445]

[442] *See supra* Part II, B.1.b(3) and C.2.c.
[443] *See supra* note 191.
[444] For similar statements, see, *e.g.*, Bonell, *supra* note 25, at Art. 6, 1.1; Winship, *supra* note 277, at 9-31; and Samson, *supra* note 47, at 234.
[445] *See* Official Records, *supra* note 52, at 247-48; Documentary History, *supra* note 52, at 468-69.

A suggestion that the principle of party autonomy be limited by the concept of good faith was rejected with relatively little debate.[446] Accordingly, not only may the parties determine the content and extent of their obligations by adopting contractual provisions that vary from the default rules in the Convention, but they may also indicate the circumstances under which the failure to perform by one party amounts to a fundamental breach. The principle of party autonomy thus requires looking at the *nature of the contractual obligation* for which strict performance might be essential.

2. Cross-References to the Concept of Fundamental Breach

There are several cross-references to the concept of fundamental breach in the Convention: articles 46(2), 49(1)(a), 51(2), 64(1)(a), 72(1),

---

See also ¶ 1 of the Secretariat Commentary on art. 5 of the 1978 Draft Convention (antecedent to art. 6 of the Official Text)(stating that the parties "may derogate or vary the effect of any of its provisions by adopting provisions in their contract providing solutions different from those in the Convention").

Art. 12 aims at serving the special demands of those states the legal systems of which impose written form for contracts of international sales for purposes of validity, evidence, and administrative control. It provides:

> Any provision of article 11, article 29 or Part II of this Convention that allows a contract of sale or its modification or termination by agreement or any offer, acceptance or other indication or intention to be made in any form other than in writing does not apply where any party has his place of business in a Contracting State which has made a declaration under article 96 of this Convention. The parties *may not derogate from or vary the effect of this article.* [emphasis added]

[446] The proposal of the Canadian delegation aimed at limiting the principle of party autonomy was rejected after little debate. See the critical comments by the delegations of Norway (Rognlien, ¶ 57), Sweden (Hjerner, ¶ 58), United States (Farnsworth, ¶ 60), the Republic of Korea (Kim, ¶ 61), and Belgium (Dabin, ¶ 62). The Canadian proposal (U.N. DOC. A/CONF.97/C.1/L.10) to revise Draft art. 5, as orally amended by the delegation of the German Democratic Republic, read as follows:

> (1) The parties may exclude the application of this Convention or, subject to [Draft] article 11, derogate from or vary the effect of any of its provisions. However, except where the parties have wholly excluded the Convention, *the obligations of good faith*, diligence and reasonable care *prescribed by this Convention may not be excluded.* [emphasis added]

For the Canadian Proposal, as orally amended, see Official Records, *supra* note 52, at 86; Documentary History, *supra* note 52, at 658. For the critical comments, see Official Records, *supra* note 52, at 247-48; Documetnary History, *supra* note 52, at 468-69.

73(1), and (2).[447] Except for article 46(2), which is concerned with substitute delivery, all of the provisions deal with the right of the parties to avoid the contract in specific situations. First, we will examine the various avoidance provisions and then we will analyze the buyer's right to demand substitute delivery.

a. Fundamental Breach and Avoidance of the Contract

(1) Seller's Fundamental Breach: Articles 49(1)(a) and 51(2)

Articles 49(1)(a) and 51(2) deal with fundamental breach committed by the seller.

According to article 49(1)(a), the buyer may declare

> the contract avoided if the failure by the seller to perform any of his obligations under the contract or this Convention amounts to a fundamental breach of contract.

When the seller delivers only a part of the goods, or if only a part of the goods delivered conforms to the contract, article 51(2) provides that:

> The buyer may declare the contract avoided in its entirety only if the failure to make delivery completely or in conformity with the contract amounts to a fundamental breach of contract.

The express reference to the "obligations under the contract" in articles 49(1)(a) confirms the approach focusing on the *nature of the contract terms* in determining fundamental breach.

It has been argued that, under article 51(2), one important factor in determining whether the nonconformity of some of the goods or the incomplete delivery entitles the buyer to avoid the entire contract is if the breach renders the intended use of the remainder impossible.[448] Article

[447] Art. 70 also deals with fundamental breach but is not concerned with remedies. It is rather concerned with the effect of a breach by the seller on the passing of the risk.

[448] *See* Huber, *supra* note 106, at Art. 51, n.5 (stating that avoidance under art. 51(2) requires that partial delivery must be of no interest to the buyer). *See also* HONNOLD, *supra* note 20, at § 317 (noting that "[o]ne of the purposes of paragraph (2) of Article 51 is to make clear that paragraph (1) does not force the buyer to sort out the non-conforming

51(2) therefore seems to support, at least in situations where the failure to make delivery completely or in conformity with the contract, the approach which asks whether the *purpose of the contract* has been frustrated by the breach.

(2) Buyer's Fundamental Breach: Article 64(1)(a)

Article 64(1)(a) deals with the buyer's fundamental breach and runs parallel to article 49(1)(a).[449] It therefore does not add anything to the analysis of article 49(1)(a).

(3) Anticipatory Fundamental Breach: Article 72

Article 72 allows a contract to be avoided when one party's breach is anticipated by the other. It reads:

> (1) If prior to the date for performance of the contract it is *clear* that one of the parties will commit a fundamental breach of contract, the other party may declare the contract avoided.
> (2) If time allows, the party intending to declare the contract avoided must give reasonable notice to the other party in order to permit him to provide adequate assurance of his performance.
> (3) The requirements of the preceding paragraph do not apply if the other party has declared that he will not perform his obligations. [emphasis added]

---

goods for separate handling"). The U.S. Uniform Commercial Code (U.C.C.) achieves a similar result by providing (§ 2-608) for the revocation of acceptance of a "commercial unit," which is defined (§ 2-105(6)) as a unit which "by commercial usage is a single whole for the purpose of sale and division of which materially impairs its character or value on the market or in use."

[449] Art. 64(1) provides in part:

> The seller may declare the contract avoided:
> (a) if the failure by the buyer to perform any of his obligations under the contract or this Convention amounts to a fundamental breach of contract;

The text of paragraph (1) itself does not offer much assistance in the determination of fundamental breach.[450] In the context of paragraph (3), it is possible to conclude that those cases where it is clear that the promisor will not perform his future obligations are envisaged by the reference to fundamental breach under paragraph (1).[451] The question remains, however, which particular act or occurrence justifies the conclusion that the promisor will not perform? Is the application of article 72(1) limited to cases in which non-performance is absolutely certain? If so, the right to avoidance should be granted only where the promisor is unable to perform. But what then would be the function of paragraphs (2) and (3)?

At first glance, it seems that paragraph (2) limits the right of avoidance to those cases in which the promisor fails to provide adequate assurance following a reasonable notice by the promisee, and that paragraph (3) exempts the promisee from the notice requirement in case of the promisor's refusal to perform.[452]

---

[450] For a similar statement, see SCHLECHTRIEM, *supra* note 45, at 95 (stating that it is not clear from the wording of ¶ 1 when a particular act or occurrence justifies the conclusion that a fundamental breach is to be expected). Neither does the official ULIS commentary on ULIS art. 76, which is basically recapitulated by art. 72(1) provide any further illumination. There it is elaborated that avoidance due to an anticipatory breach is fully justified since it would not be "right that one party remains bound by the contract when the other has, for instance, deliberately declared that he will not carry out one of his fundamental obligations or when he conducts himself in such a way that it is clear that he will commit a fundamental breach of contract." *See* André Tunc, *Commentary on the Hague Conventions of 1 July 1964 on International Sale of Goods and the Formation of Contracts of Sale, in* DIPLOMATIC CONFERENCE ON THE UNIFICATION OF LAW GOVERNING THE INTERNATIONAL SALE OF GOODS 88 (Ministry of Justice of the Netherlands eds., 1964).

[451] For a similar conclusion, see Hans G. Leser, *Art. 72, IN* COMMENTARY ON THE UN CONVENTION ON THE INTERNATIONAL SALE OF GOODS Art. 72, n.21 (Peter Schlechtriem ed. 1998) (stating that if the party threatening to breach the contract refuses to provide adequate assurance or does not react to the notice within a reasonable time, the contract may be avoided without further delay).

[452] For a different conclusion, see M. Gilbey Strub, *The Convention on the International Sale of Goods: Anticipatory Repudiation Provisions and Developing Countries,* 38 INT'L COMP.L.Q. 475, 498 (1989) (stating that a failure to respond to a request for assurances "is too vague to merit avoidance" under the text of art. 72).

The Secretariat Commentary on the Draft article 63[453] shows confirmation of such an understanding. Since article 72(1) is identical with Draft article 63, with the one exception that the Official Text refers to "a fundamental breach of contract" rather than a "fundamental breach," the Secretariat Commentary is of special relevance. It states, *inter alia*, that:

> The future fundamental breach may be *clear* either because of the words or actions of the party which constitute a repudiation of the contract or because of an objective fact, such as the destruction of the seller's plant by fire or the imposition of an embargo or monetary controls which will render impossible future performance.[454] [emphasis added]

In the absence of such "clear" cases, the Secretary Commentary states that:

> The *failure by a party to give adequate assurance* that he will perform when properly requested to do so under [Draft] article 62(3) may help make it "clear" that he will commit a fundamental breach.[455] [emphasis added]

Draft Article 62(3) [antecedent to article 71(3) of the Official Text], which deals with the parties' right to suspend performance, on the other hand, provides that:

> A party suspending performance, whether before or after the dispatch of the goods, must immediately give notice thereof and must continue with performance if the other party provides adequate assurance of his performance.[456]

The text of Draft article 62(3) does not substantially differ from paragraph (2) of article 72. It was added to this article only at the Vienna Diplo-

---

[453] Draft art. 63 reads as follows (*see* Official Records, *supra* note 52, at 53; Documentary History, *supra* note 52, at 443):

> If prior to the date for performance of the contract it is clear that one of the parties will commit a fundamental breach, the other party may declare the contract avoided.

[454] *See* ¶ 2 of the Secretary Commentary on Draft art. 63, Documentary History, *supra* note 52, at 443.

[455] *Id.*

[456] Official Records, *supra* note 52, at 52; Documentary History, *supra* note 52, at 442.

matic Conference in order to address concerns of developing countries who expressed fears that the power of avoidance might be abused.[457] In the light of these comments, it is therefore possible to conclude that the promisor's failure to provide adequate assurance in accordance with paragraph (2) of article 72 makes it "clear" that he will commit a fundamental breach.[458]

This conclusion, however, gives rise to further questions: (1) Under which circumstances is the promisee entitled to demand adequate assurance of performance from the promisor and what constitutes an adequate assurance? (2) Is the right of avoidance under article 72, where there is no indication that performance is impossible or that the promisor will fail to perform, limited to those cases in which the promisor fails to provide adequate assurance?

What constitutes an adequate assurance varies depending on the circumstances, including the standing and integrity of the promisor, his previous conduct in relation to the contract, and the nature of the event that

[457] The delegate of Egypt (Shafik, ¶ 2), Official Records, *supra* note 52, at 420; Documetnary History, *supra* note 52, at 641, introducing his delegation's amendments said that "the remedy [in ¶ 1] whereby a party might proceed directly to avoidance of contract was rather drastic; even if the other party had already been declared bankrupt, his creditors might still be prepared to fulfill the contract. . . notification should be given in all cases." *Id.*

[458] For the same conclusions, see Bennet, *supra* note 141, at Art. 71, 3.7; HONNOLD, *supra* note 52, at § 394. See also the decisions of the Düsseldorf Court of Appeal and the Berlin District Court where both courts held that failure to provide adequate assurance by the buyer makes it clear that he would not pay the purchase price. See OLG Düsseldorf , 14 January 1994, 17 U 146/93, *supra* note 248; LG Berlin, 30 September 1992, 99 O 123/92, *supra* note 249.

Ziegel, *supra* note 115, at 9-35, takes another position. He argues that a party's failure to provide an adequate assurance of performance is not unequivocal evidence of his unwillingness to perform, "particularly when he may question the validity of the requesting party's feeling of insecurity to bring with." *Id.* S.K. Date-Bah, *The Convention on Contracts for the International Sale of Goods from the Perspective of the Developing Countries, in* LA VENDITA INTERNAZIONALE 34 (Giuffré ed., 1981), agrees with Ziegel's opinion in that anticipatory breach under art. 72(1) "requires proof by the person seeking to avoid the contract of facts from which a conclusion can logically and rationally be reached by induction that the other party is likely to commit a fundamental breach. Mere appearances are not good enough." *Id. See also* SCHLECHTRIEM, *supra* note 45, at 96 (stating that refusal to provide adequate assurance "should not in itself be regarded as 'clear' evidence of an impending breach of contract").

creates uncertainty as to his ability and willingness to perform.[459] In general, for such an assurance to be "adequate," it must give reasonable security to the promisee that either the promisor will perform in fact, or that the promisee will be compensated for all losses incurred in executing his own performance.[460] In practice, there will be very few cases where a mere statement of intention and ability to perform provides adequate assurance to the promisee.[461]

In most instances a new term of payment against documents, a guarantee by a reputable bank, or a letter of credit issued by a reputable bank will be required.[462]

When the promisor must provide such assurance depends on the circumstances surrounding the risk of non-performance. In light of the serious economic consequences arising out of the failure to comply with the assurance obligation, a subjective fear by the promisee will not justify a demand for adequate assurance.[463] Rather, as under article 71(1),[464] which sets out the circumstances permitting the parties' right to suspend performance, there must be objective grounds showing a high degree of probability that the promisor will not perform a substantial part of his obligations.[465] It is required that there be a serious deficiency in the promisor's ability to perform or in his creditworthiness or it must follow from his conduct in preparing to perform or in performing the contract.[466]

[459] *See* HONNOLD, *supra* note 20, at § 392 (emphasizing that threats of non-performance may develop under a wide variety of circumstances).

[460] *See* ¶ 13 of the Secretariat Commentary on Draft art. 62, Official Records, *supra* note 52, at 53; Documentary History, *supra* note 52, at 443.

[461] For a similar statement, see HONNOLD, *supra* note 20, at § 392 (stating that "reassuring words" alone cannot provide adequate assurance).

[462] For further examples, see the examples 62E and 62F by the Secretariat Commentary on Draft art. 62(3), Official Records, *supra* note 52, at 53; Documentary History, *supra* note 52, at 443.

[463] For a similar conclusion, see HONNOLD, *supra* note 20, at § 388; and SCHLECHTRIEM, *supra* note 45, at 95 (stating that art. 72(2) should primarily apply to situations where the performance of the promisor is jeopardized by objective circumstances).

[464] For the text of art. 71(1), see *supra* note 214.

[465] For a similar conclusion, see HONNOLD, *supra* note 20, at § 388.

[466] For a similar conclusion, see Leser, *supra* note 451, at Art. 72, n.10 (stating that the reasons mentioned under art. 71(1) are also applicable to art. 72). For examples of deficiencies in seller's ability to perform and the buyer's creditworthiness, see Bennet, *supra* note 141, at Art. 71, 2.6 (*e.g.*, where the production at the seller's factories was held up by

For example, a buyer's history of making late payments on other contracts might indicate a serious deterioration in his creditworthiness, entitling the seller to ask for adequate assurance.[467] On the other hand, the mere fact that the seller made defective deliveries to other buyers with similar needs does not authorize the buyer to ask for assurance. However, if the cause of the seller's defective deliveries to other buyers was the result of using a raw material from a particular source, indications that the seller is preparing to use the raw material from the same source would give the buyer the right to demand adequate assurance.[468]

It is unclear whether avoidance based on article 72 is limited to those cases where the promisor fails to provide adequate assurance after having received a reasonable notice. Neither the wording nor the legislative history supports or excludes such a reading.[469] With regard to anticipated non-delivery, non-payment, or failure to take delivery, the synchronism between article 72 and articles 49(1)(b), 64(1)(b) seems to support it. Failure to pro-

---

a strike, which is likely to continue for some time; or where buyer falls behind in his payments to a seller in respect of other contracts).

[467] For a similar example with regard to the promisee's right to suspend his performance, see ¶ 6 of the Secretariat Commentary on Draft art. 62 [antecedent to art. 71 of the Official Text], Official Records, *supra* note 52, at 52; Documentary History, *supra* note 52, at 442.

[468] *See id.*

[469] It is true that the proposed amendment by Egypt to link the remedies of avoidance and suspension by replacing Draft art. 63 was rejected by 19 votes in favor and 19 against. This amendment reads as follows (see U.N. DOC. A/CONF.97/C.1/L.249; U.N. DOC. A/CONF.97/C.1/L.250; *reprinted* in Official Records, *supra* note 52, at 130; Documentary History, *supra* note 52, at 702):

> (1) If the seller has already dispatched the goods before the grounds described in paragraph (1) of [Draft] article 62 become evident, he may prevent the handing over of the goods to the buyer even though the buyer holds a document which entitles him to obtain them. This paragraph relates only to the rights in the goods as between the buyer and the seller.
>
> (2) The seller who prevents the handing over of the goods to the buyer under paragraph (1) of this article must immediately give notice to the buyer of his intention to declare the contract avoided should the buyer fail, within a reasonable time, to provide adequate assurance of properly performing his obligations.

The rejection, however, was mainly based on the grounds that the developed countries did not want to lump together the remedies of avoidance and suspension. It therefore does not rule out the conclusion that a failure to provide adequate assurance always constitutes a fundamental breach. For a fuller review of the discussion about the Egyptian proposal, see Strub, *supra* note 452, at 492-93 and Vilus, *supra* note 469, at 245.

vide adequate assurance and to respond to a *Nachfrist* notice present analogous questions because the underlying purposes and function of a *Nachfrist* notice and a demand for adequate assurance are analogous. Both are aimed at preserving the contract by giving the promisor the opportunity to remove the performance obstacles which give rise to the right to avoidance.[470] While the "*Nachfrist*-type" procedure eliminates uncertainty when performance is overdue, the adequate-assurance procedure eliminates uncertainty concerning performance that is not yet due.[471]

Although the "*Nachfrist*-type" procedure is not applicable to the delivery of non-conforming goods, the arguments supporting an interpretation of article 72 analogous to articles 49(1)(b) and 64(1)(b) also apply to the anticipated delivery of non-conforming goods. Making avoidance dependent on a failure to provide adequate assurance would not only help preserve the enforceability of the contract, but also eliminate uncertainty as to when the anticipated delivery of non-conforming goods justifies avoidance. Therefore, it seems plausible to argue that, except for cases where the promisor is unable[472] or unwilling[473] to perform or where the circum-

---

[470] According to art. 72(2), the promisor "must give reasonable notice to the [promisee] *in order to permit him to provide adequate assurance.*" [emphasis added]

[471] This point has been emphasized by Flechtner, *supra* note 300, at 53-108, fn.194, where the author notes that "[i]mperfect assurances and imperfect responses to a *Nachfrist* notice present analogous questions because the functions of a *Nachfrist* notice and a demand for adequate assurance are analogous: the "*Nachfrist*-type" procedure eliminates uncertainty when performance is overdue; the adequate-assurance procedure eliminates uncertainty concerning performance that is not yet due."

[472] For example, A promises to deliver oil to B by ship in Hamburg on Jan. 9. On Jan. 4 the ship is still 2000 kilometers from Hamburg. At the speed it is making it will not arrive in Hamburg on Jan. 9, but at the earliest on January 15. If time is of the essence, B may terminate the contract before Jan. 9.

[473] Whether a demand for new terms or an alleged breach of contract amounts to a declaration not to perform is doubtful. For a similar conclusion, see HONNOLD, *supra* note 20, at § 396 (stating that "[a]voidance should not be triggered if A informs B of the need to negotiate a modification of their agreement"); and Magnus, *supra* note 28, at Art. 72 n.27.

For a different conclusion, see SCHLECHTRIEM, *supra* note 45, at 95, where the author notes that art. 72(3) also covers those cases "in which a demand for new terms or alleged contract violations by the other side are used as pretext for not performing one's own obligations;" Stoll, *supra* note 138, at 642 (stating that cases where a party without justification put forward defenses or demands to have the contract modified or renegotiated require similar treatment than repudiation).

stances would not allow for reasonable notice,[474] avoidance may *only* be based on the failure of the promisor to provide adequate assurance in compliance with a reasonable notice.[475]

In sum, article 72 confirms the approach that employs the parties' (in)ability and (un)willingness to perform as a relevant factor in the determination of fundamental breach prior to the date of performance. It also confirms the approach that focuses on whether a party's behavior may give cause to the other not to rely on his future performance. In this writer's opinion, the absence of reliance, however, must be founded on a failure to provide adequate assurance of one party's performance so as to allow the other party to avoid the contract.

Making performance depend on a modification of the contract, however, must be considered as a refusal to perform. For a similar conclusion, see HONNOLD, *supra* note 20, at § 396; and Magnus, *supra* note 28, at Art. 72, n.27.

[474] It has been argued that where the date of delivery is so near that assurances cannot be procured in time, there is no need to notify the other party. *See* SCHLECHTRIEM, *supra* note 45, at 95. HONNOLD, *supra* note 20, at § 403, believes that "modern methods of communication" would normally allow the provision of notice without impinging on the aggrieved party's "freedom of action."*Id.*

[475] Such an understanding would arrive at the same result as when one treats the failure to provide adequate assurance itself as an actual fundamental breach. This course is followed by the UNIDROIT Principles as well as the Principles of European Contract Law.

See art. 8:105(2)(Assurance of Performance) of the European Contract Principles [antecedent to art. 3.105(2) of the first version], *supra* note 69, at <http://www.ufsia.be/~estorme/PECL2en.html>:

> Where this assurance [of performance] is not provided within a reasonable time, the party demanding it may terminate the contract if he still reasonably believes that there will be a fundamental non-performance by the other party and gives notice of termination without delay.

UNIDROIT Principles art. 7.3.4. (Adequate Assurance of Due Performance), at <http://www.unidroit.ord/english/principles/princ.html>:

A party who reasonably believes that there will be a fundamental non-performance by the other party may demand adequate assurance of due performance and may meanwhile withhold its own performance. Where this assurance is not provided within a reasonable time the party demanding it may terminate the contract.

(4) *Fundamental Breach and Installment Sales: Article 73(1)(2)*

Article 73 governs the avoidance of installment sales. While paragraph (1) of article 73 basically repeats the contents of articles 49(1)(a) and 64(1)(a) with respect to the parties' failure to perform a particular installment,[476] paragraph (2) deals with future installments. The latter paragraph entitles the aggrieved party to declare the installment contract avoided for the future if the promisor's

> failure to perform any of his obligations in respect of any delivery gives [the aggrieved party] good grounds to conclude that a fundamental breach of contract will occur with respect to future installments.

As under article 72(1), paragraph (2) of article 73 does not itself provide any assistance to determine when a particular act or occurrence justifies the conclusion that a fundamental breach is to be expected.[477] The formulation "good grounds to conclude" seems to require a less strict and more subjective standard for avoidance than under article 72(1).[478] This

[476] Art. 73 (1) provides:

> In the case of a contract for delivery of goods by instalments, if the failure of one party to perform any of his obligations in respect of any installment constitutes a fundamental breach of contract with respect to that instalment, the other party may declare the contract avoided with respect to that installment.

[477] According to ¶ 6 of the Secretariat Commentary on Draft art. 64 [antecedent to art. 73 of the Official Text], Official Records, *supra* note 52, at 54; Documentary History, *supra* note 52, at 444, "the test does not look to the seriousness of the current breach. This is of particular significance where a series of breaches, none of which in itself is fundamental or would give good reason to fear a future fundamental breach, taken together does give good reason for such a fear."

[478] There is a dispute among scholars whether the different formulations under art. 71(1)("it becomes apparent"), art. 72(1)("clear") and art. 73(2)("good grounds to conclude") require different degrees of certainty. Some authors hold the view that there is a gradation of remedies, increasing from art. 71(1) via art. 73(2) to art. 72, in the sense that the latter requires the highest degree of certainty. They argue that it is not the different wording itself that enables any distinction to be drawn, but the severity of the remedy's interference with the contract. Avoidance of the contract in the future under art. 73(2), as a reaction to a breach of contract, although not necessarily fundamental in nature, is at a lesser level than avoidance of the whole contract. *See* Leser, *supra* note 451, at Art. 73, n.23; Magnus, *supra* note 28, at Art. 73, n.22 and Art. 72, n.9.

Other authors conclude from the wording and the fact that in the setting of art.

reading is confirmed by the Secretariat Commentary on the 1978 Draft version of article 73(2), which is identical with the Official Text. It is expressly stated with reference to the 1978 Draft version of article 72(1) that avoidance of the contract in respect of future deliveries is permitted even though it is not "clear" that there will be a fundamental breach.[479]

The grounds for the assumption that a fundamental breach will occur are different under article 73 from those under article 72. Neither the promisor's failure to provide adequate assurance on demand due to a deterioration of creditworthiness, nor his declaration that he will not perform, give the promisee the right to avoid the contract. An actual failure to perform must instead be the basis for avoidance of future installments.[480]

Thus, as far as it concerns future installments, article 73(2) does not support the approach that considers a party's refusal to perform itself as a fundamental breach. It confirms, however, the no-reliance approach based on an actual breach.

b. The Concept of Fundamental Breach and the Duty to Deliver Substitute Goods (Article 46(2))

(1) Fundamental Breach in the Light of the Text of Article 46(2)

Article 46(2) specifically addresses the buyer's right to demand specific performance.[481] It gives the buyer the right to substitute delivery

---

73(2)(unlike the situations invoking arts. 71 and 72) a breach of contract has already occurred, that a less strict and more subjective standard for avoidance is required. *See, e.g.*, HONNOLD, *supra* note 20, at § 401; and Bennett, *supra* note 141, at Art. 73, 3.3.

SCHLECHTRIEM, *supra* note 45, at 96, takes the view that the different formulations under arts. 71(1), 72(1) and art. 73(2) do not require different degrees of certainty. He argues that the decisive factor is "whether a reasonable person would be convinced that a breach of contract is certain to occur." *Id.*

[479] *See* the Secretariat Commentary on Draft art. 64, *supra* note 16, at ¶ 5, Official Records, *supra* note 52, at 54; Documentary History, *supra* note 52, at 444.

[480] For this conclusion, see Bennett, *supra* note 141, at Art. 73, 3.3 (stating that it is doubtful whether the grounds for the assumption that a fundamental breach will occur can derive from the bankruptcy of the other party or a statement by him that he does not intend to perform his obligations with respect to future installments). *See also* ENDERLEIN & MASKOW, *supra* note 106, at Art. 73, 7.

[481] Art. 46(2) provides:

where the lack of conformity constitutes a fundamental breach of contract.[482]

Since this remedy applies only to the delivery of non-conforming goods and requires that delivery actually have occurred, article 46(2) does not apply when the seller has not delivered at all. In such a case the buyer has "only" the general right to demand specific performance under article 46(1). Consequently, the approach focusing on one party's (in)ability or (un)willingness to perform as relevant factors in the determination of fundamental breach cannot be employed. Neither can the no-reliance approach be employed under article 46(2) since, as under articles 49(1)(a), 51(2) and 64(1)(a), no future performance is due other than the remedying of the non-conforming goods.

(2) *Fundamental Breach and the Legislative History of Article 46(2)*

The approach of the UNIDROIT Principles, which focuses on whether the breaching party will suffer disproportionate loss as a result of the preparation for performance if the contract is avoided, has not been introduced into the Convention. The rationale for that approach, namely to regard non-performance after the preparation as factor in favor of fundamental breach (as opposed to non-performance before such preparation),[483] has not been reported as subject of deliberations within UNCITRAL or at the Vienna Diplomatic Conference.

As for the buyer's right to substitute delivery, however, consideration was given to limit the exercise of this right to avoid hardship on the seller. Since the seller is in the same economic position as when the buyer chose avoidance of the contract,[484] it seems useful to examine the legislative his-

---

If the goods do not conform with the contract, the buyer may require delivery of substitute goods only if the lack of conformity constitutes a fundamental breach of contract and request for substitute goods is made either in conjunction with notice given under article 39 or within a reasonable time thereafter.

[482] *See* ENDERLEIN & MASKOW, *supra* note 106, at Art. 46, 3.

[483] *See* UNIDROIT Principles, *supra* note 68, at art. 7.3.1, comment e (stating that "[n]on performance is less likely to be treated as fundamental if it occurs late, after the preparation of performance, than if it occurs early before such preparation").

[484] For a similar statement, see Will, *supra* note 16, at Art. 46, 2.2.1.2. Where the buyer asks for substitute delivery the seller has to cover not only the costs of disposing of the non-conforming goods, as is the case when the buyer avoided the contract, but also for shipping a second lot of goods to the buyer. The costs to the seller arising out of the ex-

tory of Article 46(2) and decide whether it can support the application of the UNIDROIT Principles approach.

(a) Deliberations within the UNCITRAL

During the preparatory work for the Convention there was some controversy as to whether or not the buyer's right to demand cure should be made explicit in the text, and whether there should be any limitations on the exercise of the buyer's rights to demand cure and substitute delivery. Under one view, the right to require cure should be limited to cases of fundamental breach and, if the goods have been delivered, the cure should not cause the seller unreasonable inconvenience or unreasonable expense.[485] Another view was that there should be no limitations on the right of the "innocent" party to require that the party in breach perform the contract.[486] A Special Working Group then proposed the following limitations on the buyer's right to demand cure and substitute delivery.[487]

> (2) The buyer may require the seller to remedy a lack of conformity in the goods by repairing them only if the seller can do so without unreasonable inconvenience or unreasonable expense.
> (5) The buyer may require delivery of substitute goods if the lack of conformity constitutes a fundamental breach and it is *reasonably practicable* for the seller to supply substitute goods. [emphasis added]

In support of the proposed text, it was stated, *inter alia*, that if the costs to the seller of curing defects or supplying substitute goods were prohibitive, then the buyer should be compelled to accept damages.[488] This rule would coincide with the principle of mitigation of damages set forth in article 59 [antecedent to article 77 of the Convention].[489] Those who opposed the pro-

---

ercise of the remedy of substitute delivery thus might be considerably higher than of the avoidance remedy.

485 See UNCITRAL Yearbook VIII (1977), at 43 (¶ 247); Documentary History, *supra* note 52, at 336.

486 *See id.* at 43 (¶ 248).

487 *See id.* at 43 (¶ 251).

488 *See id.* at 44 (¶ 254).

489 *See id.* at 42 (¶ 254); Documentary History, *supra* note 52, at 335.

Likewise, the United States proposed amending Draft art. 73 (antecedent to art. 77

posed text reiterated that the right to demand performance should not be subject to any pre-conditions.[490] UNCITRAL did not retain the proposal[491] and accordingly no limitation on the exercise of the buyer's right to substitute delivery was introduced in the text of the 1978 Draft Convention.[492]

(b) First Committee Deliberations and the Decisions by Plenary Conference

The controversy continued at the Vienna Diplomatic Conference. The amendments submitted by the delegations of Norway,[493] Denmark,[494] Fin-

---

of the Official Text) to reduce a claim against the party in breach if the injured party failed to mitigate damages. As presented, the proposal would have applied to any form of relief. The proposal was defeated. *See* U.N. DOC. A/CONF.97/C.1/L.288, Official Records, *supra* note 52, at 133; Documentary History, *supra* note 52, at 705. *See also* Secretariat Commentary on Draft art. 73, *supra* note 16, at ¶ 3, Official Records, *supra* note 52, at 61; Documentary History, *supra* note 52, at 451 (mitigation applies only to damage awards).

[490] *See* UNCITRAL Yearbook VIII (1977), at 42 (¶ 256); Documentary History, *supra* note 52, at 335.

[491] *See id.* at 42 (¶ 257).

[492] Draft art. 42 provides (*see* Official Records, *supra* note 52, at 9; Documentary History, *supra* note 52, at 386):

> (1) The buyer may require performance by the seller of his obligations unless the buyer has resorted to a remedy which is inconsistent with such requirements.
>
> (2) If the goods do not conform with the contract, the buyer may require delivery of substitute goods only if the lack of conformity constitutes a fundamental breach and a request for substitute goods is made either in conjunction with [Draft] article 37 or within a reasonable time thereafter.

[493] The Norwegian delegation proposed to replace ¶ 2 of Draft art. 42 with the following text of ¶¶ 2 and 3 (*see* U.N. DOC. A/CONF.97/C.1/L.79; *reprinted* in Official Records, *supra* note 52, at 112; Documentary History, *supra* note 52, at 684):

> (2) Where the goods do not conform with the contract, the buyer may require *the seller to remedy the lack of conformity by repair, unless this is not reasonably practicable for the seller, or to deliver* substitute goods if the lack of conformity constitutes a fundamental breach. [emphasis in the original]
>
> (3) Any request *for repair* or substitute goods *may be* made *only* in conjunction with notice given under [Draft] article 37 within a reasonable time thereafter. [emphasis in the original]

[494] The Danish delegation proposed to replace ¶ 2 of Draft art. 42 with the following text of ¶¶ 2 and 3 (*see* U.N. DOC. A/CONF.97/C.1/L.138; *reprinted* in Official Records, *supra* note 52, at 112; Documentary History, *supra* note 52, at 684):

land,[495] and Sweden[496] to Draft article 42(2) proposed that the buyer should have the right to require that the seller bring non-conforming goods into conformity by repair. Such a remedy was viewed as in the interest of the buyer in cases where no substitute goods could be obtained, and generally in the interests of both parties, in that it allowed a fairly lenient remedy which would remove obstacles to a contract.[497] The Norwegian and Swedish delegations pointed out that paragraph (1) of Draft article 42 did not specify the nature or means of performance regarding the buyer's right to repair. Therefore a specific provision on the buyer's right to repair was required.[498] None of the proposals, however, focused on curtailing the exercise of the buyer's right to substitute delivery.

---

(2) Where the goods do not conform with the contract, the buyer may require the seller to remedy the lack of conformity by repair unless this is not reasonably practicable for the seller, or if the lack of conformity constitutes a fundamental breach, to deliver substitute goods.

(3) Any request for repair or substitute goods may be made only in conjunction with notice given under [Draft] article 37 or within a reasonable time thereafter.

[495] The Finnish delegation proposed to replace ¶ 2 of Draft art. 42 with the following text of ¶¶ 2 and 3 (*see* U.N. DOC. A/CONF.97/C.1/L.139; *reprinted* in Official Records, *supra* note 52, at 112; Documentary History, *supra* note 52, at 684):

(2) Where the goods do not conform with the contract, the buyer may require the seller to remedy the lack of conformity by repair if such a repair does not cause the seller unreasonable costs or harm. If the lack of conformity constitutes a fundamental breach, the buyer may require the seller to deliver substitute goods.

(3) Any request for repair or substitute goods may be made only in conjunction with notice given under article 37 or within a reasonable time thereafter.

[496] The Swedish delegation proposed to replace ¶ 2 of Draft art. 42 with the following text of ¶¶ 2 and 3 (*see* U.N. DOC. A/CONF.97/C.1/L.173; *reprinted* in Official Records, *supra* note 52, at 112; Documentary History, *supra* note 52, at 684):

(2) The buyer may require the seller to remedy the lack of conformity in the goods by *repairing* them only if the seller can do so without unreasonable inconvenience or unreasonable expense. [emphasis in the original]

(3) The buyer may require delivery of substitute goods only if the lack of conformity constitutes a fundamental breach and it is reasonably practicable for the seller to supply substitute goods.

[497] See comments of the Finnish delegation (Sevon, ¶ 74), Official Records, *supra* note 52, at 332; Documentary History, *supra* note 52, at 553.

[498] See comments of the Norwegian (Rognlien, ¶ 77) and Swedish delegation (Hjerner, ¶ 81), Official Records, *supra* note 52, at 333; Documentary History, *supra* note 52, at 554.

Only the proposal made by the Federal Republic of Germany[499] purported to limit the buyer's right. It was to a large extent identical with the Scandinavian proposals and their approach to the buyer's right to require the seller to repair the goods. There was a difference, however, in that the buyer's right to require substitute goods did not depend on whether the lack of conformity constituted a fundamental breach of contract. The German delegation took the view that this right should be excluded only if it was not reasonably practicable for the seller to deliver the substitute goods.[500]

An *ad hoc* Working Group was established to prepare a common text.[501] A compromise, however, was reached only in respect to the buyer's right to demand repair, the exercise of which was made subject to the condition that *repair be reasonably practicable for the seller.*[502]

The joint proposal was generally welcomed by several delegations with the exceptions of France,[503] the former USSR,[504] and the United

---

[499] The delegation of the Federal Republic of Germany proposed to revise ¶ 2 to read as follows (*see* U.N. DOC. A/CONF.97/C.1/L.135; *reprinted* in Official Records, *supra* note 52, at 112; Documentary History, *supra* note 52, at 684):

> If the goods do not conform with the contract, the buyer may require the seller to remedy a lack of conformity in the goods by repairing them or to deliver substitute goods unless it is reasonably not practicable for the seller to repair the goods or to deliver substitute goods. Any request to repair the goods or to deliver substitute goods may be made only in conjunction with notice given under [Draft] article 37 or within a reasonable time thereafter.

[500] See comments of the German delegation (Klingsporn, ¶ 76), Official Records, *supra* note 52, at 333; Documentary History, *supra* note 52, at 554.

[501] The *ad hoc* working group was composed of the representatives of Finland, the Federal Republic of Germany, Norway and Sweden.

[502] Their joint proposal was mainly based on the wording of the original amendment by the Federal Republic of Germany except for the question of the delivery of substitute goods, on which the member of the *ad hoc* Working Group held differing views. It added as a new ¶ 3 the following text (*see* U.N. DOC. A/CONF.97/C.1/L.173; *reprinted* in Official Records, *supra* note 52, at 112; Documentary History, *supra* note 52, at 684):

> If the goods do not conform with the contract, the buyer may require the seller to remedy the lack of conformity by repair *unless this is not reasonably practicable for the seller.* A request for repair must be either in conjunction with notice given under [Draft] article 37 or within a reasonable time thereafter. [emphasis added]

[503] The French delegation proposed the addition of the words "due account being taken of the legitimate interests of the buyer" at the end of the first sentence. *See* Official Records, *supra* note 52, at 335 (Ghestin, ¶ 15); Documentary History, *supra* note 52, at 556.

[504] The Soviet delegation proposed the deleting the words "for the seller" at the end of

States,[505] which proposed amendments aimed at taking into account that in some cases the buyer should have the right to repair, *even if repair would put the seller to considerable inconvenience.*[506] The three delegations finally agreed on a joint text, which was unanimously adopted.[507] It revised the new paragraph (3) to read:

> If the goods do not conform with the contract, the buyer may require the seller to remedy the lack of conformity by repair unless this is not reasonable, taking account of all the circumstances. A request for repair must be made either in conjunction with notice given under [Draft] article 37 or within a reasonable time thereafter.[508]

The representative of the Federal Republic of Germany then suggested that his delegation's draft amendment should be brought into line with newly adopted paragraph (3).[509] Paragraph (2) would accordingly be revised to read:

> If the goods do not conform with the contract, the buyer may require the seller to deliver substitute goods *unless this is not reasonable*, taking account of all the circumstances. A request to deliver substitute goods may be made only in conjunction with notice given under Draft article 37 or within a reasonable time thereafter.[510] [emphasis added]

---

the first sentence of the new ¶ 3. *See* Official Records, *supra* note 52, at 336 (Medvedev, ¶ 24); Documentary History, *supra* note 52, at 557.

505 The U.S. delegation suggested introducing a phrase such as "taking account of the circumstances of the seller and the buyer." *See* Official Records, *supra* note 52, at 336 (Farnsworth, ¶ 28); Documentary History, *supra* note 52, at 557.

506 See comments by the French (Ghestin, ¶ 15), Russian (Medvedev, ¶ 24) and U.S. delegations (Farnsworth, ¶ 28), Official Records, *supra* note 52, at 335-36; Documentary History, *supra* note 52, at 556-57.

507 *See* Official Records, *supra* note 52, at 336 (¶ 38); Documentary History, *supra* note 52, at 557.

508 *See* Official Records, *supra* note 52, at 336 (¶ 37); Documentary History, *supra* note 52, at 557.

509 See the comments by the German delegation (Landfermann, ¶ 47), Official Records, *supra* note 52, at 337; Documentary History, *supra* note 52, at 558.

510 *Id.* The proposal was welcomed by the Italian delegation whose representative pointed out that ¶¶ 2 and 3 dealt only with specific cases and that the general right was set out in ¶ 1. The choice between the two possible remedies described in ¶¶ 2 and 3, basically depended on the nature of the goods and not, as the existing text of ¶ 3 provided, on the nature of the breach. *See* Official Records, *supra* note 52, at 337 (Bonell, ¶ 51);

The German representative argued that his delegation's proposal would allow the courts to consider the circumstances of each particular case, including the difficulties of both the seller and the buyer. This proposal was criticized by several delegations, primarily on the grounds that the delivery of substitute goods and avoidance were, from an economic perspective, very similar situations,[511] and that the delivery of substitute goods might turn out to be even more onerous to the seller than simple avoidance.[512] For these reasons, it was argued, the requirement of fundamental breach should be kept. In the light of that criticism the German proposal was rejected.[513]

(c) Conclusion

Neither UNCITRAL nor the delegates at the Vienna Diplomatic Conference adopted proposals that took account of consequences arising out of the buyer's exercise of his right to demand substitute delivery. It seems that the delegates viewed the seller's interests as sufficiently protected by the fundamental breach requirement, and wanted the interests of the buyer in

---

Documentary History, *supra* note 52, at 558.

See, on the other hand, the comments of the Swedish delegation, Official Records, *supra* note 52, at 337 (Hjerner, ¶ 52); Documentary History, *supra* note 52, at 558, which criticized the German proposal for confusing the situation, since it collapsed two ideas, substitution and repair.

[511] See comments of the Bulgarian delegation (Stalev, ¶ 49), Official Records, *supra* note 52, at 337; Documentary History, *supra* note 52, at 558.

[512] See comments of the French delegation (Stalev, ¶ 49), Official Records, *supra* note 52, at 337; Documentary History, *supra* note 52, at 558. *See also* the Secretariat Commentary, *supra* note 16, at ¶12, Draft art. 42, Official Records, *supra* note 52, at 38; Documentary History, *supra* note 52, at 428:

> If the goods which have been delivered do not conform to the contract, the buyer may want the seller to deliver substitute goods which do conform. However, it could be expected that the costs to the seller of shipping a second lot of goods to the buyer and of disposing of the non-conforming goods already delivered might be considerably greater than the buyer's loss from having non-conforming goods. Therefore, paragraph (2) provides that the buyer can "require delivery of substitute goods only if the lack of conformity constitutes a fundamental breach. . . ."

[513] *See* Official Records, *supra* note 52, at 337 (¶¶ 54, 55); Documentary History, *supra* note 52, at 558.

exercising his right to substitute delivery to prevail over those of the seller.[514]

Such an interpretation is confirmed by the drafting history of the disposition governing the buyer's right to demand repair, which does not require a fundamental breach but may be limited in view of the consequences to the seller. In this context, it should also be noted that the delegates adopted an amendment to the effect that the buyer's right to repair is not automatically barred by the fact that repair would significantly inconvenience the seller.

Bearing in mind that in most cases substitute delivery is likely to generate greater costs and thus cause even more hardship to the seller than avoidance, it therefore seems plausible that if the consequences of substitute delivery are not considered in determining fundamental breach, then no consideration should be given to any hardship suffered by the seller as a result of the contract avoidance (*argumentum a maiore ad minus*).

3. Avoidance Situations Where No Fundamental Breach Is Required

a. Non-Performance within Time Fixed by *Nachfrist* Notice: Articles 49(1)(b), 64(1)(b)

According to article 49(1)(b), non-delivery does not *per se* allow the buyer to declare the contract avoided. Likewise, article 64(1)(b) provides that non-payment or failure to take delivery itself does not entitle the seller to declare the contract avoided. In both cases a *Nachfrist* must be fixed,[515] and only when the breaching party fails to perform within this fixed period or declares that he will not perform is avoidance permitted. This "*Nachfrist*-

[514] For a similar conclusion, see Vivian Curran Grosswald, *Cross Reference and Editorial Analysis of CISG Article 46*, at *Pace University database*, <http://www.cisg.law.edu/cisg/text/cross/cross-46.html> (stating that elements of reasonableness are built into art. 46(2) and (3) in that the buyer may not require the seller to remedy a lack of conformity by repair pursuant to art. 46(3) when "this is unreasonable having regard to all the circumstances" and in that the buyer may only require delivery of substitute goods pursuant to art. 46(2) when there is a lack of conformity that constitutes a fundamental breach of contract.

[515] *See* arts. 47(1) and 63(1) (permitting the setting of a time limit for late performance on the side of the seller and buyer, respectively).

type" requirement leads to the question of whether it is reconcilable with articles 49(1)(b) or 64(1)(b), respectively, to treat non-performance due to the parties' (in)ability or (un)willingness as fundamental breach without having set such a *Nachfrist.*

In the present writer's view this question must be answered in the affirmative. The objective of the "*Nachfrist*-type" requirement is to exert pressure on the breaching party in case of late delivery and to give him a second chance to perform. However, where the party refuses to perform and thus expresses his unwillingness to perform the fixing of a *Nachfrist* makes no sense.[516] The same is true where it is clear from the circumstances that the party is or will not be able to perform.[517] The scope of article 49(1)(b) and 64(1)(b) is thus actually limited to cases of late delivery,[518] and it follows that the factors focusing on the parties' (in)ability or (un)willingness to perform are not excluded by articles 49(1)(b) and 64(1)(b).

b. Avoidance of Installments Based on Interdependence with a Defective Installment: Article 73(3)

Paragraph (3) of article 73 provides for cases where one installment is avoided in accordance with paragraph (1) of article 73 and it has interdependence with other past or future deliveries. In such case, the buyer may,

---

[516] For the same conclusion, see Huber, *supra* note 106, at Art. 49, n.22 and Will, *supra* note 16, at Art. 49, 2.1.3. *See also* Treitel, *supra* note 418, at 16-149 to 16-150 (stating with regard to the *Nachfrist* requirement under German, Austrian and Swiss law that the main purpose of the requirement of a *Nachfrist* is to protect the promisor by giving him a further period of grace within which to perform, but that in case of the seller's refusal, "no useful purpose would be served by the *Nachfrist*"). [emphasis in the original]

[517] *See id.* at 16-150 (stating that the *Nachfrist* requirement is not applicable where the default does not consist of delay but of impossibility).

[518] *See* the Secretariat Commentary *supra* note 16, at Draft art. 43, ¶ 4 [antecedent to art. 47 of the Official Text], Official Records, *supra* note 52, at 39; Documentary History, *supra* note 52, at 429:

> This Convention specifically rejects the idea that in a commercial contract for the international sale of goods the buyer may, as a general rule, avoid the contract merely because the contract delivery date has passed and the seller has not as yet delivered the goods. In these circumstances the buyer may do so if, and only if, the failure to deliver on the contract delivery date causes him substantial detriment and the seller foresaw or had reason to foresee such a result.

> at the same time, declare [the contract] avoided in respect of deliveries already made or of future deliveries if, *by reason of their interdependence*, those deliveries *could not be used for the purpose contemplated by the parties* at the time of the conclusion of the contract. [emphasis added]

This wording seems to support the approach that focuses on the purpose of the contract in determining fundamental breach, even though it is not expressly stated that the lack of utility of past or future deliveries can alone constitute a fundamental breach. It could be argued, however, that article 73(3) is the counterpart of article 51(2) as far as delivery is made in installments and that it clearly contemplates a fundamental breach situation.[519]

4. Limitations on the Concept of Fundamental Breach

a. Foreseeability of the Consequences of the Breach

The systematic interpretation of the foreseeability element, for several reasons, strongly supports the approach that focuses on the conclusion of the contract as the relevant point in time. First of all, except for those provisions concerning the loss of remedial rights as a result of a delay by the aggrieved party,[520] whenever knowledge or foreseeability is required under the Convention, the time of the conclusion of the contract is relevant.[521] It should also be noted that article 73(3), dealing with the avoidance of installment contracts, expressly refers to the time of the conclusion of the contract.

Moreover, businessmen calculate potential transactional risks at the time of the formation of the contract.[522] Taking account of events occur-

[519] *See* Huber, *supra* note 106, at Art. 51, n.3 (stating that art. 51(2) is not applicable to installment contracts).

[520] *See, e.g.* arts. 40, 43, 49(2)(b), and 64(2)(b).

[521] *See* Holthausen, *supra* note 105, at 105 (concluding from the very similar wording of articles 25 and 74 that the time of the conclusion of the contract is the relevant point in time for knowledge or foreseeability and emphasizing, with reference to arts. 9(2), 31(b), 42(2)(a), 73(3), and 79(1), that under the Convention, whenever knowledge and foreseeability is required, the time of the conclusion of the contract is relevant, except for those provisions which deal with the loss of remedial rights as a result of a delay by the aggrieved party, such as arts. 40, 43, 49(2)(b), and 64(2)(b). Those provisions, however, apply by their nature only at a later point in time).

[522] This point has been emphasized by those authors viewing the time of the conclusion of the contract as relevant. *See, e.g.* Schlechtriem, *supra* note 106, at Art. 25, n.15.

ring after the closure, however, would allow one party to increase the risks of the other party. A buyer, for example, could transform a contract, in which the time of delivery is not fundamental, into a transaction where time is of the essence of the contract by simply informing the seller that he has promised to sell the goods at a particular time.[523] Such a reading of article 25 would hardly contribute to a greater acceptance of the Convention in the business world.[524]

Finally, the foreseeability requirement under article 25 is similar to article 74, which contains the foreseeability test for the recovery of damages. It provides that the

> damages may not exceed the loss which the party in breach foresaw or ought to have foreseen *at the time of the conclusion of the contract*. . . . [emphasis added]

As one Canadian author, who represented Canada at the Vienna diplomatic conference, rightfully pointed out: it would be "anomalous" if a party could take the radical step of avoiding the contract on the basis of consequences for which it could not even recover damages.[525]

---

[523] For a similar example, see SCHLECHTRIEM, *supra* note 45, at 60.

[524] Both the black letter rules of the UNIDROIT Principles and the European Principles do not expressly state the time when the party in breach had to have or should have foreseen the detrimental consequences to the other side. The official commentaries, however, expressly refer to the time of the formation of the contract. *See* European Principles, *supra* note 69, at 126; UNIDROIT Principles, *supra* note 68, at comment on art.7.3.2(a).

[525] *See* Ziegel, *supra* note 115, at 9-20. Flechtner, *supra* note 300, at II. A, takes a different view. With reference to the U.C.C., which, on the one hand, limits consequential damages to losses foreseeable at the time of contracting (art. 2), while on the other hand permits the buyer to revoke acceptance of non-conforming goods — an action equivalent to avoidance under the Convention — if the non-conformity "substantially impairs [their] value to him" (§ 2-608(1)), he argues that there is a precedent for the "anomaly" feared by Ziegel in the U.S. sales law. Furthermore, he argues that this alleged "anomaly" could be justified on the ground that the foreseeability requirements in arts. 25 and 74 serve different purposes. While the foreseeability limitation on damages is designed to limit the financial exposure of the parties to a contract for sale by excluding liability for remote consequences, the foreseeability requirement in the definition of fundamental breach, in contrast, is meant to limit avoidance to appropriate circumstances.

b. Seller's Right to Cure: Article 48

Consideration of an offer to cure is not expressly required in the determination of fundamental breach, and an American proposal to include such language in article 25 was not adopted by UNCITRAL.[526] Thus, consideration of an offer to cure as a limiting factor in determining fundamental breach, in view of its present definition, is only permissible if one argues that, where cure of a breach is feasible and the breaching party is willing to cure, the aggrieved party is not substantially deprived of his expectations under the contract. With regard to the buyer's right to avoidance, such an interpretation, though plausible,[527] cannot be justified by the Convention's legislative history of the concept of fundamental breach, as illustrated above.[528] It is also incompatible with the text of article 48(1).[529]

The opening words of article 48(1) make the seller's right to cure "[s]ubject to article 49." Giving these words their ordinary and plain meaning, it appears that the buyer's right to declare the contract avoided in accordance with article 49(1)(a) prevails over the seller's right to cure.[530] The determination of fundamental breach in the light of any offer to cure, however, would enable the seller to prevent the buyer from avoiding the contract and would, therefore, actually allow the seller's right to cure to prevail over the buyer's right to avoid. Even if one argues that the opening words do not clarify their exact relationship, the position that the right to cure is paramount ignores the fact that the majority of the delegations at the Vienna Diplomatic Conference took the exact opposite view.[531]

---

526 *See supra* Part III, B.2.b.(1)(a)(ii), note 400.

527 *See* Huber, *supra* note 106, at Art. 46, n.23 (stating that where the cure of a breach is feasible the aggrieved party is not generally substantially deprived of its expectations under the contract) and SCHLECHTRIEM, *supra* note 45, at 78 (stating that when time is not of the essence of the contract, the seller's cure within a reasonable time after the due date will normally prevent the delay from constituting a fundamental breach).

528 *See supra* Part III, B. 3.

529 For the text of art. 48(1), see *supra* note 256.

530 For a similar conclusion, see Ziegel, *supra* note 115, at 9-22; Schnyder & Straub, *supra* note 105, at Art. 48, n.29. HONNOLD, *supra* note 20, at § 296, takes a very different position. He argues, with reference to the legislative history, that the amendment to art. 48(1) "leaves little room for doubt" that the right to cure is the paramount provision and that the cure provision of art. 48(1) could be frustrated "by an unqualified application of article 49(1)." *Id.*

531 *See supra* Part III, B.2.b.(1)(a)(ii), note 395.

Another argument against the determination of fundamental breach in light of an offer to cure can be found in the text of article 50, where it is expressly stated that the seller's right to cure prevails over the buyer's right to reduce the price. In view of such clear wording, it's plausible to conclude that if the delegates to the Diplomatic Conference had really wanted the right to cure to prevail over the right to declare the contract avoided, they would have used similar words either in article 48 or 49.

Furthermore, the employment of an offer to cure as a relevant factor in determining fundamental breach would cause both theoretical and practical problems. The notion of an offer retrospectively frustrating the buyer's existing right of avoidance is difficult to justify in theory.[532] As a practical matter, this approach gives rise to the question of whether the seller must make his offer to cure before the buyer makes his notice of avoidance. If priority were decisive, one would provoke a competition between buyer and seller and produce purely arbitrary results.[533] Ignoring that such competition in exercising a remedy should not be a consideration under law, it would also leave the seller in limbo as long as he does not know of the defect.[534]

The only way to avoid such consequences (and to protect the seller's interests) would be either to impose on the buyer the duty to notify the seller of the breach and to give the seller the opportunity to invalidate the declaration of avoidance retroactively through an offer to cure, or to not treat his right to cure as precluded by the notice of avoidance. The latter way has been adopted by the UNIDROIT Principles[535] but, at least as a gen-

---

[532] *See* Karollus, *supra* note 143, at 495; Huber, *supra* note 106, at Art. 46, n.18 (both criticizing the curability approach on the grounds it enables the seller retrospectively to frustrate the buyer's right of avoidance). See also the critical comments by Will, *supra* note 106, at Art. 48, 3.2.2, where the author asks the question of whether there is any "need to resort to so unconvincing a construction" to protect the seller's right to cure by giving the following illustration:

> Suppose that yesterday [the buyer] concluded that a certain breach was fundamental; today he is awaiting the seller's offer to cure — the very breach has changed its nature and become a non-fundamental one; and if tomorrow all hope vanishes — the breach is automatically reconverted into a fundamental breach. Fundamental — non-fundamental — from day to day does not allow for any legal certainty in international transactions.

[533] This point is rightly emphasized by Schnyder & Straub, *supra* note 105, at Art. 49, n.22 and Karollus, *supra* note 143, at 495.

[534] For the same criticism, see Karollus, *supra* note 143, ar 495.

[535] *See supra* note 194.

eral rule, there is no room for it under the Convention. According to the Official Records of the Convention it was not even discussed during the preparatory work for the Convention.

Both approaches seem difficult to reconcile with the character of the avoidance remedy, which initially releases both parties from their obligations after notice of avoidance has been given. To make the fundamental nature of the breach dependent on an offer to cure would give the seller the opportunity to reinstate the buyer's obligations. Consequently, the buyer would be retroactively burdened with the duty to mitigate the loss resulting from the breach. This result does not seem fair to the buyer since he already bears the risk of evaluating the gravity of the breach.[536]

For all these reasons, it is this writer's view that consideration of an offer to cure as a decisive factor in the determination of fundamental breach is not permissible. It would result in more uncertainty and, as one author rightfully points out, indeed "contribute to the further weakening of the notion of fundamental breach."[537] Although it has been argued, it is untrue that the seller's right to cure would be frustrated through an unqualified application of the buyer's right to avoidance. The right to cure is simply limited to those cases where the breach is not fundamental or where the buyer decides not to avoid the contract despite the occurrence of a fundamental breach.

c. Duty to Mitigate Losses

Article 77 imposes a duty on the aggrieved party to take reasonable steps to mitigate his loss.[538] Those steps include the resale of the goods by

---

[536] *See* Will, *supra* note 16, at Art. 48, 2.1.1.1.1 (stating that "the buyer who has already suffered the seller's fundamental breach of contract should not, in addition, be burdened with the entire range of uncertainties as to the same seller's ability and willingness to cure").

[537] For this statement, see *id.* at Art. 48, 3.2.2 , where the author criticizes the "offer-to-cure" approach for not being very precise.

[538] Art. 77 provides:

> A party who relies on a breach of contract must take such measures as are reasonable in the circumstances to mitigate the loss, including loss of profit, resulting from the breach. If he fails to take such measures, the party in breach may claim a reduction in the damages in the amount by which the loss should have been mitigated.

an aggrieved buyer as well as the purchase of substitute goods by an aggrieved seller.[539] If this provision were applicable under articles 46(2), 49(1)(a), and 64(1)(a), then article 77 would effectively preclude the buyer from exercising the right to substitute delivery and avoidance whenever substitute goods were reasonably available and would bar the seller from declaring the contract avoided whenever it was reasonably possible to resell the goods.[540] In other words, the effect of article 77 would be that the aggrieved party must mitigate loss through the choice of remedy.[541]

The suggestion that article 77 limits the right to substitute delivery and avoidance is contradicted, however, by the wording of article 77, the remedial structure of the Convention, and its drafting history. In the first instance, the second sentence of article 77 provides that

> the party in breach may claim a reduction in the *damages* in the amount by which the loss should have been mitigated. [emphasis added]

Under this wording, the duty to mitigate applies only when the aggrieved party claims damages, not when that party demands substitute delivery or avoidance.[542]

Second, article 77, as enacted, is placed within the section of the Convention entitled "Damages."[543] Articles 46(2), 49(1)(a), 51(2), and 64(1)(a),

---

[539] For similar conclusions, see V. Knapp, *Art. 77, in* COMMENTARY ON THE INTERNATIONAL SALES LAW, THE 1980 VIENNA SALES CONVENTION 2.2 (C. Bianca & M. Bonell eds., 1987); Peter Schlechtriem, *Gemeinsame Bestimmungen über Verpflichtungen des Verkäufers und des Käufers, in* LAUSANNER KOLLOQUIUM 169 (Schweizerisches Institut für Rechtsvergleichung ed., 1985); E. Allan Farnsworth, *Damages and Specific Relief,* 27 AM.J.COMP.L. 247, 251 (1979); HONNOLD, *supra* note 20, at § 418; Stoll, *supra* note 138, at Art. 77, n.10; ENDERLEIN & MASKOW, *supra* note 106, at Art. 77, 2; HERBER & CZERWENKA, *supra* note 16, at Art. 77, n.6; and PILTZ, *supra* note 100, at § 5 n.462.

[540] For a similar conclusion, see Farnsworth, *supra* note 27, at 251 (commenting on Draft art. 73 [antecedent to art. 77 of the Official Text] that "the most common step to be taken in avoidance of loss under a contract for the sale of goods is a substitute sale or 're-sale' to another buyer in the case of breach by the buyer and a substitute purchase or 'cover' from another seller in case of breach by the seller").

[541] For the same conclusion with regard to the availability of the specific performance remedy under arts. 46(1) and 62, see Amy H. Kastely, *The Right to Require Performance in International Sales,* 63 WASH.L.REV. 607, 622 (1988).

[542] *See* Feltham, *supra* note 180, at 355 (stating that art. 77 "is hardly expressed as a bar to requiring performance").

[543] *See* Kastely, *supra* note 540, at 622 and Steven Walt, *For Specific Performance Under the*

on the other hand, appear in the sections governing remedies for breach of contract, and are not concerned with the availability of damages. Under the Convention, there is a clear distinction between the remedies available to the buyer in articles 46 to 52 and damages as provided in articles 74 to 77.[544] A similar distinction can be found in the seller's remedies.[545] The organization of the remedial provisions constitutes a significant distinction between the right to substitute delivery and avoidance and a claim for damages, including the duty to mitigate damages under article 77.[546]

Finally, the drafting history clearly indicates that article 77 does not limit the right to avoidance or substitute delivery. At the Vienna Diplomatic Conference, the United States proposed to amend the Draft version of article 77 to the effect that the words "or a corresponding modification or adjustment of any other remedy" should be added to the provision.[547] It was argued that an aggrieved party's failure to mitigate loss should relieve the party in breach not only of liability for damages but also other remedies.[548] This proposal was rejected by a large majority of the delegates.[549] Article 77, therefore, is not applicable to the right to substitute delivery and avoidance. The question of whether the duty to mitigate loss, as an expression of good faith in international trade, requires that the aggrieved party should refrain from exercising these remedies, will be discussed later.[550]

United Nations Sales Convention, 26 TEX.INT'L L. J. 211, 215-16 (1991)(both emphasizing that art. 77 is placed in the section that deals only with the damages remedy).

544 *See* Art. 45(1), *supra* note 271.

545 *See* Art. 61, *supra* note 271.

546 For a similar assertion in respect to the parties' right to specific performance, see Kastely, *supra* note 541, at 622.

547 *See* U.N. DOC. A/CONF.97/C.1/L.288, Official Records, *supra* note 52, at 133; Documentary History, *supra* note 52, at 705. The U.S. proposed to revise the second sentence of Draft art. 73 [antecedent to art. 77 of the Official Text] to read as follows:

> If he fails to take such measures, the party in breach may claim a reduction in the damages in the amount which should have been mitigated, or *a corresponding modification or adjustment of any other remedy.* [emphasis in the original]

548 The U.S. proposal was aimed at cases where the seller, despite the buyer's wish to the contrary, continue to manufacture a thing which has become useless for the buyer, solely in order to claim the full contract price. See the comments by the U.S. delegate (Honnold, ¶ 55), Official Records, *supra* note 52, at 396; Documentary History, *supra* note 52, at 617.

549 For the discussion of the proposal, see Official Records, *supra* note 52, at 396-98 (¶¶ 55–78); Documentary History, *supra* note 52, at 617-19. The proposal was rejected by 24 votes to 8.

5. Fundamental Breach in the Light of the Regime Governing the Seller's Obligations under the Convention

Under the Convention, a breach is not necessarily fundamental whenever the seller violates a specific obligation or provision, and the availability of remedies does not generally depend on the violation of a specific obligation, except for the seller's duty to deliver the goods.[551] In the latter case, the buyer's right to avoidance is subject to the "*Nachfrist*-type" procedure, which allows avoidance after having fixed a time of reasonable length for the defaulting party to remedy his non-performance.[552]

The fact that the fundamental nature of a breach does not depend on the violation of a specific provision of the Convention calls into question the approach focusing on whether the buyer's expectations have been frustrated due to the breach. Those who support this approach take the view that, where the goods do not possess the features necessary for the use intended by the buyer, or where a third party claims a right to possession or prohibits their use by virtue of a patent or other intellectual property right, a fundamental breach has been committed. Since these cases constitute a breach of the seller's obligation under articles 35(2)(a)(b),[553] 41,[554] and

---

[550] See *infra* Part III, E.2.b.c.d.

[551] Unlike the Common Law of England, the Convention does not adopt a system of *a priori* characterization of the seller's obligations into condition and warranties with respect to implied terms of title, description, merchantability, fitness, and sale by sample. Nor does the Convention, like German law, differentiate between "main" and "subordinate" obligations, nor between different forms of breach (impossibility, delay, so-called "positive violation of a contractual duty," *culpa in contrahendo*). For a brief summary of the Common Law remedial system, see Treitel, *supra* note 418, at 16-167, and for a brief summary of the German system, see, *e.g.*, DANNEMANN, *supra* note 60, at 27 — 33.

[552] *See supra* Part III, C.3.a.

[553] Art. 35(2)(a)(b) provides:

> (1) Except where the parties have agreed otherwise, the goods do not conform with the contract unless they:
>
> (a) are fit for the purposes of which goods of the same description would ordinarily be used;
>
> (b) are fit for any particular purpose expressly or impliedly made known to the seller at the time of the conclusion of the contract, except where the circumstances show that the buyer did not rely, or that it was unreasonable for him to rely, on the seller's skill and judgement

[554] Art. 41 provides:

> The seller must deliver goods which are free from any right or claim of a third party, unless the buyer agreed to take the goods subject to that right or claim. However, if such right or claim is

42,[555] this approach leads to the result that any violation of these provisions must be regarded as a fundamental breach.[556]

This conclusion, however, is supported neither by the text of article 25 nor by its legislative history. It also seems inconsistent with the legislative history of article 49(1)(b). At the Vienna Diplomatic Conference, a Dutch proposal to extend the *Nachfrist*-type avoidance mechanism under the 1978 Draft version of article 49(1)(b)[557] to cover important breaches of contract other than non-delivery was rejected by a substantial margin.[558]

---

based on industrial property or other intellectual property, the seller's obligation is governed by article 42.

[555] Art. 42 provides in part:

(1) The seller must deliver goods which are free from any right or claim of a third party based on industrial property or other intellectual property, of which at the time of the conclusion of the contract the seller knew or could not have been unaware, provided that the right or claim is based on industrial property or other intellectual property:

[556] See Peter Schlechtriem, *Einheitliches UN-Kaufrecht,* JZ 1037, 1045 (1988), where the author takes the view that any violation of art. 35(2)(b) and (c) constitutes a fundamental breach. Lack of fitness for the ordinary use, in his eyes, cannot be regarded as a fundamental breach.

[557] Draft art. 45(1)(b) [antecedent to art. 49(1)(b) of the Convention] provides:

(1) The buyer may declare the contract avoided:

(a) . . .

(b) if the seller has not delivered the goods within the additional period of time fixed by the buyer in accordance with paragraph (1) of [Draft] article 43 or has declared that he will not deliver within the period so fixed.

[558] See Report on the proceedings in the First Committee, Official Records, *supra* note 52, at 117; Documentary History, *supra* note 52, at 689 (9 votes in favor and 31 against). The Dutch amendment (U.N. DOC. A/CONF.97/C.1/L.165; *reprinted* in Official Records, *supra* note 52, at 116; Documentary History, *supra* note 52, at 688) were to the following effect:

Revise subparagraph (b) of paragraph (1) to read as follows:

[I]f the seller has not, within the additional period of time fixed by the buyer in accordance with paragraph (1) of [Draft] article 43, *performed his obligations*, or has declared that he will not *do so* within the period so fixed. [emphasis in the original]

After this proposal was amended orally by Canada by the insertion of the word "important" immediately before the word "obligations," the Canadian delegation withdrew its own proposal in favor of the Dutch amendment. See Report on the proceedings in the First Committee, Official Records, *supra* note 52, at 117; Documentary History, *supra* note 52, at 689.

The Canadian amendment (U.N. DOC. A/CONF.97/C.1/L.150; *reprinted* in Official Records, *supra* note 52, at 116; Documentary History, *supra* note 52, at 688) reads as follows:

The effect of that proposal would have been to authorize the buyer to transform a lack of conformity into a fundamental breach and, as the Official Records of the discussion of the proposals show, this was the decisive factor leading to its rejection.[559]

From this rejection, it is plausible to infer that there should be no *automatism* in the sense that a certain lack of conformity or that third party claims should always be regarded as a fundamental breach. As the case law on fundamental breach confirms, lack of conformity is, in practice, most often invoked by buyers on the grounds that the goods are not fit for the intended use. Had the delegations to the Diplomatic Conference viewed such unfitness as a fundamental breach, the discussion of the extension of the *Nachfrist*-type avoidance mechanism to cases of lack of conformity would have been superfluous. In this writer's view, therefore, the approach, focusing on whether the purpose of the contract has been frustrated in order to determine fundamental breach, is not reconcilable with the regime governing the seller's obligations under the Convention.[560]

6. Conclusion (The Concept of "Fundamental Breach" in Context)

We have scrutinized the concept of fundamental breach under article 25 in the context of the Convention's remedial system, the various cross-references to fundamental breach, those provisions under the Convention giving the parties the right of avoidance without requiring a fundamental breach, and the regime of the seller's obligations under the Convention. Also discussed were potential limitations on the concept of fundamental breach

[I]f the seller has not delivered the goods or *performed any other material obligation* within the additional period of time fixed by the buyer in accordance with [Draft] article 43 or has declared that he will not deliver within the period so fixed.

[559] See the comments by the delegations of Sweden (Hjerner, ¶ 69), the Federal Republic of Germany (Schlechtriem, ¶ 71), the United States (Farnsworth, ¶ 76), Greece (Krispis, ¶ 77), International Chamber of Commerce (Bortolotti, ¶ 82), Spain (Olivencia Ruiz, ¶ 83) and the United Kingdom (Feltham, ¶ 84), Offical Records, *supra* note 52, at 354-55; Documentary History, *supra* note 52, at 575-76.

[560] The German Supreme Court's finding in the New Zealand mussels case that, in the absence of an agreement as to the merchantability of the goods, unmarketability does not constitute fundamental breach thus corresponds with this conclusion. *See* BGH, 8 March 1995, VIII ZR 159/94, *supra* note 217.

and their effect on the availability of those remedies requiring a fundamental breach. The results of this examination can be summarized as follows:

The Remedial System of the Convention

The remedial system of the Convention supports the approach that focuses on the *nature of the contractual obligation* and the *remedy-oriented* approach. The approach, focusing on the gravity of the consequences as measured by the *contract's overall value and the monetary loss suffered by the aggrieved party*, is not supported by the Convention's remedial system. It disregards the fact that the damages remedy, apart from the right of avoidance, is always available to the aggrieved party. Moreover, it cannot explain why avoidance is necessary, above and beyond the damages remedy, to protect the expectation interests of the aggrieved party under the contract. Additionally, the application of the additional criteria provided for by the UNIDROIT Principles cannot be supported, according to which a breach is fundamental because it was committed *intentionally or recklessly*. It disregards the fact that under the Convention's remedial system fault is not generally a condition of contractual liability and that no remedy depends on fault in the sense of deliberate or negligent wrongdoing.

Cross-References to Fundamental Breach

The criterion employed by the UNIDROIT Principles, which looks at whether the breaching party would suffer a *disproportionate loss* as a result of the avoidance in determining fundamental breach, cannot be supported by the various cross-references to fundamental breach. To the contrary, the drafting history of article 46(2) gives good reason to view recourse to this criterion, in general, as prohibited. The different cross-references do, however, confirm the *no-reliance* approach (articles 72, 73(2)) and the approaches looking at one party's *(in)ability/(un)willingness to perform* (article 72) or whether the goods are fit to their *intended purpose* (article 51(2)).

Avoidance Situations Where No Fundamental Breach Is Required

None of the various approaches to determine fundamental breach is excluded by the provisions entitling the parties to avoid the contract without requiring a fundamental breach (articles 49(1)(b), 64(1)(b)). As far as it concerns installment sales, article 73(3) supports the approach focusing on the intended purpose.

Regime of the Seller's Obligations under the Convention

The approach, which asks whether the aggrieved party can use the goods for their *intended purpose*, can be supported by article 51(2) and 73(3). However, it is challenged by the Convention's concept that the fundamental nature of a breach does not automatically follow from the breach of a certain obligation under the Convention. One way to avoid any inconsistency could be to apply this approach only within the scope of articles 51(2) and 73(3), and to consider unfitness for the intended purpose outside their scope as a fundamental breach only where the parties have agreed on fitness for a particular use. In that case, the parties' will prevails over conceptual concerns.

Limitations on the Concept of Fundamental Breach

As far as the *foreseeability* requirement is concerned, the systematic interpretation supports the notion that the conclusion of the contract is the relevant point in time. Consideration of an *offer to cure* in determining fundamental breach, in so far it concerns avoidance of the contract, is not permitted in the light of the wording and legislative history of article 48(1) and its relationship to articles 49(1)(a). The same is not true under an approach that looks only at whether *cure is possible*. It follows from the wording[561]

[561] "[t]he *seller* may . . . remedy at his own expenses any failure to perform his obligations. . . ." [Emphasis added].

and the legislative history of article 48(1) that the scope of this provision is limited to situations where the seller or a third party appointed by him remedies the defect.[562] This approach, however, does not require the seller to remedy the defect. Nor do the theoretical concerns about the retroactive effect of an offer to cure apply to that approach.

D. Underlying Purposes and Policies of the Term "Fundamental Breach" within the Remedial System of the Convention

The purpose of the fundamental breach requirement can best be understood in the context of the remedial system of the Convention and especially in the context of those remedies whose availability depends on the existence of a fundamental breach, namely avoidance and substitute delivery. From the Convention's legislative history it is possible to conclude that the limitation of the right of avoidance and substitute delivery is primarily aimed at avoiding hardship to the party in breach.[563]

With regard to the remedy of substitute delivery, there is no doubt that in many cases it will cause hardship to the seller. He must not only take back the delivered goods but also deliver substitute goods, which necessarily involves the risk of damages or loss and expenses such as transportation and storage.[564] Regarding the avoidance remedy, however, there are situations where avoidance produces only little hardship to the seller. This is the case,

---

[562] Accordingly the buyer himself, based on art. 48, cannot charge a third party to remedy the defect at the seller's expense. The costs of repair effected by a third party are only recoverable as damages when the requirements of art. 74 are met. For the same conclusion, see Magnus, *supra* note 28, at Art. 48, n.35.

[563] *See* Will, *supra* note 16, at Art. 49, 2.1.2 (stating that the purpose of restricting the buyer's choice of avoidance serves primarily the interests of the seller who must take back the goods supplied and bears all risks of damages or loss).

[564] At the Vienna Diplomatic Conference, the French representative (Ghestin, ¶ 53), in support of the fundamental breach requirement, pointed out that the remedy of substitute delivery might be even more onerous on the seller than avoidance of the contract. *See* Official Records, *supra* note 52, at 337 (¶ 53), Documentary History, *supra* note 52, at 559. For a similar statement see also Will, *supra* note 16, at Art. 46, 2.2.1.2.

for example, in situations of future performance, where the goods have not been dispatched and the buyer declares the contract avoided. Unless the goods are of a specific nature, or are especially designed for the needs of the buyer, and for those reasons they are difficult to sell to third parties, avoidance does not mean hardship to the seller.[565]

Similarly, where the seller declares the contract avoided due to the buyer's failure to pay, the costs of returning the goods will cause the buyer hardship only in exceptional cases. Moreover, in a situation where the buyer is close to going bankrupt the seller will be content to at least get back the goods, even at his own risk and expense.[566] To a certain extent the Convention seems to take into account these different situations by allowing the buyer to avoid the contract before delivery has been made and before the occurrence of an actual fundamental breach. However, there is no assumption under the Convention that the seller is generally in a better position to dispose of the goods than the buyer. It seems, therefore, that the underlying

---

[565] *See* Audit, *supra* note 28, at 150 (emphasizing that recession can be a great inconvenience, particularly where the goods were made specifically for the buyer).

[566] Art. 64(1), which establishes the seller's right to avoidance, does not distinguish between his right to avoid the contract before or after the goods have been delivered. If he does so, art. 81(2) entitles him to seek restitution from the buyer. When the seller is not the only unpaid creditor, however, his claim to restitution is likely to conflict with the claims of other creditors and the question arises as to which right prevails. The Convention does not deal with any rights that third persons may have acquired on the goods concerned. Whether, for instance, a creditor of the buyer, the buyer's receivers in bankruptcy, or a purchaser in good faith, may oppose the restitution of goods sold is to be determined by the applicable national law. The effect of a retention of title clause may be influenced by three legal systems: the *lex contractus* decides whether the parties can contractually defer the transfer of title and the third party effect on the title is determined by the *lex rei sitae.* Finally, the *lex concursus* decides to what extent the retention of title must be recognized. And under these various applicable domestic rules, the right of an unpaid seller under art. 81(2) as against the rights of other creditors of a buyer in possession, the buyer's receivers, or a purchaser in good faith will be often prejudiced. *See* HONNOLD, *supra* note 20, at §§ 356.1, 448-49; JOSEPH LOOKOFSKY, UNDERSTANDING THE CISG IN EUROPE 115-16 (1997) (stating that art. 81(2) is not intended to prejudice the rights of third parties as defined by other applicable rules); Denis Tallon, *Art. 81, in* COMMENTARY ON THE INTERNATIONAL SALES LAW, THE 1980 VIENNA SALES CONVENTION Art. 81, 2.7 (C. Bianca & M. Bonell eds., 1987) (pointing out that restitution may be thwarted by the bankruptcy of the party who has to return the goods); and Ziegel, *supra* note 115, at 9-32 — 33.

purpose of the fundamental breach requirement is not so much concerned with protecting the interests of the breaching party as much as preserving the enforceability of the contract if it all feasible and to avoid economic waste in trade.[567] This policy is also reflected in offering the breaching party the possibility to cure and requiring the aggrieved party wishing to avoid the contract due to late delivery to provide a *Nachfrist*.

All factors employed in determining fundamental breach limit the availability of the remedies of avoidance and substitute delivery and thus serve the Convention's objective. However, none of the factors is applicable to every possible situation of fundamental breach and, for that reason, the extent of the limitation differs depending on the factors employed. Some of the factors, such as *(in)ability* or *(un)willingness*, for example, can only be applied to the remedy of avoidance in cases of non-delivery, non-payment or failure to take delivery. They cannot be employed to determine under which circumstances the delivery of non-conforming goods amounts to a fundamental breach. The *no-reliance* approach is only applicable where future performance is due.

The approaches looking at an *offer-to-cure/possible cure* or whether the failure to perform was *intentional or reckless* are applicable to both the avoidance and the substitute delivery remedy. Since their application requires actual delivery, however, they cannot be employed in non-delivery situations or future performance situations. The same holds true for the *remedy-oriented* approach and the factor looking at the *intended purpose* of the goods. Finally, the approach in the UNIDROIT Principles that looks at whether the breaching party suffers *disproportionate loss* if the non-performance is treated as fundamental, is applicable to actual as well as to

---

[567] *See* Robert A. Hillman, *Applying the United Nations Convention on Contracts for the International Sale of Goods: The Elusive Goal of Uniformity, in* REVIEW OF THE CISG 21-49 C.1 (Cornell Law Review ed., 1995) (stating that the Convention's goal of saving deals promotes important international values pertinent to the contracting process); Audit, *supra* note 28, at 150 (stating that avoidance leads to the unwanted inconvenience and expense of litigation); Georges Dubé, *The Civil Code of Quebe and the Vienna Convention on International Contracts for the Sale of Goods,* in CONFÉRENCES SUR LE NOUVEAU CODE CIVIL DU QUÉBEC 205, 219 (Yvon Blais ed., 1992); Michida, *supra* note 143, at 283; Kappus, *supra* note 111, at 530; and Ulrich Magnus, *The General Principles of the CISG*, 3 INT'L TRADE & BUS. L.A. 33-56, at ¶ 9 (1997) (concluding from the fact that the Convention allows contract avoidance only under narrow conditions and as a last resort, that the *favor contractus* rule is one of the Convention's general principles).

future performance situations but is limited in its scope to the avoidance remedy.

In view of the limitations on each of these factors, it seems that their accumulated application would serve the underlying purposes and policies of the fundamental breach requirement best. In determining the relevant point in time for measurement of foreseeability of the consequences of the breach, the approach focusing on the time of contract formation limits the availability of the remedies of avoidance and substitute delivery more than the approach that also takes into account the breaching party's subsequent knowledge.

E. The Concept of Fundamental Breach and the Observance of Good Faith

This section is concerned with the final requirement to be observed in the interpretation of the Convention, namely the promotion of the observance of good faith in international trade. In particular, we will examine whether the promotion of the observance of good faith requires a modification of the contractual or statutory right of the parties to avoid the contract or demand substitute delivery. In this context, we will further examine whether the various factors employed in determining fundamental breach correspond with the requirement of good faith.

1. The Application of the Principle of Good Faith in Area of Remedies in General

As pointed out above, the requirement of good faith not only operates as an additional criterion in interpreting the Convention, but is also directed to the conduct of the parties to an individual contract of sale.[568] Consequently, it has been argued by scholars to construe fundamental breach and the exercise of the remedies requiring a fundamental breach in the light of the Convention's many references to standards of reasonableness and the general duty to mitigate damages.[569]

---

568 *See supra* Part I, C.

569 *See, e.g.*, Dore & Defranco, *supra* note 89, at 61 (stating that the good faith requirement also applies in circumstances in which the right to declare a contract avoided is lost); HONNOLD, *supra* note 20, at 95 (stating that "avoiding a contract after a market change that permits a party to speculate at the other's expense, may well be inconsistent

The following four specific cases, especially worthy for consideration because of their practical relevance and partially because of the controversy they provoked at UNCITRAL as well as at the Vienna Diplomatic Conference, will be examined as they relate to the principle good faith.

2. Four Specific Cases for the Application of the Principle of Good Faith

a. Minor Breaches of Contract

It has been argued that the good faith requirement precludes a party from automatically invoking his right of avoidance or substitute delivery after a minor deviation in performance by the other.[570] None of the various approaches applicable to the delivery of non-conforming goods considers a breach of contract causing few if any damages, where the goods can still be used for their intended purpose, or where the defect can be easily and cheaply repaired as fundamental. These approaches thus take the requirement of good faith in the proposed form sufficiently into account.

Such is not the case, however, where the parties have expressly agreed that any deviation from all or specific contract terms constitutes a fundamental breach. The application of the approach focusing on the *nature of the contract* would entitle the aggrieved party to avoid the contract or to demand substitute delivery even if the breach is minor as described above. The issue in a such case is whether the Convention's principle of party autonomy is limited by the Convention's good faith requirement to act reasonably.

---

with the Convention's provisions governing [this remedy] when they are construed in the light of the principle of good faith"); Huber, *supra* note 106, at Art. 48, n.9 (stating that the seller's right to choose between different methods of cure follows from the principle of good faith); Jianming Shen, *The Remedy of Requiring Performance under the CISG and the Relevance of Domestic Rules,* 13 ARIZ.J.INT'L & COMP.L. 253, 276 (1996) (concluding that art. 7 subjects the exercise of the right to specific performance to the general "good faith" obligation).

[570] *See e.g.* Rosett, *supra* note 42, at 290 (stating that good faith is an interpretive tool that precludes a perfect tender approach to interpretation of the seller's obligations of delivery and does not treat minor deviations by either side as an event that terminates the contract).

Unlike under the UNIDROIT[571] and the European Principles,[572] however, the principle of party autonomy is not expressly limited under the Convention, and attempts at the Vienna Diplomatic Conference to limit this principle by the concept of good faith were rejected.[573] Within the scope of the Convention, the parties' freedom to determine the content of their individual contract is only restricted by otherwise applicable mandatory rules, be they of national, international, or supranational origin. It seems, therefore, that the Convention's principle of party autonomy prevails over the Convention's good faith requirement and that the breaching party cannot invoke good faith to invalidate a clause providing for avoidance or substitute delivery for any deviation from the contract, no matter how trivial.[574] This view is confirmed by article 4, according to which the Convention is not concerned with the validity of the contract or of any of its provisions.[575]

---

[571] UNIDROIT Principles *supra* note 68, arts. 1.5 and 1.7 provide:

Article 1.5 ("Mandatory rules")

The parties may exclude the application of these Principles or derogate from or vary the effect of any of their provisions, except as otherwise provided in the Principles.

Article 1.7 ("Good faith and fair dealing")

(1) Each party must act in accordance with good faith and fair dealing in international trade.

(2) The parties may not exclude or limit this duty.

[572] European Principles *supra* note 69, (completed and revised second version), art. 1:102 (1), provides (*see* http://www.ufsia.be/~estorme/PECL2en.html):

(1) Under these Principles, parties are free to enter into a contract and to determine its contents, subject to the requirements of good faith and fair dealing, and the mandatory rules established by these Principles.

[573] *See supra* Part III, C.1.b., n. 443, 444.

[574] For a similar conclusion, see ENDERLEIN & MASKOW, *supra* note 106, at Art. 7, 5 (stating that a contract with clear wording cannot be modified based on the principle of good faith). For a different conclusion without giving any reason, see Babiak, *supra* note 60, at 142; Bonell, *supra* note 25, at Art. 7, 2.4.1 (stating that even contractual agreements might be disregarded if their application in accordance with art. 6 would in the specific case appear to be contrary to good faith); Magnus, *supra* note 567, at 5(b)(1) (stating that except for the provision of art. 12 CISG, the validity issues to be determined in conformity with national law and the principle of good faith, the parties' authority to regulate their relationship is unlimited).

[575] According to art. 4, the Convention merely lays down rules for the objective agreement necessary to create a contract of sale. All other questions concerning the validity of the contract are to be determined according to domestic law. Art. 4 provides:

This Convention governs only the formation of the contract of sale and the rights and obligations of the seller and the buyer arising from such a contract. In particular, except as other-

b. The Fundamental Breach is Curable and the Seller Offers Cure before/after the Buyer Declared the Contract Avoided

Professor Honnold, who argues that whether a breach is fundamental should be decided in light of an offer to cure, holds the view that the principle of good faith imports affirmative obligations on the parties to communicate during performance and to cooperate in the repairing of defects.[576] He argues that, in case of the delivery of defective goods, where cure is feasible, the principle of good faith requires that the buyer not avoid the contract before giving the seller the opportunity to remedy the defect. To that end the buyer must communicate the defect to the seller and request information regarding the seller's plans concerning cure. The seller then is "obliged" to respond to the buyer's request.[577] Other authors more generally take the view that an aggrieved party must act reasonably to mitigate damages and this duty may require accepting an offer to cure from the breaching party, possibly even after a fundamental breach has been committed.[578]

If one follows these propositions to their logical conclusion, as far as the avoidance remedy is concerned, in fact, only the *offer-to-cure* approach would be the decisive factor in the determination of fundamental breach where non-conforming goods have been delivered. All other approaches applicable to the delivery of non-conforming goods would need to be interpreted in a non-decisive way when the seller offers cure and the requirements of article 48(1) are met. To apply the good faith requirement in such a manner, however, is not permitted since it disregards the text of article 48(1) and the intention of the majority of the delegates at the Vienna Diplomatic Conference.[579] As we noted above, the principle of good faith may not modify a statutory provision of the Convention in order to justify

---

wise provided in this Convention, it is not concerned with:

(a) the validity of the contract or of any of its provisions or of any usage;

[576] *See* HONNOLD, *supra* note 20, at § 296 (arguing that the good faith requirement obliges on the one hand the buyer to inform the seller of the defect and to ask him whether he will remedy it, and on the other one, it obliges the seller to respond to the buyer's request for early information about his plans to remedy).

[577] *See id.*

[578] *See, e.g.*, Hillman, *supra* note 567, at C. 1 (stating that the aggrieved party's duty to minimize loss may require it to accept new offers from the breaching party, possibly even after a fundamental breach).

[579] *See supra* Part III, B.2.b, C.4.b.

a result that is contrary to its wording and the intent of the drafting parties. Therefore, the proposition that the principle of good faith always requires accounting for an "offer-to-cure" in determining fundamental breach cannot be supported.

c. The Fundamental Breach Is Curable and the Buyer Demands Substitute Delivery while the Seller Offers Cure

In the context of the buyer's demand for substitute delivery when at the same time the seller offers cure, some authors take the view that if the seller can meet the buyer's expectations by repairing as well as by delivering substitute goods, then the decisive consideration will be the cost, and consequently in choosing his remedy, the buyer must observe the duty to mitigate losses and allow the seller to cure.[580]

This situation seems to be a stronger case for considering an offer to cure. The opening words of article 48(1) refer only to the buyer's right of avoidance but not to his right of substitute delivery, and the theoretical concerns about the retroactive effect of an offer to cure do not apply to the remedy of substitute delivery.[581]

The only objection to such an application of the principle of good faith would be that the U.S. proposal to amend the 1978 Draft version of article 48 and to allow the seller to cure a defect, regardless of the buyer's right

[580] *See e.g.* Will, *supra* note 16, at Art. 48, 3.1.1; Huber, *supra* note 106, at Art. 46, n.56 and Art. 48, n. 9 (stating that it follows from the principle of good faith that art. 46(2) does not give the buyer a right to compel the seller to deliver substitute goods, if the defect could be remedied just as well by repair and repair would be reasonable for the buyer and more favorable to the seller). *See also* NEUMAYER & MING, *supra* note 117, at 322 (arguing that the Convention prefers to prevent the additional economic burdens involved in the restitution of previously delivered goods and conclude that the seller's right to repair should prevail over the buyer's right to require substitution, provided that the other conditions of art. 48(1) are met); and Grosswald Curran, *supra* note 514, at "Another reasonableness issue" (with reference to the principle of reasonableness arguing that "a solution is to handle [the interplay between art. 46(2) and art. 48] according to the formula recited in art. 46(3): in a manner that is not regarded as unreasonable having regard to the circumstances of each case").

[581] *See* Grosswald Curran, *supra* note 514, at "Another reasonableness issue" (with regard to the text of arts. 48(1) and 50 (buyer's right to reduce the price) pointing out that interplay between art. 46(2) and art. 48 is not accompanied by either type of express language).

to substitute delivery, was rejected at the Vienna Diplomatic Conference. However, the proposal was only rejected by 10 votes in favor and 10 against and, according to the Official Records of the Conference, without further discussion.[582] In view of the outcome of this vote, it seems, therefore, permissible to apply the good faith requirement in the proposed form.[583] Where repair is feasible without causing the buyer unreasonable inconvenience, it is indeed plausible to argue that the general principle of reasonableness requires consideration of an offer to cure in the determination of fundamental breach when the buyer demands substitute delivery while the seller offers repair.[584]

d. Substitute Delivery Is Impossible or Exceptionally Burdensome

In regard to the right of specific performance under article 46(1), some authors argue that the principle of good faith requires that the breaching party be relieved of the obligation to make a delivery if it is physically impossible or exceptionally burdensome.[585] Since substitute delivery under article 46(2) is a particular case of specific performance, this proposition also applies to that right. Where substitute performance is physically impossible, however, recourse to the principle of good faith is not necessary. In that case the remedy of substitute delivery is meaningless and will not be sought by the buyer.[586] It only becomes relevant when the exercise of

---

[582] *See supra* Part III, B.2. b (2)(a)(ii), notes 396 — 400.

[583] *See* Schneider, *supra* note 143, at 82 (pointing out that the question of whether the Convention places a serious limit on the seller's right to cure by giving the buyer the right to dictate the terms of the cure under art. 48 with a demand for substitute goods is still open to debate).

[584] The consequence of such application of the good faith requirement is that the buyer's right to substitute delivery depends on the seller's failure to remedy the defect within a reasonable time.

[585] *See* Kastely, *supra* note 541, at 621(concluding from the Secretariat Commentary on Draft art. 65 [antecedent to art. 79 of the Official Text] that the principle of good faith is an essential aspect of the right to performance. *See also,* the Secretariat Commentary, *supra* note 16, at ¶ 8, art. 65, Official Records, *supra* note 52, at 55; Documentary History, *supra* note 52, at 445.

[586] *See* SCHLECHTRIEM, *supra* note 45, at 103 (stating that in cases where obligations are physically impossible to fulfill, domestic legal doctrine –"*impossibilum nulla est obligatio*"–generally prevent a demand for performance).

the right to substitute performance is exceptionally burdensome for the breaching party.

There are, however, two objections to the proposed application of the good faith principle to the buyer's right to substitute delivery. The first follows from the legislative history of article 46(2) and the context of article 46(3). Proposals aimed at taking into account the consequences to the seller when the buyer demands substitute delivery were rejected.[587] The second objection follows from article 28,[588] according to which the exercise of the right to specific performance, and also to the buyer's right to substitute delivery, is subject to the law of the *forum*, which includes a domestic doctrine of good faith.[589] Hence, there is no room for the application of the *Convention's* principle of good faith in the proposed form to limit the availability of the right to substitute delivery. Its application would entail broadening the scope of the Convention.

3. Conclusion (The Concept of Fundamental Breach and the Observance of Good Faith)

The main objective of this section was to examine whether the Convention's requirement to promote the observance of good faith in international trade requires a modification of the contractual or statutory right of the parties to avoid the contract or demand substitute delivery. To that end, four specific cases were illustrated in which such a modification has been suggested. The result of this examination is that the principle of good faith cannot set aside express terms of the contract according to which any deviation from the contract is deemed fundamental. With regard to statutory

---

[587] *See supra* Part III, C. 2.b (2).

[588] Art. 28 provides:

> If, in accordance with the provisions of this Convention, one party is entitled to require performance of any obligation by the other party, a court is not bound to enter a judgement for specific performance unless the court would do so under its own law in respect of similar contracts of sale not governed by this Convention.

[589] There is general agreement that the right to substitute delivery, as a specific form of the right to require performance, is subject to art. 28. *See, e.g.*, LOOKOFSKY, *supra* note 566, at 86; Magnus, *supra* note 28, at Art. 46, n.31; Dubé, *supra* note 567, at 219. HONNOLD, *supra* note 20, at § 285, however, takes the view that "in the absence of evidence that UNCITRAL and the Diplomatic Conference faced this problem and evidenced a decision to give an unqualified reading to Article 28, Articles 46(2) and 46(3) should be regarded as *lex specialis* qualifying the general provisions of Article 28."

rights, it was shown that the principle of good faith limits the buyer's right to substitute delivery, but not his right to avoid the contract, when the seller offers cure, provided that the requirements of article 48(1) are met. It therefore modifies the effect of article 46(2) and by the same token supports, in part, the approach that determines fundamental breach in light of an offer to cure. In all other above discussed cases, the good faith principle may modify the effect of the avoidance or substitute delivery provisions or take precedence over them only under exceptional circumstances, but not as a general rule.

F. Conclusion (Part III: The Meaning of the Concept of Fundamental Breach in Light of the Text of Article 25, the Convention's Legislative History, Context within the Convention, Underlying Purposes and the Observance of Good Faith)

In this Part, following the Convention's rules of interpretation, we have examined the concept of fundamental breach under article 25 in light of its structure, legislative history, context within the Convention, underlying purposes, and the observance of good faith. We have attempted to demonstrate that all approaches employed in determining fundamental breach support the underlying purpose of this concept, namely to preserve the enforceability of the contract by limiting the remedies of avoidance and substitute delivery. However, the approaches which focus on the *monetary loss of the aggrieved party*, *intentional or reckless non-performance* and *disproportionate loss*, cannot be supported by means of literal, historical and systematic interpretation of fundamental breach and, therefore, their application must be ruled out. The results of our examination of the various approaches can be summarized as follows:

1) Consideration of the *nature of the contractual obligation violated* in determining fundamental breach is confirmed by the text of article 25, its legislative history and the principle of party autonomy, which allows the parties to determine the circumstances under which a breach of contract will be fundamental. The supremacy of that principle is confirmed by the reference to the parties' obligation under the contract in the various cross-references to fundamental breach. The principle of party autonomy is not

limited by the Convention's requirement to observe good faith in international trade.

2) The approach which focuses on the *contract's overall value and the monetary loss suffered by the aggrieved party* cannot be supported by the wording of article 25. While the *travaux préparatoires* remain silent as to the permissibility of that approach, it cannot be supported by the remedial system of the Convention. It is therefore not a relevant factor to be considered in determining fundamental breach.

3) Consideration of the *fitness of the goods for their intended purpose* as relevant factor in determining fundamental breach is supported by the text of article 25. According to the preparatory works, the drafters of the Convention did not discuss whether the fitness of goods for the intended purpose is of such importance that unfitness always constitutes a fundamental breach. The cross-reference to article 51(2) confirms such an approach as far as partial non-performance is concerned, and article 73(3) confirms it in respect to installment sales. It is, however, rejected by the Convention's regime governing the seller's obligations. This approach, therefore, cannot be applied outside the scope of articles 51(2) and 73(3).

4) The *remedy-oriented* approach can be supported by the language of article 25 and is not excluded by its legislative history. It is strongly supported by the Convention's remedial system.

5) The wording of article 25 can support the approach that determines fundamental breach in light of an offer-to-cure. It is, however, excluded by the opening words of article 48(1), its legislative history, and the systematic interpretation of fundamental breach. While the "observance of good faith" requirement under article 7(1) cannot modify article 48(1) contrary to the express intent of the legislator in avoidance situations, it requires consideration of an *offer-to-cure* where the buyer demands substitute delivery and the seller offers to cure.

6) To consider whether *cure is possible* without requiring an offer by the breaching party can be supported by the text of article 25. This approach, unlike the offer-to-cure approach, is not excluded by the language of article 48(1). Nor is it ruled out by the drafting history of article 48(1).

7) The wording of article 25 can support the approach that looks at the parties' (in) ability and (un) willingness to perform. It is further supported by the legislative history of article 49(1)(b) and article 64(1)(b), by their wording, and by the various cross-references to fundamental breach in article 72 and article 73(2).

8) Consideration of whether the *breach or conduct by one party gives the other party reason to believe that it cannot rely on the other party's future performance* can be supported by the language of article 25 and the cross-references to fundamental breach in article 72 and article 73(2).

9) The approach that focuses on whether the breach was committed *intentionally or recklessly* can be supported by the text of article 25. It is, however, incompatible with the remedial system of the Convention under which fault is not a condition of contractual liability and of no importance in the availability of either remedy. Recourse to this approach to determine fundamental breach is thus not permissible.

10) Consideration of the extent to which the breaching party suffers *disproportionate loss* in determining whether a breach is fundamental is supported neither by the wording of article 25 nor by its drafting history. This factor, therefore, cannot be employed in the determination of fundamental breach.

11) The language of article 25 supports the approach which holds the time of the formation of the contract as the relevant point in time at which the party in breach had to foresee or should have foreseen the detrimental consequences to the other party. This approach is not supported by the legislative history, but it should it not be excluded, since the deliberations at the Vienna Diplomatic Conference based on the Draft version of article 25 differs from the final text. The systematic interpretation of the foreseeability requirement as well as the underlying purposes of article 25 strongly endorse this approach.

Part IV — Critique of the Remaining Approaches

Part III has examined whether the employment of the different approaches employed by scholars and the courts in determining fundamental breach can be justified by means of the Convention's rules of interpretation. This examination has shown that only the following criteria are applicable to determine the fundamental nature of a breach:

- the nature of the contractual obligation violated, namely whether the non-performed obligation was an essential term of the contract;
- in case of the delivery of non-conforming goods, the gravity of the consequences of the breach in light of

- partial non-performance, the fitness of the goods for their intended purpose; and
- whether it is reasonable for the aggrieved party to retain the defective goods, make use of them and then claim damages for any loss suffered as a result of the breach ("remedy-oriented"-approach);
- consideration of fundamental breach as a prerequisite for the availability of the buyer's right to substitute delivery, the existence of an offer to cure, when the requirements of article 48(1) are met;
- the possibility of cure;
- the parties' (in)ability or to perform;
- the parties' (un)willingness to perform; and
- whether a breach or conduct of one party gives the other party reason to believe that it cannot rely on the other party's future performance.

There are three principal objections to the remaining approaches employed in determining fundamental breach. These objections are based on the assumption that the existence of various and partially conflicting approaches do not correspond to the business community's need for certainty and predictability in contractual relationships. They originate from the placement of the definition of fundamental breach in the first chapter of Part III under the heading "General Provisions."[590] Part III (articles 25-88) not only regulates the substance of the contract of sale, including the respective rights and obligations of the buyer and the seller, but also deals with the remedies available to the seller and the buyer. Giving this heading its plain and ordinary meaning, there is only one concept of fundamental breach to be applied to any provision in Part III.[591]

The first objection to the various approaches is their applicability. The *no-reliance* approach, as applied by the scholars and the courts, for example, is only applicable to cases where future performance is due. But where no future performance is due from the breaching party other than the rem-

[590] For a similar conclusion, see Schnyder & Straub, *supra* note 105, at Art. 49, n.21; and Magnus, *supra* note 28, at Art. 48, n.29; (concluding from the placement of the definition of the term "fundamental breach" makes clear that it needs to be interpreted uniformly throughout the Convention).

[591] *See* Schnyder & Straub, *supra* note 105, at Art. 49, n.21 and Flechtner, *supra* note 300, at I.D. (emphasizing that "the Convention replaces U.C.C. Article 2's byzantine rules on material breach with a single standard applicable in all circumstances").

edying of the breach itself, the aggrieved party cannot invoke no-reliance.[592] The approach, which looks at one party's (in) ability or (un) willingness to perform, applies only to non-delivery, non-payment, or failure to take delivery situations, and not where non-conforming goods were delivered.

On the other hand, the approach that asks whether the goods are fit for their *intended purpose* requires some form of delivery of the goods. The same is true for the *remedy-oriented* and the *offer-to-cure* approach, as well as the *possibility to cure approach*, but none require an offer by the breaching party. None of these approaches is applicable when the seller has not delivered the goods or when performance is not yet due.

The approach that is focused on the nature of the contractual obligation, in theory, applies to all possible situations of fundamental breach. However, where there are no express or implied terms of the contract from which it can be deduced that a certain failure to perform constitutes a fundamental breach or no terms that give the other party the right to avoidance or substitute delivery, this approach provides no assistance.

Consequently, the limited scope of the different factors leads to the conclusion that fundamental breach is to be interpreted differently depending on which remedy is sought and whether or not performance was due.[593] For example, when the buyer demands substitute delivery, only those approaches which are applicable where delivery actually took place can be employed in determining fundamental breach. Neither the no-reliance approach nor that which looks at a party's (in)ability or (un)willingness to perform are applicable when the remedy of substitute delivery is sought. They apply only to the avoidance remedy. On the other hand, the approach focusing on the existence of an offer to cure cannot be employed when the buyer has declared the contract avoided, but is relevant in the determining fundamental breach when he demands substitute delivery.

The second objection arises from the fact that the application of the various approaches applicable to the delivery of non-conforming goods may lead to conflicting results. For example, where the goods were bought for processing, there would be a fundamental breach under the purpose approach if processing were impossible due to the delivery of partially defective goods. The remedy-oriented approach, on the other hand, would reach

[592] This point has been emphasized by the German Supreme Court, see BGF, 15 November 1995; VIII ZR 18/94, *supra* note 232.

[593] Such an interpretation has been suggested by Karollus, *supra* note 143, at 495.

this result only if the sale of the goods were unreasonable for the aggrieved party. Another conflict may potentially arise from the application of the remedy-oriented approach and the approach looking at whether cure is possible, *e.g.* where the defect in the goods sold is not curable, but their resale is reasonable, as was the case in the "African cobalt sulfate" decision by the German Supreme Court.[594] In those cases the question arises as to which of the conflicting approaches should prevail. A concurrent application of the different approaches, in the absence of any order, must necessarily lead to arbitrary results and is unduly onerous to the aggrieved party, since it increases the risk of misevaluating whether a breach was in fact fundamental.

The third objection to the various approaches is that they are not applicable to any possible actual fundamental breach in situations where no future performance is due. For example, none of the various approaches can be applied where the seller has violated the buyer's exclusive right to market the goods sold where no further deliveries are due. Nor can they be employed when one of the parties to a contract of sale has violated his obligation to inform or to co-operate with the other party.[595] The approach that looks at one party's (in)ability or (un)willingness to perform is limited to non-delivery, non-payment, or failure to take delivery situations. The approach that looks at whether the breach is curable is limited in its application to the delivery of non-conforming goods and documents, but cannot be employed to determine the nature of other forms of breach. The same holds true regarding the remedy-oriented approach and that which asks whether an offer to cure was made in determining fundamental breach. Finally, the approach focusing on whether the goods are fit for their intended use can be only employed with regard to the delivery of partially non-conforming goods.

In the light of these objections, it seems necessary not only for both practical and theoretical reasons, but also on grounds of certainty and predictability, to rethink the existing approaches in determining fundamental breach and to replace them by a more coherent unified concept.

---

[594] *See* BGF, 3 April 1996, VIII ZR 51/95, *supra* note 223.

[595] For example, S in Montreal agrees to sell goods to B in Hamburg at a stated price f.o.b. Montreal. B fails to nominate a vessel to carry the goods thereby preventing S from performing his own obligation to ship the goods. Does, in the absence of any contract terms from which it follows that failure to nominate a vessel is to be regarded as fundamental breach, B's failure constitute a fundamental breach entitling S to terminate the contract?

Part V — Introduction of a New Methodology

In this final part, a new methodology for the determination of fundamental breach will be introduced. This new methodology would cover all possible breach of contract situations; would be applicable to both the avoidance and substitute delivery remedy; and is a justifiable interpretive method in accordance with article 7(1). To that end, it is first necessary to examine in greater detail how the Convention balances the parties' competing interests, with regard to the availability of these particular remedies.

Many legal systems, in meting out justice in private law matters, assume that merchants generally enter into commercial contracts for purely economic reasons and can, therefore, be fully compensated with damages for any breach of contract, whether fundamental or not.[596] The Convention, however, accepts this premise only once the parties have performed their obligations to deliver the goods, paid the price for the goods, and taken delivery of them. Only then are damages the primary remedy in case of a breach, whereas all other remedies, with the exception of reduction in price, are available only after additional requirements have been met. Before the parties have fulfilled their obligations, at least in terms of its placement in the Convention's overall scheme, specific performance is the primary remedy although damages are equally available.[597]

If the assumption is right that in commercial relations most things can indeed be reduced to monetary damages, then one must confront the question of why should the aggrieved party ever wish to pursue the remedy of avoidance and substitute delivery? The most important reason, in commercial practice, is that these remedies yield a more favorable result in monetary terms.[598] This will be so where the loss suffered is wholly or partly

---

[596] *See* Treitel, *supra* note 418, at at 16-10 — 16-31 (illustrating the different approaches towards the availability of specific performance as opposed to damages in various common and civil law jurisdictions).

[597] This point has been emphasized by Treitel, *supra* note 27, at § 72 (stating that the Convention adopts the Civil Law principle that the aggrieved party is entitled to require performance).

[598] For other possible reasons which the aggrieved party has for terminating the contract, see Treitel, *supra* note 27, at § 241 (stating that while the most obvious reason of the aggrieved party is the hardship which he may suffer in having to accept or retain a performance different from that for which he bargained, the right to terminate is often asserted for quite different reasons, such as that termination is the speedier remedy than a suit for performance or damages).

irrecoverable, e.g. because the aggrieved party violated his duty to mitigate, or where the party in breach is exempted from damages for failure to perform due to an impediment beyond his control, or where damages are hard to quantify, to prove or to enforce, or are too remote. Another case in which the aggrieved party, in particular, might wish to avoid the contract is where he has made a bad bargain, which would still have been bad, even if the contract had been duly performed. Moreover, in principle, avoidance may favor the aggrieved party in the event of the other party's insolvency. Finally, with regard to substitute delivery, a further reason to seek this remedy is that the buyer needs the goods and only the seller produces them; or where no adequate substitute goods are available elsewhere.

On the other hand, the party in breach may have equally obvious reasons for wishing to resist avoidance and substitute delivery. Once the contract has been avoided the party in breach must make restitution of whatever the aggrieved party has supplied or paid under the contract. That may mean that he has to bear a risk, which, by the terms of the contract or by its very nature, was one that was undertaken by the aggrieved party.[599] This will generally be the position when a buyer seeks to avoid a forward sale in a falling market, or when a seller seeks to avoid such a sale in a rising market. The party in breach may even lose all or most of his performance when there is no market for it elsewhere. Moreover, in attempting to perform he may have incurred expenses, which will be wholly or largely wasted as a result of avoidance. In addition, both substitute delivery and avoidance necessarily involve risks of damage or loss and expenses such as costs for the transport of the (substitute) goods. When other remedies, such as damages or price reduction are available, these remedies will often safeguard the interests of the aggrieved party sufficiently so that avoidance should be not be employed.

The Convention, on the one hand, protects the interests of the aggrieved party by recognizing in principle the right to avoidance and substitute delivery. By providing these remedies the Convention takes into account that there are situations where the interests of the aggrieved party are not sufficiently protected by an award of damages. However, by requiring that the defect substantially deprive the aggrieved party and that the deprivation be foreseeable to the party in breach, the Convention also considers the interests of the party in breach. When the party in breach is able and willing to perform, he enjoys further protection in that a formal

[599] This point has been emphasized by Treitel, *supra* note 27, at § 241.

notice either in the nature of a *Nachfrist* (after performance was due) or a demand for adequate assurance (before performance was due) is required. Where the party in breach is unable or unwilling to perform at all, the Convention allows the aggrieved party to avoid the contract without requiring any formal notice or the existence of a fundamental breach. Ignoring these particular cases, one may conclude that the Convention, in the determination of fundamental breach, incorporates a dual test based on a certain degree of severity of the breach and focuses on whether the aggrieved party especially *needs* these remedies — as opposed to damages — to compensate for impairment.

Of the existing approaches, only the remedy-oriented approach takes into account these two factors. This approach focuses not only on whether the goods do not possess the features necessary for their intended use by the buyer (*"severity of the breach"* factor), but also on whether the interests of the buyer are sufficiently protected by damages (*"need"* factor). All other approaches focus exclusively on the severity of the default in evaluating the degree of the breach. The remedy-oriented approach, however, is limited in its scope to the delivery of non-conforming goods and, at least in its current form as proposed by scholars, only takes into account the risk of the *buyer* of engaging in a dispute with the seller as to whether he sold the goods for a reasonable price thereby observing his duty to mitigate losses. Moreover, it is of no assistance in the determination of fundamental breach when the *seller* is seeking the avoidance remedy. On the other hand, this approach is a good basis for developing a more comprehensive methodology.

In order to cover all possible situations of fundamental breach, past, present or future, in determining the severity of the breach, one should not exclusively consider whether the breach has frustrated the buyer's expectations with respect to the intended use of the goods. Rather one should ask whether a breach by one party has frustrated the expectations of the other party with regard to the purpose of the contract *as a whole*. Such an approach would not only be applicable to the delivery of non-conforming goods, but also to other cases of non-performance enumerated in the Convention, such as late delivery or late payment, failure to deliver in full, defect in title, and missing or defective documents. Moreover, it would also apply to (anticipated) breaches of other obligations which "frustrate" the aggrieved party's purpose in entering into the contract, such as: the failure to obtain certain permits, test certificates, or other documents;[600] protection

[600] *See* BGH, 3 April 1996, VIII ZR 51/95, *supra* note 223.

of trademarks[601] or preventing the buyer from parallel importing[602] or the seller from selling goods inside a certain territory;[603] a violation of the duty to provide information; and the failure to co-operate in order to give full effect the contract, etc.[604]

If the purpose of the contract has indeed been frustrated, the question that remains is whether there should be any limitations on the possible reasons indicating the aggrieved party's "need" of the remedy of avoidance and substitute delivery as outlined above. In the present writer's view, if the party in breach loses the benefit of the mitigation rule, the aggrieved party should be deprived of exercising these particular remedies. Moreover, problems with regard to the obtainment and enforcement of a damages award should not be taken into account, since such considerations also concern the remedy of avoidance and substitute delivery, the enforcement of which also requires taking legal action. One instance of when substitute delivery is not preferable to a damages award is when performance of the contract would be illegal, for example, where after the delivery of the defective goods the seller's government has imposed an export ban on selling goods of that kind. The buyer should then be barred from exercising this remedy even if he cannot obtain a satisfactory substitute.

On the other hand, where the party in breach is exempted from paying damages under article 79 for failure to perform due to an impediment beyond his control, the aggrieved party should be entitled to avoid the contract or, if possible, demand substitute delivery.[605] The same is true where damages cannot compensate the aggrieved party when they are hard to quantify, difficult to prove, or where the buyer runs the risk that, when cal-

---

[601] *See* OLG Frankfurt a.M., 17 September 1991, 5 U 164/90, *supra* note 237.

[602] *See* CA, *Chambre commerciale*; *S.A.R.L. Bri Production "Bonaventure,"* 22 February 1995, *supra* note 207.

[603] *See* LG Frankfurt a.M., 16 September 1991, 3/11 O 3/91, *supra* note 238.

[604] *See* Schlechtriem, *supra* note 106, at Art. 25, n.24 (emphasizing that "the fact an obligation is stated to be 'ancillary' is irrelevant to the importance of the corresponding interest which the promisee has in its performance"); LOOKOFSKY, *supra* note 566, at 88, where the authors state, that "even the breach of an ancillary duty can amount to a fundamental breach if it is so seriously jeopardizes the purpose of the transaction that the aggrieved party cannot reasonably be expected to further trust the party in breach".

[605] For the same conclusion, see HONNOLD, *supra* note 20, at § 308.2 (stating that "when Article 79 exempts a party from damages for failure to perform, the *appropriate* remedy is usually avoidance of the contract") [Emphasis added]

culating the loss, there will be a dispute with the seller regarding the reasonableness of the resale price. Such is the case where no market price for the non-conforming goods is ascertainable, or where the aggrieved party suffered or is likely to suffer immaterial harm for injury of his business reputation, for example, when the buyer of luxury goods designated to be sold in a high-end markets sells them to ordinary drugstores.

Another case where avoidance is the more appropriate remedy is continuing or successive contracts, calling for repeated acts of performance over a period of time, in particular exclusive distribution agreements. Such contracts presuppose the continuation of a relationship involving personal confidence, and, therefore, a breach of one party, which destroys that confidence, should justify avoidance by the other.

The buyer's insolvency is a further case for avoidance though in most instances restitution will be thwarted by the applicable *lex concursus*.[606] Where the damages are too remote under article 74 and assuming that the formation of the contract is the relevant point in time at which foreseeability is measured, in most instances the grounds invoked by the aggrieved party to justify avoidance will also be regarded as too remote under article 25. Therefore, this case will not become very practical. Finally, the fact that a bad bargain was made should not be taken into account when determining the aggrieved party's need of avoidance, since the risk of making a bad bargain has been undertaken by the aggrieved party.

It was the object of this Paper to elucidate the concept of fundamental breach and to replace the various approaches introduced by the courts and scholars with a methodology that would provide the parties to a contract governed by the Convention greater assistance in determining whether a fundamental breach has occurred. To that end we critically examined the existing approaches. We have concluded that it is necessary not only for both practical and theoretical reasons, but also on grounds of certainty and predictability, to rethink the existing approaches in determining fundamental breach and to replace them by a more coherent unified concept. The new methodology incorporates a test that asks whether the purpose of the contract has been frustrated due to the breach, and whether the aggrieved party needs the remedy of avoidance or substitute delivery — as opposed to damages — in determining fundamental breach. In case of a breach and in the absence of any contractual provision providing for fundamental

[606] *See supra* note 564.

breach, with the help of this new methodology, it should not be difficult for the aggrieved party to determine whether this breach is fundamental. Moreover, with regard to the remedy of substitute delivery, this methodology promotes the uniform application of the Convention in both Common Law and Civil Law jurisdictions since the factors indicating the buyer's need for substitute delivery would give him in Common Law jurisdictions, subject to the court's discretion, the right to a judgement entitling the buyer to this form of specific relief. By the same token, the new methodology is appropriate to reconcile the conflict in the Convention's remedial provisions created by article 28, which limits the buyer's right to (substitute) performance in Common Law jurisdictions.

PART II

Case Translations

Translation from German

Federal Supreme Court (Bundesgerichtshof), Civil Panel VIII

December 4, 1996
Index No. VIII ZR 306/95

Translation by Walter, Conston, Alexander & Green, P.C.

Editors: William M. Barron, Esq. & Birgit Kurtz, Esq.

Key CISG provisions at issues:
Article 39(1)
[Also cited: Articles 3(1); 6; 26; 35; 38(1); 49(1)(a);
57(1)(a); 57(1)(b); 64(1)(a); 81(1)]

Facts:

Plaintiff [seller's assignee] demands payment of the purchase price from defendant [buyer] for a computerized printing system including software arising out of an assigned right.

On November 11, 1992, the [buyer], located in Vienna, ordered a printing system called "dynamic page printer" from Company A, located in P. near N. (hereinafter Company A) for the total price of DM 65,100. The unit consisted of a thermal transfer printer, a color monitor, a computer and a software package. Company A confirmed the order by letter dated November 22, 1992. With respect to the warranty, the order confirmation contained the following arrangement, which indisputably became part of the contract:

"The warranty covers software and hardware as a unit. The warranty period is 6 months and starts with the non-defective functioning of the system. The start of the warranty period is calculated from the installation and operational handover.

In the event that a subsequent malfunction or a defect appears later, the buyer shall give prompt written notice of this fact to Company A. . . . If cure of the defect fails twice, the buyer may then, according to his choice, reduce the purchase price or declare the contract avoided."

On January 30, 1993, the printing system was installed at the [buyer's] offices, and on February 8, 1993, it was handed over for the purpose of commencing operation. By letter dated February 9, 1993, the [buyer] informed Company A of eight defects. Four were listed as "open points," and one defect, outlined under Point 4, referred to "Documentation of the Printer," about which [buyer] requested resolution by February 25, 1993 at the latest. Company A commented on this by letter dated February 11, 1993; it announced that the delivery of the documentation would take place during the 7th calendar week 1993.

By further letter dated March 2, 1993, the [buyer] complained that despite the additional period of time set until February 25, 1993, Company A had not remedied the defects listed under Points 1, 2, 3, 5 and 8 of the letter dated February 9, 1993; at the same time, [the buyer] declared the contract avoided "because of non-compliance with the additional time period granted." [The buyer] did not mention the Documentation of the Printer any more.

Until this point, the [buyer] had neither in total nor in part paid the purchase price, which was due in installments of 20% upon receipt of the confirmation of the order, 60% upon announcement of delivery, and 20% after the installation and operational handover. The Regional Court [Landgericht] granted the claim for payment of DM 65,100 in all respects. On appeal by the [buyer], the Higher Regional Court [Oberlandesgericht] revised the decision of the Regional Court and dismissed the complaint. On appeal, the [seller's assignee] requests that the judgment of the trial court be reinstated.

Grounds for the decision:

I.

The appeals court stated: It was not necessary to decide whether the Regional Court had wrongfully assumed its local, and through that, its international jurisdiction, as the [buyer] argues. Pursuant to ZPO[1] § 512, the appeal cannot be based upon this assertion.

On the merits, however, [the court held] the appeal of the defendant was successful. The defendant did not owe the purchase price because it was

[1] [Translator's Note: "ZPO" stands for "Zivilprozeßordnung," the German Code of Civil Procedure.]

entitled to declare the contract avoided under Art. 49(1)(a) of the Uniform U.N. Sales Law (CISG), which is applicable here; the reason was that the delivered printing system did not meet the requirements of the contract within the meaning of CISG Art. 35 because there was no delivery of a complete documentation. No handbook for the computer was ever delivered. The instructions to the user software given to the [buyer] only partially met the requirements of complete documentation. According to the jurisprudence of the Federal Court of Justice, a complete user handbook was part of the supplier's principal obligation to perform, and the (partial) failure to perform this principal obligation entitles the buyer generally to repudiate pursuant to BGB[2] § 326.

[The court stated that] the [buyer] had given timely notice of the defect of incomplete documentation. Under an objective and reasonable view, the chosen term "Documentation of the Printer" referred to the entire system, i.e., to the hardware as well as to the software; it was timely and sufficiently detailed. Since Company A did not deliver complete documentation despite the [buyer's] notice of the defect, the [buyer] repudiated the conract rightfully on account of a fundamental breach of contract.

[The court held that,] nevertheless, the second attempt to cure the defect failed as well, since the [seller's assignee] also remained inactive after the [buyer's] second demand of August 24, 1994. This letter by the [buyer] was also timely; specifically, the claim for delivery of complete documentation was not time-barred. Finally, the failure to mention the insufficient documentation in the [buyer's] letter of repudiation dated March 2, 1993 did not constitute a waiver of the right to assert the defect. After all this, the [buyer] (once again) declared the contract avoided by letter dated October 12, 1994, which amounts to an avoidance under CISG Art. 64(1)(a). Therefore, pursuant to CISG Art. 81(1), it was freed from the obligation to pay the purchase price.

II.

These statements do not withstand legal scrutiny.

1. The international jurisdiction, which must be analyzed sua sponte at every stage of the proceeding (BGH,[3] decision of February 3, 1993 — XII

[2] [Translator's Note: "BGB" stands for "Bürgerliches Gesetzbuch," the German Civil Code.]

[3] [Translator's Note: "BGH" stands for "Bundesgerichtshof," the Federal Court of Justice.]

ZB 93/90 = BGHR[4] ZPO before § 1 / Competence, international, alimony 1), wrongfully was not considered by the court of appeals. The rule in ZPO § 512a cited by the court does not apply to the question of international jurisdiction (BGHZ[5] 44, 46).

The international jurisdiction of German courts follows from the general rules of jurisdiction. Accordingly, the Regional Court of Nürnberg-Fürth, acting as the trial court and constituting the venue of the contractual place of performance, had local and international jurisdiction (ZPO § 29(1)). Pursuant to CISG Art. 57(1), which applies in this case, the disputed purchase price claim (obligation which must be fulfilled at the debtor's address) had to be satisfied at the location of the seller's seat — P. near N.; the regulation of CISG Art. 57(1)(b), according to which, under certain circumstances, the payment must take place at the location of the handover of the goods, does not apply because the conditions of payment agreed upon — also regarding the last installment payable after the installation and operational handover of the system — do not contain a reciprocal and simultaneous [performance] provision in the sense of the mentioned rule.

2. On the merits, the appeal is successful. The court of appeals based its opinion on the, [buyer] rightfully declaring the contract avoided after [seller's] failure to deliver complete documentation, of which the [buyer] gave notice. The appealed decision cannot be based upon this reasoning.

a) It can be left open, whether the contract concluded between Company A and the [buyer] is a pure sales contract or a contract for the supply of goods to be manufactured or produced. Pursuant to CISG Art. 3(1), contracts for the supply of goods to be manufactured or produced generally should be deemed sales contracts; therefore, the warranty provisions of the CISG apply without restriction (Schlechtriem/Herber, CISG, 2d ed., Art. 3 ¶ 3).

b) If the [buyer] has warranty claims against the seller — and of what kind — primarily depends upon the warranty terms and conditions of Company A, which became part of the contract. They have priority over the CISG provisions (CISG Art. 6).

---

[4] [Translator's Note: "BGHR" stands for "Systematische Sammlung der Entscheidungen des Bundesgerichtshofs (LBl)," the Systematic Collection of Decisions of the Federal Court of Justice (looseleaf).]

[5] [Translator's Note: "BGHZ" stands for "Entscheidungen des Bundesgerichtshofes in Zivilsachen (amtliche Sammlung)," the official reporter for Decisions of the Federal Court of Justice in Civil Matters.]

The contractual provisions merely regulate the extent, the beginning and the duration of the warranty, the obligation of the buyer to give immediate notice of the defects occurring after the handover, as well as the buyer's right to reduce the purchase price or to declare the contract avoided after two failed attempts to cure. Apart from that, the warranty provisions of the CISG remain applicable.

aa) The latter initially applies to the timeliness of the notice of those defects that already exist at the time of the goods' handover. To that extent, CISG Art. 38(1) provides that the buyer must examine the goods within as short a period of time as the circumstances will allow. He must give notice to the seller of any defect within a reasonable period after this point in time (CISG Art. 39(1)).

The [buyer] complained about the "Documentation of the Printer" as an "open point" by letter dated February 9, 1993, i.e., one day after the February 8, 1993 handover of the system and instructions by an employee of the seller. Therefore, the timeliness of the notice is beyond question.

bb) We cannot agree, however, with the court of appeals insofar as it deemed the [buyer's] notice to be detailed enough with respect to the lack of complete documentation for the printer unit.

Pursuant to CISG Art. 39(1)(last clause), the buyer must, in his notice, describe with particularity the kind of lack of conformity with the contract. That way, the seller shall be able to get an idea of the kind of breach of contract and take the necessary steps, e.g. to initiate a substitute or subsequent delivery. On the other hand, the demands of specificity must not be carried too far (Schlechtriem/Schwenzer, supra, Art. 39, ¶ 6). The determination as to whether a notice of defects complies with this standard is primarily made by the trial judge.

The court of appeals held that the term "Documentation of the Printer" under Point 4 of the [buyer's] notice of defects dated February 9, 1993 referred to the whole unit including the software. This interpretation does not withstand the arguments on appeal [here].

Since the printer unit delivered by the [seller] consisted of a thermal transfer printer, a color monitor, a computer and a software package, the term "printer" — as the court of appeals did not correctly see — was, without further specification, at least ambiguous because it could relate to the unit as well as to the individual element. Therefore, in order to meet the requirements of CISG Art. 39(1), the [buyer] would have been obligated to describe the defect in such a detailed manner that any misunderstandings were impossible and to enable the seller to determine unmistakably what was meant. Special knowledge on the part of the [buyer] was not necessary for this task because anyone who handles these kinds of systems is able to distinguish the printing system from the printer itself as an individual component. Therefore, the ambiguity of the term "printer" goes against the [buyer].

Up to now, the court of appeals has not reached any findings from which one could discern that the parties nevertheless understood the [buyer's] notice of defects unambiguously in the sense of the missing documentation for the entire printer unit. The [seller's assignee's] submission in the lower courts indicates the opposite, i.e., that the notice of defect really only covered the documentation for the printer. The [seller's assignee] already claimed at trial that Company A had sent the demanded documentation for the printer by letter dated February 22, 1993 in order to settle the notice of defects concerning Point 4 of the letter dated February 9, 1993. It additionally referred to this allegation in its reply to the notice of appeal in an admissible manner (BGH, decision dated October 20, 1992 — VI ZR 361/91 = BGHR ZPO § 520(2)(1), reply to notice of appeal 1, with further citations). If the seller, in reaction to the [buyer's] notice of defects, sent documentation for the "printer" as an individual component — which must be presumed for the appeal to this court — and if the [buyer] did not mention Point 4 anymore in its letter of rescission dated March 2, 1903 but objected to five of the formerly eight defects as "not cured," one must infer that what the [buyer] received from Company A corresponded to what it had asked for in its letter dated February 9, 1993.

In any event, we cannot assume, based on the facts known so far, that the notice of defects dated February 9, 1993 referred to the documentation for the entire printer system with the clarity CISG Art. 39(1) requires in the interests of the seller.

c)

aa) In the opinion of the court of appeals, however, the [buyer] had the right to revive the notice of defective documentation by letter dated August 24, 1994 — after the issuance of the first judgment dated July 26, 1994 — and to grant the [seller] another period for subsequent improvement.

In this respect, the legal starting point of the court of appeals is already incorrect: It assumes that the beginning of the time period is the time of the delivery of the complete documentation and relies on the decision of the

Federal Court of Justice dated November 4, 1992 — VIII ZR 165/91 (NJW[6] 1993, 461, 462). In doing so, it overlooks that HGB[7] § 377, upon which the decision was based, refers to the time of "delivery," which requires the complete delivery of the goods into the buyer's sphere of influence (decision of the Federal Court of Justice, supra, at II 2 b). In contrast, CISG Art. 39(1) speaks of a "reasonable time after (the buyer) has discovered or ought to have discovered (the lack of conformity of the goods)." Recourse to the mentioned jurisprudence is, therefore, for this reason alone not possible.

It is obvious, that the limitations period of CISG Art. 39(1) had run by August 1994; upon a reasonable examination, the [buyer] could have, within a short period of time, recognized the complained-of alleged breach of contract regarding "the documentation, i.e., the operating or service instructions," which was noticed in the letter dated August 24, 1994. The question whether this period of time had expired on the day of the [buyer's] letter of repudiation dated March 2, 1993, can be left open (for the calculation of the time period during which to give notice, compare BGHZ 129, 75, 85 et seq.). It can further be left open whether the [buyer] has forfeited its right to give notice of defects by basing its repudiation exclusively on other defects, without reserving its right to raise warranty claims concerning any defects with respect to the documentation. The court of appeals' assumption that the [buyer] validly declared the contract avoided in its letter dated October 12, 1994 after the notice of defects dated August 24, 1994 and the failure to cure, is therefore incorrect.

bb) Insofar as the court of appeals reasons that the [buyer's] repudiation "amounts to an annulment within the meaning of CISG Art. 64(1)(a)," it must be noted for clarity purposes that this provision refers to the seller's right to repudiate. Here, however, we are only looking at the question of whether the [buyer] in his role as the buyer was able to declare the contract avoided. As long as we do not deal with contractual conditions that have precedence, this must be answered pursuant to CISG Art. 49.

Moreover, the court of appeals did not consider — as the appeal has rightly claimed — whether the [buyer's] repudiation dated October 12, 1994, was already null and void simply because it was not declared vis-à-vis

---

[6] [Translator's Note: "NJW" stands for "Neue Juristische Wochenschrift," a weekly law journal.]

[7] [Translator's Note: "HGB" stands for "Handelsgesetzbuch," the German Commercial Code.]

the seller but only vis-à-vis the [seller's assignee]. The [seller's assignee] only became the owner of the purchase price claim by assignment. A transfer of the contract did not take place.

3. The court of appeals' judgment can therefore not be valid (ZPO § 564). This panel cannot finally decide the matter because the determination of further facts is necessary. In both lower courts, the [buyer] gave notice of further defects concerning the functioning of the system. On remand, the court of appeals will have to consider whether those defects of the system justify the repudiation of the contract because of a fundamental breach of contract pursuant to CISG Art. 49(1)(a) or a repudiation pursuant to the seller's terms and conditions of warranty. Therefore, the matter must be remanded to the lower court (ZPO § 565(1)(1)).

Translation from German

Federal Supreme Court (Bundesgerichtshof)

February 15, 1995

Index No. VIII ZR 18/94

By Walter, Conston, Alexander & Green, P.C.

Editors: William M. Barron, Esq.; Birgit Kurtz, Esq.

Key CISG provisions at issue:

Article 49 -

[Also cited: Articles 3(1); 47(1); 53; 72; 80]

Headnote

Time limitations of a right to declare a contract avoided due to anticipatory fundamental breach of contract.

Main Holding

Upon appeal by plaintiff [seller], the judgment of the Sixth Division for Civil Matters of the Higher Regional Court [Oberlandesgericht] of Düsseldorf dated November 18, 1993 is reversed with regard to costs and to the extent that the judgment found against the [seller]. The cross-appeal is dismissed.

To the extent that the judgment was reversed, the case is remanded to the court of appeals for another hearing and decision, and for calculation of the costs of the appeal.

Facts

On March 4, 1991, defendant [buyer] ordered a key-embossing machine with a round switch-table from the [seller] for a purchase price of DM 259,900. The [seller] accepted the order by confirmation dated March

22, 1991. The purchase price was payable in three installments of 30% each: Upon confirmation of the order, at the time of notice of readiness for delivery, and at the time of invoicing. The remaining 10% was payable after acceptance of the equipment; until the full purchase price was paid, the [seller] retained title to the machine, which was to be delivered in September 1991 "subject to the usual reservation."

The manufacturer of the machine, with whom the [seller] was connected through the distribution agreement dated February 21/23, 1979, was the intervenor [manufacturer]; the machine was supposed to be accepted in advance by the [buyer] at the manufacturer's place of business. The [buyer] paid the [seller] the down payment in the amount of DM 77,970, which was due at the time of the confirmation of the order. After disputes arose between the manufacturer and the [seller] during the subsequent period of time, the manufacturer terminated the distribution agreement for cause without notice by letter dated July 18, 1991 and imposed, by letter dated August 14, 1991, a halt of delivery of goods against the [seller] until claims described in detail were satisfied. By letter dated August 26, 1991, the manufacturer notified the [buyer] that it was ready to make delivery to the [buyer] and attached its own invoice for the second installment in the amount of DM 77,970. Thereafter, the [buyers] employees performed the pre-acceptance of the machine in the absence of the [seller] at the manufacturer's factory on September 11, 1991; following that, the [buyer] paid the requested second installment to the manufacturer. The latter delivered the machine including accessories in the beginning of October 1991 to the [buyers] business, who accepted the machine on October 18, 1991 after installation and training.

By facsimile dated November 4, 1991, the [seller] requested from the [buyer] payment of the remaining purchase price in the amount of DM 181,930 setting a deadline for payment. After the manufacturer asserted that it had "stepped into" the existing orders after the termination of the distribution agreement and after it required payment to itself, the [buyer] made no further payments to either the [manufacturer] or the [seller]. In its complaint, the [seller] demands that the [buyer] pay to the [seller] the remaining purchase price in the amount of DM 181,930 plus interest. The [buyer], supported by the manufacturer as the intervenor, claimed that the machine had been delivered to it by the [manufacturer] under retention of title in the [manufacturer's] own name and on the [manufacturer's] account. Arguing that the [seller] had not performed its fundamental obligation to deliver the purchased item and to transfer ownership, the [buyer] further declared the contract avoided pursuant to Art. 49(1)(a) of the U.N. Sales Convention. Alternatively, it set off the [seller's] claim against the claim that arose under the agreement for services, in favor of the key-embossing machine in the amount of DM 102,240.35, which had been assigned to it by the [manufacturer] on April 2, 1992.

The trial court [Landgericht] granted the complaint except for part of the interest. After filing the appeal, the [buyer] declared a set-off against all of the payment claims of the [manufacturer] arising from the manufacture of the key-embossing machine and amounting to DM 186,333, based on the additional contract of assignment dated July 29, 1993 which was submitted by the [manufacturer's] brief dated September 7, 1993. Furthermore, the [buyer], by facsimile of its attorney dated October 16, 1992, set a deadline of November 16, 1992 for the [seller] to prove that the [seller] was entitled to transfer ownership of the delivered key-embossing machine in order to remove the existing defect of title, and after the time limit had expired without result, the [buyer] again, in the alternative, declared the contract avoided. With regard to the [buyer's] alternative set-off, the [seller] asserted that the assignment of the [manufacturer's] claim to the [buyer] had no effect because the [manufacturer] had already assigned this claim to someone else after the order was made, and, additionally, that it [the seller] had set off the [manufacturer's] claim arising under the agreement for services against claims of higher amounts by letter of its attorney dated November 22, 1991.

The court of appeals [Oberlandesgericht] amended the decision of the trial court and merely ordered the [buyer] to pay DM 3,577 plus interest and otherwise dismissed the claim. On appeal, the [seller] demands the reinstatement of the trial court's decision. By brief dated November 22, 1991, the [manufacturer] filed a cross-appeal on behalf of the [buyer], requesting full dismissal of the claim irrespective of the alternative set-off.

Grounds

I. In the opinion of the court of appeals, which applies the United Nations Convention on Contracts for the International Sale of Goods of April 11, 1980 (CISG) to the legal relationship between the parties, the [seller] had a claim for the balance of the purchase price in the amount of DM 181,930 pursuant to CISG Art. 53 until the [buyer] declared the set-off. Because of the [seller's] lack of cooperation and consent, [the court ruled that] the [buyer] and the [manufacturer] were unable to replace the contracting party in such a way that, from then on, the [manufacturer] had become the contracting partner of the [buyer] instead of the [seller]. [The court found that] the [buyer] also did not effectively declare the contract avoided because the requirements of CISG Art. 49(1) were not met. The court held that, as anticipated, the [buyer] first obtained possession of the machine and, taking into account the retention of title, a legal expectancy right of the machine ordered by it; in this respect, [the court reasoned that] its legal position was no different than if the [buyer] had considered the [seller] its supplier. The [buyer] should have given the [seller] an additional delivery deadline according to CISG Art. 47(1) after the [manufacturer] refused to deliver in the [seller's] name; then, after expiration of the time-limit without result, it could have declared the contract avoided under CISG Art. 49(1)(b); but it failed to do this. [The court stated that] after obtaining possession of the machine and using it, it was no longer possible to set an additional time-limit for the purpose of declaring the contract avoided.

[The court ruled that] the [buyer] could not successfully rely on the facsimile dated October 16, 1992. [It held that] it does not constitute a fundamental breach of contract that the [seller] was not yet able to transfer full ownership of the machine to the [buyer]. [The court stated that] the [buyer] itself did not comply with its contractual duties, because it refused to fulfil its obligation to pay the purchase price to the [seller]; furthermore, the [buyer] was supposed to perform in advance considering the retention of title to which the [seller] and the [buyer] had agreed. [The court found that] in any case, according to CISG Art. 80, the [buyer] could not rely on the still outstanding transfer of ownership, because the transfer of ownership had failed, among other things, for the reason that the [buyer] had not given the [seller] the opportunity, by granting a certain time-limit according to CISG Art. 47(1), to meet the requirements for the transfer of ownership after complete payment of the purchase price.

[The court held that] the [seller's] claim for the balance of the purchase price in the amount of DM 181,930 had, however, become void by way of set-off against a claim arising out of a right assigned by the [manufacturer] in the amount of DM 178,353, so that the [buyer] only had to pay DM 3,577.

II. These elaborations do not withstand legal scrutiny on all points.

1. The court of appeals correctly assumes that, pursuant to CISG Art. 1(1)(a) in connection with CISG Art. 3(1), the United Nations Con-

vention on Contracts for the International Sale of Goods of April 11, 1980 (BGBl.[1] 1989 II, 588) applies to the contract between the parties dated March 4/22, 1991 concerning the delivery of a key-embossing machine.

2. As the court of appeals further correctly states, the [seller's] claim for the purchase price has not become void because of the alleged agreement between the [buyer] and the [manufacturer], since, due to the lack of the [seller's] participation, the consent of all the parties (BGHZ[2] 96, 302, 308 with further citations) required for such an assignment of the contract is missing.

3. With respect to the result, there is no objection to the assumption of the court of appeals that the contract between the parties continues to exist, because the [buyer] has neither in its answer to the complaint nor in its appeals brief effectively declared the contract avoided.

a) It need not be decided whether the [buyer] was entitled to declare the contract avoided pursuant to CISG Art. 72 after it had obtained knowledge of the [manufacturer's] imposing a halt on the delivery of goods and whether there was, therefore, a risk that the [seller] would possibly no longer be able to transfer ownership of the machine to the [buyer]. It is true that, according to CISG Art. 72, the other party may declare the contract avoided if, prior to the date of performance of the contract, it is apparent that one of the parties will commit a fundamental breach of contract. The purpose of this provision, however, is only to protect a party against a future breach of contract, and it therefore takes place before the delivery and its different forms of disruptions (*see* von Caemmerer/Schlechtiem, Kommentar zum Einheitlichen UN Kaufrecht, 1990, Art. 72 & 4).

With respect to breaches of contract that occur only after the obligation has become due, the ordinary provisions applicable hereto remain in force, especially the right of the buyer to declare the contract avoided pursuant to CISG Art. 49.

After the [buyer] had accepted the machine on October 18, 1991 and valid delivery had thereby taken place, it was obligated to pay the balance of the purchase price after another six weeks, at the latest, pursuant to the contract entered into by the parties on March 4/22, 1991, i.e., it was obligated to pay by November 29, 1991, in order to cause the transfer of ownership of

---

[1] [Translator's note: "BGBl." stands for "Bundesgesetzblatt," the federal law gazette.]

[2] [Translator's note: "BGHZ" stands for "Die amtliche Sammlung der Entscheidungen des Bundesgerichtshofes in Zivilsachen," the official reporter of Decisions of the German Federal Court of Justice in Civil Matters.]

the machine. Therefore, performance of the contract was set by both parties for the end of November 1991, so that the [buyer] was able to exercise its right to declare the contract avoided pursuant to Art. 72 CISG only until that point. Although the [seller] had demanded, by facsimile dated November 11, 1991, that the [buyer] pay the balance of the purchase price in the amount of DM 181,930, so that the [buyer] had to assume that the [seller] insisted on the performance of the contract, the [buyer] exercised its right to declare the contract avoided for the first time in its answer to the complaint dated March 30, 1992.

b) The [buyer's] claim to declare the contract avoided is also not justified under CISG Art. 49, as the court of appeals has correctly found in the outcome. In this respect, it can be left undecided here as well, whether the [seller] committed a fundamental breach of contract by failing to perform its obligations, which would have given the [buyer] the right to declare the contract avoided according to CISG Art. 49(1)(a). In any case, the [buyer] lost this right because it did not exercise it within a reasonable period of time (CISG Art. 49(2)(b)). At the latest, when the [buyer] received notification that the [manufacturer] had imposed a halt of delivery of the goods to the [seller] in November 1991, it was apparent to the [buyer] that the [seller] would not be able to perform its obligation of transferring ownership even after receiving payment of the purchase price. If, however, the [buyer] let approximately five months pass until it declared the contract avoided for the first time during the lawsuit commenced by the [seller], it lost its right to declare the contract avoided, the exercise of which should not be delayed unreasonably in the interest of quick clarification of the legal relationships between the parties. Therefore, the [buyer's] cross-appeal properly was unsuccessful.

4. The court of appeals is, however, wrong in assuming that the [seller's] claim for the balance of the purchase price in the amount of DM 181,930 is voided by the [buyer's] set-off against a claim in the amount of DM 178,353 arising out of an assigned right.

a) Nevertheless, on appeal, the [seller] argues unsuccessfully that the set-off does not hold up because the [buyer] has not submitted evidence showing that the claim for the balance due under the agreement for services was assigned effectively to the [buyer] by the [manufacturer]. The appeal thus refers to the [seller's] allegation that the [manufacturer] had already assigned its claim against the [seller] arising under the order dated March 26, 1991 to the G.-Bank in B. after the order was placed; the court of appeals considered this statement irrelevant because an allegation of the point in time of the alleged other assignment was missing.

aa) It is true that the [seller's] allegation may be interpreted as the defense of another prior assignment because a subsequent (further) assignment would not have affected the preceding assignment.

bb) Even if the [seller] had denied the validity of the assignment to the [buyer] by arguing that there was a prior assignment of the claim of the [manufacturer] to G.-Bank and that, consequently, the [buyer] had the burden of proof regarding the absence of the alleged assignment as a negative fact, the principles established by case law with respect to furnishing so-called negative evidence are of advantage to it. According to these principles, the [seller] first had to deny the validity of the assignment of the claim to the [buyer] by substantiated specification of the alleged prior assignment, while the [buyer] then had to prove the falsity of the other party's argument (compare BGH[3], decision dated February 5, 1987 IX ZR 65/86 = WM 1987, 590 at II 1 = BGHR[4] ZPO[5] ' 286 Negativbeweis 1 with further citations; *see also* Zöller/Greger, *ZPO*, 19th ed., before ' 284 & 24). A substantiated specification of the alleged prior assignment to G.-Bank, which the [buyer] denied by pleading lack of knowledge and which the [manufacturer] denied as false, is, however, missing so that the court of appeals has rightly assumed, at least with respect to the result, that this argument was irrelevant.

b) The court of appeals has, however, as the appeal correctly argues, made a procedural error by rejecting the [seller's] argument as untimely under ZPO " 527, 520(2), 296(1), that it [the seller] had set off the claim assigned to the [buyer][6] against claims amounting to more than DM 218,000 by letter of its attorney dated November 22, 1991.

aa) Insofar as the [buyer] has, with reference to the [manufacturer's] brief dated September 9, 1993, declared a set-off exceeding the assignment

[3] [Translator's note: "ABGH" stands for ABundesgerichtshof,@ the Federal Court of Justice.]

[4] [Translator's note: "BGHR" stands for "Systematische Sammlung der Entscheidungen des Bundesgerichtshofs (LBl)," the Systematic Collection of Decisions of the German Federal Court of Justice (looseleaf).]

[5] [Translator's note: "ZPO" stands for "Zivilprozeßordnung," the German Code of Civil Procedure.]

[6] [Translator's note: The original German text states "the claim assigned to plaintiff [seller]," which does not make sense in this context.]

dated April 2, 1992, for the first time on appeal in accordance with the submitted assignment agreement dated July 29, 1993, a failure to observe the deadline to answer set for March 1, 1993 (ZPO ' 520(2)) cannot be considered in any event, because, until this time, the set-off had not yet been declared in this respect. If the [seller], therefore, by brief dated September 22, 1993, substantiated, for the first time, its counter-claims, with which, according to its submissions, it declared a set-off against the [manufacturer's] claim by letter from its lawyer dated November 22, 1991, this was not too late.

bb) The question, whether the [seller's] argument was late with respect to the partial amount of DM 102,240.35, which was designated for set-off at trial because of the assignment dated April 2, 1992, does not have to be decided. Because the [seller's] contention that the [manufacturer's] claim arising under the agreement for services was void because of the counter-set-off pursuant to the letter dated November 22, 1991, must be investigated as explained above, a delay of the proceedings according to ZPO '' 527, 520(2), 296(1) will equally not be considered insofar as the [seller's] objection is aimed at the assignment of the claim to the partial amount of DM 102,240.35 according to the assignment declaration dated April 2, 1992.

5. The challenged decision therefore must be reversed upon the [seller's] appeal insofar as it found against the [seller], and the matter must be remanded to the court of appeals to that extent for clarification of the question whether the alleged counter-set-off dated November 22, 1991 was valid.

Prior decisions: OLG[7] Düsseldorf November 18, 1993, 6 U 228/92; LG[8] Düsseldorf July 9, 1993, 31 O 223/91.

---

[7] [Translator's note: "OLG" stands for "Oberlandesgericht," the Higher Regional Court, a court of appeals.]

[8] [Translator's note: "LG" stands for "Landgericht," the trial court.]

Translation from German

Court of Appeals (Oberlandesgericht) of Düssseldorf, Germany

October 2, 1994
Index No. 6U 32/93

by Walter, Conston, Alexander & Green, P.C.
Editors: **William M. Barron, Esq. & Birgit Kurtz, Esq.**

Key CISG provisions at issue:
Articles 6; 38(1); 39(1); 53; 74; 78
[Also cited: Articles 35; 44; 45; 46; 49(1)(a); 50; 81; 95]

Extract from the decision:

Plaintiff [seller] has a claim against defendants [buyers] for payment of the amount of FF 61,646.40 as set forth in the complaint — subject to a decision on the set-off. The [seller] can claim this amount from the OHG[1] operated by the [buyers] as the balance of the purchase price for the textiles it had delivered, in accordance with Art. 53 of the United Nations Convention on Contracts for the International Sale of Goods of April 11, 1980 (CISG; compare BGBl.[2] 1989 II, p. 588 et seq.) [. . .]. The [buyers], as partners in the OHG, are jointly and severally liable for this purchase price claim. This follows from HGB[3] § 128 [. . .].

[. . .]

Thus, the [buyers] are liable under HGB Section 128 for the purchase price claim that the [seller] has against the OHG operated by the [buyers]. This purchase price claim is based on CISG Art. 53.

It is uncontested that, in 1989, the [seller] and the OHG operated by the [buyers] concluded several sales contracts for the delivery of textiles, and a part . . . of the agreed-upon, total purchase price . . . remains outstanding.

---

[1] [Translator's Note: "OHG" stands for "Offene Handelsgesellschaft," a type of German partnership.]

[2] [Translator's Note: "BGBl." stands for "Bundesgesetzblatt," the German Federal Law Gazette.]

[3] [Translator's Note: "HGB" stands for "Handelsgesetzbuch," the German Commercial Code.]

The provisions of the above-mentioned UN Convention on the International Sale of Goods apply to the legal relationships resulting from contracts of sale. It is true that the applicability does not follow from the direct force of these regulations as domestic German law, as this Convention only came into force in the Federal Republic of Germany on January 1, 1991 (compare Announcement dated October 23, 1990, BGBl. 1990 II, p. 1477), whereas the sales contracts in question date back to 1989. The applicability of the Convention in this case results from the fact that the general German conflict of laws rules apply to the present contracts, with the consequence that, under EGBGB[4] Arts. 28(1)&(2), French law, in principle, applies to the contracts, which, in turn, has provided for the application of the Convention since January 1, 1988.

The aforementioned general conflict of law provisions, as set forth in the German Introductory Law to the Civil Code, apply to the present case, because the transactions at issue do not come within the scope of application of the Uniform Law on the International Sale of Goods (ULIS) of July 17, 1973 (BGBl. 1973 II, p. 885). For, under ULIS Art. 1, this law applies only to specified international contracts for the sale of movable goods if the parties have their registered offices in the territory of different signatory states. Under ULIS Art. 102, signatory states within the meaning of ULIS are countries that have ratified, or acceded to, the Agreement Relating to the Introduction of a Uniform Law on the International Sale of Goods. Since France was not a signatory state to this Convention, the special conflict of law provisions embodied in ULIS Art. 1, which normally had priority over the general German conflict of law rules, do not apply in this case (compare BGHZ[5] 96, 313, 3164; MüKo[6]/Martiny, 2d ed., App. I to EGBGB Art. 28, ¶ 43, with further citations).

Hence, within the framework of the applicable general German conflict of law rules, EGBGB Arts. 28(1)&(2) apply here. This stems from the fact that it cannot be assumed that the contracting parties made a choice of law within the meaning of EGBGB Art. 27 — for instance for the applica-

[4] [Translator's Note: "EGBGB" stands for "Einführungsgesetz zum Bürgerlichen Gesetzbuch," the German Introductory Law to the Civil Code.]

[5] [Translator's Note: "BGHZ" stands for "Entscheidungen des Bundesgerichtshofes in Zivilsachen," the Official Reporter of Decisions of the German Federal Court of Justice for Civil Matters.]

[6] [Translator's Note: "MüKo" stands for "Münchener Kommentar," a well-known commentary to the Civil Code.]

bility of German law — either at the conclusion of the contract or subsequently. None of the parties has expressly set forth that, at the conclusion of the contract, the applicability of German law was expressly agreed to. A tacit choice of law also cannot be assumed. There are no indications that point to the contracting parties tacitly relying on the application of German law at the conclusion of the contract. Similarly, no tacit choice of law with respect to German law can be found in the parties' conduct during the litigation. It is true that it can suffice that both parties tacitly assumed the applicability of German law. However, sufficiently clear and unambiguous statements by the parties as to which law should be applied here are not discernable.

Because there is no choice of law, the analysis of the contracts is therefore, under EGBGB Art. 28(1), governed by the law of the country to which they show the closest connection; under the guidance of EGBGB Art. 28(2), this is the country in which the contracting party that is to undertake the characteristic performance has its main administrative or head registered office at the time of the contract's conclusion. The present contracts are contracts of sale in which the characteristic performance is undertaken by the seller (compare OLG[7] Frankfurt NJW[8] 1991, 3102; Palandt[9]/Heldrich, 52d ed., EGBGB Art. 28, ¶ 8, with further citations; MüKo/Martiny, supra, EGBGB Art. 28, ¶ 112, with further citations). That means that, in the present case, French law is applicable, because the [seller] has its registered commercial office in France and the performance was to be undertaken from there as well.

Since France has been a signatory state to the CISG since January 1, 1988 and has declared no reservation under CISG Art. 95 (compare MüKo/Martiny, supra, App. II to EGBGB Art. 28, ¶ 2; von Caemmerer/Schlechtriem, Kommentar zum einheitlichen UN-Kaufrecht (Commentary to the Uniform UN Sales Law), preceding CISG Art. 1-6, ¶ 17), the analysis of the parties' legal relationships is subject to this Convention.

Moreover, the additional requirements with respect to the scope of application of the Convention as to the subject matter are met. Namely, the requirements of CISG Art. 1(1)(b) are present, because this case involves

---

[7] [Translator's Note: "OLG" stands for "Oberlandesgericht," the Higher Regional Court or court of appeals.]

[8] [Translator's Note: "NJW" stands for "Neue Juristische Wochenschrift," a well-known weekly legal publication.]

[9] [Translator's Note: "Palandt" is the most renowned and influential commentary to the German Civil Code.]

contracts for the sale of goods between parties that have their registered offices in different countries — the [seller] in France and the [buyers] in Germany.

The fact that the [buyers] have asserted warranty claims in response to the [seller's] claim for the purchase price under CISG Art. 53 does not bar — for instance under CISG Art. 81 — the [seller's] claim.

[. . .]

In this respect, the provisions of the CISG are also applicable pursuant to the above-mentioned provisions. In the case of a purchase of fungible goods, as is the case here, the buyer can, under these provisions, upon the delivery of goods that do not conform to the contract, either demand subsequent improvement (CISG Art. 35, Art. 45(1)(a), Art. 46(1) & (3)), replacement (CISG Art. 35, Art. 45(1)(a), Art. 46(1) & (2)), a reduction of the purchase price (CISG Art. 35, Art. 45(1)(a), Art. 50), or damages (CISG Art. 35, Art. 45(1)(b), Art. 74), or declare the contract avoided (CISG Art. 35, Art. 45(1)(a); Art. 49(1)(a)).

The requirement for raising the warranty claims is, according to CISG Arts. 38 and 39, that the buyer have examined the goods without delay and have reported any defects within a reasonable time after their discovery or the possibility of their discovery, and then provide a specific description of the kind of non-compliance with the contract. If these requirements are not met, the buyer loses the right to assert the lack of conformity of the goods, unless he has a reasonable excuse for his failure to give notice of defects (CISG Art. 39(1), Art. 44). The point in time at which the buyer was obligated to have determined the breach of contract is governed by the provisions regulating the duty to examine. In this context, CISG Art. 38 provides that the goods must be examined within as short a period of time as the circumstances permit. This means that for the determination of the length of the period permitted to examine and give notice, which begins upon the delivery of the goods to the buyer, the circumstances of the individual case and the reasonable possibilities of the contracting parties are crucial, as to which a strict standard must be applied (compare BGH NJW 1982, 2730, 2732, with further citations on the largely analogous provisions of ULIS Arts. 38 & 39; von Caemmerer/Schlechtriem, supra, CISG Art. 38, ¶ 5, with further citations).

In the present case . . . , it was easily possible to examine the shirts — at least by way of sampling — immediately after their delivery and to give notice of the defects discovered during the examination at least within a few days after the delivery of the goods. The [buyers] have not demonstrated conclusively that this happened. . . . [The] alleged [. . .] point in time [. . .] that notice of the defects was given [. . .] need not be further specified. This is so because, at that time, more than two months had already elapsed since the delivery of the goods. This period can no longer be regarded as "reasonable" within the meaning of CISG Art. 39(1).

[. . .]

With respect to the [. . .] collection costs, which the [seller] has raised as an ancillary claim [. . .], it must be considered on remand that it is true that the [seller], in the case of a breach of contract, could be entitled to damages under CISG Art. 74, where a breach of contract is understood to mean every form of objective failure to perform a contractual obligation, without the debtor first having to be given notice of default (compare von Caemmerer/Schlechtriem, supra, CISG Art. 74, ¶ 6, with further citations). However, it will have to be considered whether, and to what extent, the costs represented necessary expenditures for the collection of the claim. Regardless of the fundamental considerations that have to be made in this context with respect to the reimbursement of collection costs for the collection of foreign claims, the amount of the potentially reimbursable collection costs depends at any rate on whether, and in what amount, there is a set-off. This results from the fact that the amount of the collection costs possibly paid by the [seller] is determined conclusively by the amount of the claim to be collected.

Within the scope of the main claim, to which the [seller] is entitled, it is at any rate entitled, under CISG Art. 78, to interest for the asserted period of time. In this regard, the interest rate is calculated under French law, which, according to the contract and EGBGB Arts. 28(1) and (2), applies to the contract at issue. [. . .].

[. . .]

Original language (French) and English translation

COUR D'APPEL DE GRENOBLE

R.G. n° 93/3275 — 22 February 1995

Translation by Gary F. Bell, 1998. ©
Assistant Professor, Faculty of Law, National University of Singapore

Thanks to my colleagues Loy Wee Loon (NUS), David Lametti
and Geneviève Saumier (McGill) for their help.

Key CISG provisions at issue:

Articles 7; 8(1); 25; 64(1)(a); 73(2)

*[text in square brackets is added by the translator]

Chambre commerciale Au Nom du Peuple Français
Arrêt du mercredi 22 février 1995

E N T R E:
SARL BRI PRODUCTION "BONAVENTURE", dont le siège est 44 rue de la Libération — BP 35 à GIERES (38610)

APPELANTE d'un jugement rendu par le Tribunal de Commerce de GRENOBLE en date du 14 mai 1993, suivant déclaration d'appel du 29 juin 1993.

Représenté par la SCP d'Avoués PERRET & POUGNAND
Assisté de Me FESSLER, Avocat
E T :
Société PAN AFRICAN EXPORT, dont le siège est 27 Commander boulevard Nesconset 11767 NEW YORK ETATS UNIS

Commercial Chamber In the Name of the French People
Decision of Wednesday 22 February 1995

BETWEEN:
SARL BRI PRODUCTION "BONAVENTURE", with its head office at 44 rue de la Libération — BP 35 à GIERES (38610)

Appellant of a judgement delivered by the Tribunal of Commerce of GRENOBLE on 14
May 1993, following a declaration of appeal issued on 29 June 1993.
Represented by SCP d'Avoués PERRET & POUGNAND
Assisted by Me FESSLER, Avocat
AND :
Société PAN AFRICAN EXPORT, with its head office at 27 Commander Boulevard,
Nesconset NEWYORK, USA, 11767

INTIME
Représenté par la SCP d'Avoués GRIMAUD
Assisté de Me KAPLAN, Avocat au barreau de Paris

RESPONDENT
Represented by SCP d'Avoués GRIMAUD
Assisted by Me KAPLAN, Avocat at the Bar of Paris

COMPOSITION DE LA COUR :
Lors des débats et du délibéré:
Monsieur BERAUDO, Président
Monsieur BAUMET, Conseiller
Monsieur FALLET, Conseiller
Assistés lors des débats de Mme COMBE, Greffier.

CORAM :
At the pleadings and during the deliberations
Monsieur BERAUDO, Président
Monsieur BAUMET, Conseiller
Monsieur FALLET, Conseiller
Assisted during the pleadings by Mme COMBE, Greffier (Clerk).

DEBATS:
A l'audience publique du 18 janvier 1995 les Avoués ont été entendus en leurs conclusions, et les Avocats en leurs plaidoiries, l'arrêt a été rendu à l'audience du mercredi 22 février 1995

PLEADINGS:
At the public hearing of 18 January 1995, the solicitors having been heard in their [written] conclusions and the advocates in their pleadings, the decision was delivered at the session on Wednesday 22 February 1995

La Cour statue sur l'appel interjeté par la société BRI PRODUCTION à l'encontre d'un jugement du Tribunal de Commerce de Grenoble en date du 14 mai 1993 qui l'a condamnée à payer diverses sommes à titre de dommages-intérêts à la société PAN AFRICAN EXPORT pour avoir refusé d'honorer des commandes qu'elle avait acceptées.

The Court rules on the appeal by BRI PRODUCTION against the judgement of the Tribunal of Commerce of GRENOBLE rendered on 14 May 1993 which orders it to pay some sums of money as damages to PAN AFRICAN EXPORT for refusing to honor orders it had accepted.

Lors des premiers contacts entre BRI PRODUCTION et la société PAN AFRICAN, cette dernière avait écrit, dans une télécopie datée du 27 mai 1991, qu'elle n'était pas intéressée par l'importation de Jeans aux États-Unis mais qu'elle était intéressée par des achats pour ses clients en Afrique et en Amérique du Sud.
La correspondance se terminait par une demande de catalogue et de listes de prix.

At the time of the first contacts between BRI PRODUCTION and PAN AFRICAN, the latter had written, in a fax dated 27 May 1991, that it was not interested in importing jeans to the USA but that it was interested in buying for clients in Africa and South America.
The correspondence ended with a request for a catalogue and price lists.

Les 06 et 11 juin 1991, dans des télécopies adressées à la société BONAVENTURE, en Espagne, la société PAN AFRICAN écrit ceci: "Nous avons des clients en Afrique et certains en Amérique du Sud et nous souhaiterions pouvoir nous mettre d'accord avec vous afin de pouvoir acheter des Jeans Bonaventure pour eux."
Ne recevant pas de réponse de BONAVENTURE ESPAGNE, la société PAN AFRICAN adresse une copie à BRI PRODUCTION et lui fait connaître son désir de se fournir auprès d'elle.

On 6 and 11 June 1991, in faxes sent to BONAVENTURE in Spain, PAN AFRICA wrote the following: "We have clients in Africa and in South America and we would like to reach an agreement with you so that we can buy Bonaventure Jeans for them."
Having received no answer from BONAVENTURE SPAIN, PAN AFRICAN sent a copy to BRI PRODUCTION and informed BRI PRODUCTION that it would like to get supplies from it.

Le 13 août 1991, une commande est passée par la société PAN AFRICAN pour la Boutique Petete de Guayaquil (EQUATEUR). Sur les six bons de livraison établis les 10 et 17 octobre 1991 figure comme adresse de livraison Petete Boutique, Guayaquil.

On 31 August 1991, PAN AFRICAN orders for Boutique Petete in Guayaquil (ECUADOR). The delivery address on the six delivery slips dated 10 and 17 October 1991, is Petete Boutique, Guayaquil.

Le 14 octobre 1991, à 9 h 36 la société PAN AFRICAN indique à BRI PRODUCTION qu'elle envisage une seconde commande. Dans une télécopie du même jour, 18 h 05, BRI PRODUCTION demande quelle sera la destination de la marchandise.

On 14 October 1991, at 9:36 a.m., PAN AFRICAN informs BRI PRODUCTION that it is considering a second order. In a fax on the same day, at 6:05 p.m., BRI PRODUCTION asks what will be the destination of the goods.

Dans une seconde télécopie du lendemain, BRI PRODUCTION fixe des conditions de prix et de quantité et demande à nouveau à être informé sur la destination des marchandises.

In a second fax the next day, BRI PRODUCTION sets the price and the quantity and again requests to be informed of the destination of the goods.

Par télécopie du 17 octobre 1991, PAN AFRICAN passe une commande mentionnant des quantités à être livrées sans retard pour le 15 novembre, et demande confirmation. L'identité du client final n'est pas mentionnée.

By fax on 17 October 1991, PAN AFRICAN makes an order specifying the quantities to be delivered without delay by 15 November and asks for a confirmation. The identity of the final client is not mentioned.

Le 21 octobre 1991, BRI PRODUCTION demande à nouveau le nom et l'adresse du client.

On 21 October 1991, BRI PRODUCTION again requests for the name and address of the client.

Par une mention manuscrite sur la Télécopie, reçue le 21 octobre, la société PAN AFRICAN indique "La Palestina N.A. DE RYDERKADE CURACAO NA."

By a hand written note on the fax received on 21 October, PAN AFRICAN indicates "La Palestina N.A. DE RYDERKADE CURACAO NA."

Le 24 octobre 1991, BRI PRODUCTION accepte de livrer et mentionne sur la télécopie l'adresse du client, "La Palestina . . . ," indiquée par la société PAN AFRICAN.

On 24 October 1991, BRI PRODUCTION agrees to deliver and indicates on the fax the address of the client "La Palestina . . ." as indicated by PAN AFRICAN.

Le 27 octobre 1991, la société PAN AFRICAN indique à BRI PRODUCTION qu'elle s'occupera de l'expédition et qu'elle l'informera des clients et de la destination.

On 27 October 1991, PAN AFRICAN informs BRI PRODUCTION that it will take care of the shipping and that it will inform BRI PRODUCTION of the clients and destination.

Le bon de commande établi le 29 octobre 1991 mentionne comme nom du client et adresse de livraison "PAN AFRICAN EXPORT La Palestina. . . ." Les mêmes indications figurent sur la facture pro-forma établie le 04 novembre 1991.

The order slip of 29 October 1991 indicates the name of the client and delivery address as "PAN AFRICAN EXPORT La Palestina. . . ." The same appears on the pro-forma invoice of 4 November 1991.

Début novembre 1991, la société BRI PRODUCTION demande à la société PAN AFRICAN de justifier de la livraison à Guayaquil des marchandises vendues fin octobre 1991.

In early November, BRI PRODUCTION asks PAN AFRICAN to prove the delivery to Guayaquil of the goods sold at the end of October 1991.

La société PAN AFRICAN répond que cette demande n'a pas été clairement formulée au début et qu'elle autorisait, pour l'avenir, son transitaire, LEPP INTERNATIONAL, à fournir les documents que BRI PRODUCTION réclamerait.

PAN AFRICAN answers that this request was not clearly formulated from the beginning and that for the future, it authorizes its forwarding agent LEPP INTERNATIONAL to provide the documents that BRI PRODUCTION will require.

Elle précise que pour la livraison passée, le client a exigé qu'elle renonce à cette demande mais indique qu'elle est disposée à présenter le connaissement établissant que la marchandise a été embarquée.

PAN AFRICAN adds that for the past delivery, the client had demanded that it abandon this request [for documents] but indicates that it is willing to show the bill of lading establishing that the goods were put on board.

Le 15 novembre 1991, la société BRI PRODUCTION PRODUCTION fait connaître que sans preuve écrite de la destination finale des marchandises livrées fin octobre 1991, elle ne procéderait plus à des nouvelles livraisons.

On 15 November 1991, BRI PRODUCTION indicates that without written evidence of the final destination of the goods delivered at the end of October 1991, it would not make any new deliveries.

Le 18 novembre 1991, BRI PRODUCTION indique qu' "avant de parler de l'avenir et de nouvelles livraisons nous voulons que vous nous donniez la preuve de votre fiabilité."

On 18 November 1991, BRI PRODUCTION states that "before talking about the future and about new deliveries, we want you to give us evidence that we can rely on you" [literally: we want you to give of the evidence of your reliability].

PAN AFRICAN répond en bas de la demande que les documents peuvent être examinés au cabinet de son avocat, Me Philip KAPLAN.

PAN AFRICAN answers at the bottom of the request that the documents can be inspected at the office of its advocate, Me Philip Kaplan.

Il résulte d'une lettre de Me KAPLAN à la société BONAVENTURE qu' "un connaissement maritime de la CGM concernant la première vente de marchandises à (sa cliente) suivant facture pro-forma en date du 26 septembre 1991" a été présentée au Directeur Commercial de BRI PRODUCTION. La copie demandée du connaissement a été refusée.

It is learned from a letter of Me Kaplan to BONAVENTURE that a "maritime bill of lading of CGM concerning the first sale of goods with pro forma invoice of 26 September 1991" was shown to the commercial director of BRI PRODUCTION. The request for a copy of this bill of lading was denied.

Aucun document relatif à cette expédition n'est produit aux débats.

No document relating to this shipping was produced in this court.

La société BRI PRODUCTION verse aux débats une déclaration en Douane, à l'exportation, portant le cachet de la douane française du 25 octobre 1991, mentionnant comme expéditeur PAN AFRICAN EXPORT Cordova Guayaquil Equateur et comme destinataire LEP Madrid. La déclaration concerne trois palettes de Jeans.

BRI PRODUCTION produced a Customs declaration, for export, bearing the stamp of the French Customs of 25 October 1991, mentioning as shipper PAN AFRICAN EXPORT Cordoya Guayaquil Ecuador and as recipient LEP Madrid. The declaration is regarding three pallets of Jeans.

Dans une télécopie du 16 novembre 1989, la société PAN AFRICAN avait proposé à M. Ricardo PELAEZ, destinataire final de la marchandise expédiée en octobre 1991, la livraison de pantalons Jeans à Madrid.

In a fax on 16 November 1989, PAN AFRICAN proposed to deliver some jeans trousers to Madrid to Mr Ricardo PELAEZ, the final recipient of the goods sent in October 1991.

* * *

* * *

Devant la Cour, la société BRI PRODUCTION conclut à la réformation en faisant valoir, en substance, qu'elle est liée par des contrats avec plusieurs distributeurs à l'étranger, que, spécialement en Espagne où la marque de Jeans Bonaventure est recherchée, elle a intérêt à éviter que soit créé un réseau parallèle de vente.

In this Court, BRI PRODUCTION concludes [i.e. argues] that there is avoidance [of the contract] after arguing, essentially that it is bound by contracts with many foreign distributors and that, more specifically in the case of Spain where the brand name "Jeans Bonaventure" is sought after, it has an interest in not allowing a parallel network of sale [parallel imports].

Elle précise qu'elle a reçu de nombreuses plaintes de ses distributeurs espagnols qui déplorent que des Jeans Bonaventure inondent le marché et qu'elle a été confrontée à des problèmes de contrefaçon. Elle ajoute que, pour les Etats-Unis, elle n'est pas propriétaire de la marque Bonaventure et risque la saisie de sa production.

It adds that it has received numerous complaints by its Spanish distributors who complain that Bonaventure Jeans have flooded the market and that it has encountered counterfeiting problems. It adds that, with respect to the USA, it is not the owner of the trade mark "Bonaventure" and that it risks having its products seized.

Elle affirme donc que, pour elle, la destination finale de la marchandise est une condition essentielle du contrat.

It therefore asserts that, for itself, the final destination of the goods is an essential condition of the contract.

Elle indique que les marchandises, objet du contrat conclu en septembre 1991, destinées à la boutique Petete à Guayaquil (Equateur) ont été en fait livrées au magasin "Moda Joven Vaquero" à Madrid, en Espagne. Elle explique que le détournement a eu lieu sur instructions données par PAN AFRICAN au transitaire en France et que les marchandises ont été expédiées en Espagne avec une facture de PAN AFRICAN de sorte qu'elle-même n'a jamais reçu de documents douaniers de nature à lui permettre de justifier d'une exportation auprès de l'administration fiscale.

It further states that the goods that were the object of the contract of September 1991, destined [literal translation] for Petete in Guayaquil (Ecuador) were in fact delivered to the store "Moda Joven Vaquero" in Madrid, in Spain. It explains that this diversion took place because PAN AFRICAN so instructed its forwarding agent in France and that the goods were shipped to Spain with an invoice by PAN AFRICAN such that it has never received custom documents that would allow it to prove an export to the Tax Authorities.

La société BRI PRODUCTION déduit du comportement de la société PAN AFRICAN qu'elle était fondée à lui demander de justifier de la destination effective des marchandises avant de procéder à de nouvelles livraisons et, faute de ce faire, à refuser de livrer.

BRI PRODUCTION deduces from the behaviour of PAN AFRICAN that it is justified to require PAN AFRICAN to prove the actual destination of the goods before proceeding to any new deliveries and, in cases of refusal to do so, to refuse to deliver.

Elle demande 10 000 Ffrs à titre de dommages-intérêts, 10 000 Ffrs au titre de l'article 700 du nouveau code de procédure civile et la distraction des dépens au profit de la SCP d'Avoués PERRET & POUGNAND.

It seeks 10,000 francs as damages, 10,000 francs under article 700 of the new code of civil procedure and the payment of cost to the benefit of SCP d'Avoués PERRET & POUGNAND.

* * *

* * *

La société PAN AFRICAN EXPORT conclut à la confirmation du jugement, demande la capitalisation des intérêts échus, "la somme de US $ 118 000 ou sa contre-valeur en francs au jour du paiement à titre de dédommagement des pertes de bénéfices sur commandes futures", 20 000 Ffrs à titre de dommages-intérêts, 20 000 Ffrs au titre de l'article 700 du nouveau code de procédure civile et la distraction des dépens au profit de la SCP d'Avoués GRIMAUD.

PAN AFRICAN EXPORT concludes that the judgement should be confirmed, seeks the capitalisation of the cumulated interest, "the sum of US $118,000 or its equivalent in francs on the day of payment as compensation for the loss of profits on future orders", 20,000 francs as damages, 20,000 francs under article 700 of the new code of civil procedure and the payment of cost to the benefit of SCP d'Avoués PERRET & POUGNAND.

Elle fait valoir, en substance, qu'elle a indiqué, comme la société BRI PRODUCTION le lui demandait, la destination finale des marchandises et que l'exigence de documents prouvant que la commande antérieure avait bien été livrée à Quayaquil pour procéder aux livraisons concernées par des commandes ultérieures ainsi que la demande d'un chèque de garantie de la destination sont tardives, remettent en cause un contrat définitivement conclu et caractérisent une faute contractuelle.

It argues, essentially, that, as requested by BRI PRODUCTION, it had revealed the final destination of the goods, and that [BRI PRODUCTION was late in requesting] as a condition for delivery pursuant to later orders, that documents be produced proving that the earlier order was indeed delivered in Quayaquil, and [late] in requesting a cheque guaranteeing the destination, and that these requests put in question [i.e. reopen] a contract that had been agreed as final and they constitute a contractual fault.

Dans des conclusions additionnelles en réponse, la société PAN AFRICAN déclare ne pouvoir confirmer l'authenticité du document douanier produit par l'appelant mais "reconnaît que les marchandises avaient été prises en charge par leur destinataire . . . en Espagne où il avait un établissement". Elle précise que "l'Espagne n'avait jamais été une destination explicitement interdite".Elle ajoute à titre subsidiaire, que "même si par impossibile [impossibilité?] la Cour estimait qu'il y aurait eu non formation des nouveaux contrats de vente et que les nouvelles exigences de BRI PRODUCTION seraient justifiées d'un point de vue contractuel, ces mêmes exigences seraient nulles en droit communautaire, comme constituant une interdiction d'exporter vers un autre pays de l'Union Européenne."

In its additional conclusions in rebuttal, PAN AFRICAN EXPORT declares it is unable to confirm the authenticity of the custom documents produced by the appellant but "concedes that the recipient of the goods took responsibility for them [= took possession of them] in Spain where it had a place of business." It adds that "Spain never was an explicitly forbidden destination." It adds, as a subsidiary argument, that "even if (and it considers this impossible) the Court would be of the opinion that there was no formation of new contracts of sale and that the new demands of BRI PRODUCTION are justified from a contractual point of view, they would be null under Community law as it would amount to a prohibition of exportation to another country of the European Union."

* * *

* * *

SUR CE, LA COUR

Attendu, sur le droit applicable au contrat de vente, que par lettres du 23 janvier 1995, les parties ont été invitées à conclure, si elles le souhaitaient, sur l'application aux contrats de vente de la convention de Vienne du 11 avril 1990 sur les contrats de vente internationale de marchandises.

ON THIS, THE COURT

Whereas, on the law applicable to the contract of sale, by the letters of 23 January 1995, the parties have been invited to conclude [i.e. to argue], if they so wished, on the application of the Vienna Convention of 11 April 1990 [sic] on contracts for the international sale of goods.

Que l'applicabilité de cet instrument résulte de l'établissement du vendeur en France et de l'acheteur aux États-Unis, États différents, également parties à la convention ainsi que le prévoit l'article 1er, paragraphe 1, alinéa a de la convention.

Whereas the applicability of this instrument comes from the seller having a place of business in France and the buyer in the USA, two different States, both parties to the convention as provided by article 1 paragraph 1, sub paragraph a of the convention.

Que les parties ont fait connaître qu'elles n'entendaient pas conclure sur l'application au litige des dispositions de ce texte.

Whereas the parties informed us that they did not intend to conclude [argue] on the application to this case of the provisions of this text.

* * *

* * *

Attendu, sur la portée juridique de la stipulation relative à la destination figurant dans les contrats conclus en septembre et en octobre 1991 à destination de

Guayaquil (Equateur) et de Curacao (Antilles Néerlandaises), que l'article 8, paragraphe 1 de la convention de Vienne dispose ceci:

Whereas, on the juridical effect of the stipulation relating to the destination found in the contracts concluded in September and October 1991 for shipping to Guayaquil (Ecuador) and Curacao (Dutch Indies), article 8 paragraph 1 of the Vienna Convention states:

"Au fins de la présente convention, les indications et les autres comportements d'une partie doivent être interprétés selon l'intention de celle-ci lorsque l'autre partie connaissait ou ne pouvait ignorer cette intention."

"For the purposes of this Convention, statements[*] made by and other conduct of a party are to be interpreted according to his intent where the other party knew or could not have been unaware what that intent was." *[Please note that the official French version that the court uses, "indications," is probably much broader than term "statement." "Indication" in French corresponds roughly to this definition of indication in the Oxford English Dictionary: "The action of indicating, pointing out, or making known; that in which this is embodied; a hint, suggestion, or piece of information from which more may be inferred." To remind you of this, I will translate references to the word "indication" in the French version of article 8 as "indication," but remember that it refers to the French version of the convention, which in the English version is "statement"].

Que ce texte appliqué au présent litige signifie que les indications et les comportements de BRI PRODUCTION doivent interprêtés selon l'intention de leur auteur, BRI PRODUCTION, lorsque la société PAN AFRICAN connaissait ou ne pouvait ignorer cette intention.

Whereas this text, when applied to the present case, means that the indications and conduct of BRI PRODUCTION must be interpreted according to the intention of their author, BRI PRODUCTION, where PAN AFRICAN knew or could not have been unaware what that intent was.

Qu'il résulte de la première prise de contact, en vue de l'établissement de relations d'affaires suivies, entre BRI PRODUCTION et PAN AFRICAN que cette dernière savait que les relations commerciales ne pouvaient être nouées que pour des marchandises destinées à l'Amérique du Sud ou à l'Afrique et que la télécopie de PAN AFRICAN du 27 mai 1991 a rassuré BRI PRODUCTION sur ce point.

Whereas from the first contract with a view to establishing long-term business relations between BRI PRODUCTION and PAN AFRICAN, one can see that the latter knew that the commercial relations could be only with respect to goods to be shipped to South America or Africa, and that the fax of PAN AFRICAN dated 27 May 1991 reassured BRI PRODUCTION on this point.

Qu'il s'ensuit que les mentions de l'adresse du client final sur les différents documents relatifs aux ventes ne peuvent pas être comprises comme des indications abstraites dont la réalité aurait été indifférente à la société BRI PRODUCTION.

Whereas it follows that the mention of the ultimate client's address on the various documents relating to the sales cannot be understood as abstract indications, the truth of which would be immaterial [would make no difference] to BRI PRODUCTION.

Que dans l'intention de cette dernière, l'adresse du client final devait être celle de la livraison effective; Que l'insistance mise par BRI PRODUCTION pour connaître l'identité du client final démontrait à la société PAN AFRICAN que les affirmations qu'elle avait elle-même formulées dans plusieurs correspondances (télécopies du 27 mai 1991, des 6 et 11 juin 1991) de revendre à des destinataires d'Afrique et d'Amérique du Sud devaient être conformes à la réalité.

Whereas, in the intent of the latter, the ultimate client's address had to be the actual address of delivery; whereas the insistence of BRI PRODUCTION to know the identity of the final client demonstrated to PAN AFRICAN that the assurances that it had itself made in numerous communications (faxes of 27 May 1991, 6 and 11 June 1991) to resell to recipients in Africa and South America had to be truthful.

Attendu en conséquence, que la société BRI PRODUCTION était fondée à demander des justificatifs établissant que les lieux de livraison figurant sur les documents contractuels étaient les lieux de livraison effective; Qu'avant le procès, la société PAN AFRICAN n'a pas contesté le principe d'une telle vérification ; Que, dans un premier message du 08 novembre 1991, elle a garanti à

BRI PRODUCTION qu'elle lui remettrait un document sous huitaine; Qu'elle s'y est dérobée, ensuite, en faisant valoir l'opposition de son client; Qu'elle a prétendu y consentir enfin en faisant intervenir son avocat pour présenter au Directeur Commercial de BRI PRODUCTION un connaissement maritime ; Que par son comportement, la société PAN AFRICAN démontre qu'elle avait également compris que les lieux indiqués pour la destination des marchandises devaient être sincères et qu'une preuve de l'effectivité de la livraison à la destination déclarée par elle-même pouvait lui être demandée.

Whereas, as a consequence of this, BRI PRODUCTION was justified in asking for evidence establishing that the places of delivery stated on the contractual documents were the actual places of delivery; whereas before the trial, PAN AFRICAN did not contest the principle of such verification; whereas in a first message of 8 November 1991, it guaranteed to BRI PRODUCTION that it would provide a document within a week. It then avoided this commitment saying that its client opposed it; it then pretended to agree to it in the end by having its advocate intervene to show a maritime bill of lading to the commercial director of BRI PRODUCTION. Whereas, by its conduct, PAN AFRICAN shows that it also understood that places mentioned as the destination of the goods had to be truthful and that evidence of the actual delivery at the destination by it might be requested.
* * *

* * *

Attendu sur la sanction de l'absence de justification du lieu de livraison effective que cette absence de justification ou la justification par un connaissement, simplement présenté, non remis en copie, dont des investigations ultérieures et l'aveu de PAN AFRICAN ont démontré la falsification, prive substantiellement la société BRI PRODUCTION de ce qu'elle était en droit d'attendre du contrat ; Que le comportement de la société PAN AFRICAN constitue une contravention essentielle au contrat au sens de l'article 25 de la convention de Vienne.

Whereas, regarding the remedy for the lack of evidence of the place of actual delivery, this lack of evidence or the mere production as evidence of a bill of lading without providing any copy, and which upon further investigation and the admission of PAN AFRICAN proves to be falsified, deprives substantially BRI PRODUCTION of what it was entitled to expect from the contract; whereas the conduct of PAN AFRICAN amounts to a fundamental breach of contract as provided by article 25 of the Vienna Convention.

Que l'article 64 de cet instrument stipule que "le vendeur peut déclarer le contrat résolu . . . si l'inexécution par l'acheteur de l'une quelconque des obligations résultant pour lui du contrat ou de la présente convention constitue une contravention essentielle au contrat."

Whereas article 64 of this instrument states that "the seller may declare the contract avoided . . . if the failure of the buyer to perform any of his obligations under the contract or this convention amounts to a fundamental breach of contract."

Qu'en outre la société BRI PRODUCTION a accordé à la société PAN AFRICAN un délai raisonnable, compte tenu des circonstances, du 21 octobre au 25 novembre 1991, pour se conformer aux obligations contractuelles;

Whereas, moreover, BRI PRODUCTION granted PAN AFRICAN an additional period of time of reasonable length considering the circumstances, from 21 October 1991 to 25 November 1991, to abide by its contractual obligations;

Attendu qu'en l'absence d'exécution satisfaisante du premier contrat, la société BRI PRODUCTION était fondée à rompre les relations contractuelles pour les opérations suivantes assorties des mêmes obligations;

Whereas, in the absence of a satisfactory performance of the first contract, BRI PRODUCTION is justified to break the contractual relations for further operations that entail similar obligations;

Que l'article 73, alinéa 2, de la convention de Vienne autorise en effet, dans les contrats à livraisons successives, une partie victime d'une contravention essentielle pour une livraison qui a de sérieuses raisons de penser que la méconnaissance des obligations se reproduira, de déclarer le contrat résolu pour l'avenir, si elle le fait dans un délai raisonnable ; Que la réaction de BRI PRODUCTION, sans être brutale, a été faite dans un délai permettant à PAN AFRICAN de trouver un fournisseur de remplacement;

Whereas article 73, paragraph 2 of the Vienna Convention indeed authorizes, in cases of contracts for delivery of goods by installments, a party who is the victim of a fundamental breach for a delivery and who has [*]serious reasons to think[*] that the disregard of the obligations will recur, to declare the contract avoided for the future if it does so within a reasonable time; Whereas the reaction of BRI PRODUCTION, without being abrupt [sudden and strong], occurred after a period of time allowing PAN AFRICAN to find another supplier; *[The English version of art. 73 says "good grounds to conclude" but the French version, which the court uses, says "de sérieuses raisons de penser" which leads the court to talk of "serious reasons to think."]

* * *

* * *

Attendu, sur la méconnaissance par BRI PRODUCTION des règles de concurrence communautaire, que la société PAN AFRICAN qui a déclaré faire du commerce en Afrique et en Amérique du Sud et a conclu des contrats mentionnant ces destinations n'a pas d'intérêt à revendiquer leur respect;

Whereas, regarding the disregard by BRI PRODUCTION of the rules regarding competition within the Community, PAN AFRICAN which declared that it was conducting its business with Africa and South America and has entered into contracts mentioning these destinations has no standing to ask for the enforcement of such rules;

Que dans la mesure où la fraude commise par PAN AFRICAN serait de nature à lui conférer un intérêt juridiquement protégé pour veiller au respect des règles communautaires sur le marché espagnol, il lui appartiendrait d'indiquer précisément en quoi le contrat de distribution exclusive de la marque Bonaventure conclu entre la société BRI PRODUCTION et la société espagnole NO WAY OUT, approuvé le 11 mars 1991 par le Directeur de la Chambre de Commerce et d'Industrie de Bilbao, contrevient à l'article 85 du traité CEE, notamment au troisième paragraphe de ce texte; Qu'en effet, les concessions exclusives ne sont pas nulles en tant que telles et que, s'agissant de produits génériques comme les pantalons, les Jeans de marque Bonaventure, eux-mêmes en concurrence avec de nombreuses autres marques de Jeans, sont facilement substituables;

Whereas, to the extent that the fraud committed by PAN AFRICAN could be of such a nature as to confer on it a legally protected interest in the enforcement of Community rules on the Spanish market, it would have to show precisely how the contract of exclusive distribution of the brand name Bonaventure entered into by BRI PRODUCTION and the Spanish company NO WAY OUT, approved on 11 March 1991 by the Director of the

Chamber of Commerce and Industry of Bilbao contravenes article 85 of the EEC treaty, notably the third paragraph of that text; whereas, in fact exclusive concessions are not null in themselves and whereas with respect to generic products such as trousers, jeans of the Bonaventure brand name, these products are competing with many other brands of Jeans and can easily be substituted [by other products];

Qu'une atteinte aux règles de concurrence communautaire a donc besoin d'être démontrée; Qu'en l'absence de précision, il y a lieu de juger que l'exigence par BRI PRODUCTION que les destinations mentionnées par la société PAN AFRICAN soient respectées et que les marchandises ne soient pas détournées vers le marché espagnol n'encourt pas la nullité;

Whereas a violation of Community rules regarding competition must be demonstrated; whereas in the absence of more details, we must rule that the requests of BRI PRODUCTION that the destinations mentioned by PAN AFRICAN be complied with and that the goods not be diverted to the Spanish market, are not null;

* * *

* * *

Attendu que le jugement déféré doit être réformé; Que la société PAN AFRICAN doit être déboutée de l'ensemble de ses demandes;

Whereas the judgement appealed from must be reformed; Whereas we must deny all of the remedies requested by PAN AFRICAN;

Attendu, sur la somme de 10 000 Ffrs réclamée par la société BRI PRODUCTION pour procédure abusive et injustifiée, que le comportement de la société PAN AFRICAN, contraire au principe de bonne foi dans le commerce international, édicté par l'article 7 de la convention de Vienne, aggravé par la prise de position judiciaire de demandeur au procès, caractérise l'abus de procédure; Que le trouble causé par le procès à la société BRI PRODUCTION justifie l'allocation de la somme demandée;

Whereas, regarding the sum of 10,000 francs claimed by BRI PRODUCTION for abusive and unjustified actions, the conduct of PAN AFRICAN, going against the principle of good faith in international trade promulgated by article 7 of the Vienna Convention, made worse by the judicial position taken by the plaintiff at trial constitutes an abuse of procedure; Whereas the inconvenience caused by this trial to BRI PRODUCTION justifies the sum requested;

Attendu, sur la demande de 10,000 Ffrs au titre de l'article 700 du nouveau Code de procédure civile, qu'il y a lieu d'y faire droit;

Whereas, regarding the request for 10,000 francs under article 700 of the new code of civil procedure, it is appropriate to grant it;

PAR CES MOTIFS, LA COUR:
Statuant publiquement et par arrêt contradictoire, après en avoir délibéré conformément à la loi, REFORME le jugement attaqué;
DEBOUTE la société PAN AFRICAN de l'ensemble de ses demandes;
LA CONDAMNE à payer à la société BRI PRODUCTION
** 10 000 Ffrs à titre de dommages-intérêts pour procédure abusive;*
** 10 000 Ffrs au titre de l'article 700 du Nouveau Code de Procédure Civile ;*
PRONONCE publiquement par Monsieur BERAUDO, Président qui a signé avec Madame COMBE, Greffier.

FOR THESE REASONS, THE COURT:
Pronouncing judgement publicly and on a contested case after deliberations as required by law;
REFORMS the judgement appealed from;
REJECTS all the remedies sought by PAN AFRICAN
ORDERS it to pay to BRI PRODUCTION:
* 10,000 francs as damages for abusive actions [abuse of process];
* 10,000 francs under article 700 of the new Code of Civil Procedure
PRONOUNCED publicly by Monsieur BERAUDO, Président who signed with Madame COMBE, Greffier.

Translation from German

ICC Arbitration Award 8611/HV/JK of 1997

1997.01.23 (23 January 1997)

Translation: Beate Satory
University of Cologne, Germany

Key CISG provisions at issue:
Articles 4; 7(1); 7(2); 9(1); 18(1); 19(3); 33(c); 39(1); 71(3); 74; 78
[Also cited: Articles 19(2); 44]

Arbitrator: Dr. Roland Loewe

Award

In International Chamber of Commerce Arbitration Proceeding 8611/HV/JK of 1997 between the [claimant] W (formerly I), Germany [seller], and the respondent R, Spain [buyer], regarding claims of DM 161,558.82, deducting the amount of the counterclaim of the [buyer], interest and cost, the arbitrator has decided:

The [seller] is to be awarded the sum of DM 161,538.82.

The counterclaims of the [buyer] against the [seller] rightly exist to the sum of DM 54,500.

The [buyer] is required to pay the [seller] the amount of DM 107,058.82 plus 5% interest from 1 October 1992 as well as to compensate [seller] $3,333.33 for the costs of arbitration and DM 2,333.33 for the costs of [seller] for his participation in the proceedings.

The additional demand for capital, interest and costs is to be dismissed.

Opinion

In the claim of 24 March 1995 the [seller] requests the payment of a number of invoices between 12 June 1991 and 2 July 1992 amounting to

DM 157,430.27 and interest payable on arrears to the sum of DM 4,128.55, thus making a total of DM 161,568.82, as well as further interest at a rate of 13.25 % since 1 October 1992.

In [buyer's] defense statement of 12 June 1995 the [buyer] does not dispute having received the goods specified in the invoices, yet without paying. However, the [buyer] claims to have been damaged by the behavior of the [seller]. Therefore, the [buyer] maintains a right to set-off damages against the [seller]'s claim.

On 15 January 1988 the [seller] and the [buyer] entered into a so-called "contract of representation." This contract included the agreement of the [seller] to grant the [buyer] the exclusive right of preemption for all I-products with the exception of a certain [type of machine] in Spain including the Balearic Islands but not the Canary Islands. Subsequently, numerous individual purchases were transacted.

The contract contains the following Clause 13: "Any dispute will be settled under the Rules of the International Chamber of Commerce; the place of arbitration will be A (a location in Germany)."

On 24 July 1996 in A at the oral hearing, the representatives of the parties signed the following statement:

> "The parties correspondingly declare that by the 'Rules of the International Chamber of Commerce' in Clause 13 of the contract dated 25 January 1988 they meant the arbitration rules of the International Chamber of Commerce. Furthermore, they submit to settle all disputes in arbitration concerning the contract of representation as well as all later individual purchases."

Moreover, the contract between the parties contains the following clauses significant to this proceeding:

§ 4 para. 2: "[Seller] I will not supply other companies in Spain with its products."

§ 8 para. 4: "Date of payment: 120 days from date of invoice, 90 days from date of delivery less 2 % cash discount."

§ 10: "This contract is valid until 31 December 1990 beginning on 1 April 1988 and will be automatically renewed for another year provided that there has been no earlier written termination of the contract by either party."

§ 11: a) "[Seller] may terminate the contract at the end of the year provided that the following net purchase values have not been attained:

1988 DM 750,000
1989 DM 1,000,000
1990 DM 1,000,000

"In this case, the contract will expire after 6 months of the year in question."

b) "In the case of termination after 3 years, no reasons will be required; the period of notice will then be 6 months."

c) "The contract may be terminated by either party at any time, without notice, for the following serious reasons:

1. Bankruptcy, insolvency or liquidation of one of the parties of the contract;

2. Breach of contract by one of the parties of the contract.

§ 15: "The language of contract is German."

On 8 January 1992, the [seller] informed the [buyer] of the future impossibility of shielding the Spanish market from [seller's] I-products by other suppliers.

This was justified by the argument that in 1991 the [buyer] had purchased only DM 203,000 worth of goods from [seller] representing approximately half of their purchase of 1990 and this figure was far behind the [seller]'s expectations. Furthermore, due to a takeover by the W-group in November 1991, [seller's] I-products would also be sold by S-Espana (another company of the same group).

At the same time, [seller] promised to continue fulfilling all orders of the [buyer], however not on an exclusive basis.

The [buyer] justified its counterclaims, stating that the [seller] had breached the exclusive contract glutting the Spanish market via company S, as well as failing to supply ordered goods. Moreover, the [seller] not only supplied defective goods, which [seller] refused to take back, but also did not supply required replacement parts.

The decisive criterion of rights and duties can only be the contract itself. Regarding any questions not determined by the contract, the arbitrator must apply the law resulting from the suitable conflict-of-law norm (Art. 13(3) of the ICC Rules of Procedure).

The language of the contract is German; the parties have chosen the German residence of the [seller] as being the place of arbitration. Therefore, it would seem advisable to apply German rules of conflict of law. Article 28 para. 2 of the Introductory Law of the German Civil Code (in the version of the law governing international private law from 25 July 1986,

BGBl II 809), assumes that the closest connection of a contract exists with the State in which the party with the characteristic performance (i.e., not the paying party) has its residence or, if the party concerned is a company or a legal person, its headquarters. In the present case, this is the Federal Republic of Germany and, since there is nothing to be said against this assumption, German law is applicable.

The contract of 25 January 1985 also applies to the individual contracts as far as contract-affecting clauses are concerned (Contract Art. 8: setting of the price and terms of payment; Contract Art. 12: no obligation to take back unsold goods or to issue credit notes for them after conclusion of the contract; Contract Art. 13: dispute settlement).

The [seller] maintains that [seller] attached [seller's] sales and delivery conditions to every invoice, which the [buyer] never contradicted. [Seller] has presented two different examples of those conditions. One of these examples shows simply from the citing of the bank accounts and the name of the manager (before the merger with W) that it concerned conditions of I; the other is headed "W S — I" and is more detailed. The latter could not have been used for sales before the takeover. No information has been given by the [seller] concerning the time that the forms were changed.

Although sales and delivery conditions probably were not attached to every single invoice, it is likely that at least from time to time sales and delivery conditions were attached to invoices. After all, the conditions were printed so they could be announced to the business partners. They must have been imparted to the [buyer] at least in the old version, possibly also in the new version. The [buyer] has not asserted that [buyer] had contradicted any point of this version, or that [buyer] had transmitted [buyer's] own purchase conditions.

Questions concerning the individual contracts which are not dealt with by the contract of sole representation will be handled by the UN Convention of 11 April 1980 on Contracts for the International Sale of Goods (CISG). As stated in CISG Art. 1(1)(a), this relates to sales after 1 August 1991 (effective date for Spain) and, on the basis of CISG Art. 1(1)(b), to sales after 1 January 1991 (effective date for Germany), considering that German law is applicable for international sales contracts as of 1 January 1991.

There are doubts as to whether the attached sales and delivery conditions constitute a deviation from the offer thus turning the purported acceptance into a refusal combined with a counter-offer. In the present case, this problem is only of theoretical importance. If one were to consider the deviation an essential modification, then the contract was concluded with the acceptance of the delivered goods together with the copy of the sales and delivery conditions. However, if the modification was not essential, in accordance with Art. 19(2) CISG, the contract would be concluded with the delivery of the goods. This also refers to the first sending of the sales and delivery conditions, thus it became a practice between the parties (Art. 9(3) CISG).

Disputes not settled by the general principles of the CISG (Art. 7(2) CISG) will be decided by internal German law.

After the effective date of the terms of reference, by the sending of the letter of 15 May 1996 the arbitrator ordered the parties to address all issues of the proceedings as well as to produce all documents of evidence by 20 June 1996. On 24 July 1996 in A, the parties attended the oral hearing which took place in the presence of a sworn translator. At first, the parties intended to interrogate witnesses but did not name any specific person and finally waived an interrogation altogether. They neither moved for interrogation of the parties nor the appointing of an expert to examine the delivered goods which the [buyer] had designated as faulty. This examination would more than likely have been useless simply causing excessive costs, since any expert would hardly have judged with certainty the condition of the goods four or five years after the time of delivery.

A further extension until 1 September 1996 was granted to the [buyer] for production of documents. Finally, the arbitrator instructed the [buyer] to present all evidence for the notice of defects which [buyer] had presented. The [seller] was ordered to present all evidence of [seller's] response to these notices of defects as well as all evidence justifying the claimed interest rate. This extension, too, expired without any document having been produced.

Mainly, this arbitration suffered from general assertions (such as "all defects notified;" "no defects notified or, by way of exception, removed by exchange;" "no replacement parts delivered;" "all replacement parts delivered"). However, none of these assertions have been proven, or at best only insufficiently. This has considerably impeded the arbitrator's duty to discover the facts of the case (Art. 14(1) of the ICC Rules of Procedure). Furthermore, it would not have been wise to provoke assertions or denials by the parties through specific questions the truth of which could not have subsequently been proven.

The [seller] then asked for still another extension for the purpose of making a statement concerning the documents produced by the [buyer].

However, this request was unfounded, since the [buyer] had not produced any further documents. Therefore, the arbitrator pronounced the proceedings concluded.

Since none of the reasons of Contract Art. 11(c) are relevant, a termination was only feasible within 6 months. The [buyer] lost its monopoly in the first half of 1992 because of the [seller's] action. Therefore, the [seller] is liable for damages. In accordance with Art. 249-252 of the German Civil Code, damages to assets are reparable (Heinrichs in Palandt, Bürgerliches Gesetzbuch 253, § 249, margin no. 7, preliminary remarks (1995)). According to Art. 253 of the German Civil Code the reparation includes the lost profit which could in all probability have been expected in the normal course of business or under special circumstances, especially after the arrangements were made and the precautions taken.

In the first 3 years of the contract, the [buyer] received DM 730,000 worth of goods, including around DM 40,000 in 1990 and DM 200,000 in 1991. In the first 6 months of 1992, the [buyer] bought DM 100,000 worth of goods from the [seller]. The question therefore arises as to how much more of the goods [buyer] would have bought if company S had not entered the market as a competitor. A presentation of evidence had been blocked due to a lack of access to the documents of company S. The [seller], too, made no reference to the turnover of company S. Moreover, one has to bear in mind that, on the one hand, the [buyer] had carried out an expensive advertising campaign for I-products with the result that [buyer's] sales of the [seller]'s goods had rapidly increased as shown in one of the diagrams. On the other hand, due to Company S's numerous branches in Spain, Company S probably obtained a turnover of the I-products which the [buyer] could not have achieved.

Therefore, the arbitrator must be free to judge the damages following his own convictions on the basis of the known data and on the assumption of a normal course of business (see Art. 287 of the German Civil Procedural Code). It can be assumed that the turnover of the [buyer] for I-products would have equaled that of its best sales year, namely 1990, yet not surpassed it. In that time, the [buyer] achieved a turnover of DM 400,000 worth of goods. This would mean DM 200,000 worth of goods per six-month period. In the hearing of 24 July 1996, the [buyer] maintained that it achieved a net profit on I-products between 18 and 20%, yet it did not prove these figures. However, the [seller] did not dispute a net profit of no more than 15%. Therefore, the [buyer]'s counterclaim of DM 15,000 arises from the irregular termination of the contract of sole representation.

After 2 July 1992, the [seller] did not accept any further orders from the [buyer] because, in the meantime, there had been no payments by the [buyer] for the above mentioned claims of the delivered goods.

Furthermore, the [buyer] demands a setting off against damages caused by defective machines. In this connection, the [buyer] maintains that it provided notice of the defects either immediately in writing or at the date when [buyer] was informed of the defect by [buyer's] customers. However, there are also complaints about defects that were not taken care of by the [seller]. At this stage, the [buyer] had stopped all correspondence with the [seller] since [buyer] planned to assert the issue in the arbitration. However, the [seller] alleges that it handled every received complaint. These complaints, however, concern only an insignificant part of the range of products.

A list of the 2,265 sold and 51 returned machines was mailed on 3 December 1992 to the [seller], i.e., five months after the [seller] had refused to accept further orders from the [buyer]. A certificate (dated 16 November 1992) from Notary D was attached to the list confirming an inventory of the stock delivered by the [seller], and also comprising goods in stock to the alleged amount of DM 100,000. The Notary had not judged and was not able to judge whether the goods were defective or not and why they had not been sold. Finally, the [buyer] submitted a file of credit notes totaling 7,693,487 Pesetas, allegedly granted to customers because of defective goods that had been supplied to the [buyer] by the [seller]. This file concerns documents drawn up by the [buyer] only, the authenticity and correctness of which could only be proven through an interrogation of every one of the 105 customers. As shown above, there had been no application for witness interrogation.

Point 5 of the old version of the sales and delivery conditions concerning defects and notice of defects states:

> "The existence of defects does not entitle a withholding of payment. There is no set-off for counterclaims. The legal regulation applies to the admission and effectiveness of possible notices of defects."
>
> "Complaints may cause claims regarding warranty only if the buyer can prove the proper use of the delivered machines or tools until the assertion of the notice of defects. Furthermore, he has to allow the inspection of the goods still in stock and the used machines."

Concerning warranties, the new version of the sales and delivery conditions states:

> 6.1 "Notices of mechanical defects, false delivery and incorrect number of delivered goods detected by reasonable inspection of the goods must be made in writing within 8 days of arrival of the goods at the final destination. In the case of a later detection of the defect, the notice must be made after its discovery without delay. If the goods are no longer in the condition of delivery, the buyer must prove that the defects had been existent at the moment of delivery. Any essential interference or modification of the goods will exclude notices of defect, which will also be excluded if there has been an express or tacit waiver to inspect the goods."
>
> 6.2 "Our right of plea for delay will not be waived by negotiations."

Regarding the old version (concerning admission and effectiveness of the notices of defect) as well as the new version (concerning the content of the notices of defect), Art. 39(1) of the CISG subsidiarily applies. Accordingly, the buyer must notify the supplier of the defect within a reasonable delay at the time of actual or possible detection, thereby specifying the breach of contract.

In the proceedings, too, the [buyer] did not maintain or prove any defects of precisely designated goods. It is therefore of no importance which of the goods are covered by the old version of the sales and delivery conditions. No claim for damages by the [buyer] will arise due to defects of delivered goods, especially since the [buyer] neither alleged nor proved a reasonable excuse for the omission of the required notice (Art. 44 CISG). Therefore, the question of a valid setting off in the old version of the sales and delivery conditions is unfounded.

The [buyer] urged several times for the delivery of replacement parts of the goods delivered and sold by the [seller]. In [buyer]'s letter dated 16 July 1991 it is stated:

> "Replacement Parts for Machinery"
>
> "Despite our repeated request, there has been no delivery; on the contrary, we were forced to remove them from new machines in order to provide our customers with the expected service. In doing so, new difficulties were caused: we cannot sell those machines as long as you do not deliver the replacement parts.
>
> You have to take into consideration that R has not yet claimed the replacement parts to which it is entitled in several cases under the conditions of the warranty.

> There had also been changes of the machinery parts without forewarning. Furthermore, you did not send any current sketches with performed or planned changes.
>
> You have advised that the replacement of our stock is cancelled for machines of previous types; the machines we asked you to send on 23 April 1991 have not been delivered.
>
> Likewise, the parts ordered by Mr. H from C 91 have not been delivered. For instance: the new [parts] of the [machinery] in order to now update your recent delivery of the old type machinery. Otherwise, this delivery would become obsolete, unless you prefer to have this sent back as well.
>
> Ultimately, you have announced a break in delivery . . . and, as announced on the phone and hereby confirmed, we do regret to inform you that we will hold back payment of a certain outstanding part until we receive the missing up-to-date material ordered on 23 April 1991.
>
> Finally, your Mr. H promised to fulfill the order — at least as far as the replacement parts are concerned — in order to prevent further damages to our customers because of the poor service you have rendered so far. And, up to this very moment, you have not kept this promise either. . . ."

The arbitrator has no doubts concerning the authenticity of this letter. However, the translation of the Spanish original regarding the last two lines of the penultimate paragraph is not quite suitable. It seems that the [buyer] means to hold back the payment for certain deliveries until delivery of the ordered replacement parts as well as the up-to-date machinery.

Apparently, the [buyer] has always believed in the [seller]'s obligation to continue delivering replacement parts for the sold machinery. At the oral hearing on 24 July 1996, the [seller] acknowledged the obligation to deliver replacement parts for the delivered goods for another seven years, and stated that [seller] would have carried out those deliveries if the [buyer] had paid the numerous outstanding invoices. Regarding machines no longer produced by the [seller], the [seller] stated that replacement parts are still specially made and stored in a warehouse in order to provide customers with corresponding replacement parts.

In accordance with literature and jurisprudence concerning Art. 433 of the German Civil Code, the producer of series-produced automobiles, machines and technical equipment has a collateral obligation to have replacement parts ready for delivery even if there has been no special agreement, but only for a certain period of time. In most cases, this results from the principle of good faith according to Art. 242 of the German Civil Code; but also, in a few cases, according to Art. 26(2) of the Law governing Competition Limitation (see amongst others: Kühne, Der Betriebsberater 1527 (1986)). In the present case, neither of the following issues are relevant: whether the enumeration of the seller's obligations in the CISG is final and therefore excludes the national law (including the national jurisprudence), or whether the obligation to deliver replacement parts is a question not expressly settled by the CISG and hence to be judged by the applicable national law. Since the provisions of Art. 7(1) CISG concern only the interpretation of the Convention, no collateral obligation may be derived from the "promotion of good faith" (as foreseen by Loewe, Internationales Kaufrecht 33 (1989). Notably the American, but also the German, literature on the CISG supports a different view. *See e.g.*, v. Caemmerer/Schlechtriem, Kommentar zum Einheitlichen UN-Kaufrecht 90-92, margin numbers 17-27 (2d ed., 1995) and Herber/Czerwenka, Internationales Kaufrecht 48, margin number 6 (1991); however, they do not go so far as to regard every collateral obligation derived from Art. 242 of the German Civil Code as covered by Art. 7(1) CISG; essentially reduced to "interpretation" Enderlein/Maskow/Stargardt, Kaufrechtskonvention der UNO, 47, margin number 5 (1985)).

Nevertheless, regarding the relationship between the parties, a prompt delivery of replacement parts had become normal practice as defined by Art. 9(1) of the CISG by which the [seller] was bound.

In accordance with Art. 33(c) of the CISG, the seller has to deliver the goods within a reasonable time after the conclusion of the contract. From Art. 7(2) it can be derived that the obligation to deliver subsequent replacement parts would have to be fulfilled within a reasonable time after receiving the buyer's order. The letter of 16 July 1991 gives evidence of the [seller]'s failure to meet this obligation, or at least not within a reasonable time period. In fact, this failure appeared before the [buyer] was in arrears for payment justifying a nonperformance according to Art. 71(1)(b) of the CISG. Therefore, in accordance with Art. 74 of the CISG, the [seller] is liable to pay damages equal to the loss including the loss of profit since the [seller] ought to have foreseen damages as a possible consequence of [seller's] breach of contract.

Considering the arbitrator's lack of reliable documents concerning the number and value of the machines for which [buyer's] customers did not pay because of non-delivery of replacement parts, the arbitrator must judge the damages according to his own conviction having taken into consideration the circumstances of this case.

After all, the [buyer] maintains (page 2 of the statement of defense) having suffered such damages only in 1991. The letter of 16 July 1991 can only concern the first six months, i.e., in total DM 100,000 worth of machines. Conceding that a quarter of those goods have become worthless, the loss of the [buyer] amounts to DM 25,000 plus 15 % loss of profit, thus DM 28,750 in total.

The [buyer] is also requesting Pesetas 5,410,428 (equivalent to DM 60,000) spent on canvassing of customers. Furthermore, the [buyer] complained of having lost numerous customers (having built a clientele of 1,100) due to the [seller]'s non-delivery of the requested replacement parts. This loss also had been foreseeable to the [seller]. Nevertheless, the [buyer] had to take into consideration that the delivery by the [seller] could not have been everlasting and that [buyer] would lose certain customers due to the non-delivery of the replacement parts for I-products. The advertising costs for the final third of 1991 and for 1992 must be, however, deducted from the total advertising costs, which are divided into yearly totals. Concerning the delivery of whole machinery, this deduction already results from the lack of liability (not provided for in the contract of representation either) to accept sales offers (see Art. 18(3) CISG) and, concerning component parts, from the expiry of the aforementioned usage which includes the immediate payment for the replacement parts. In either case, there has been no need for a statement in accordance with Art. 71(3) CISG despite the promise of delivery dated 8 January 1992.

Thus, the excluded advertising costs amount to Pesetas 1,500,000 or DM 17,000. It also can be assumed that the [buyer] has lost a quarter of its clientele established through advertising costs of DM 43,000 and therefore DM 10,750 of the expenditure on advertising.

With respect to the updating of the delivered machinery mentioned in the letter of 16 July 1991, no reason is to be found to oblige the [seller] to update machinery or to pay damages for failure to do so.

The justified claims of the [seller] will be reduced by a set off of DM 54,500 to a total sum of DM 107,058.82.

The [seller] demands that this amount be charged at a rate of interest of 13.25% from 1 October 1992. Art. 78 CISG provides "If a party fails to pay the price or any other sum that is in arrears, the other party is entitled to interest on it. . . ." Some invoices were due prior to 1 October but the arbitrator cannot grant interest prior to that date as the [seller] has not asked for it. The demand, recognized by the [buyer], for interest on arrears totaling DM 4,128.55 from earlier purchases is excluded from the general payment of interest because this would lead to interest on interest, which is prohibited in Art. 78 CISG, and which, through Art. 289 of the German Civil Code and Art. 353 of the German Commercial Code, is not expressly provided for. This demand is the first to be included in the setting off because, according to the basic principle of German law, the consequences of the setting off should be backdated to the moment when the demands were first made (Heinrichs in Palandt, loc cit, Art. 389, 453, margin number 1).

The sales and delivery conditions of the first version designate an interest rate of 2% above the rate of the [seller]'s bank, whereas the conditions of the second version establish the rate that banks use for current accounts on condition that it is at least 2% above the respective discount rate of the central bank of the State in question. The [seller] has not supplied any evidence of these rates of interest within the granted grace period and there is no obligation for the arbitrator to investigate this matter. Any certificate provided by the bank can no longer be taken into consideration after the end of the extension. Because Art. 78 CISG does not, for obvious reasons, define the interest rate, the law applicable to this matter, in certain circumstances the monetary law, comes into force. Both are part of German law which, in Art. 352 of the Commercial Code concerning trade transactions, fixes the interest rate at 5%.

The [seller] won two-thirds of the total claims, the [buyer] one-third. The [buyer] therefore must compensate [seller] $3,333.33 for the costs of arbitration and DM 2,333.33 for the costs of [seller] for his participation in the proceedings.